The Derrick Bell Reader

CRITICAL AMERICA

General Editors: Richard Delgado and Jean Stefancic

The Derrick Bell *Reader*

Edited by
Richard Delgado and Jean Stefancic

NEW YORK UNIVERSITY PRESS
New York and London

NEW YORK UNIVERSITY PRESS
New York and London
www.nyupress.org

Library of Congress Cataloging-in-Publication Data
Bell, Derrick A.
The Derrick Bell reader / edited by
Richard Delgado and Jean Stefancic.
p. cm. — (Critical America)
Includes bibliographical references and index.
ISBN–13: 978–0–8147–1969–5 (cloth : alk. paper)
ISBN–10: 0–8147–1969–4 (cloth : alk. paper)
ISBN–13: 978–0–8147–1970–1 (pbk. : alk. paper)
ISBN–10: 0–8147–1970–8 (pbk. : alk. paper)
1. Race discrimination—Law and legislation—United States.
2. Race discrimination—United States.   3. African Americans—
Civil rights.   4. United States—Race relations.   I. Delgado,
Richard.   II. Stefancic, Jean.   III. Title.   IV. Series.
KF4755.B45   2005
305.896'073—dc22   2005006790

New York University Press books are printed on acid-free paper,
and their binding materials are chosen for strength and durability.

Manufactured in the United States of America

c 10 9 8 7 6 5 4 3 2 1
p 10 9 8 7 6 5 4 3 2 1

I have not always been right, but I have been sincere.

—W. E. B. Du Bois

Contents

Acknowledgments

The editors gratefully acknowledge the contributions of University of Pittsburgh law students Kevin Jayne and Jeanette Oliver in framing, assembling, and editing this book, and of Susan Broms, University of Pittsburgh law librarian, in locating hard-to-find materials. We thank Derrick Bell for responding patiently and warmly to our endless inquiries. We are grateful to Salwa Jabado for securing permissions for this book and to Deborah Gershenowitz for keeping the project on course. LuAnn Driscoll, Karen Knochel, Darleen Mocello, Valerie Pompe, and Barbara Salopek prepared the manuscript with precision and dispatch. The University of Pittsburgh School of Law and the Center for the Study of Law and Society at the University of California, Berkeley, Law School provided support and a stimulating work environment.

The Derrick Bell Reader

Introduction

The bespectacled, 59-year-old law professor leaned back in his chair and looked out his office window, a pensive expression clouding his scholarly, unlined features. Outside, groups of students walked across a grassy quad framed by stately, traditional buildings. One, wearing a maroon sweat-shirt with "Harvard" emblazoned on the front, gesticulated animatedly to a friend on their way to a morning class.

Viewing, almost breathing in, the bucolic scene, he smiled. He loved teaching and felt that a college campus was as close to a fountain of youth as he would ever get. And it didn't hurt that the world believed the school where he now held a named chair was the finest in the world. That young woman out there, black like him, might be in law school one day. She might excel, even aspire to be a law professor. How receptive would that world be to candidates like her?

He reached for a yellow pad and began scribbling notes for the talk he planned to give at the student rally scheduled for noon. It had been at least two weeks since he had written a letter to the dean with copies to every faculty member. Coming at the end of a full year of unsuccessful efforts by student groups, the letter announced his decision to take an unpaid leave until the school hired and tenured a woman of color. He had not made that letter public, but neither had he heard back from the dean or the faculty. Their silence, as he had learned from earlier protests, was tantamount to rejection.

A few faculty members had privately expressed concern as to how he would pay his bills. He replied quietly that at this point, he was more concerned about saving his soul. A well-meaning faculty friend came by his office, closed the door, and told him that he and his wife would pay one month of his home mortgage, insisting that Bell keep the payment confidential. Bell thanked him and promised to get in touch if he needed the help. He never did. The friend did not understand that Bell needed his *public support for his protest far more than his private financial aid. A former student, now a member of the faculty, did call and offer to join Bell in his protest. Bell responded that he appreciated his offer, but urged him to remain on the faculty, where he was developing a clinical program that the students badly needed.*

Believing it might be useful to the student activists and faculty of color, he gave the letter to the leaders. One of them, Keith Boykin, negotiated an exclusive to the New York Times, *resulting in a front-page story that very morning. Keith predicted, accurately as it turned out, that the media would be out in force covering the rally.*

While styled a protest, his action turned out to be a deferred resignation. For that was what he would, in effect, be doing by taking an unpaid leave until the school hired and tenured its first female law professor of color. His colleagues, mainly confident white men, were unlikely to yield to what they would see as pressure tactics, especially from the school's first tenured African American law professor, someone who wrote provocative, counterintuitive essays on race and racism rather than more traditional law review articles loaded with footnotes about contracts, corporations, and other mainstream legal subjects.

No matter that his text on race and the law, first published in 1973 and then in its third edition, had been adopted for civil rights courses across the country. His many writings, including a trade book based on a Harvard Law Review Foreword, were widely read, and his courses were among the most popular in the law school. None of these accomplishments would move more than a small number of the faculty to take seriously his insistence that the absence of women of color on the faculty deprived the school of unique perspectives.

In part because of his continuing efforts, five other black men now served on the faculty, three of them tenured. Paradoxically, their long-resisted presence now served as proof to most observers that the faculty did not discriminate and would, as they promised, hire a woman of color when one surfaced who met their standards.

He stood up and began to pace. He had good friends on the faculty. If even one or two of those with prestigious reputations were to agree to join his protest, its prospects would have been much improved. His colleagues might see that many black woman lawyers, including some teaching at other schools, easily met their standards—something he could not say for some of his colleagues who had not written a thing in years but nevertheless adamantly opposed the appointment of one black woman after another, many of whose names he had brought forward himself.

But he stood alone. A few of his liberal colleagues had told him, in private, that they were with him. But when it came time to vote, most invariably melted away, switching sides or abstaining. As a result, no black woman candidate was able to gain the requisite vote.

Despite all the battles, mostly lost, he realized that he would really miss this place, particularly the students, many of whom showed him a level of love and respect that brightened even the more difficult times. "Is it possible," he muttered to himself, "that some of my friends are right, and with almost fifteen years of service here, I can do more working from within?" He smiled, recalling that he had rejected similar advice more than thirty years earlier when he had chosen to leave the Justice Department over its ultimatum that he resign from the NAACP and that he had asserted for years that civil rights lawyers and activists need to stand ready to supplement petitions, lawsuits, and other forms of polite supplication with street protests and other forms of militancy. He turned to his computer and began writing his speech to what he expected would be a large and supportive gathering of students.

Birth of an Activist-Scholar

Derrick Bell grew up in a black neighborhood of Pittsburgh known as "The Hill." The oldest of four children, Bell credits his mother for inspiring him to work hard, succeed, and stand ready to challenge unjust authority. He cites conversations with his father for his early training in the white man's world. Both parents insisted that because of racial discrimination, black people had to be twice as good to get half as much. His father, born in Alabama, had been forced to leave as a teenager. Attending a county fair, and snapping a small toy whip, he had angered two white boys who, proclaiming that "no nigger should have a whip," whipped him with a bull whip they were carrying. He later came upon them without the whip and beat up both of them. Fearing for his safety, his family sent him north to stay with relatives in Pittsburgh. There he met Bell's future mother, whose plans for a college education were postponed permanently when the two married in early 1930. Bell was born in November.

After graduating from public high school in 1948 and Duquesne University in Pittsburgh in 1952, Bell served two years in the Air Force, including one in Korea. He returned to his home city to study law at the University of Pittsburgh, earning his degree in 1957. In addition to family support, Bell cites his experience delivering newspapers during his high school years as a key source for his interest in law. Two of his customers were lawyers and a third, the only black judge in western Pennsylvania. Bell was impressed by their lifestyle and valued the encouragement they and their wives provided.

In his class of 120 students, he was the only black, and in the school, only one of three. In those days, the school had no women students of any race. Bell was a determined student, studying long hours, speaking up in class, and earning good grades that won him a position on the school's law review. He published several pieces in his first year on the review, impressing his contemporaries enough that they selected him associate editor in chief.

As graduation loomed, the young Bell's academic credentials carried little weight in his home town, whose leading law firms did not then hire blacks. The few black practitioners were not able to take on a young, inexperienced lawyer, and he had little interest in setting up an office on his own. On the recommendation of a few of his professors, he gained a position in the Honor Graduate Recruitment Program recently established at the United States Department of Justice, where he worked for a year on appeals by men seeking exemption from the draft as conscientious objectors.

Because of his continued interest in racial issues, he obtained a transfer to the newly formed Civil Rights Division in 1958, but his tenure there proved short. After several months, his superiors learned that he was a member of the NAACP. Considering this affiliation to be a conflict of interest, and probably fearful of controversy with southern members of Congress, they demanded that he surrender his two-dollar membership. When he refused, they took him off race cases and assigned him to perform routine work, moving his desk to the hall outside his former office. He took their hint, and muttering a few choice words about *Sweatt v. Painter*, soon resigned.

Returning to Pittsburgh, he obtained a position as executive director of the local branch of the NAACP, a nonlegal position. While working there, he met Thurgood Marshall, then director of the organization's legal arm, the NAACP Legal Defense and Education Fund, when the famous lawyer visited Pittsburgh on a speaking tour. Marshall knew about Bell's resignation from the Justice Department and, impressed with the young attorney-without-portfolio, offered him a position on his staff. Bell immediately accepted, moved to New York, and soon was working on important civil rights cases with a small but elite cadre of four attorneys: Thurgood Marshall, Constance Baker Motley, Jack Greenberg, and James Nabrit III. It was an ideal position, one he recognized he would have not obtained had he not challenged the Justice Department's conservative personnel policy.

During his years with the fund, 1960–1966, Bell litigated or supervised almost three hundred school desegregation cases throughout the South. During these dangerous and unsettled times, local police officials kept close track of his activities in their towns, and federal judges not only rejected his arguments—although they were based on settled legal principles—but would also turn their backs on him while he was arguing in open court.

Travel was risky, particularly when Bell went to meet with clients in rural areas where the roads were narrow and often unmarked. Even plane flights could be harrowing. On one occasion, a snow storm prevented his plane from landing in Jackson, Mississippi. It landed instead in Memphis and Bell took a late night train that was crowded and unheated. Cold and tired, he tried to call a local attorney to come for him. Unwittingly, he had entered a telephone booth in the whites-only waiting room. White policemen showed up and dragged the young attorney off to jail, where he spent the night.

Bell left the Legal Defense Fund in 1966 but continued his school desegregation work as deputy director of the federal Health, Education, and Welfare Department's Office for Civil Rights. By this time, he had become interested in teaching law, but inquiries to several schools led nowhere. In 1967, Bell agreed to serve as the first executive director of the newly established Western Center on Law and Poverty, a public interest and litigation center sponsored by the University of Southern California Law School in Los Angeles, California. His new position afforded him the opportunity to run a public interest law program as well as to teach civil rights as an adjunct professor at USC.

He moved his family to Los Angeles and settled in for what he thought would be a long stay. Then, the urban rebellions broke out across the country in the wake of Dr. Martin Luther King's assassination in the spring of 1968. Soon, many law schools, along with corporations and government agencies, recognized the need to add a few blacks to their all-white professional staffs. Bell began receiving urgent expressions of interest from a half-dozen top schools. Following a personal recruitment effort by its then dean, Derek Bok, he agreed to join the Harvard Law faculty in the fall of 1969 with the understanding, as the dean put it, "that he would be the first, but not the last black" they would hire.

Finding His Voice

The next few years were filled with challenges. These included the usual ones a new professor faces. He had to come to terms with teaching and students, earn his colleagues' respect, and write enough to justify his position on the faculty. But his status as the school's first and only black professor added a special dimension. Black students flocked to him, seeking his advice and consolation. White students recognized his interest and willingness to spend time with them. His office was seldom quiet.

He also had to earn the respect of many skeptical white and some black students who wondered—even if they did not say it—if his status as an affirmative action hire meant that he was not as qualified as the other professors. Bell worked hard at his teaching, developing innovative approaches to constitutional law and race courses. Over time, his courses became among the most popular in the curriculum.

The faculty proved more resistant. He and his colleagues differed over many issues, particularly faculty hiring and promotion. They also differed in their background and experiences. Not only were they white and Bell black. Class separated them as well. Bell, unlike many on the Harvard Law faculty, had not come from a well-to-do family, attended a prestigious college and law school, and clerked for a U.S. Supreme Court justice. Few of them considered race and racism, his areas of teaching and scholarship, of significant intellectual value.

Bell's contract provided that, as a senior recruit, he would come up for tenure at the end of his second year. Although he had published a number of essays in law reviews, publication was not a consideration in the tenure decision. Rather, tenure would be based on his teaching and mentoring of students. His civil rights course had gone well, but in response to some black students' concerns about no blacks teaching in the basic curriculum, he had agreed to teach a large first-year criminal law course. Choosing to focus on what he felt were inadequacies in this course, the chair of the appointments committee counseled him to defer the tenure decision for a year while he strengthened his teaching in that course. After consulting with his wife, Jewel, he decided to ignore this advice and go up for tenure at the agreed time. "After all," she reminded him, "Harvard needs us more than we need Harvard." His wife's grasp of the situation proved accurate. The faculty tenure vote was affirmative and Bell became the first black law professor at the Harvard Law School.

Two years later, Bell published the first edition of his text, *Race, Racism, and American Law.* Its success seemed to lessen rather than increase interest in hiring more blacks. Frustrated, Bell threatened to resign unless the school honored the "first but not last" promise the dean had made to him when he had been hired. A second black man, C. Clyde Ferguson, was appointed, but the dean made it clear that Bell's resignation threat had nothing to do with it.

Bell's activism did not come at the cost of his writing. A few years later he published two law review articles of startling originality that won him widespread attention in the law school world. The first was "Serving Two Masters: Integration Ideals and Client Interests in School Desegregation Litigation," published in *Yale Law Journal* in 1976. Bell had became convinced that the black community did not need—or, in many cases, want —busing, the school desegregation remedy that civil rights lawyers had been pursuing for at least a dozen years. Instead, they wanted better schools. This kind of talk was heresy within the NAACP, which at that time was staunchly committed to enforcing the mandate of *Brown v. Board of Education*, their great legal breakthrough.

Bell sounded what turned out to be one of his signature themes: the conflict of interest inherent in much public interest litigation. American law requires a flesh-and-blood plaintiff, usually an ordinary person, with "standing"—a specific, concrete grievance with a specific actor or defendant. Much public interest litigation, however, is maintained by specialized litigation centers, like the NAACP Legal Defense Fund or the National Organization of Women. These litigators must represent victims of the policies they want to change. The idea is to file a case challenging the unjust policy, determined to take it to the Supreme Court in the hope that it will announce new law.

In all this, the attorney's overarching objective is to change the law. He or she wants to bring about a great breakthrough, one that will move things in the direction the litigation center wants. For example, when feminist attorneys litigated and won the abortion decision, *Roe v. Wade,* they were as interested in the legal principle of reproductive privacy as the fortunes of the plaintiff, Roe. And when Thurgood Marshall and his colleagues at the NAACP Legal Defense and Education Fund argued *Brown v. Board of Education*, they were as interested in establishing the principle that separate but equal schools violated the Fourteenth Amendment as they were in improving the lives of the specific parents who brought suit and of their children.

What Bell noticed was that in many school desegregation cases, what the black community wants and what the law-reform-bent lawyers want are subtly different. The clients want better schools, while the lawyer wants integrated schools. In the early years after *Brown,* these objectives coincided. Later, they did not. What if desegregating a large school district results in the loss of many jobs by black teachers and administrators? What if the district closes down the black school, which formerly served as a refuge and nerve center for the black community, and buses black school children to hostile white schools located on the other side of town? Can an attorney, in good conscience, advocate for a remedy that his or her law-reform organization believes is best but that the client community does not really want or need? Or must he or she be guided exclusively by the client's interest, and, if so, how does one go about ascertaining what that interest is?

While the legal community was considering those issues, Bell published a second article a few years later in the pages of the *Harvard Law Review.* Entitled "*Brown v. Board of Education* and the Interest Convergence Dilemma," this second article explored a further aspect of that famous case, namely, its place in history and what brought it about. Bell began by asking why the Supreme Court decided the famous case when it did. After all, Bell's old organization, the NAACP Legal Defense Fund, had been arguing school desegregation cases for decades and had been either losing or winning only narrow, incremental victories. Yet, in 1954, the Court declared that in pupil assignment cases, separate is never equal.

What caused the Court to take this audacious step just then? Most Americans, indeed most lawyers, probably thought that American society had finally achieved a moral breakthrough and realized that separation was demeaning and harmful to black school children. The Court merely followed suit. Bell's answer—that international appearances and the self-interest of elite whites dictated that blacks receive a spectacular breakthrough—provoked cries of outrage and condemnation as being too cynical.

Still, it rang true for many of his readers and constituted an early, and impressive, statement of a key critical theme—revisionist history. It also may have opened a breach between Bell and many conventional liberals in the law school world. After his first major article in *Yale Law Journal* came out, discussing the conflict of interest between lawyer and client in public interest litigation, Bell recounts how Paul Bator, a famous colleague, made a trip to his office. Bator told Bell that he had read the article and had come by to congratulate him. "This is really good," he said. Few of his colleagues reacted that way to his realist demotion of *Brown v. Board of Education,* a mainstream of liberal jurisprudence and a crown jewel of American legal thought.

A New Challenge: University Administration and Politics

Soon after publication of the Harvard article, Bell's life took a different turn. During a sabbatical year teaching at the University of Washington Law School in Seattle, he received an invitation from Eugene Scoles, a former dean at the University of Oregon Law School, to come to Eugene for a visit and perhaps put his hat in the ring for the deanship there. Bell liked Eugene and the school, and with the reluctant approval of his wife and three now teenage children, he decided to apply for and was named to the position.

Life in Eugene proved eventful and full of new challenges. Bell had to learn how to conduct faculty meetings, decide upon pay raises for the faculty, raise funds from alumni and wealthy patrons, and deal with the usual range of student complaints. He seems to have been a successful, if somewhat unconventional, dean. Despite an administrative style that featured an emphasis on teaching and increasing student and faculty diversity, he lasted five years, considerably longer than the average. In particular, he seems to have been a better fundraiser than anyone expected.

The many demands of a dean's life did, however, require putting aside his scholarship. For the first few years, he wrote little, none of it pathbreaking. Then, one day the telephone rang. It was the president of the *Harvard Law Review,* inviting him to compose the prestigious annual Foreword to the 1984 Supreme Court issue. His draft was due in a matter of months and could deal with any issue having to do with recent Supreme Court developments.

Such an honor comes rarely to a legal scholar. Bell, wondering where he would find the time, finally agreed and then began casting about for a novel approach and a focus. All the previous Forewords featured the predictable cases-and-policies format that identified various emerging or implicit models in Supreme Court jurisprudence and weighed in on the side of the author's favorite. Bell hit upon the idea of using legal storytelling, discussing legal problems and issues in the form of dialogues between himself and a fictional super-lawyer, Geneva Crenshaw, who had known Bell in their former lives when they had practiced law at the NAACP Legal Defense Fund, but whose life since that time had taken a dramatic turn. The two old friends discuss racial remedies, the search for justice, affirmative action, and many other topics—all in the pages of *Harvard Law Review.* Bell later turned the format of his fictional chronicles into a series of books, one of which, *Faces at the Bottom of the Well,* briefly made it onto the *New York Times* bestseller list.

Bell resigned his position as dean when he and his faculty found themselves in fundamental disagreement over the hiring of a young Asian American teaching candidate, whom the appointments committee had listed third in a list of over one hundred candidates for an open teaching position. When the top two candidates declined, instead of offering the position to the Asian woman, the committee convinced a majority of faculty to reopen the search. Knowing she was fully qualified and convinced that hiring the school's first Asian American law professor was the right thing to do, Bell announced his resignation effective at the end of the school year.

Paradoxically, Bell's Supreme Court Foreword had just come out, so his academic star had never shone more brightly. His wife, Jewel, who had taken a position heading a University of Oregon academic support program for minority students, wanted another year to continue her work. To accommodate her wish, Bell remained in Eugene but accepted an invitation to deliver a series of lectures at other law schools around the country. Then John Ely, a former colleague at Harvard serving as dean at Stanford Law School, invited Bell to visit and teach constitutional law there for the spring semester.

Bell had taught the subject at Harvard and was both an accomplished teacher and a well-known scholar in that field, so the assignment seemed like a good idea. His wife could wind up her work and the children could complete the school year in Eugene. Bell rented a room in the home of a

Stanford Law School administrator and commuted many weekends back to Eugene.

When school started, Bell found himself in front of a class of new students. At Stanford, Constitutional Law is a required first-year course to which students are assigned. Of three sections, two were taught by members of the regular faculty. As he had done at Harvard, he used a standard casebook but emphasized that to understand the Constitution, one had to keep in mind that the Framers were men of wealth with investments in land, slaves, manufacturing, and shipping. The document they fashioned served their primary interest in protecting vested property. When students suggested that he was being too hard on the Framers, he referred them to the classic work of Charles Beard, *The Economic Interpretation of the Constitution*. The students were unfamiliar with Beard and uncomfortable with any criticism of the country's origins, particularly from this unknown visitor from Oregon.

After a few weeks, Bell noticed that a number of students were not attending his class. Then he received an invitation from a student group inviting him to join other faculty members in a series of enrichment lectures about current constitutional issues. Asked to speak on race, Bell readily agreed, considering it an indication of his acceptance in his new community, and set about preparing his speech. His happiness turned to chagrin a little later when a delegation of black law students visited him to warn him that the lecture series was actually designed by a faculty member who, without discussing it with him, accepted student complaints that Bell was teaching them constitutional law in a strange and unconventional way. The lecture series, in short, was aimed at rectifying his own perceived weaknesses as an instructor.

The black students wanted to protest the series and Bell urged them to do so, promising to express his outrage with the dean. When at the start of the first lecture the black students condemned the series as racist, the lecturer refused to go on and the series was promptly canceled. In addition, Bell learned that in clear violation of school rules, the other two constitutional law teachers had permitted his students to sit in on their classes. The faculty member who had set up the lecture later apologized to Bell, explaining that every teacher loses a class from time to time, and he was just trying to ensure that Bell's students would not miss out on the basics of this important course.

Bell explained that every black teacher potentially loses the class when he or she walks in and students see an unfamiliar black face. The challenge is to prove that competent teaching can come in all colors, and the lecture series as well as other faculty who had allowed his students to attend their classes had interfered with Bell's effort to do just that.

Dean Ely apologized and urged Bell to forget the incident. After pondering this advice, Bell resolved instead to make an issue of it. In a long column entitled "The Price and Pain of Racial Remedies," published in *The Stanford Lawyer,* Bell described the incident and challenged the Stanford community to reflect on what it meant about themselves and the school's racial climate. In addition, with the help of a few friends teaching at other law schools, he prepared and mailed letters detailing the incident to law school deans across the country, urging that to avoid similar situations that could destroy a young, inexperienced teacher, they schedule the matter for discussion at their faculty meetings.

After responding at first defensively, Stanford took Bell's challenge to heart, holding a series of town hall meetings to discuss the institution's own receptiveness to innovative teaching, racial minorities, and diverse viewpoints. The self-searching continued well after Bell left Stanford.

Over the years of his deanship, Harvard had made it clear that he would be welcome to return there. Hoping that his academic achievements would provide him with a status that had eluded him during his earlier time at Harvard, he decided to do so.

Back at his old school, Bell resumed his teaching, writing, and advocacy on racial issues. By then, three additional black men were teaching at Harvard Law School, but no woman of color. Prompted by women students of color, Bell reluctantly came to agree with their position that a black man, like him, or a white woman, like those few on the Harvard faculty, could not fully understand the pressures women of color faced in law school and would encounter in practice. The school needed law professors who could both serve as role models for minority women and provide unique perspectives to the law school community at large.

Bell, who had championed the cause of minority hiring both at Harvard and at Oregon, began assisting a group of progressive students urging Harvard to hire its first woman professor of color. He refused to accept his faculty colleagues' usual excuses: "The pool is so small." "All the good ones have a myriad of opportunities, some paying much more than we can offer." "We may have to wait a while until really good ones come along—you don't want us to sacrifice quality, do you? How fair would that be for the students, white or black?"

Tenured professors from other law schools often received invitations to spend a semester or a year in what are referred to as "look-see" visits, trial periods during which the Harvard faculty could interact with them and see if they measured up. During the 1989–90 school year, a black woman from a top school came for one of these visits. Bell felt she had brought all the qualities that had prompted the years-long effort. The faculty disagreed. The student advocates were disappointed; Bell, disgusted. With the school year drawing to a close, he announced that he would take an unpaid leave of absence until Harvard Law School hired its first woman of color.

His decision did not come lightly. His wife, Jewel, his major support for thirty years, was seriously ill with breast cancer. She did not oppose this latest action, but wondered why he was always the one who took risks to protest what he considered racial injustices. Bell, devastated by her death three months later, remained determined to see his battle through.

For the next year, Bell supported his children and himself with lectures, book royalties, and consultancies. He then sought and obtained a second year of leave, but the school warned him about a university rule limiting tenured members of the faculty to two consecutive years of absence. During that year, John Sexton, a former student who had taken Bell's class years earlier while a Harvard law student, got in touch with Bell. Now dean at New York University Law School, Sexton offered Bell a visiting position at the school, which he accepted.

A year later, his situation still unresolved with no woman of color appointed, Bell asked Harvard for a further extension. The answer came back quickly: denied. Bell's appeals were unsuccessful. Sexton offered to request his faculty to vote Bell a tenured appointment. Bell declined, but indicated his willingness to teach on a year-to-year basis. Sexton worked out the details, referring to Bell as the Walter Alston of legal academe. (Alston had managed the Brooklyn and later the Los Angeles Dodgers for twenty years, never receiving more than a one-year contract.) Bell is now working on his fourteenth year of one-year contracts.

New York University turned out to be a good home for Bell. He continues to be popular with the students, who flock to his courses. He developed what he calls a participatory teaching method that enables students to learn by doing, as they would in a clinical course, and by teaching one another. In addition to his demanding teaching schedule and several lectures at other schools, Bell has completed nearly a book a year in his period at NYU, an extraordinary pace for a law professor, young or old.

As a permanent visitor, Bell does not attend faculty meetings or participate in faculty governance—which, he ruefully admits, helps keep him out of trouble. When he turned sixty-five, his second wife, Janet, whom he married in 1992, raised money to establish an annual Derrick Bell Lecture. Attended by a huge and growing crowd of former students and current friends, the Bell Lecture features an invited speaker discussing Bell's work in the context of current developments in race law. He rides the subway to the law school on the days he teaches but does most of his writing at home. Now in his mid-seventies, Bell has no plans to retire and will continue teaching and writing as long as his health permits.

Major Themes in Bell's Writing

Easily among the most productive and innovative legal scholars of his generation, Bell has pioneered at least three areas of scholarship: critical race theory, narrative scholarship, and economic-determinist analysis of racial history. In the law school world, he has few peers. In the world of public affairs, he stands with Cornel West and his former students Charles Ogletree and Patricia Williams. As a teacher and innovator of classroom methods, he stands alone.

A great many young scholars view him as a model, but he himself seems to have had no academic mentor who shepherded his early career. Even William Hastie discouraged him from entering the civil rights field on the theory that *Brown v. Board of Education* had solved everything. His inspiration is W. E. B. Du Bois, a black genius who wrote prodigiously and whose views on race and American society brought rejection by black leaders and harassment by the government. Judge Robert L. Carter is a life mentor, admired for his many accomplishments in law and his willingness to recognize new developments and reassess even strongly held earlier views.

This book is divided into fifteen chapters, each corresponding to a theme or emphasis in Bell's writing. The excerpts cover a wide range of topics, from revisionist history and interest convergence to school desegregation and black nationalism. Some are written in elegant expository prose; others, in the narrative form for which Bell is famous.

Each section opens with a short introduction by the editors, describing the material to follow and placing it in the context of Bell's thought. Most of the excerpts contain very few footnotes; the reader seeking the full versions is encouraged to consult them at any major law library or bookstore.

This volume collects works of Bell that we considered either exemplary —his best work—or illustrative. Bell has written over one hundred articles and ten books. Accordingly, we were forced to make some hard choices and left out some very good material. A bibliography at the end of the book contains a list of his works, as well as information regarding the Derrick Bell Archive at the NYU Bobst Library.

[Eds. The actual letter Bell wrote, announcing his intention to take an unpaid leave as a protest against his school's refusal to hire its first black woman law professor, appears in chapter 6, this volume.]

Prologue
The Chronicle of the
Constitutional Contradiction

Excerpted from one of Bell's signature volumes, And We Are Not Saved, *this famous Chronicle serves as an entry point for Bell's work. Clearly and simply written, it introduces Bell's fictional interlocutor and alter ego, Geneva Crenshaw, as well as several of Bell's themes that the reader will meet elsewhere in this book—economic determinism, racial realism, revisionist history, and the role of white racism in maintaining the country's social equilibrium. It also introduces legal storytelling, a device Bell pioneered to render complex legal concepts comprehensible to the average reader.*

In the Chronicle, Geneva time-travels back to the Constitutional Convention of 1787. Once there, she challenges the Framers to reconsider the contradiction they are creating as they incorporate slavery into the U.S. Constitution, which promises liberty and justice for all.

At the end of a journey back millions of light-years, I found myself standing quietly at the podium at the Constitutional Convention of 1787. . . . The three dozen or so convention delegates looked tired. . . . They knew this was a closed meeting, and thus could not readily take in the appearance, on what had just been an empty platform, of a tall stranger—a stranger who was not only a woman but also, all too clearly, black.

. . . .

"Gentlemen," I said, "my name is Geneva Crenshaw, and I appear here to you as a representative of the late twentieth century to test

From *And We Are Not Saved* by Derrick Bell 26 (1987). Copyright © 1987 by Basic Books, Inc. Reprinted by permission of Basic Books, a member of Perseus Books, L.L.C.

whether the decisions you are making today might be altered if you were to know their future disastrous effect on the nation's people, both white and black."

For perhaps ten seconds, a shocked silence reigned. Then the chamber exploded with shouts, exclamations, oaths. . . . A warm welcome would have been too much to expect, but their shock at my sudden presence turned into an angry commotion unrelieved by even a modicum of curiosity.

. . . When I remained standing, unmoved by their strong language and dire threats, several particularly robust delegates charged toward the platform, determined to carry out the shouted orders: "Eject the Negro woman at once!"

Suddenly the hall was filled with the sound of martial music, blasting trumpets, and a deafening roll of snare drums. At the same time a cylinder composed of thin vertical bars of red, white, and blue light descended swiftly and silently from the high ceiling, nicely encapsulating the podium and me.

. . . As each man reached and tried to pass through the transparent light shield, a loud hiss broke out, quite like the sound that electrified bug zappers make on a warm summer evening. While not lethal, the shock each attacker received was sufficiently strong to knock him to the floor, stunned and shaking.

The injured delegates all seemed to recover quickly, except one who had tried to pierce the light shield with his sword. The weapon instantly glowed red hot and burned his hand. At that point, several delegates tried to rush out of the room either to escape or to seek help—but neither doors nor windows would open.

"Gentlemen," I repeated, but no one heard me in the turmoil of shouted orders, cries of outrage, and efforts to sound the alarm to those outside. Scanning the room, I saw a swarthy delegate cock his long pistol, aim carefully, and fire directly at me. But the ball struck the shield and ricocheted back into the room. . . .

At that, one of the delegates, raising his hand, roared, "Silence!" and then turned to me. "Woman! Who are you and by what authority do you interrupt this gathering?"

"Gentlemen," I began, "delegates, . . . fellow citizens, I—like some of you—am a Virginian, my forefathers having labored on the land holdings of your fellow patriot, the Honorable Thomas Jefferson. I have come to urge that, in your great work here, you not restrict the sweep of Mr.

Jefferson's self-evident truths that all men are equal and endowed by the Creator with inalienable rights, including 'Life, Liberty and the pursuit of Happiness.'" It was, I thought, a clever touch to invoke the name of Thomas Jefferson who, then serving as American minister to France, was not a member of the Virginia delegation. But my remark could not overcome the offense of my presence.

"How dare you insert yourself in these deliberations?" a delegate demanded.

"I dare," I said, "because slavery is an evil that Jefferson, himself a slave owner and unconvinced that Africans are equal to whites, nevertheless found introduced 'a perpetual exercise of the most boisterous passions, the most unremitting despotism on the one part, and degrading submissions on the other.' Slavery, Jefferson has written, brutalizes slave owner as well as slave and, worst of all, tends to undermine the 'only firm basis' of liberty, the conviction in the minds of the people that liberty is 'the gift of God.'"

. . . .

A hush settled in the group. No one wanted to admit it, but Jefferson's ambivalence on the slavery issue obviously bore meaning for at least some of those in the hall. . . .

"The stark truth is that the racial grief that persists today," I ended, "originated in the slavery institutionalized in the document you are drafting. Is this, gentlemen, an achievement for which you wish to be remembered?"

Oblivious to my plea, a delegate tried what he likely considered a sympathetic approach. "Geneva, be reasonable. Go and leave us to our work. We have heard the petitions of Africans and of abolitionists speaking in their behalf. Some here are sympathetic to these pleas for freedom. Others are not. But we have debated this issue at length, and after three months of difficult negotiations, compromises have been reached, decisions made, language drafted and approved. The matter is settled." . . .

. . . "Sirs," I said, "I have come to tell you that your compromises will not settle the matter of slavery. And even when it is ended by armed conflict and domestic turmoil far more devastating than that you hope to avoid here, the potential evil of giving priority to property over human rights will remain. Can you not address the contradiction in your words and deeds?"

"There is no contradiction," replied another delegate. ". . . Life and liberty were generally said to be of more value than property, . . . [but] an accurate view of the matter would nevertheless prove that property is the main object of Society."

"A contradiction," another delegate added, "would occur were we to follow the course you urge. We are not unaware of the moral issues raised by slavery, but we have no response to General Pinckney, who has admonished us that 'property in slaves should not be exposed to danger under a Govt. instituted for the protection of property.'"

"Of what value is a government that does not secure its citizens in their persons and their property?" inquired another delegate. "Government, . . . was instituted principally for the protection of property and was itself . . . supported by property. . . . The security the Southern states want is that their negroes may not be taken from them."

"Your deliberations here have been secret," I replied. "And yet history has revealed what you here would hide. The Southern delegates have demanded the slavery compromises as their absolute precondition to forming a new government."

"And why should it not be so?" a delegate in the rear called out. "I do not represent the Southern point of view, and yet their rigidity on the slavery issue is wholly natural, stemming as it does from the commitment of their economy to labor-intensive agriculture." . . .

"Then," I countered, "you are not troubled by the knowledge that your Southern colleagues will defend this document in the South Carolina ratification debates by admissions that 'Negroes were our wealth, our only resource'?"

"Why, in God's name," the delegate responded, "should we be troubled by the truth, candidly stated? . . . The blacks are the laborers, the peasants of the Southern states."

At this, an elderly delegate arose and rapped his cane on his chair for attention. . . . "If a record be made, that record should show that the economic benefits of slavery do not accrue only to the South. Plantation states provide a market for Northern factories, and the New England shipping industry and merchants participate in the slave trade. Northern states, moreover, employ slaves in the fields, as domestics, and even as soldiers to defend against Indian raids."

I shook my head. "Here you are then! Representatives from large and small states, slave states and those that have abolished slavery, all of you are protecting your property interests at the cost of your principles. . . . Are you not concerned with the basic contradiction in your position: that you . . . in fact represent and constitute major property holders? Do you not mind that your slogans of liberty and individual rights are essentially guarantees that neither a strong government nor the masses will be able to interfere with your property rights and those of your class? Future citizens of this nation will hold this contradiction, between what you espouse and what you here protect, against you."

"Unless we continue on our present course," a delegate called out, "no nation will come into existence whose origins can be criticized. These sessions come about because the country is teetering between anarchy and bankruptcy." . . .

"Indeed," I said, . . . "I understand the nature of the crisis that brings you here, but the compromises you make on the slavery issue are—"

"Young woman!" interrupted one of the older delegates. "You say you understand. But I tell you that it is nearly impossible for anybody who has not been on the scene to conceive what the delicacy and danger of our situation . . . [have] been. I am President of this Convention, drafted to the task against my wishes. I am here and I am ready to embrace any tolerable compromise that . . . [is] competent to save us from impending ruin."

. . . .

"Thank you, General Washington," I responded. "I know that you, though a slave owner, are opposed to slavery. And yet you have said little during these meetings. . . . Future historians will say of your silence that you recognize that to throw the weight of your opinion against slavery might so hearten the opponents of the system, while discouraging its proponents, as to destroy all hope of compromise. This would prevent the formation of the Union, and the Union, for you, is essential."

"I will not respond to these presumptions," said General Washington, "but I will tell you now what I will say to others at a later time. The new document contains some things, I will readily acknowledge, that never did, and I am persuaded never will, obtain my cordial approbation; but I did then conceive, and do now most firmly believe, that in the aggregate it is the best constitution that can be obtained at this epoch, and that this, or a dissolution, awaits our choice, and is the only alternative."

"Do you recognize," I asked, "that in order to gain unity among yourselves, your slavery compromises sacrifice freedom for the Africans who live amongst you and work for you? Such sacrifices of the rights of one group of human beings will, unless you arrest them here, become a difficult-to-break pattern in the nation's politics."

"Did you not listen to the general?" This man, I decided, must be James Madison. . . .

"I expect," Madison went on, "that many will question why I have agreed to the Constitution. And, like General Washington, I will answer: 'because I thought it safe to the liberties of the people, and the best that could be obtained from the jarring interests of States, and the miscellaneous opinions of Politicians; and because experience has proved that the real danger to America & to liberty lies in the defect of *energy & stability* in the present establishments of the United States.'"

"Do not think," added a delegate from Massachusetts, "that this Convention has come easily to its conclusions on the matter that concerns you. . . . Many of us share concerns about basing apportionment on slaves as insisted by the Southern delegates. . . ."

. . . .

"Even so," I said, "the Convention has acquiesced when representatives of the Southern states adamantly insisted that the proposed new government not interfere with their property in slaves. And is it not so that, beyond a few speeches, the representatives of the Northern states have been, at best, ambivalent on the issue?"

"And why not?" interjected another delegate. "Slavery has provided the wealth that made independence possible. . . . At the time of the Revolution, the goods for which the United States demanded freedom were produced in very large measure by slave labor. Desperately needing assistance from other countries, we purchased aid from France with tobacco produced mainly by slave labor. The nation's economic well-being depended on the institution, and its preservation is essential if the Constitution we are drafting is to be more than a useless document. . . ."

. . . "The real crisis you face," I said, "should not be resolved by your recognition of slavery, an evil whose immorality will pollute the nation as it now stains your document. Despite your resort to euphemisms like *persons* to keep out of the Constitution such words as *slave* and *slavery,* you cannot evade the consequences of the ten different provisions you have placed in the Constitution for the purpose of protecting property in slaves.

. . . .

"Gentlemen," I continued, "how can you disagree with the view of the Maryland delegate Luther Martin that the slave trade and 'three-fifths' compromises 'ought to be considered as a solemn mockery of, and insult to that God whose protection we had then implored, and . . . who views with equal eye the poor African slave and his American master'? . . ."

"Again, woman," a Northern delegate assured me, "we have heard and considered all those who oppose slavery. Despite the remonstrations of the abolitionists—of whom few, I must add, believe Negroes to be the equal of white men, and even fewer would want the blacks to remain in this land were slavery abandoned—we have acted as we believe the situation demands."

"I cannot believe," I said, "that even a sincere belief in the superiority of the white race should suffice to condone so blatant a contradiction of your hallowed ideals."

. . . .

Finally, a delegate responded to my challenge. "You have, by now, heard enough to realize that we have not lightly reached the compromises on slavery you so deplore. Perhaps we, with the responsibility of forming a radically new government in perilous times, see more clearly than you in hindsight that the unavoidable cost of our labors will be the need to accept and live with what you call a contradiction. . . . This contradiction is not lost on us. Surely we know, even though we are at pains not to mention it, that we have sacrificed the rights of some in the belief that this involuntary forfeiture is necessary to secure the rights for others in a society espousing, as its basic principle, the liberty of all.

. . . "It grieves me," he continued, "that your presence here confirms my worst fears about the harm done to your people because the Constitution, while claiming to speak in an unequivocal voice, in fact promises freedom to whites and condemns blacks to slavery. But what alternative do we have? Unless we here frame a constitution that can first gain our signatures and then win ratification by the states, we shall soon have no nation. For better or worse, slavery has served as the backbone of our economy, the source of much of our wealth. The colonies condoned it, just as the Articles of Confederation recognized it. The majority of the delegates to this convention own slaves and must have that right protected if they and their states are to be included in the new government."

He paused and then asked, more out of frustration than defiance, "What better compromise on this issue can you offer than that which we have fashioned over so many hours of heated debate?"

. . . .

I thanked the delegate for his question and then said, "The processes by which Northern states are even now abolishing slavery are known to you all. What is lacking here is not legislative skill but the courage to recognize the evil of holding blacks in slavery. . . . You fear that unless the slavery of blacks receives protection, the nation will not survive. And my message is that the compromises you are making here mean that the nation's survival will always be in doubt. For now in my own day, after two hundred years and despite bloody wars and the earnest efforts of committed people, the racial contradiction you sanction in this document remains and threatens to tear this country apart."

"Mr. Chairman," said a delegate, a colonel from the deep South, "this discussion grows tiresome and I resent to my very soul the presence in our midst of this offspring of slaves. If she accurately predicts the future fate of her race in this country, then our protection of slave property, which we deem essential for our survival, is easier to justify than in some later time when, as she implies, negroes remain subjugated even without the threats we face.

. . . .

"It's all hypocrisy! . . . Our Northern colleagues bemoan slavery while profiting from it as much as we in the South, meanwhile avoiding its costs and dangers. And our friends from Virginia, where slavery began, urge the end of importation—not out of humanitarian motivations, as their speeches suggest, but because they have sufficient slaves, and expect the value of their property will increase if further imports are barred. . . . We speak easily today of liberty, but the rise of liberty and equality in this country has been accompanied by the rise of slavery. . . ."

. . . .

"So, Colonel," I interrupted, "you are saying that slavery for blacks not only provided wealth for rich whites but, paradoxically, led also to greater freedom for poor whites. . . . In effect, what I call a contradiction you deem a solution. Slavery enables the rich to keep their lands, arrests discontent and repression of other Englishmen, strengthens their rights and nourishes their attachment to liberty. . . . You preserve the rights of Englishmen by destroying the rights of Africans. . . ."

. . . .

"The Colonel," I continued, "has performed a valuable service. He has delineated the advantages of slavery as an institution in this country. And your lengthy debates here are but prelude to the struggles that will follow your incorporation of this moral evil into the nation's basic law."

"Woman! We implore you to allow us to continue our work. While we may be inconsistent about the Negro problem, we are convinced that this is the only way open to us. You asked that we let your people go. We cannot do that and still preserve the potential of this nation for good—

a potential that requires us to recognize here and now what later generations may condemn as evil. And as we talk I wonder—are the problems
of race in your time equally paradoxical?"

I longed to continue the debate, but never got the chance. Apparently
someone outside had summoned the local militia. I turned to see a small
cannon being rolled up, pointing straight at me. Then, in quick succession, the cannoneer lighted the fuse; the delegates dived under their desks;
the cannon fired; and, with an ear-splitting roar, the cannonball broke
against the light shield and splintered, leaving me and the shield intact.

My mission over, I returned to the twentieth century.

CHAPTER I

Economic Determinism
and Interest Convergence

*What accounts for the uneven trajectory of black fortunes, with periods
of advance followed inexorably by ones of steady retreat? The selections
that follow illustrate one of Bell's signature theses—that it is white interests, particularly economic ones, and not advancing morality or the im-
peratives of law that call the tune. Some of the selections make this point
by means of a broad review of black history, showing that what we call
civil rights breakthroughs really came about because of white needs. One,
reprinted from the* Harvard Law Review, *focuses on a single case,* Brown
v. Board of Education. *The concluding selection asks what would happen
if blacks threw in the towel and let whites commit acts of racism, but only
after paying a racial licensing fee that would go to improve conditions in
the black community. As the reader will see, Bell not only puts forward
his audacious thesis; he documents it by resort to both history and imaginative thought experiments.*

White Superiority in America
Its Legal Legacy, Its Economic Costs

A few years ago, I was presenting a lecture in which I enumerated the myriad ways in which black people have been used to enrich this society and made to serve as its proverbial scapegoat. I was particularly bitter about the country's practice of accepting black contributions and ignoring the contributors. Indeed, I suggested, had black people not existed, America would have invented them.

From the audience, a listener reflecting more insight on my subject than I had shown, shouted out, "Hell man, they did invent us." The audience responded with a round of applause in which I joined. Whether we are called "colored," "Negroes," "Afro-Americans," or "blacks," we are marked with the caste of color in a society still determinedly white. . . .

Racial discrimination has placed and continues to place a heavy burden on all black people in this country. A major function of racial discrimination is to facilitate the exploitation of black labor, to deny us access to benefits and opportunities that would otherwise be available, and to blame all the manifestations of exclusion-bred despair on the asserted inferiority of the victims.

But the costs and benefits of racial discrimination are not so neatly summarized. Two other inter-connected political phenomena emanate from the widely shared belief that whites are superior and have served critically important stabilizing functions in the society: First, whites of widely varying socio-economic status employ white supremacy as a catalyst to negotiate policy differences, often through compromises that sacrifice the rights of blacks. Second, even those whites who lack wealth and power are sustained in their sense of racial superiority and thus rendered

33 Vill. L. Rev. 767 (1988). Used by permission.

more willing to accept their lesser share by an unspoken but no less certain property right in their "whiteness." This right is recognized and upheld by courts and society like all property rights under a government created and sustained primarily for that purpose.

Let us look first at the compromise-catalyst role of racism in American policy-making. When the Constitution's Framers gathered in Philadelphia, it is clear that their compromises on slavery were the key that enabled Southerners and Northerners to work out their economic and political differences.

The slavery compromises set a precedent under which black rights have given way throughout the nation's history to further white interests. Those compromises are far more than an embarrassing blot on our national history. Rather, they are the original and still definitive examples of the ongoing struggle between individual rights reform and the maintenance of the socioeconomic *status quo*.

Why did the Framers do it? . . .

They felt—and likely were right—that a government committed to the protection of property could not have come into being without the race-based slavery compromises placed in the Constitution. The economic benefits of slavery and the political compromises of black rights played a major role in the nation's growth and development. In short, without slavery, there would be no Constitution to celebrate. This is true not only because slavery provided the wealth that made independence possible, but also because it afforded an ideological basis to resolve conflict between propertied and unpropertied whites.

According to historians, including Edmund Morgan[1] and David Brion Davis,[2] working-class whites did not oppose slavery when it took root in the mid-1660s. They identified on the basis of race with wealthy planters, even though they were and would remain economically subordinate to those able to afford slaves. But the creation of a black subclass enabled poor whites to identify with and support the policies of the upper-class. And large landowners, with the safe economic advantage provided by their slaves, were willing to grant poor whites a larger role in the political process. Thus, paradoxically, slavery for blacks led to greater freedom for poor whites, at least when compared with the denial of freedom to African slaves. Slavery also provided propertyless whites with a property in their whiteness.

My point is that the slavery compromises set a precedent under which black rights have been sacrificed throughout the nation's history to further white interests. Consider only a few examples:

- The long fight for universal male suffrage was successful in several states when opponents and advocates alike reached compromises based on their generally held view that blacks should not vote. Historian Leon Litwack reports that "utilizing various political, social, economic, and pseudo-anthropological arguments, white suffragists moved to deny the vote to the Negro. From the admission of Maine in 1819 until the end of the Civil War, every new state restricted the suffrage to whites in its constitution."[3]
- By 1857, the nation's economic development had stretched the initial slavery compromises to the breaking point. The differences between planters and business interests that had been papered over 70 years earlier by mutual dangers could not be settled by a further sacrifice of black rights in the *Dred Scott* case.[4]

Chief Justice Taney's conclusion in that case that blacks had no rights whites were bound to respect represented a renewed effort to compromise political differences between whites by sacrificing the rights of blacks. The effort failed, less because Taney was willing to place all blacks—free as well as slave—outside the ambit of constitutional protection, than because he rashly committed the Supreme Court to one side of the fiercely contested issues of economic and political power that were propelling the nation toward the Civil War.

When that war ended, the North pushed through constitutional amendments, nominally to grant citizenship rights to former slaves, but actually to protect its victory. But within a decade, when another political crisis threatened a new civil war, black rights again gave way in the Hayes-Tilden Compromise of 1877. Constitutional jurisprudence fell in line with Taney's conclusion regarding the rights of blacks *vis-à-vis* whites even as it condemned his opinion. The country moved ahead, but blacks were cast into a status that only looked positive when compared with slavery itself.

. . . Throughout our history, whites of widely varying socio-economic status have employed deeply set beliefs in white supremacy as a catalyst to negotiate and resolve policy differences, often through compromises that sacrifice the rights of blacks.

A connected point is that even those whites who lack wealth and power are sustained in their sense of racial superiority and thus rendered more willing to accept their lesser share by an unspoken but no less certain property right in their "whiteness." This right is recognized and upheld by courts and society like all property rights under a government created and sustained primarily for that purpose.

In the post-Reconstruction era, the constitutional amendments initially promoted to provide rights for the newly emancipated blacks metamorphosed as the major legal bulwarks for corporate growth. The legal philosophy of that era espoused liberty of action untrammelled by state authority, but the only logic of the ideology—and its goal—was the exploitation of the working class, whites as well as blacks.

Consider *Lochner v. New York*,[5] where the Court refused to find that the state's police powers extended to protecting bakery employees against employers who required them to work in physically unhealthy conditions for more than 10 hours per day and 60 hours per week. Such maximum hour legislation, the Court held, would interfere with the bakers' inherent freedom to make their own contracts with the employers on the best terms they could negotiate. . . .

For blacks, of course, we can compare *Lochner* with the decision in *Plessy v. Ferguson*.[6] In that case, the Court upheld the state's police power to segregate blacks in public facilities even though such segregation must, of necessity, interfere with the liberties of facilities' owners to use their property as they saw fit.

Both opinions are quite similar in the Court's use of Fourteenth Amendment fictions: the assumed economic "liberty" of bakers in *Lochner*, and the assumed political "equality" of blacks in *Plessy*. Those assumptions, of course, required the most blatant hypocrisy. Both decisions, though, protected existing property and political arrangements while ignoring the disadvantages to the powerless caught in those relationships: the exploited whites (in *Lochner*) and the segregated blacks (in *Plessy*).

Efforts to form workers' unions to combat the ever-more-powerful corporate structure failed because of the active antipathy against blacks practiced by all but a few unions. Excluded from jobs and the unions because of their color, blacks found jobs as scab labor during strikes, a fact that simply increased the hostility of white workers that should have been directed toward their corporate oppressors.

The Populist Movement in the latter part of the nineteenth century attempted to build a working-class party in the South strong enough to overcome ruling class exploitation. But when neither Populists nor the conservative Democrats were able to control the black vote, they agreed to exclude blacks entirely through state constitutional amendments, thereby leaving whites to fight out elections themselves. With blacks no longer a force at the ballot box, conservatives dropped even the semblance of opposition to Jim Crow provisions pushed by lower-class whites as their guarantee that the nation recognized their priority due to their whiteness.

Southern whites rebelled against the Supreme Court's 1954 decision declaring school segregation unconstitutional precisely because they felt it endangered the long-standing priority of their superior status to blacks. . . . But in the late twentieth century, the passwords for gaining judicial recognition of the still viable property right in being white include "higher entrance scores," "seniority," and "neighborhood schools." Consider, as well, the use of impossible-to-hurdle intent barriers to deny blacks remedies for racial injustices where the relief sought would either undermine white expectations and advantages gained during years of overt discrimination, or expose the deeply imbedded racism in a major institution, such as the criminal justice system.

The continuing resistance to affirmative action plans, set-asides, and other meaningful relief for discrimination-caused harm is based in substantial part on the perception that black gains threaten the main component of status for many whites: the sense that as whites, they are entitled to priority and preference over blacks. The law has mostly encouraged and upheld what Mr. Plessy argued in *Plessy v. Ferguson* was a property right in whiteness, and those at the top of the society have benefitted because the masses of whites are too occupied in keeping blacks down to note the large gap between their shaky status and that of whites on top.

. . . .

Today—even in the midst of outbreaks of anti-black hostility on our campuses and elsewhere—an increasing number of working-class whites are learning what blacks have long known: that the rhetoric of freedom is no substitute for economic justice.

True, it may be that the structure of capitalism . . . will never provide real economic justice for all. But in the beginning, the Constitution deemed those who were black as the fit subject of property. The miracle of that document—too little noted today—is that those same blacks and their allies have in their quest for racial justice brought to the Constitution much of its current protection of individual rights.

The challenge is to move the document's protection into the sacrosanct area of economic rights, this time to insure that opportunity in this sphere is available to all. Progress in this critical area will require continued civil rights efforts, but may depend to a large extent on whites coming to recognize that their property right in being white has been purchased for too much and has netted them only the opportunity, as C. Vann Woodward put it, "to hoard sufficient racism in their bosoms to feel superior to blacks while working at a black's wages."

. . . .

The cost of racial discrimination is levied against us all. Blacks feel the burden and strive to remove it. Too many whites have felt that it was in their interest to resist those freedom efforts. That temptation, despite the counter-indicators provided by history, logic and simple common sense, remains strong. But the efforts to achieve racial justice have already performed a miracle of transforming the Constitution—a document primarily intended to protect property rights—into one that provides a measure of protection for those whose rights are not bolstered by wealth, power, and property.

NOTES

1. Edmund Morgan, American Slavery, American Freedom: The Ordeal of Colonial Virginia (1975).

2. David Brion Davis, The Problem of Slavery in the Age of Revolution: 1770–1820 (1975).

3. Leon Litwack, North of Slavery: The Negro in the Free States 1790–1860, at 79 (1967).

4. Dred Scott v. Sandford, 60 U.S. 393 (1857).

5. 198 U.S. 45 (1905).

6. 163 U.S. 537 (1896).

Brown v. Board of Education
and the Interest-Convergence
Dilemma

The year was 1959, five years after the Supreme Court's decision in *Brown*. If there was anything the hard-pressed partisans of the case did not need, it was more criticism of a decision ignored by the President, condemned by much of Congress, and resisted wherever it was sought to be enforced. Certainly, civil rights adherents did not welcome adding to the growing list of critics the name of Professor Herbert Wechsler, an outstanding lawyer, a frequent advocate for civil rights causes, and a scholar of prestige and influence. Nevertheless, Professor Wechsler chose that time to deliver Harvard Law School's Oliver Wendell Holmes Lecture raising new questions about the legal appropriateness and principled shortcomings of *Brown* . . . .

Courts, Wechsler argued, "must be genuinely principled, resting with respect to every step . . . on analysis and reasons quite transcending the immediate result that is achieved."[1] . . . Wechsler found difficulty with Supreme Court decisions where principled reasoning was in his view either deficient or, in some instances, nonexistent. He included the *Brown* opinion in the latter category.

Wechsler concluded the Court in *Brown* must have rested its holding on the view that "racial segregation is, *in principle,* a denial of equality to the minority against whom it is directed; that is, the group that is not dominant politically and, therefore, does not make the choice involved." Yet, Wechsler found this argument untenable because it seemed to require an inquiry into the motives of the legislature, a practice generally foreclosed to the courts.

93 Harv. L. Rev. 518 (1980). Used by permission.

Wechsler then asserted that the legal issue in state-imposed segregation cases was not one of discrimination at all, but rather of associational rights: "the denial by the state of freedom to associate, a denial that impinges in the same way on any groups or races that may be involved." Wechsler reasoned that "if the freedom of association is denied by segregation, integration forces an association upon those for whom it is unpleasant or repugnant." And concluding with a question that has challenged legal scholars, Wechsler asked:

> Given a situation where the state must practically choose between denying the association to those individuals who wish it or imposing it on those who would avoid it, is there a basis in neutral principles for holding that the Constitution demands that the claims for association should prevail?[2]

The Search for a Neutral Principle: Racial Equality and Interest Convergence

Scholars had little difficulty finding a neutral principle on which the *Brown* decision could be based. Indeed, from the hindsight of a quarter century of the greatest racial consciousness-raising the country has ever known, much of Professor Wechsler's concern seems hard to imagine. To doubt that racial segregation is harmful to blacks, and to suggest what blacks really sought was the right to associate with whites, is to believe in a world that does not exist now and could not have existed then. Professor Charles Black, therefore, correctly viewed racial equality as the neutral principle which underlay the *Brown* opinion. Black's major premise is that "the equal protection clause of the Fourteenth Amendment should be read as saying that the Negro race, as such, is not to be significantly disadvantaged by the laws of the states."[3] The equal protection clause clearly bars racial segregation because segregation harms blacks and benefits whites in ways too numerous and obvious to require citation.

Logically, the argument is persuasive, and Black has no trouble urging that "[w]hen the directive of equality cannot be followed without displeasing the white[s], then something that can be called a 'freedom' of the white[s] must be impaired."[4] It is precisely here, though, that many whites part company with Professor Black. Whites may agree in the abstract that blacks are citizens entitled to constitutional protection against racial discrimination, but few are willing to recognize that racial segregation is much more than a series of quaint customs that can be remedied effectively without altering the status of whites. The extent of this unwillingness is illustrated by the controversy over affirmative action programs, particularly those where identifiable whites must step aside for blacks they deem less qualified or less deserving. Whites simply cannot envision the personal responsibility and the potential sacrifice inherent in Professor Black's conclusion that true equality for blacks will require the surrender of racism-granted privileges for whites.

This sober assessment of reality raises concern about the ultimate import of Black's theory. On a normative level, as a description of how the world *ought* to be, the notion of racial equality appears to be the proper basis on which *Brown* rests, and Wechsler's framing of the problem in terms of associational rights thus seems misplaced. Yet, on a positivistic level—how the world *is*—large segments of the American people do not deem racial equality legitimate, at least to the extent it threatens to impair the societal status of whites. Hence, Wechsler's search for a guiding principle in the context of associational rights retains merit in the positivistic sphere, because it suggests a deeper truth about the subordination of law to interest-group politics with a racial configuration.

Although no such subordination is apparent in *Brown,* it is possible to discern in more recent school decisions the outline of a principle, applied without direct acknowledgment, that could serve as the positivistic expression of the neutral statement of general applicability. Its elements rely as much on political history as legal precedent and emphasize the world as it is rather than how we might want it to be. Translated from judicial activity in racial cases both before and after *Brown,* this principle of "interest convergence" provides: The interest of blacks in achieving racial equality will be accommodated only when it converges with the interests of whites. However, the Fourteenth Amendment, standing alone, will not authorize a judicial remedy providing effective racial equality for blacks where the remedy sought threatens the superior societal status of middle and upper class whites.

It follows that the availability of Fourteenth Amendment protection in racial cases may not actually be determined by the character of harm suffered by blacks or the quantum of liability proved against whites. Racial remedies may instead be the outward manifestations of unspoken and perhaps subconscious judicial conclusions that the remedies, if granted, will secure, advance, or at least not harm societal interests deemed important by middle and upper class whites. Racial justice—or its appearance—may, from time to time, be counted among the interests deemed important by the courts and by society's policymakers.

In assessing how this principle can accommodate both the *Brown* decision and the subsequent development of school desegregation law, it is necessary to remember that the issue of school segregation and the harm it inflicted on black children did not first come to the Court's attention in the *Brown* litigation: blacks had been attacking the validity of these policies for 100 years. Yet, prior to *Brown*, black claims that segregated public schools were inferior had been met by orders requiring merely that facilities be made equal. What accounted, then, for the sudden shift in 1954 away from the separate but equal doctrine and towards a commitment to desegregation?

The decision in *Brown* to break with the Court's long-held position on these issues cannot be understood without some consideration of the decision's value to whites, not simply those concerned about the immorality of racial inequality, but also those whites in policymaking positions able to see the economic and political advances at home and abroad that would follow abandonment of segregation. First, the decision helped to provide immediate credibility to America's struggle with Communist countries to win the hearts and minds of emerging third world peoples. Advanced by lawyers for both the NAACP and the federal government, this point was not lost on the news media. *Time* magazine, for example, predicted that the international impact of *Brown* would prove scarcely less important than its effect on the education of black children: "In many countries, where U.S. prestige and leadership have been damaged by the fact of U.S. segregation, it will come as a timely reassertion of the basic American principle that 'all men are created equal.'"[5]

Second, *Brown* offered much needed reassurance to American blacks that the precepts of equality and freedom so heralded during World War II might yet be given meaning at home. Returning black veterans faced not only continuing discrimination, but also violent attacks in the South which rivalled those that took place at the conclusion of World War I. Their disillusionment and anger found poignant expression when black actor, Paul Robeson, in 1949 declared: "It is unthinkable . . . that American Negroes would go to war on behalf of those who have oppressed us for generations . . . against a country, the Soviet Union, which in one generation has raised our people to the full human dignity of mankind."[6] It is not impossible to imagine that fear of the spread of such sentiment influenced subsequent racial decisions made by the courts.

Finally, some whites realized that the South could make the transition from a rural, plantation society to the sunbelt with all its potential and profit only when it ended its struggle to remain divided by state-sponsored segregation. Thus, segregation was viewed as a barrier to further industrialization in the South.

. . . For those whites who sought an end to desegregation on moral grounds or for the pragmatic reasons outlined above, *Brown* appeared to be a welcome break with the past. When the Supreme Court finally condemned segregation, however, the outcry was nevertheless great, especially among poorer whites who feared loss of control over their public schools and other facilities. Their fear of loss gained force from the sense that they had been betrayed. They relied, as had generations before them, on the expectation that white elites would maintain lower class whites in a societal status superior to that designated for blacks. In fact, legislatures initially established segregated schools and facilities [in many cases] at the insistence of the white working class. Today, little has changed. Many poorer whites oppose social reform as "welfare programs for blacks" although, ironically, they have employment, education, and social service needs that differ from those of poor blacks by a margin that, without a racial scorecard, is difficult to measure.

Interest-Convergence Remedies under Brown

The question still remains as to the surest way to reach the goal of educational effectiveness for both blacks and whites. I believe that the most widely used court-ordered programs may in some cases be inferior to plans focusing on "educational components," including the creation and development of "model" all-black schools. . . . The remedies set forth in the major school cases following *Brown*—balancing the student and teacher populations by race in each school, eliminating one-race schools, redrawing school attendance lines, and transporting students to achieve racial balance—have not in themselves guaranteed black children better schooling than they received in the pre-*Brown* era. Such racial balance measures have often altered the racial appearance of dual school systems without eliminating racial discrimination. Plans relying on racial balance to foreclose evasion have not eliminated the need for further orders protecting black children against discriminatory policies, including resegregation within desegregated schools, the loss of black faculty and administrators, suspensions and expulsions at much higher rates than white students, and varying forms of racial harassment ranging from exclusion from extracurricular activities to physical violence. Antidefiance remedies, then, while effective in forcing alterations in school system structure, often encourage and seldom shield black children from discriminatory retaliation.

The educational benefits of mandatory assignment of black and white children to the same schools are also debatable. If benefits did inure, they have begun to dissipate as whites flee in alarming numbers from school districts ordered to implement mandatory reassignment plans. In response, civil rights lawyers sought to include entire metropolitan areas within mandatory reassignment plans in order to encompass mainly white suburban school districts where so many white parents sought sanctuary for their children.

Thus, the antidefiance strategy was brought full circle from a mechanism for preventing evasion by school officials of *Brown*'s antisegregation mandate to one aimed at creating a discrimination-free environment. This approach to the implementation of *Brown*, however, has become increasingly ineffective; indeed, it has in some cases been educationally destructive. A preferable method is to focus on obtaining real educational effectiveness which may entail the improvement of presently desegregated schools as well as the creation or preservation of model black schools.

. . . .

Desegregation remedies that do not integrate may seem a step backward toward the *Plessy* "separate but equal" era. Some black educators, however, see major educational benefits in schools where black children, parents, and teachers can harness the real cultural strengths of the black community to overcome the many barriers to educational achievement. As Professor Laurence Tribe argued, "[J]udicial rejection of the 'separate but equal' talisman seems to have been accompanied by a potentially troublesome lack of sympathy for racial separateness as a possible expression of group solidarity."[7]

This is not to suggest that educationally oriented remedies can be developed and adopted without resistance. Policies necessary to obtain effective schools threaten the self-interest of teacher unions and others with vested interests in the status quo. But successful magnet schools may provide a lesson that effective schools for blacks must be a primary goal rather than a secondary result of integration. Many white parents recognize a value in integrated schooling for their children but they quite properly view integration as merely one component of an effective education. To the extent that civil rights advocates also accept this reasonable sense of priority, some greater racial interest conformity should be possible.

NOTES

1. Herbert Wechsler, Toward Neutral Principles of Constitutional Law, 73 Harv. L. Rev. 1, 15 (1959).

2. Id. at 34.

3. See, e.g., Charles Black, The Lawfulness of the Segregation Decisions, 69 Yale L.J. 421, 421 (1960).

4. Id. at 429.

5. See Derrick Bell, Racial Remediation: An Historical Perspective on Current Conditions, 52 Notre Dame Law. 5, 12 (1976).

6. D. Butler, Paul Robeson 137 (1976) (unwritten speech before the Partisans of Peace, World Peace Congress in Paris).

7. Laurence Tribe, American Constitutional Law § 16-15, at 1022 (1978) (footnote omitted).

The Role of Fortuity in Racial Policy-Making

Blacks as Fortuitous Beneficiaries of Racial Policies

. . . .

The involuntary sacrifice of black rights can serve as a catalyst enabling whites to settle serious policy differences. I now see that these silent covenants that differ so much in result are two sides of the same coin. The two-sided coin with involuntary racial sacrifice on the one side, and interest-convergent remedies on the other can be called: racial fortuity.

Racial fortuity resembles a contract law concept: the third-party beneficiary. In brief, two parties may contract to provide goods or services to a third. For example, a husband wishing to have flowers delivered to his wife on a weekly basis contracts with a florist to provide this service. If the florist fails to do so, the husband can sue, but a large and complicated body of law governs when the wife can sue the florist. While she was the intended beneficiary, she was not a party to the contract and may not even have known about it.

One aspect of this body of law is clear. The contracting parties must intend to confer a benefit on a third-party. As one court put it, "The test is whether the benefit to the third person is direct to him or is but an incidental benefit to him arising from the contract. If direct, the third party may sue on the contract."[1] Thus, in many states, the wife could sue the florist. If the benefit were incidental, however, the third party has no right of recovery.

. . . .

Sometimes the parties are identifiable. Often, though, one finds no technical contract as such. Rather, policy makers weigh various options and come to agreements or silent covenants. The *Brown* decision reflects the Supreme Court justices' consensus that for reasons of foreign policy and domestic tranquility constitutional protection for segregation must end. At the Constitutional Convention, the Framers sacrificed black hopes for freedom because they knew that they could not gain support for the Constitution unless it recognized slavery and protected slave owners' property in slaves.

As I have said, racial policy actions may be influenced, but are seldom determined, by the seriousness of the harm blacks are suffering, by the earnest petitions they have argued in courts, by the civil rights bills filed in legislative chambers, or even by impressive street protests. None of these change blacks' status as fortuitous beneficiaries. As with incidental beneficiaries in contract law, "The test is whether the benefit to the third person is direct to him or is but an incidental benefit to him arising from the contract. If direct he may sue on the contract; if incidental he has no right of recovery thereon."[2] Racial fortuity.

But, aren't racial policies often justified as remedies for discrimination? Didn't Lincoln's Emancipation Proclamation, by its very terms, claim to abolish slavery? Didn't the post–Civil War Amendments grant rights of citizenship to the former slaves? And didn't *Brown v. Board* grant the relief the NAACP lawyers sought by striking down racial segregation in the public schools?

All true, but these commitments came about when those making them saw that they, those they represented, or the country could derive benefits that were at least as important as those blacks would receive. Blacks were not necessary parties to these commitments. Lincoln acted in an understanding with his generals and other supporters that if he abolished slavery, it would disrupt the Confederate work force, foreign governments would not enter the Civil War on the side of the Confederacy, and Union armies could enlist the freed slaves to fill their badly depleted ranks.

The post–Civil War Amendments were adopted with the understanding that by doing so, Republicans would maintain control of the federal government for years to come. And the Supreme Court determined to decide *Brown* as it did because it agreed with the State Department that invalidating segregation in the public schools would benefit the nation's foreign policy. While blacks complained bitterly when each of these "civil rights" arrangements was not enforced because policy makers moved on to new concerns, blacks were, as fortuitous beneficiaries, unable to gain meaningful enforcement despite their good faith expectation that commitments set out in the law, even in the Constitution, would be honored.

. . . .

Whites as Fortuitous Beneficiaries of Racial Policies

While the economic, political, and psychic benefits whites gained from slavery and segregation are demonstrable, the real costs to whites of those benefits are unacknowledged. As with blacks, most whites are not directly engaged in racial policymaking. This is true even though the racial policymakers are usually white, and whites generally identify with these policymakers assuming their influence is pivotal—as it often is. But their preferences, often their insistence on laws that undermine black rights and provide legal standing to various forms of discrimination, do not ensure the maintenance of these discriminatory policies when conditions change. In this sense, whites too are fortuitous beneficiaries to the racial policies that they seek and hold dear.

Recall how Jim Crow laws that would eventually segregate blacks in every aspect of public life began to emerge out of a series of unofficial racial agreements between white elites and poorer whites who demanded laws segregating public facilities to insure official recognition of their superior status over blacks with whom, save for color, they shared a similar economic plight. For the most part, courts readily upheld these laws.

Then in the late 1940s, policy makers and the Supreme Court began to revoke support for segregation in its most blatant forms. President Truman, under pressure from civil rights groups, issued executive orders providing for equal treatment and opportunity in the armed services, and abolishing racial discrimination in federal employment. The Supreme Court began finding unconstitutional rather obvious infringements on basic rights to vote. Courts struck down white primaries through which southern whites excluded blacks from meaningful participation in electoral politics. Resisting whites saw these decisions as peremptory revocation of policies they considered permanent. Yet while deeming themselves the prime motivations for policies of white preference, whites could no longer use the law to require continued enforcement of white preferences.

Thus, whites, too, became fortuitous beneficiaries of racial policies adopted and abandoned for reasons beyond race.

Racial Fortuity and Reparations

In light of foreign and domestic concerns that likely influenced the *Brown* decision, consider what interest-convergence factors might move policy-makers to look favorably on the reparations-for-slavery claims that have drawn media and scholarly attention. After affirmative action, reparations could become the next area of major racial activism and controversy.

. . . .

Reparations has a history that began even before the Civil War. Its proponents have been many and their arguments varied, but in general they assert: 1) slaves were not paid for their labor for over 200 years, depriving their descendants of their inheritance; 2) the descendants of slave owners wrongfully inherited the profits derived from slave labor; 3) the U.S. government made and then broke its promise to provide former slaves with 40 acres and a mule; 4) systematic and government-sanctioned economic and political racial oppression since the abolition of slavery impeded and interfered with the self-determination of African Americans and excluded them from sharing in the nation's growth and prosperity; 5) the reparations that Germany gave to Jews and the United States to Native Americans and Japanese Americans are precedents for the payment of reparations to African Americans.

Opponents dismiss racial reparations as a pipedream. None of those who were slaves or slave masters is still alive. Serious procedural barriers bar suits intended to require the descendants of slave owners to pay the descendants of slaves. Yale Law School Professor Boris Bittker conducted a thorough review of the legal difficulties facing reparations litigation, concluding that it is highly unlikely that blacks living today will obtain direct payments in compensation for their forebears' subjugation as slaves before the Emancipation Proclamation.[3]

Hidden by the often outraged opposition to reparations is that this country compensates for generalized loss all the time: certainly large corporations through bankruptcy laws, re-structuring, tax provisions, and—in the case of some worthy corporations like Chrysler or Lockheed—outright government grants. The Japanese reparations program and that sought by blacks differ, but even so, the Japanese precedent might be helpful to black reparations' advocates.

As I write, Harvard Law Professor Charles Ogletree, Charles Garry, Johnnie Cochran, and a host of other lawyers have filed a reparations suit against the City of Tulsa and the state of Oklahoma on behalf of hundreds of survivors of the total destruction of Greenwood, the prosperous black section of that city, in 1921. Plaintiffs filed litigation following failure of negotiations for a reparations settlement. The history is clear. In 1921, a young black man who had accidentally stepped on the toe of a white female elevator operator was charged with molesting her. Fearing he might be lynched, armed black men volunteered to help the sheriff protect the youth. A scuffle with whites resulted, shooting started, and two blacks and ten whites were killed. When the outnumbered blacks retreated to the black community, whites looted hardware and sporting goods stores, arming themselves with rifles, revolvers, and ammunition. Large groups of whites and blacks fired on each other. Whites then decided to invade what they called "Niggertown" and systematically wipe it out.

To accomplish this end, more than 10,000 armed whites gathered, 60 to 80 automobiles filled with armed whites formed a circle around the black section, while airplanes were used to spy on the movements of blacks and—according to some reports—drop bombs on the blacks. Black men and women fought valiantly but vainly to defend their homes against the hordes of invaders who, after looting the homes, set them on fire. Blacks seeking to escape the flames were shot down.

Fifty or more blacks barricaded themselves in a church where they resisted several massed attacks. Finally, a torch applied to the church set it ablaze, and the occupants began to pour out, shooting as they ran. Several blacks were killed. The entire black belt became a smoldering heap of blackened ruins. Hardly a shanty, house, or building was left standing. Domestic animals wandering among the wreckage were the only signs of life. Unofficial estimates put the death toll at 50 whites and 150 to 200 blacks, many of whom were buried in graves without coffins. Other victims incinerated in the burning houses were never accounted for.

In recent years, the City of Tulsa raised a memorial to the victims of the massacre, but the city is actively defending against the litigation. The judge in the case granted the plaintiffs' request to take depositions of some of their clients, all of whom are in their 80s or older in order to preserve critical testimony about the tragedy. . . . The Tulsa litigation, by narrowing reparations claims to a specific and undeniable racial attack that caused the deaths of countless blacks and the destruction of a whole community, quiets opponents and exerts pressure for relief.

According to Randall Robinson: "The issue here is not whether or not we can, or will, win reparations. The issue rather is whether we will fight for reparations, because we have decided for ourselves that they are our due."[4] Here is the activist strategy for responding to the restraints of racial fortuity. It is based on the conviction that a cause is worth pursuing despite the obstacles of law and public opinion. The pursuit can create conditions that convince policy makers, unmoved by appeals to simple justice, that relief is a prudent necessity.

NOTES

1. See, e.g., Cherry for Use of Trueblood v. Aetna Cas. & Sur. Co., 300 Ill. App. 392, 21 N.E.2d 4 (3d Dist. 1939).

2. Id.

3. Boris Bittker, The Case for Black Reparations (1973).

4. Randall Robinson, The Debt 206 (2000).

The Racial Preference
Licensing Act

At an elaborate Rose Garden signing ceremony witnessed by the many right-wing groups that worked for its passage, the President assured the nation that the new Racial Preference Licensing Act represented a realistic advance in race relations. "It is," he insisted, "certainly not a return to the segregation policies granted constitutional protection under the 'separate but equal' standard of *Plessy v. Ferguson.*" "And," he added, "it is no more than an inopportune coincidence that the Act was passed exactly a century after the Court announced the *Plessy* decision. Rather, the new law embodies a bold new approach to the nation's oldest problem. It does not assume a nonexistent racial tolerance, but boldly proclaims a commitment to moral justice through the workings of a marketplace undisturbed by government interference."

Indeed, the new Act ratified discriminatory practices that by the early 1990s had become the de facto norm. Under the new Act, all employers, proprietors of public facilities, and owners and managers of dwelling places on application to the federal government could obtain a license authorizing the holders or their agents to exclude or separate persons on the basis of race and color. The license itself was expensive, though not prohibitively so. After obtaining a license, the holder was required to pay to a government commission a tax equal to three percent of the income derived from employing, serving, or selling to whites during each quarter in which a policy of racial preference was in effect.

Holders were required to display their licenses prominently, and to operate their businesses in racially selective fashion. Discrimination had to

Foreword: The Final Civil Rights Act, 79 Cal. L. Rev. 597 (1991). © 1991 by the *California Law Review.* Reprinted from the *California Law Review* by permission of the Regents of the University of California, Berkeley.

be practiced on a nonselective basis. Licenses were not available to those not planning to discriminate but seeking to use a license as a form of insurance against discrimination suits. Minority group members carried the burden of proof when charging discrimination against a facility not holding a license, but the minority group members could meet that burden with statistical and circumstantial as well as direct evidence. Under the Act, successful complainants were entitled to damages and attorney's fees.

. . . License fees and commissions were placed in an "equality fund" used to underwrite black businesses, offer no-interest mortgage loans for black home buyers, and provide scholarships for black students seeking college and vocational education. To counter charges that black people would be segregated and would never gain any significant benefit from the equality fund, the commission overseeing collection and distribution of license fees consisted of five members—each a representative from a major civil rights organization—appointed by the President to their posts for three-year terms.

The President committed himself and his administration to effective enforcement of the new Racial Preference Licensing Act. He warned that those found guilty of discriminating without a license or who failed to comply with the license provisions were subject to civil penalties as stiff as those under the RICO statutes.

"It is time," the President declared, "to bring hard-headed realism rather than well-intentioned idealism to bear on our long-standing racial problems. Policies adopted because they seemed right have usually failed. Actions taken to promote justice for blacks brought injustice to whites without appreciably improving the status or standards of living for blacks, particularly those members of the group who most needed protection.

"Within the memories of many of our citizens, this nation has both affirmed polices of racial segregation and advocated polices of racial integration. Neither approach has been either satisfactory or effective in furthering harmony and domestic tranquility. Today, I sign what may be the final civil rights law. It maximizes freedom of racial choice for all our citizens while guaranteeing that people of color will benefit either directly from equal access or indirectly from the fruits of the license taxes paid by those who choose policies of racial exclusion.

"I respect the views of those who vigorously opposed this new law. And yet the course we take today was determined by many forces too powerful to ignore, too popular to resist, and too pregnant with potential to deny. We have vacillated long enough. We must move on toward what I predict will be a new and more candid and collaborative relationship among all our citizens. May God help us all as we seek in good faith a new way of resolving our oldest and most ineluctable problem."

Debating the Final Civil Rights Act

To: Ms. Geneva Crenshaw (proponent and drafter of the Act)
Electronic Mail Route 47-782

Dear Geneva,

My God, woman! What are you trying to do to me? . . . Your allegorical racial chronicles, despite their rather radical critiques of the civil rights movement, have become quite well-known both among lawyers and laypersons. As you predicted, they have stirred a healthy and much-needed debate. . . .

But give me a break! . . . Your odious proposal will earn me permanent enmity from the civil rights community. Of course, the right-wing conservatives whom you accurately designate as the sponsors and supporters of this anti–civil rights law will hail me as the "The Black Savior" of racial reform.

. . . But suggesting a black-bonus-based return to state-supported racial segregation is simply going too far. God may be dead, but the Fourteenth Amendment, though wounded by the current Supreme Court, still lives.

Realistically,
Derrick

To: Professor Derrick Bell

Dear Doubting Thomas,

Oh ye of little faith! Even after all these years, you remain as suspicious of my truths as you are faithful to the civil rights ideals that events long ago rendered obsolete. Whatever its cost to your relationship with your civil rights friends, why can't you accept the inevitability of my Final Civil Rights Act?

As to the viability of the Fourteenth Amendment, or, for that matter, any civil rights law, you—not I—wrote that the first Rule of Race Relations Law is that:

Racial remedies are the outward manifestations of unspoken and perhaps unconscious conclusions that such remedies—if adopted—will secure, advance, or at least not harm the interests of whites in power.

What I assume you are saying is that while blacks struggle for legal protection against one or another form of racial discrimination, the country responds only when the requested relief will serve some societal interest deemed important to whites. Virtually every piece of civil rights legislation beginning with the Emancipation Proclamation supports your position.

. . . .

Your second Rule of Race Relations Law, if you remember, is that:

The benefits to blacks of civil rights policies are often symbolic rather than substantive, and when the crisis that prompted their enactment ends, they will infrequently be enforced for blacks, though in altered interpretations they may serve the needs of whites.

. . . .

Now, I can hear you asking, "How do the rules justify my Racial Preference Licensing Act, which looks like a new, more subtle, but hardly less pernicious 'separate but equal' law?" Let me try and explain.

Derrick, today as it did in the mid-1890s, the Supreme Court is reacting to a range of social forces that are hardening racial attitudes. Whites, as they did a century ago, are concluding that the country has done enough for its racial minorities. The never-vigorous enforcement of civil rights laws has slowed, encouraging open violations and discouraging victims from filing complaints they fear will only add futility and possible retaliation to their misery.

What the President calls the Final Civil Rights Act *is, in fact, a manifestation of your Rule Two. The society—or much of it—has tired of its commitment to protect blacks against the preference of whites. It believes that the return of legal protection of racially discriminatory policies is in its interest. And it seeks to give that interest legitimacy by claiming that the notion—suggested early in theory—that whites have a right of nonassociation should be recognized in law.*

However, the Act is attractive to many whites because it seems to contain provisions that conform to an inversion of your Rule One. That is, because of the Equality Fund, they are able to ratio-nalize a return to legalized segregation by viewing this as the neces-sary means to reach the black reparations end long sought by black groups.

Your challenge is to determine whether in this, as in any seem-ingly hostile, racial policymaking lies unintended potential that African Americans can exploit. Think about it, Derrick. Legisla-tion like the Final Civil Rights Act *may be all African Americans can expect, and could prove all that they need.*

Prophetically,
Geneva

To: Ms. Geneva Crenshaw
Electronic Mail Route 47-782

Dear Geneva,

Even as a vehicle for discussion, I cannot accept the legalized reincarnation of Jim Crow. Too many of our people suffered and sacrificed to bury those obnoxious signs: "Colored" and "white."
. . . Your Final Civil Rights Act *will simply squander our high prin-ciples in return for a mess of segregation-tainted pottage. Victory on such grounds is no victory at all.*

Resolutely,
Derrick

To: Professor Derrick Bell

Dear Derrick,

Tell me: What principle is so compelling that you continue your support for obsolete civil rights strategies while ignoring the con-temporary statistics regarding black crime, broken families, devas-tated neighborhoods, alcohol and drug abuse, out-of-wedlock births, illiteracy, unemployment, and welfare dependency? Segrega-tion was hateful, but if I knew that its return would reduce the devastation of black communities to the ante-desegregation levels, I would think such a "trade" entitled to serious thought, not self-righteous dismissal.

. . . You and other civil rights policymakers must realize that you have been formulating your strategies without any real assessment of the continuing importance of racial subordination of black people

to the stability of the American economic and political system. It is not that you civil rights advocates do not admit the existence of racism. You know it exists and assert on every public occasion that no social fact in America is more salient than racial difference. You readily and pessimistically recount the developments marking the end of the second reconstruction and the parallels with the end of the first reconstruction a century ago. But you do not see the critical connection between the social subordination of blacks and the social stability of whites.

"The fact is, friend, you do not have forever to see my point."

"What!" I said, startled. I had been reading Geneva's words from my computer screen when I became conscious of a low, melodious voice saying those very words. I turned, and. . . .

There she was. Seated on the small couch in my study, her over six-foot, slender frame gave her a regal presence. Geneva's strong features were framed by her intricately braided hair that was now quite gray and made a striking contrast with her still smooth skin that was almost translucent in its blue-black glory. She greeted me with that smile of hers that conveyed both warmth and authority.

"Welcome," I said, trying to mask my shock with what I hope was savoir-faire. "Is it now your practice to visit folks who are still at work at 2 a.m.?"

"If you spent more time worrying about our people and less meddling in my business, we would all be better off and I would not have to visit you at any time.

. . . .

"I decided our computer correspondence was inadequate to convey the real significance of the *Final Civil Rights Act.*"

"Well," I said, "I am more than delighted to see you, but you did not have to come back to lecture me about the reasons for the continuing and increasingly virulent vitality of American racism. I understand, moreover, the importance of race as a stabilizing force in American society. . . ."

. . . .

". . . Racism is more than a group of bad white folks whose discriminatory tendencies can be controlled by well-formed laws, vigorously enforced. It is a nonnegotiable essential element of America as we know it. Belief in the superiority of their whiteness leads many whites to accept unthinkingly a status that is often as disadvantaged as that involuntarily held by blacks. It is tied to the existing economic system and serves as a principal stabilizer of that system."

"Whatever happened to 'We Shall Overcome'?"

"Racist opposition has polluted and transformed the dream that phrase once inspired into a myth that comforts and distracts you from the harsh racial reality that is closing in around us and ours."

. . . Geneva continued. "Don't you see? Just as parents used to tell children stories about the stork to avoid telling them about sex, so we hold to dreams about a truly integrated society. . . . In his recent book, *Love's Executioner and Other Tales of Psychotherapy,*[1] Dr. Irvin Yalom reports that a fundamental principle in psychotherapy is the inevitability of death for each of us and for those we love. He describes the myriad ways we devise to escape or deny the terrible reality of death. . . . We chuckle and agree with Woody Allen when he says, 'I'm not afraid of death. I just don't want to be there when it happens.' The fact is, 'full awareness of death ripens our wisdom and enriches our life.' A dying patient recognized this when he stated, 'though the *fact,* the physicality of death destroys us, the *idea* of death may save us.'[2]

"Derrick, the analogy is not exact, but just as death is inevitable and inherent in life, so racism in America, while not inherent, is intractable. It is socially constructed, but no less real. We must deal directly with American racism, just as we do with death. Civil rights advocates and their organizations must face the unavoidable truth that this nation's social stability is built on a belief in and a determination to maintain white dominance. Racism is the manifestation of this deeply entrenched determination. It plays a key role in a capitalist society where the growing gap between the wealth of the rich and the poverty of the rest of the populace is both large and obscene. But even a total reform of our economy would not erase—and might intensify—the need of whites to measure their self-worth by maintaining blacks in a subordinate status."

"Geneva. What you are saying sounds like a prescription for terminal despair. As applied to your Racial Preference Licensing Law, it is simply too risky."

"It is risky," Geneva agreed, defiantly. "It is an approach with risks quite like those we must face as we seek the salvation in life that comes when we accept the reality of death."

"But, Geneva, if death and racial subordination are inevitable and unavoidable, if all our efforts and accomplishments will come to nothing, then what is the meaning of life and what then is the value of working for civil rights?"

Geneva brightened. "As discouraging as that sounds," she explained, "it seems to me that when we ask that question aloud, we are dealing directly with the unstated question that has bedeviled us all along. Out in the open, we can forthrightly deal with the seeming paradox of a people long oppressed by law continuing to look to law for remedies that elude our grasp, deceive our minds, and frustrate our hopes."[3]

. . . .

"I agree with the need for a more realistic perspective, Geneva, but how do you move from realism to your Racial Preference Licensing Law?"

"In the face of disaster, the person who is truly liberated from the fear of death looks for redeeming possibilities. Civil rights advocates, freed of the 'We Shall Overcome' syndrome, should and can make a similar assessment of all racial policies—including the Racial License Preference Act.

"Consider that by authorizing racial discrimination, the Act removes the long-argued concern that civil rights laws deny a right of nonassociation. By requiring the discriminator to publicize his actions and to pay all blacks a price for that 'right,' the law may dilute both the financial and psychological benefits of racism. Most whites pay a tremendous price for their unthinking and often unconscious racism, but they are less willing to make direct payments for the privilege. Today, even the worst racist denies that he is a 'racist.'

"Black people, moreover, will no longer have to divine whether an employer, realtor, or proprietor wants to exclude them. The license will give them—and the world—ample notice. Those who seek to discriminate without a license will place their businesses at risk of serious, even ruinous, penalties.

"It may seem crazy, but racism is hardly based on logic. We need to fight racism with racism the way a forest ranger fights fire with fire. . . .

. . . .

"Civil rights advocates must face up to the racial realities of American social and economic stability and try to structure initiatives and responses in the light of the racial world as it is rather than as they would like it to be."

. . . .

Geneva, still smiling, stood, ready to head toward the door when she delivered this last zinger. Bending to give me a kiss, she said, "Write soon. You are as impossible as ever, but I've missed you nonetheless."

The usually squeaky door to my study opened and closed silently as she departed. My two large Weimaraner hounds—usually alert to the slightest sound—had slept soundly through Geneva's visit.

Could I have fallen asleep and imagined what had happened? But no. There on my monitor was all of our conversation, miraculously transcribed and ready to insert into my now completed chapter. The notion of a license to practice racial discrimination in the 1990s seemed absurd, but no more so than the reality of worsening racism as we approach the twenty-first century.

NOTES

1. Irvin Yalom, Love's Executioner and Other Tales of Psychotherapy (1989).
2. Id. at 7.
3. See id. at 12.

CHAPTER 2

Racial Realism

The pieces in this chapter, which opens with Bell's famous Space Traders Chronicle, sound a second signature theme in Bell's writing—the permanence of racism. If whites in this country hold most of the power and manipulate civil rights advances for blacks to maintain their ascendancy, no force known to humanity is likely to change this state of affairs. Hoping for more is foolhardy; the best one can do is come to terms with one's destiny and find what meaning one can in struggle itself. Power ineluctably asserts and reasserts itself, treating ruthlessly those (like Paul Robeson) who get in its way. Yet, a certain nobility attends refusing to submit meekly to one's fate. And, by mobilizing its own resources, the black community even without white help may accomplish much for its own, for example, its children. Bell thus addresses the "so what" question about what blacks should do in light of their predicament. He also describes his role in inspiring a movement, Critical Race Theory, that struggles with many of these issues.

The Chronicle
of the Space Traders

Hypotheticals are a staple of discussion in law school classrooms. . . .
Building on this foundation, I began extending these fictional stories to
reflect the contradictions and dilemmas faced by those attempting to
apply legal rules to the many forms of racial discrimination. . . . I am
not sure who coined the phrase "Critical Race Theory" to describe
this form of writing. I know that I have received more credit than I
deserve for the movement's origins. I rather think that this writing is
the response to a need for expressing views that cannot be communicated effectively through existing techniques. And I agree with two
major writers of this genre regarding the purpose and goal of narrative writing:

> Legal storytelling is a means by which representatives of new commu-
> nities may introduce their views into the dialogue about the way soci-
> ety should be governed. Stories are in many ways more powerful than
> litigation or brief-writing and may be necessary precursors to law re-
> form. They offer insights into the particulars of lives lived at the mar-
> gins of society, margins that are rapidly collapsing toward a disappear-
> ing center. This is not true just of our times. In Biblical history, story-
> tellers for oppressed groups told tales of hope and struggle—for
> example, that of the Promised Land—to inspire and comfort the com-
> munity during difficult times. Reality could be better—and, perhaps,
> will be. Other storytellers have directed their attention to the oppres-
> sors, reminding them of a day when they would be called to account.
> Stories thus perform multiple functions, allowing us to uncover a more

The Power of Narrative, 23 Legal Stud. F. 315 (1999). Used by permission.

layered reality than is immediately apparent: a refracted one that the legal system must confront.[1]

. . . .

The Space Traders' Solution

1 JANUARY.

The first surprise was not their arrival. The radio messages had begun weeks before, announcing that one thousand ships from a star far out in space would land on 1 January in harbors along the Atlantic coast from Cape Cod to North Carolina. . . . The first surprise was the ships themselves. The people who lined the beaches of Cape Cod saw huge vessels, the size of an aircraft carrier, which the old men in the crowd recognized as being pretty much like the box-shaped landing craft that carried Allied troops to the Normandy beachheads during the Second World War. . . . Then came the second surprise. The leaders of this vast armada could speak English. Moreover, they spoke in the familiar comforting tones of a former U.S. president, having dubbed his recorded voice into a computerized language-translation system. After the initial greetings, the leader of the U.S. delegation opened his mouth to read his welcoming speech. . . . But before he could begin, the principal spokesperson for the space people . . . raised a hand and spoke crisply, and to the point.

And this point constituted the third surprise. Those mammoth vessels carried within their holds treasure of which the United States was in most desperate need: gold, to bail out the almost bankrupt federal, state, and local governments; special chemicals capable of unpolluting the environment, . . . and a totally safe nuclear engine and fuel, to relieve the nation's all-but-depleted supply of fossil fuel. In return, the visitors wanted only one thing—and that was to take back to their home star all the African Americans who lived in the United States.

They would wait sixteen days for a response to their offer. That is, on 17 January—the day when in that year the birthday of Martin Luther King, Jr., was to be observed—they would depart carrying with them every black man, woman, and child in the nation and leave behind untold treasure. . . . Then the visitors turned and glided back over the waves to their ships.

The phones of members of Congress began ringing. . . . A definite split opened up in the nature of the calls—one that reflected distinctly different perceptions of the Space Traders. Most white people were, like the welcoming delegation that morning, relieved and pleased to find the visitors from outer space unthreatening. . . . On the other hand many American blacks had seen the visitors as distinctly unpleasant, even menacing in appearance. While their perceptions of the visitors differed, black people all agreed that the Space Trade looked like bad news and burned up the phone lines urging black leaders to take action against it.

"Will the blacks never be free of their silly superstitions?" whites asked one another with condescending smiles. "Here, in this truly historic moment, when America has been selected as the site for this planet's first contact with people from another world, the blacks just revert to their primitive fear and foolishness." . . .

It was a time of crisis. Not only because of the Space Traders' offer per se, but because that offer came when the country found itself in dire straits. Decades of conservative, laissez-faire capitalism had emptied the coffers of all but a few of the very rich. The nation that had funded the reconstruction of the free world had given itself over to greed and willful exploitation of its natural resources. Massive debt had curtailed all but the most necessary services. The air was so polluted that the sick and elderly had to wear special masks whenever they ventured out-of-doors. In addition, supplies of crude oil and coal were almost exhausted. . . . Though few gave voice to their thoughts, many were thinking that the trade offer was, indeed, the ultimate solution to the nation's troubles.

2 JANUARY.

. . . As soon as the President heard the space visitors' proposition on television, his political instincts immediately locked into place. . . . He had framed the outline of his plan by the time his cabinet members gathered at 8 o'clock the next morning.

His cabinet contained no blacks. . . . Although he had followed the practice of keeping one black on the Supreme Court, it had not won him many minority votes. Furthermore, the few black figures in the party always seemed to him overly opportunistic and, to be frank, not very smart. But now, as the cabinet members arrived, he wished he had covered his bases better.

In the few hours since the Space Traders' offer, the White House and the Congress had been inundated with phone calls and telegrams. The President was not surprised that a clear majority spontaneously urged acceptance of the offer. . . . At least a third of the flood of phone calls and faxes urging quick acceptance of the offer insisted that loss of what the nation would relinquish—its African American citizens—was as worthwhile as what it would receive. The statements accurately reflected relations at the dawn of the new century. . . .

. . . .

[The President] had asked Gleason Golightly, a conservative black economics professor, to attend the meeting. Highly intelligent, Golightly seemed to be truly conservative, not a man ready to sing any political tune for a price. His mere presence as a person of color at this crucial session would neutralize any possible critics in the media, if not in the black civil rights community. . . .

"I think we all know the situation," the President said. "Those extraterrestrial beings are carrying in their ships a guarantee that America will conquer its present problems and prosper for at least this new century."

"I would venture, sir," the Vice-President noted, "that the balance of your term will be known as 'America's Golden Age.' Indeed, the era will almost certainly extend to the terms of your successor."

The President smiled at the remark and, on cue, so did the cabinet. "The VP is right, of course," the President said. "Our visitors from outer space are offering us the chance to correct the excesses of several generations. . . . They are offering not only a solution to our nation's present problems but also to what might be called the great American racial experiment. That's the real issue before us today. Does the promise of restored prosperity justify our sending away fifteen percent of our citizens to Lord knows what fate?"

"There are pluses and minuses to this 'fate' issue, Mr. President," interjected Helen Hipmeyer, Secretary of Health and Human Services. . . . "A large percentage of blacks rely on welfare and other social services. Their departure would ease substantially the burden on our state and national budgets. Why, the cost of caring for black AIDS victims alone has been out of sight. On the other hand, the consternation and guilt among many whites if the blacks are sent away would take a severe psychological toll with medical and other costs that might also reach astronomical levels. To gain the benefits we are discussing, without serious side effects, we must have more justification than I have heard thus far."

"Good point, Madame Secretary," the President answered, "but every opportunity comes with risks."

"I've never considered myself a particularly courageous individual, Mr. President." It was the Secretary of the Interior. . . . "But if I could guarantee prosperity for this great country by giving my life or going off with the Space Traders, I would do it without hesitation. And, if I would do it, I think every red-blooded American with an ounce of patriotism would as well." The Secretary sat down to the warm applause of his colleagues.

His suggestion kindled a thought in the Secretary of Defense. "Mr. President, the secretary's courage is not unlike that American men and women have exhibited when called to military service. . . . It is a call a country makes on the assumption that its citizens will respond. I think that is the situation we have here except that instead of just young men and women, the country needs all of its citizens of African descent to step forward and serve." More applause greeted this suggestion.

The Attorney General got the floor. "Mr. President, I think we could put together a legislative package modeled on the Selective Service Act of 1918. Courts have uniformly upheld this statute and its predecessors as being well within congressional power to exact enforced military duty at home or abroad by United States citizens. . . . But if the mail [Congress is] receiving is anything like ours, then the pressure for passage will be enormous."

. . . .

"What are your thoughts on all this, Professor Golightly?" asked the President. . . .

. . . .

"As you know, Mr. President. . . . I sincerely believe that black people needed to stand up on their own feet, free of the special protection of civil rights laws, the suffocating burden of welfare checks, and the stigmatizing influence of affirmative action programs. . . . Still I disagree strongly with both the Secretary of the Interior and the Attorney General. What they are proposing is not universal selective service for blacks. It is group banishment, a most severe penalty and one that the Attorney General would impose without benefit of either due process or judicial review. It is a mark of just how far out of the mainstream black people are that this proposition is given any serious consideration. Were the Space Traders asking for any other group, white women with red hair and green eyes, for example, a horrified public would order the visitors off the planet without a moment's hesitation. . . .

"Mr. President, I cannot be objective on this proposal. I will match my patriotism with that of the Secretary of the Interior. But my duty stops short of condemning my wife, my three children, my grandchildren, and my aged mother to an unknown fate. You simply cannot condemn 20 million people because they are black, and thus fit fodder for trade, so that this country can pay its debts, protect its environment, and ensure its energy supply. I am not ready to recommend such a sacrifice." . . .

. . . .

[After further discussions, Golightly continued as follows:]

"You and your cabinet must place this offer in historical perspective. This is far from the first time this country's leaders have considered and rejected the removal of all those here of African descent. Benjamin Franklin and other abolitionists actively sought schemes to free the slaves and return them to their homeland. Lincoln examined and supported emigration programs both before and after he freed the slaves. Even those Radical Republicans who drafted the Civil War Amendments wondered whether Africans could ever become a part of the national scene, a part of the American people. . . . Moreover, with all due respect, Mr. President, acceptance of the Space Traders' solution will not bring a century of prosperity to this country. What today seems to you a solution from heaven will instead herald a decade of shame and dissension mirroring the moral conflicts that precipitated this nation into its most bloody conflict, the Civil War. The deep, self-inflicted wounds of that era have never really healed. Their reopening will inevitably lead to confrontations and strife that could cause the eventual dissolution of the nation."

"You seem to assume, Professor Golightly," the Secretary of the Interior interrupted, "that the Space Traders want African Americans for some nefarious purpose. Why do you ignore alternative scenarios? Perhaps they have selected them to inhabit an interplanetary version of the Biblical land of milk and honey. Or, more seriously" the Secretary said, "they may offer your people a new start in a less competitive environment, or"—he added, with a slight smirk in the President's direction— "perhaps they are going to give your people that training in skills and work discipline you are always urging on them." . . .

"I think we get your point, Professor," the President replied smoothly. "We will give it weight in our considerations. Now," he said, rising, "we need to get to work on this thing. We don't have much time." He asked the Attorney General to draw up a rough draft of the proposed legislation by the end of the day. . . .

Long after the others had departed, Gleason Golightly sat at the long conference table. . . .

. . . .

"Oh, Golightly, glad you're still here. I want a word with you." Golightly looked up. The Secretary of the Interior, at his most unctuous, eased himself into the seat beside him.

"Listen, old man, sorry about our differences at the meeting. I understand your concerns."

Golightly did not look at the man and, indeed, kept his eyes on the wall throughout their conversation. "What do you want, Mr. Secretary?"

The Secretary ignored Golightly's coldness. "You could tell in the meeting and from the media reports that this Trade thing is big, very big. There will be debate—as there should be in a great, free country like ours. But if I were a betting man, which I am not because of my religious beliefs, I would wager that this offer will win approval. . . ."

"Why don't we simply follow your suggestion, Mr. Secretary, and tell everyone that the Space Traders are going to take the blacks to a land of milk and honey?"

The Secretary's voice hardened. "I don't think even black people are that stupid. No, Gleason, talk about patriotism, about the readiness of black people to make sacrifices for this country, about how they are really worthy citizens no matter what some may think. We'll leave the wording to you. . . ."

"And then?" Golightly asked, his eyes never moving from the wall.

"We know some blacks will escape. I understand some are leaving the country already. But if you go along with the program, Gleason, and the Trade is approved, the President says he will see to it that one hundred black families are smuggled out of the country. You decide who they are. They'll include you and yours, of course.

. . . .

. . . "Think about it, Golightly. It's the kind of deal we think you should go for."

3 JANUARY.

The Anti-Trade Coalition, a gathering of black and liberal white politicians, civil rights representatives, and progressive academics, quickly assembled early that morning. . . . The members drafted a series of legal and political steps designed to organize opposition to the Space Traders' offer.

. . . They drew up plans for direct action protests and boycotts, and, in the event that worse came to worst . . . massive disobedience.

. . . .

Professor Gleason Golightly sought the floor to propose an alternative response to the Trade offer. . . .

As he moved toward the podium, a wave of hostile murmuring broke out whose justification, Golightly acknowledged: "I am well aware that political and ideological differences have for several years sustained a wide chasm between us. But the events of two days ago have transformed our disputes into a painful reminder of our shared status. I am here because, whatever our ideological differences or our socio-economic positions, we all know that black rights, black interests, black property, even black lives are expendable whenever their sacrifice will further or sustain white needs or preferences. . . . This tradition overshadows the national debate about the Space Traders' offer and may well foretell our reply to it.

. . . .

. . . "Although you have labored here unselfishly to devise a defense against what is surely the most dangerous threat to our survival since our forebears were kidnaped from Africa's shores, I think I have a better way, and I urge you to hear it objectively and without regard to our past differences. . . . The only way we can deflect, and perhaps reverse a process that is virtually certain to result in approval of the Space Traders' offer, is to give up the oppositional stance you are about to adopt, and forthrightly urge the country to accept the Space Traders' offer."

. . . .

. . . Golightly waited until the audience quieted, then continued. "A major, perhaps the principal, motivation for racism in this country is the deeply held belief that black people should not have anything that white people don't have. Not only do whites insist on better jobs, higher incomes, better schools and neighborhoods, better everything, but they also usurp aspects of our culture that have sprung from our very subordination. . . . Whites' appropriation of what is ours and their general acquisitiveness are facts we must make work for us. Rather than resisting the Space Traders' offer, let us circulate widely the rumor that the Space Traders, aware of our long fruitless struggle on this planet, are arranging to transport us to a land of milk and honey—a virtual paradise. Remember, most whites are so jealous of their race-based prerogatives that they oppose affirmative action even though many of these programs would remove barriers that exclude whites as well as blacks. Can we not expect such whites . . . to go all out to prevent blacks from gaining access to an extraterrestrial New Jerusalem? . . . Mark my words, our 'milk and honey' story will inspire whites to institute such litigation on the grounds that limiting the Space Traders' offer to black people is unconstitutional discrimination against whites!"

. . . .

Justin Jasper, a well-known and highly respected Baptist minister, came to the microphone. "I readily concede Dr. Golightly's expertise in the psychology of whites' thinking. Furthermore, as he requests, I hold in abeyance my deep distrust of a black man whose willing service to whites has led him to become a master minstrel of political mimicry. But my problem with his plan is twofold. First, it rings hollow because it so resembles Dr. Golightly's consistent opposition in the past to all our civil rights initiatives. Once again, he is urging us to accept rather than oppose a racist policy. And, not only are we not to resist, but we are to beg the country to lead us to the sacrificial altar. God may have that power, but Dr. Golightly is not my God!"

A master orator, the Reverend Jasper quickly had his audience with him. "Second, because the proposal lacks truth, it insults my soul. In the forty years I have worked for civil rights, I have lost more battles than I have won, but I have never lost my integrity. Telling the truth about racism has put me in prison and many of my co-workers into early graves. The truth is, Dr. Golightly, that what this country is ready to do to us is wrong. . . . I can speak only for myself, but . . . I do not choose to save myself by a tactic that may preserve my body at the sacrifice of my soul. Until my Lord calls me home, I do not want to leave this country even for a land of milk and honey. My people were brought here involuntarily, and that is the only way they are going to get me out!"

The Reverend Jasper received a standing ovation. After thanking them, the minister asked everyone to join in singing the old nineteenth-century hymn, "Amazing Grace." . . .

. . . .

With the hymn's melody still resonating, the coalition's members voted unanimously to approve their defensive package. . . . Leaving the hall, everyone agreed that they had done all that could be done to oppose approval of the Space Traders' offer. As for Golightly, his proposal was dismissed as coming from a person who, in their view, had so often sold out black interests. . . .

. . . .

. . . Golightly had failed, and he knew it. Sure, he was smarter than they were—smarter even than most whites; but he had finally outsmarted himself. At the crucial moment, when he most needed to help his people, both whites and blacks had rejected as untrustworthy both himself and his plans.

4 JANUARY.

In a nationally televised address, the President sought to reassure Trade supporters that he was responding favorably to their strong messages, and to blacks and whites opposed to the Trade that he would not ignore their views. . . .

. . . .

"Of course, I am aware of the sacrifice that some of our most highly regarded citizens would be asked to make in the proposed trade. While these citizens are of only one racial group, absolutely no evidence whatsoever indicates that the selection was intended to discriminate against any race or religion or ethnic background. No decisions have been made, and all options are under review. The materials the Traders have offered us are genuine and perform as promised. Early estimates indicate that, if these materials were made available to this nation, they would solve our economic crisis, and we could look forward to a century of unparalleled prosperity. . . ."

. . . .

5 JANUARY.

. . . .

Media and business polls all reported tremendous public support for the Trade—unhappy but hardly unexpected news for the nation's richest and most powerful men. First, blacks represented 12 percent of the market and generally consumed much more of their income than did their white counterparts. No one wanted to send that portion of the market into outer space—not even for the social and practical benefits offered by the Space Traders.

Even those benefits were a mixed blessing. Coal and oil companies were not elated at the prospect of an inexhaustible energy source. Similarly, businesses whose profits were based on sales in black ghetto communities

—or who supplied law enforcement agencies, prisons, and other such institutions—faced substantial losses in sales. The real estate industry, for example, annually reaped uncounted millions in commissions on sales and rentals, inflated by the understanding that blacks would not be allowed to purchase or rent in the area. Even these concerns were overshadowed by fears of what the huge influx of gold to pay all state debts would do to the economy, or to the value of either the current money supply or gold.

Most business leaders understood that blacks were crucial in stabilizing the economy with its ever-increasing disparity between the incomes of the rich and the poor. They recognized that potentially turbulent unrest among those on the bottom was deflected by the continuing efforts of poorer whites to ensure that they at least remained ahead of blacks. If blacks were removed from the society, working and middle-class whites —deprived of their racial distraction—might look upward toward the top of the societal well and realize that they as well as the blacks below them suffered because of the gross disparities in opportunities and income.

Many of these corporate leaders and their elected representatives had for years exploited poor whites' ignorance of their real enemy. Now, what had been a comforting insulation of their privileges and wealth posed a serious barrier to what a majority saw as a first priority: persuade the country to reject the Trade. A quick survey of the media and advertising representatives was not encouraging. "It would be quite a challenge," one network executive said, "but we simply can't change this country's view about the superiority of whites and the inferiority of blacks in a week. I doubt you could do it in a decade." Even so, the corporate leaders decided to try. They planned to launch immediately a major media campaign—television, radio, and the press—to exploit both the integration achieved in America and the moral cost of its loss. . . .

Newspaper and magazine publishers promised supportive editorials, but the Vice President and other government representatives, in line with the administration's pro-Trade leanings, argued that the immediate political gains from accepting the Trade would translate into business benefits as well.

. . . .

"We need your financial support," the Vice President told corporate leaders, "but our polls show most white voters favor the Trade and the administration is under increasing pressure to do the same. . . ."

"However enticing such benefits of the Trade may be," countered a census expert from a major foundation, "the real attraction for a great many whites is that it would remove black people from this society. My staff and I have interviewed literally thousands of citizens across the country, and, though they don't say it directly, it's clear that at bottom, they simply think this will be a better country without black people. I fear, gentlemen, that those of us who have been perpetuating this belief over the years have done a better job than we knew."

"I must add what you probably already know," the Vice President responded. "The Administration is leaning toward acceptance of the Space Traders' offer. . . . [The President] knows that the working and middle-class white people in this country want the blacks to go, and if they get a chance to express their real views in the privacy of a polling place, the Trade plan will pass overwhelmingly."

"Bullshit!" roared a billionaire who had made his fortune in construction. "I'm sick of this defeatist talk! . . . Everyone says that money talks. Well dammit, let's get out there and spend some money. If this thing goes to a public referendum, we can buy whatever and whoever is necessary. It sure as hell will not be the first time," he wound up, pounding both fists on the long conference table, "and likely not the last."

. . . The business leaders began making specific plans to suspend all regular broadcasting and, through 16 January, to air nothing but anti-Trade ads and special Trade programs.

6 JANUARY.

Although the Television Evangelists of America also owned jets, they understood that their power lay less in these perks of the wealthy than in their own ability to manipulate their TV congregations' religious feelings. So, after a lengthy conference call, they announced a massive evangelical rally in the Houston Astrodome which would be televised over their religious cable network. The Trade offer was the evangelists' chance to rebuild their prestige and fortunes. . . . They would achieve this much-desired goal by playing on, rather than trying to change, the strongly racist views of their mostly working-class television audiences. True, some of the preachers had a substantial black following, but evangelical support for the Trade would not be the evangelists' decision. Rather, these media Messiahs heralded it as God's will.

The Space Traders were, according to the televised "Gospel," bringing America blessings earned by their listeners' and viewers' faithful dedication to freedom, liberty, and God's word. . . . True, a sacrifice was required if they were to obtain God's bounty—a painful sacrifice. But here, too, God was testing Americans, his chosen people, to ensure that they were worthy of His bounty, deserving of His love. . . . That night, millions of messages, all urging acceptance of the Space Traders' offer, deluged the President and Congress.

7 JANUARY.

Groups supporting the Space Traders' proposition . . . had set in motion the steps necessary to convene a Constitutional convention in Philadelphia. . . . And there, on this day, on the site of the original Constitutional convention, delegates chosen by the state legislatures quickly drafted, and by a substantial majority passed, the Twenty-seventh Amendment to the Constitution of the United States. It declared:

> Without regard to the language or interpretations previously given any other provision of this document, every United States citizen is subject at the call of Congress to selection for special service for periods necessary to protect domestic interests and international needs.

The amendment was scheduled for ratification by the states on 15 January in a national referendum. If ratified, the amendment would validate amendments to existing Selective Service laws authorizing the induction of all blacks into special service for transportation under the terms of the Space Traders' offer.

. . . .

10 JANUARY.

In the brief but intense pre-election day campaign, the pro-ratification groups' major argument exhibited an appeal that surprised even those who made it. Their message was straightforward:

> The Framers intended America to be a white country. The evidence of their intentions is present in the original Constitution. . . . We have concluded—as the Framers did in the beginning that our survival today requires that we sacrifice the rights of blacks in order to protect and further the interests of whites. The Framers' example must be our guide. Patriotism and not pity must govern our decision. . . .

In response, a coalition of liberal opponents sought to combine pragmatism and principle in what they called their "slippery Trade slope" argument. First, they proclaimed that trading away a group of Americans identifiable by race is wrong and violates our basic principles. The coalition aimed its major thrust, however, at the self-interest of white Americans: "Does not consigning blacks to an unknown fate set a dangerous precedent?" the liberals demanded. "Who will be next?"

. . . .

Astutely sidestepping the Trade precedent arguments, the response focused on the past sacrifices of blacks. "In each instance," they contended, "the sacrifice of black rights was absolutely necessary to accomplish an important government purpose. These decisions were neither arbitrary nor capricious. Without the compromises on slavery in the Constitution of 1787, there would be no America. Nor would there be any framework under which those opposed to slavery could continue the struggle that eventually led to the Civil War and emancipation."

. . . .

In countering the anti-Trade contention that the sacrifice of black rights was both evil and unprecedented, pro-Traders claimed, "Beginning with the Civil War in which black people gained their liberty, this nation has called on its people to serve in its defense. Many men and women have voluntarily enlisted in the armed services, but literally millions of men have been conscripted, required to serve their country and, if necessary, to sacrifice not simply their rights but also their lives. As for the argument that the sacrifice of black rights in political compromises was odious racial discrimination, pro-Trade forces contended that "fortuitous fate and not blatant racism" should be held responsible. . . . "All Americans are expected to make sacrifices for the good of their country. Black people are no exceptions to this basic obligation of citizenship. Their role may be special, but so is that of many of those who serve. The role that blacks may be called on to play is, however regrettable, neither immoral nor unconstitutional."

. . . The "racial sacrifice as historic necessity" argument made the pro-Trade position irresistible to millions of voters—and to their Congressional representatives.

11 JANUARY.

Unconfirmed media reports asserted that U.S. officials tried in secret negotiations to get the Space Traders to take in trade only those blacks currently under the jurisdiction of the criminal justice system—that is, in prison or on parole or probation. Government negotiators noted that this would include almost one half of the black males in the 20-to-29-year-old age bracket.[2] Negotiators were also reported to have offered to trade blacks locked in the inner cities. . . . In rejecting the American offer, the Space Traders warned that they would withdraw their proposition unless the United States halted the flight of the growing numbers of blacks who —fearing the worst—were fleeing the country.

In response, executive orders barred blacks from leaving the country until the Space Traders' proposition was fully debated and resolved. "It is your patriotic duty," blacks were told by the White House, "to allow this great issue to be resolved through the democratic process and in accordance with the rule of law." To ensure that the trade debate and referendum were concluded in a "noncoercive environment," all blacks serving in the military were placed on furlough and relieved of their weapons. State officials took similar action with respect to blacks on active duty in state and local police forces.

. . . .

14 JANUARY.

The U.S. government announced that as a result of intensive negotiations with Space Trader leaders, the visitors had agreed to amend their offer and exclude from the Trade all black people who were seventy years old and older, seriously handicapped, ill, or injured. In addition, a thousand otherwise-eligible blacks and their immediate families would be left behind as trustees of black property and possessions, all of which were to be stored or held in escrow in case blacks were returned to this country. Each of the thousand black "detainees" was required to pledge to accept a subordinate status with "suspended citizenship" until such time as the "special service inductees" were returned to the country. The administration selected blacks to remain who had records of loyalty to the conservative party and no recorded instances of militant activity. Even so, many of those blacks selected declined to remain. "We will, like the others," one black who rejected detainee status said, "take our chances with the Referendum."

15 JANUARY.

By 70 percent to 30 percent, American citizens voted to ratify the constitutional amendment that provided a legal basis for acceptance of the Space Traders' offer. In anticipation of this result, government agencies had secretly made preparations to facilitate the transfer. Some blacks escaped, and many thousands lost their lives in futile efforts to resist the joint federal and state police teams responsible for rounding up, cataloguing, and transporting blacks to the coast.

. . . .

17 JANUARY.

The last Martin Luther King holiday the nation would ever observe dawned on an extraordinary sight. In the night, the Space Traders had drawn their strange ships right up to the beaches and discharged their cargoes of gold, minerals, and machinery. They closed the doors. As the sun rose, they began to arrange in long lines some twenty million silent black men, women, and children, including babes in arms. First, the Traders directed the inductees to strip of all but a single undergarment. Then the doors swung open. Ahead, the traders directed them toward the yawning holds where they would be swallowed by what Milton might have described as a "darkness visible." Behind them, the U.S. guards, guns in hand, stood watch. There was no escape, no alternative. Heads bowed, arms now linked by slender chains, black people left the new world as their forebears had arrived.

. . . .

NOTES

1. Richard Delgado & Jean Stefancic, Derrick Bell's *Chronicle of the Space Traders: Would the U.S. Sacrifice People of Color If the Price Were Right?*, 62 U. Colo. L. Rev. 321 (1991).

2. David Savage, *1 in 4 Young Blacks in Jail Or in Court Control, Study Says*, L.A. Times, Feb. 27, 1990, p. 1, col. 1, at § A.

Racial Realism

Black people's struggle for freedom, justice, and dignity is as old as this nation. . . . In spite of dramatic civil rights movements and periodic victories in the legislatures, black Americans by no means are equal to whites. Racial equality is, in fact, not a realistic goal. By constantly aiming for a status that is unobtainable in a perilously racist America, black Americans face frustration and despair. Over time, our persistent quest for integration has hardened into self-defeating rigidity.

Black people need reform of our civil rights strategies as badly as those in the law needed a new way to consider American jurisprudence prior to the advent of the Legal Realists. By viewing the law—and by extension, the courts—as instruments for preserving the status quo and only periodically and unpredictably serving as a refuge of oppressed people, blacks can refine the work of the Realists. Rather than challenging the entire jurisprudential system, as the Realists did, blacks' challenge must be much narrower—to the principle of racial equality. This new movement— Racial Realism—is a legal and social mechanism on which blacks can rely to have their voice and outrage heard.

. . . Racial Realism is to race relations what Legal Realism is to jurisprudential thought. The Legal Realists were a group of scholars in the early part of the twentieth century who challenged the classical structure of law as a formal group of rules that, if properly applied to any given situation, lead to a right—and therefore just—result.[1] . . . Realists accept a critical and empirical attitude towards the law, in contrast to the formalists who insist that law is logically self-evident, objective, a priori valid, and internally consistent. . . . They stress the function of law, rather than the abstract conceptualization of it.

. . . .

24 Conn. L. Rev. 363 (1992). Used by permission.

Closely linked with the Realists' attack on the logic of rights theory was their attack on the logic of precedent. No two cases, the Realists pointed out, are ever exactly alike. Hence a procedural rule from a former case cannot simply be applied to a new case with a multitude of facts that vary from the former case. Rather, the judge has to choose whether or not the ruling in the earlier case should be extended to include the new case. Such a choice basically is about the relevancy of facts and is never logically compelled. Decisions about the relevance of distinguishing facts are value-laden and dependent upon a judge's own experiences.[2]

. . . .

As every civil rights lawyer has reason to know—despite law school indoctrination and belief in the "rule of law"—abstract principles lead to legal results that harm blacks and perpetuate their inferior status. Racism provides a basis for a judge to select one available premise rather than another when incompatible claims arise. Consider, for example, *Regents of the University of California v. Bakke.*[3] Relying heavily on the formalistic language of the Fourteenth Amendment, and utterly ignoring social questions about which race in fact has power and advantages and which race has been denied entry for centuries into academia, the Court held that an affirmative action policy may not unseat white candidates on the basis of their race. By introducing an artificial and inappropriate parity in its reasoning, the Court effectively made a choice to ignore historical patterns and contemporary statistics, and flee from flexible reasoning. Following a Realist approach, the Court would have observed the social landscape and noticed the skewed representation of minority medical school students. It would have reflected on the possible reasons for these demographics, including inadequate public school systems in urban ghettos, lack of minority professionals to serve as role models, and the use of standardized tests evaluated by "white" standards. Taking these factors into consideration, the Court very well may have decided *Bakke* differently.

. . . .

Black people will never gain full equality in this country. Even those herculean efforts we hail as successful will produce no more than temporary "peaks of progress," short-lived victories that slide into irrelevance as racial patterns adapt in ways that maintain white dominance. This is a hard-to-accept fact that all history verifies. We must acknowledge it and move on to adopt policies based on what I call: "Racial Realism." This mind-set or philosophy requires us to acknowledge the permanence of our subordinate status. That acknowledgment enables us to avoid despair and frees us to imagine and enact racial strategies that can bring fulfillment and even triumph.

Legal precedents we thought permanent have been overturned, distinguished, or simply ignored. All too many of the black people we sought to lift through law from a subordinate status to equal opportunity are more deeply mired in poverty and despair than they were during the separate but equal era. Despite our successful effort to strip the law's endorsement from the hated Jim Crow signs, contemporary color barriers are less visible but neither less real nor less oppressive. Today, one can travel for thousands of miles across this country and never come across a public facility designated for "colored" or "white." Indeed, the very absence of visible signs of discrimination creates an atmosphere of racial neutrality that encourages whites to believe that racism is a thing of the past.

Today, blacks experiencing rejection for a job, a home, a promotion anguish over whether race or individual failing prompted their exclusion. Either conclusion breeds frustration and eventually despair. We call ourselves African Americans, but despite centuries of struggle, none of us— no matter our prestige or position—is more than a few steps away from a racially motivated exclusion, restriction or affront.

. . . .

As a veteran of a civil rights era that is now over, I regret the need to explain what went wrong. Clearly we need to examine what it was about our reliance on racial remedies that may have prevented us from recognizing that these legal rights could do little more than bring about the cessation of one form of discriminatory conduct that soon appeared in a more subtle though no less discriminatory form. The question is whether this examination requires us to redefine goals of racial equality and opportunity to which blacks have adhered for more than a century. The answer must be a resounding "yes."

Traditional civil rights law is highly structured and founded on the belief that the Constitution was intended—at least after the Civil War Amendments—to guarantee equal rights to blacks. The belief in eventual racial justice, and the litigation and legislation based on that belief, was always dependent on the ability of believers to remain faithful to their creed of racial equality, while rejecting the contrary message of discrimination that survived their best efforts to control or eliminate it.

Despite the Realist challenge that demolished its premises, the basic formalist model of law survives. . . . The message the formalist model conveys is that existing power relations in the real world are by definition legitimate and must go unchallenged.

. . . Nearly every critique the Realists launched at the formalists can be hurled at advocates of liberal civil rights theory. Precedent, rights theory, and objectivity merely are formal rules that serve a covert purpose. Even in the context of equality theory, they will never vindicate the legal rights of black Americans. . . .

. . . The practice of using blacks as scapegoats for failed economic or political policies works every time. The effectiveness of this "racial bonding" by whites requires that blacks seek a new and more realistic goal for our civil rights activism. It is time we concede that a commitment to racial equality merely perpetuates our disempowerment. Rather, we need a mechanism to make life bearable in a society where blacks are a permanent subordinate class. Our empowerment lies in recognizing that Racial Realism may open the gateway to attaining a more meaningful status.

. . . .

While implementing Racial Realism we must simultaneously acknowledge that our actions are not likely to lead to transcendent change and, despite our best efforts, may be of more help to the system we despise than to those we are trying to help. Nevertheless, our realization, and the dedication based on that realization, can lead to policy positions and campaigns that are less likely to worsen conditions for those we are trying to help, and will be more likely to remind those in power that imaginative, unabashed risk-takers refuse to be trampled upon. Yet confrontation with our oppressors is not our sole reason for engaging in Racial Realism. Continued struggle can bring about unexpected benefits and gains that in themselves justify continued endeavor. The fight in itself has meaning and should give us hope for the future.

. . . .

A final remembrance may help make my point. The year was 1964. It was a quiet, heat-hushed evening in Harmony, a small, black community near the Mississippi Delta. Some residents were organizing to ensure implementation of a court order mandating desegregation. Walking with Mrs. Biona MacDonald, one of the organizers, up a dusty, unpaved road toward her modest home, I asked where she found the courage to continue working for civil rights. . . . "Derrick," she said slowly, seriously, "I am an old woman. I lives to harass white folks." . . .

Mrs. MacDonald did not say she risked everything because she hoped or expected to win out over the whites who, as she well knew, held all the economic and political power and the guns as well. Rather, she recognized that—powerless as she was—she had the courage and determination "to harass white folks." Her fight, in itself, gave her strength and empowerment in a society that relentlessly attempted to wear her down. Mrs. MacDonald did not even hint that her harassment would topple whites' well-entrenched power. Rather, her goal was defiance and gained force precisely because she placed herself in confrontation with her oppressors with full knowledge of their power and willingness to use it.

. . . Mrs. MacDonald understood twenty-five years ago the theory that I am espousing now for black leaders and civil rights lawyers to adopt. If you remember her story, you will understand my message.

NOTES

1. See Elizabeth Mensch, "The History of Mainstream Legal Thought," in *The Politics of Law* 18-20 (David Kairys ed., 1990).

2. Id. at 22.

3. 438 U.S. 265 (1978).

Who's Afraid of
Critical Race Theory?

As I see it, critical race theory recognizes that revolutionizing a culture begins with the radical assessment of it. Radical assessment can encompass illustration, anecdote, allegory, and imagination, as well as analysis of applicable doctrine and authorities. . . .

. . . .

"Who's Afraid of Critical Race Theory?" The interrogatory poses indirectly two questions. First, what *is* critical race theory? And second, what *ought* critical race theory to be? The distinction is useful even though the dividing line between the descriptive (what is) and the prescriptive (what it ought to be) can be quite fine.

The answers to what *is* critical race theory are fairly uniform and quite extensive. As to what critical race theory *ought* to be, the answers are far from uniform and, not coincidentally, tend to take the form of outsider criticism rather than insider inquiry. As to the *what is,* critical race theory is a body of legal scholarship, a majority of whose authors[1] are both existentially people of color and ideologically committed to the struggle against racism, particularly as institutionalized in and by law. Those critical race theorists who are white are usually committed to the overthrow of their own racial privilege.

Critical race theory scholarship is characterized by frequent use of the first person, storytelling, narrative, allegory, interdisciplinary treatment of law, and the unapologetic use of creativity. The work is often disruptive because its commitment to anti-racism goes well beyond civil rights, integration, affirmative action, and other liberal measures. This is not to

U. Ill. L. Rev. 893 (1995). The copyright to the *University of Illinois Law Review* is held by The Board of Trustees of the University of Illinois.

say that critical race theory adherents automatically or uniformly "trash" liberal ideology and method. Rather, they are highly suspicious of the liberal agenda, distrust its method, and want to retain what they see as a valuable strain of egalitarianism which may exist despite, and not because of, liberalism.

As this description suggests, critical race theory scholarship exhibits a good deal of tension between its commitment to radical critique of the law (which is normatively deconstructionist) and its commitment to radical emancipation by the law (which is normatively reconstructionist). Angela Harris views this tension—between "modernist" and "postmodernist" narrative—as a source of strength because of critical race theorists' ability to use it in ways that are creative rather than paralyzing.[2]

. . . .

Most critical race theorists are committed to a program of scholarly resistance that they hope will lay the groundwork for wide-scale resistance. Veronica Gentilli puts it this way: "Critical race theorists seem grouped together not by virtue of their theoretical cohesiveness but rather because they are motivated by similar concerns and face similar theoretical (and practical) challenges."[3] To reiterate, the similar concerns referred to here include, most basically, an orientation around race that seeks to attack a legal system which disempowers people of color.

. . . .

Critical race theorists strive for a specific, more egalitarian, world. We seek to empower and include traditionally excluded views and see all-inclusiveness as the ideal because of our belief in collective wisdom. For example, in a recent debate over "hate speech," both Chuck Lawrence and Mari Matsuda made the point that being committed to "free speech" may seem like a neutral principle, but it is not.[4] Thus, proclaiming that "I am committed equally to allowing free speech for the KKK and 2LiveCrew" is a non-neutral value judgment, one that asserts that the freedom to say hateful things is more important than the freedom to be free from the victimization, stigma, and humiliation that hate speech entails.

We emphasize our marginality and try to turn it toward advantageous perspective building and concrete advocacy on behalf of those oppressed by race and other interlocking factors of gender, economic class, and sexual orientation. When I say we are marginalized, it is not because we are victim-mongers seeking sympathy. Rather, we see such identification as one of the only hopes of transformative resistance strategy. However, we remain members of the whole set, as opposed to the large (and growing) number of blacks whose poverty and lack of opportunity have rendered them totally silent. We want to use our perspective as a means of outreach to those similarly situated but who are so caught up in the property perspectives of whiteness that they cannot recognize their subordination.

I am not sure who coined the phrase "critical race theory" to describe this form of writing, and I have received more credit than I deserve for the movement's origins. I rather think that this writing is the response to a need for expressing views that cannot be communicated effectively through existing techniques. In my case, I prefer using stories as a means of communicating views to those who hold very different views on the emotionally charged subject of race. People enjoy stories and will often suspend their beliefs, listen to the story, and then compare their views, not with mine, but with those expressed in the story.

. . . .

. . . Critical race theory writing embraces an experientially grounded, oppositionally expressed, and transformatively aspirational concern with race and other socially constructed hierarchies. Indeed, even a critical race theory critic finds that the "clearest unifying theme" of the writing is "a call for a change of perspective, specifically, a demand that racial problems be viewed from the perspective of minority groups, rather than a white perspective."[5] We use a number of different voices, but all recognize that racial subordination maintains and perpetuates the American social order. The narrative voice, the teller, is important to critical race theory in a way not understandable by those whose voices are tacitly deemed legitimate and authoritative. The voice exposes, tells and retells, signals resistance and caring, and reiterates the most fearsome power—the power of commitment to change.

Given all of this, you will not be surprised to learn that the legal academy has not warmly embraced critical race theory, particularly at the faculty level. Indeed, a small but growing body of work views critical race theory as interesting, but not a "subdiscipline" unto itself and therefore amenable to mainstream standards. These writers are not reluctant to tell us what critical race theory *ought* to be. They question the accuracy of the stories, fail to see their relevance, and want more of an analytical dimension to the work—all this while claiming that their critiques will give this writing a much-needed "legitimacy" in the academic world.

In a major critique, Daniel Farber and Suzanna Sherry urge critical race theorists to tell stories that are "accurate" and "typical," and then go on to "articulate the legal relevance of the stories" by "includ[ing] an analytic dimension."[6] The authors seem unaware of the bizarre irony in their pronouncement that "we know of no work on critical race theory that discusses psychological or other social science studies supporting the existence of a voice of color."

They do not tell us just what such a study would look like, and why centuries of testimony by people of color regarding their experiences, including individuals like Frederick Douglass, W. E. B. Du Bois, Charles Wright, and Toni Morrison, are not measure enough. Farber and Sherry also "find little support for the general claim that traditional [academic] standards are inherently unfair to work by women and minorities," and contend that "creating literature has little nexus with the specific institutional traits of law schools." They urge critical race theory writers to include more "traditional" scholarship in their approach.

Perhaps critical race theory's sharpest critic is Randall Kennedy, whose blackness lends his critique a super legitimacy inversely proportional to the illegitimacy bequeathed to critical race theory. Kennedy notes the "insurgent" quality of minority scholars whose "impatience" has succeeded in making the race question a burning issue as never before in legal academia.[7] But, he says, the writings of critical race theory reveal "significant deficiencies"; they "fail to support persuasively their claims of racial exclusion or their claims that legal academic scholars of color produce a racially distinctive brand of scholarship."

. . . .

At a time of crisis, critics serve as reminders that we are being heard, if not always appreciated. For those of us for whom history provides the best guide to contemporary understanding, criticism is a reassurance. The reason for this reassurance is contained in this final observation.

It was in the early years of African slavery, after the point where the nation decided that slaves were essential for the exploitation of the land's natural resources, but before the techniques of enslavement had been perfected. As a part of the subjugation process, newly arrived Africans were separated from those of the same tribe. They were barred from using their native language or practicing their customs. While required to learn sufficient English to understand the white masters who would rule their lives, penalties for actually learning to read and write were severe. Despite the dangers, we know that many of the enslaved did acquire basic literacy skills. The Bible was often their primer as well as the primary access to their adopted religion, Christianity.

The Africans were allowed to sing. It is said that many had voices that were pleasant to the ear, and their singing in the evening after a day of hard labor in the fields or in the master's house seemed an innocent relaxation for the slaves and their owners. It was a long time before the masters learned, if they ever did, that the slaves used their songs as a means of communication: giving warning, conveying information about escapes planned and carried out, and simply for uplifting the spirit and fortifying the soul. It was even longer before the Spirituals won recognition as a theology in song, a new interpretation of Christianity, one far closer to the original than that of those who hoped the Bible would serve as a tool of pacification, not enlightenment.

At some point, white scholars must have heard the Spirituals. It is easy to imagine their reaction. Even the most hostile would have had to admit that the sometimes joyous and often plaintive melodies had a surface attraction. The scholars would have concluded, though, that the basically primitive song-chants were not capable of complex development and were certainly too simplistic to convey sophisticated musical ideas. The music, moreover, was not in classical form, likely deemed a fatal defect. Indeed, the slave songs were not even written down by their unknown composers.

Whatever they were, the critics would conclude, these songs were not art. The music offered no potential for intellectual inspiration as opposed to purely emotional satisfaction. Of course, the critics might concede, in the hands of classically trained composers and musicians, the Spirituals might serve as folk melodies from which true art might be rendered. Stephen Foster was said to have done this, and later Antonin Dvorak, and still later, George Gershwin. Many others followed. A few of them credited the genius in the slave songs, but most simply took what they wanted and called it their own without acknowledging the sources that, when asked, they deprecated and denied.

. . . .

Comparing critical race theory writing with the Spirituals is an unjustified conceit, but the essence of both is quite similar: to communicate understanding and reassurance to needy souls trapped in a hostile world. Moreover, the use of unorthodox structure, language, and form to make sense of the senseless is another similarity. Quite predictably, critics wedded to the existing legal canons will measure critical race theory, employing their standards of excellence, and find this new work seriously inadequate. Many of these critics are steeped in theory and deathly afraid of experience. They seek meaning by dissecting portions of this writing—the autobiographical quality of some work, and the allegorical, story-telling characteristic in others. But all such criticisms miss the point. Critical race theory cannot be understood by claiming that it is intended to make critical race studies writing more accessible and more effective in conveying arguments of discrimination and disadvantage to the majority. Moreover, it is presumptuous to suggest, as a few critics do, that by their attention, even negative attention, they provide this work with legitimacy so that the world will take it seriously. Even if correct, this view is both paternalistic and a pathetically poor effort to regain a position of dominance.

I hope that those doing critical race theory, when reviewing these critiques, will consider the source. As to a response, a sad smile of sympathy may suffice. For those who press harder for explanations, both Beethoven and Louie Armstrong are available for quotation. When questioned about the meaning of his late quartets, Beethoven dismissed the critics with a prediction: "it was not written for you, but for a later age." And when asked for the meaning of jazz, Armstrong warned, "Man, if you don't know, don't mess with it."

NOTES

1. Critical race theory's founding members are usually identified as Derrick Bell, Kimberlé Crenshaw, Richard Delgado, Charles Lawrence, Mari Matsuda, and Patricia Williams.

2. Angela P. Harris, *Foreword: The Jurisprudence of Reconstruction,* 82 Cal. L. Rev. 741, 743 (1994). Richard Delgado, one of critical race theory's original writers, lists as among the attributes of critical race scholars the following:

> (1) insistence on "naming our own reality"; (2) the belief that knowledge and ideas are powerful; (3) a readiness to question basic premises of moderate/incremental civil rights law; (4) the borrowing of insights from social science on race and racism; (5) critical examination of the myths and stories powerful groups use to justify racial subordination; (6) a more contextualized treatment of doctrine; (7) criticism of liberal legalisms; and (8) an interest in structural determinism—the ways in which legal tools and thought-structures can impede law reform.

Richard Delgado, *When a Story Is Just a Story: Does Voice Really Matter,* 76 Va. L. Rev. 95, 95 n.4 (1990).

3. Veronica Gentilli, Comment, *A Double Challenge for Critical Race Scholars: The Moral Context,* 65 S. Cal. L. Rev. 2361, 2362 (1992).

4. *See generally* Charles R. Lawrence, III, *If He Hollers Let Him Go: Regulating Racist Speech on Campus,* 1990 Duke L.J. 431; Mari J. Matsuda, *Public Response to Racist Speech: Considering the Victim's Story,* 87 Mich. L. Rev. 2320 (1989).

5. Daniel A. Farber, *The Outmoded Debate over Affirmative Action,* 82 Cal. L. Rev. 893, 904 (1994).

6. Daniel A. Farber & Suzanna Sherry, *Telling Stories out of School: An Essay on Legal Narratives,* 45 Stan. L. Rev. 807, 809 (1993).

7. Randall L. Kennedy, *Racial Critiques of Legal Academia,* 102 Harv. L. Rev. 1745, 1748 (1989).

Racism Is Here to Stay
Now What?

Black people will never gain full equality in this country. Even those herculean efforts we hail as successful will produce no more than temporary
"peaks of progress," short-lived victories that slide into irrelevance as
racial patterns adapt in ways that maintain white dominance. This is a
hard-to-accept fact that all history verifies. We must acknowledge it and
move on. Armed with a perspective on our society that I call Racial Realism, we can insulate ourselves from despair based on our subordinate
status. We will then be free to imagine and activate racial strategies that
can bring fulfillment and even triumph.

My thesis is jarring, I think, because for too long we have comforted
ourselves with the myth of "slow but steady" racial progress. In fact, our
racial status in this country has been cyclical—legal rights are gained,
then lost, then gained again in response to economic and political developments over which blacks exercise little or no control. Civil rights law
has always been a part of rather than an exception to this cyclical phenomenon.

Because the dimensions of this cycle remain uncharted, we who advocate on behalf of the nation's colored people seem trapped in a giant, un-
seen gyroscope. Even our most powerful efforts are unable to divert it
from its preplanned equilibrium or alter its orientation toward dominance for whites over blacks. The symbols change, but our status remains
fixed. Society's stability strengthens rather than weakens by the movement up through the class ranks of the precious few who too quickly are
deemed to have "made it."

. . . .

35 How. L.J. 79 (1991). Used by permission.

In 1895, Booker T. Washington, another black man who had risen from the bottom—slavery itself—gained an instant and lasting status in white America by declaring in his now famous Atlanta Compromise speech that black people should eschew racial equality and seek to gain acceptance in society by becoming useful through trades and skills, developed through hard work, persistence, and sacrifice. Whites welcomed Washington's conciliatory, non-confrontational policy, and deemed it a sufficient self-acceptance for the society's involuntary subordination of blacks in every area of life. . . .

. . . .

Similarly, the most sought-after black spokespersons today are those whose views undermine affirmative action and underestimate the effects of contemporary racism—while placing the blame for blacks' ever-worsening state on characteristics that are far more the result of condition than color. Again, their homilies of self-help are not bad in themselves. They are simply grossly unrealistic in an economy where millions, white as well as black, are unemployed and where racial discrimination in the workplace is as entrenched (if somewhat less obvious) than it was when employers posted signs, "no negroes need apply."

For white people in denial, how sweet it must be for them when a black person stands in a public place and condemns as slothful and unambitious those blacks who are less successful simply because they refused to get out there and make it as the speaker did. . . .

. . . .

Actually, I am reluctant to characterize these black pseudo "Horatio Algers" as "conservatives." Hell, I consider myself a conservative. I relied on the courts as a civil rights lawyer to teach the law to the next generation of lawyers, even as the number of black folk living in poverty and dying the same way continued to mount. . . .

But Booker T. Washington and his contemporary counterparts are a reflection of and not the cause of our racial malaise. They comfort whites but should not distract blacks from the real causes of our condition. Stated simply, the deeply shared need in this nation to maintain blacks in a subordinate status serves to maintain stability and solidarity among whites whose own social and economic status varies widely. As a result, progress in our effort to gain racial equality is so hard to achieve and so easy to lose—precisely because rights for blacks are always vulnerable to sacrifice to further the needs of whites.

That is why the hard earned progress we make by enacting civil rights laws or winning cases in the courts is so transitory. Indeed, what we call "progress" in civil rights invariably depends more on the perceived benefits to whites of our proposed racial reforms than on the degree of injustice actually suffered by blacks or other people of color.

Lord knows we want progress, and we must work for it on both an individual and group level. . . . But progress is often more symbolic than real. In politics, it is tempting to look at the number of black mayors and overlook that most preside over cities with eroded tax bases, departed businesses, and entrenched civil servants. The plight of black mayors reminds us that we, as black people, gain access to political positions the way we gain access to all white neighborhoods—when the housing stock is run down, maintenance is expensive, and past abuse and mismanagement by whites make effective governance impossible for blacks who, of course, will be blamed for their failure to set things right.

In business, all but a few of our corporate executives are staff people with plenty of public exposure, little real authority, and always at risk when the need to cut budgets is high or the interest in maintaining a "minority presence" is low. We boast that we have black millionaires, but most made their money in entertainment and sports because their talents and skill entertained millions of whites and enabled some of those whites to earn billions.

. . . .

Millions of Americans, white as well as black, face steadily worsening conditions: poverty, unemployment, health care, housing, education, and the environment. The gap in national incomes has reached the point that those in the top fifth earn more than their counterparts in the bottom four-fifths combined.

Shocking. And yet, conservative white politicians are able to gain and hold even the highest office despite their failure to address seriously any of these issues. They rely instead on the time tested formula of getting needy whites to identify on the basis of their shared skin color. . . . Whites rally on the basis of racial pride and patriotism to accept their often lowly lot in life and vent their frustration by opposing any serious advancement by blacks.

It works every time. It worked when rich slave owners convinced the white working class to stand with them against the danger of slave revolts—even though slavery condemned white workers to a life of economic deprivation. It worked after the Civil War when poor whites

fought social reforms and settled for segregation rather than see those formerly enslaved blacks get ahead. It worked when most labor unions preferred to allow the plant owners to break their strikes with black scab
labor rather than allow blacks to join their unions.

It is working again as whites, disadvantaged by high stakes entrance
requirements, fight to end affirmative action policies that, in fact, have
helped more whites than blacks.

The reasons for this "Caucasian commitment" are likely both numerous and complex. But a crucial factor seems to be the unstated understanding by the mass of whites that they will accept large disparities in
economic opportunity so long as they have a priority over blacks and
other people of color for access to whatever opportunities are left.

. . . .

Even those whites who lack wealth and power are sustained in their
sense of racial superiority by policy decisions that sacrifice black rights.
The subordination of blacks seems to reassure whites of an unspoken but
no less certain property right in their "whiteness." This right receives judicial recognition like all property rights under a government created and
sustained primarily for that purpose. Thus, from the beginning of slavery,
masses of whites have supported programs that were contrary to their
economic interest as long as those policies provided them with a status superior to that of blacks. . . . Consider the case of a dirt poor southern
white, shown participating in a Ku Klux Klan rally in the movie *Resur-
gence,* who declared: "Every morning, I wake up and thank God I'm
white." For this person, and for others like him, race consciousness, man-
ifested by his refusal even to associate with blacks, provides a powerful
explanation of why he fails to challenge the current social order.

. . . .

"You made it despite being black and subject to discrimination," the
question goes, "so why can't the rest of 'them' do the same?" For those
who pose it, the question, carries its own conclusion. . . . Providing conservatives with fodder for their anti–civil rights arguments, though, is not
the only or most dangerous threat that the success of some blacks poses.
Robert L. Allen in his 1969 book, *Black Awakening in Capitalist America,* reminds us that the growing gap in income and status between those
blacks who are making it and those who are not tracks developments in
colonial countries where the colonizers maintained their control by establishing class divisions within the ranks of the colonized.

. . . .

While his book was written prior to the affirmative action era, Allen would argue that such policies co-opt a portion of the black middle class who, without their privileged positions, might provide leadership to the black masses who are now locked in poverty-stricken areas from which their potential leaders have been permitted to escape. Separated from their benighted brethren by social class and economic status, the black middle-class are often objects of deep suspicion rather than role models for those locked in poverty-based despair.

. . . .

History, I am afraid, will look at our freedom efforts as child-like, trusting, believing, and hopelessly naive. Growing up means coming to confess that many of those civil rights battles we thought we won all too frequently were transformed before our eyes into new, more sophisticated barriers for the ever elusive equality.

All now acknowledge that hopes for *Brown v. Board of Education* and the civil rights laws and precedents that followed were too optimistic. Few may agree with me that our racial equality goals may never be realized. While we must continue to work hard on individual issues of racial discrimination, we must address the reality that we live in a society in which racism has been internalized and institutionalized to the point of being an essential and inherently functioning component of that society —a culture from whose inception racial discrimination has been a regulating force for maintaining stability and growth and for maximizing other cultural values.

Deep down, most of us working in civil rights know this is as true as is the seldom acknowledged fact that each of us is going to die. Indeed, one finds a revealing similarity between how individuals deal with death and how civil rights activists deal with the minuscule possibility that "we shall overcome." . . . This is neither a prescription of despair, nor a counsel of surrender. It is not an approach without risks, quite like those we must face as we seek the salvation in life that comes when we accept the reality of death. . . .

. . . .

Here, at least, is a more realistic perspective from which to gauge the present and future worth of our race-related activities. Freed of the stifling rigidity of "live forever, we shall overcome" thinking, we may be less ready to continue blindly our faith in traditional, integration-oriented remedies as the ideal, despite the evidence accrued over the years that such policies seem to work only when it is in the interest of whites for them to work.

. . . .

You may think, "it is easy to criticize, but what would you suggest?" At the least, we should adopt the medical professions' creed: "First, do no harm." We all know better than to think racial subordination can be ended tomorrow. We need to recognize that a yearning for racial equality is fantasy. Short of the extreme of a too-bloody revolution (we know who would suffer the most), history and personal experience tell us that any forward step is likely: 1) to drive blacks backward eventually, and 2) to contribute to the reinforcing myth many white and some black Americans embrace that theirs is an ultimately successful (read humane) existence.

You will note a seeming inconsistency that plagues my argument. On the one hand, I urge you to give up the dream of real, permanent racial equality in this country. On the other hand, I urge you to continue the fight against racism. One experiences an understandable desire to choose one or the other as valid. . . . But it is not a question of pragmatism or idealism. Rather, as a former student discerned it, it is a question of both recognition of the futility of action . . . and the unblinking conviction that something must be done, that action must be taken.

. . . .

The racial philosophy that we must seek is a hard-eyed view of racism as it is and our subordinate role in it. We must realize with our slave forbearers that the struggle for freedom is, at bottom, a manifestation of our humanity that survives and grows stronger through resistance to oppression even if that oppression is never overcome. Recall the question I put to that Mississippi Delta organizer walking up a dusty, unpaved road nearly 40 years ago. I asked where she found the courage to continue working for civil rights in the face of intimidation that included her son losing his job in town, the local bank trying to foreclose on her mortgage, and shots fired through her living room window. Her answer (that she lived to harass white folks) didn't say she hoped or expected to win out over the all-powerful whites. Rather, she intended to use courage and determination as a weapon, a form of self-expression regardless of any likelihood of success—a form of defiance more potent precisely because she understood fully the oppressors' power and their willingness to use it.

Mrs. MacDonald understood many years ago what I have been trying to convey to you today. She avoided discouragement and defeat because at the point that she determined to resist her oppression, she was triumphant. Nothing the all powerful whites could do to her would diminish her triumph. . . .

Paul Robeson
Doing the State Some Service

Born in 1898, Paul Robeson rose from humble beginnings to become one of the most distinguished Americans of the twentieth century. No mere celebrity, Robeson was a modern-day Renaissance man. After graduating with Phi Beta Kappa honors from Rutgers University, where he twice received All-America football awards, he attended Columbia Law School and practiced briefly at a large law firm before becoming discouraged by the racism he encountered there.

He turned to the theater and, performing in Eugene O'Neill's plays during the early 1920s, established himself as a brilliant actor. His tremendous bass-baritone voice gave him access to concert stages, and for two decades he was hailed as one of the greatest bass-baritones in the world. In the course of his many travels abroad, he was lionized. He played the title role in the 1943 Broadway production of *Othello,* which ran a record 296 performances. His acting in that play earned him, in 1944, the Academy of Arts and Letters' Gold Medal for best diction in the American theater and the Donaldson Award for best actor.

Robeson championed the cause of the oppressed throughout his life, insisting that as an artist he had no choice but to do so. A trip to the Soviet Union early in his career had made him a life-long friend of the USSR, which in 1952 awarded him the Stalin Peace Prize. Following World War II, when he took an uncompromising stand against segregation and lynching in the United States and advocated friendship with the Soviet Union, his enemies mounted a long, intense campaign against him. Thereafter he was unable to earn a living as an artist in the United States and

Reprinted by permission from *Afrolantic Legacies* 109 by Derrick Bell. Chicago, Illinois: Third World Press, 1998.

was also denied a passport. Finally in 1958 he was allowed to go to Great Britain. He returned in 1963 in ill health and spent the last years of his life in seclusion. He died at age 78 in 1976. In my view he was one of our greatest heroes.

. . . .

Paul Robeson's life, like great art, is treasured as much for the images it evokes as for the story it portrays. At one level, one can view the obvious parallel of Robeson's contributions with those of other well-known blacks who paid a large price for their outspoken challenges to racial injustice. At another level, with Robeson's life as model, the significant but less well-known sacrifice of other blacks can be more easily recognized and appreciated.

Consider Tommie Smith and John Carlos. In accepting their gold and bronze medals in the 1968 Olympics, these black athletes mounted the victory podium and, as the national anthem played, bowed their heads, black gloved fists thrust high in protest against racial strife in America. Their protest was memorable, coming as it did at the height of the black power movement. It became a defining symbol—along with the urban rebellions—of black people's unwillingness to accept patiently the discrimination which the Supreme Court had outlawed a dozen years before.

While virtually all black people cheered the protest, most whites were appalled. They applauded when the U.S. Olympic Committee indignantly dismissed Smith and Carlos from the team. Both men suffered through years of job discrimination by employers and boycotts by sports promoters. It was the usual penalty imposed on blacks who failed to combine their success with deference acknowledging their subordinate status in life.

Significantly, the retaliatory actions against Smith and Carlos have not dimmed the memory of that event. Back in the early 1970s, I was about to publish the first law school text devoted to issues of race and racism. As both epigraph and notice that the book would treat discrimination as the evil it is rather than a subject that would be examined "neutrally," I included a photograph of the Smith-Carlos protest and dedicated the book to all those who throughout this country's history have risked its wrath to protest its faults. I called the black athletes' protest:

> The dramatic finale of an
> Extraordinary achievement
> Performed for a nation which
> Had there been a choice

Would have chosen others, and
If given a chance
Will accept the achievement
And neglect the achievers.
Here, with simple gesture, they
Symbolize a people whose patience
With exploitation will expire with
The dignity and certainty
With which it has been endured . . .
Too long.

The Olympic achievements of Carlos and Smith and the meaning of the nation's reaction to their protest are made clear by comparing them with Paul Robeson's experience. The lesson is clear. No degree of success or superiority in athletics, art, or scholarship insulates black criticism of white racism against swift and certain retaliation. Indeed, the higher the public platform provided by the society's recognition of that success, the more certain that whites will react to criticism, even though undeniably true, as an unforgivable betrayal. Robeson's experience then provides a prophetic paradigm for us all. And yet, Robeson's outspoken stance against American racism, even his too trusting attraction to communism and Russia, served well both the nation and its black citizens.

During World War II, as in earlier conflicts, blacks were at first excluded or segregated. The racial pattern was set at the start of the Revolutionary War when the Continental Congress proclaimed that it would not recruit Indians, vagabonds, or Negroes. When the enemy's challenge became threatening and the number of whites willing to serve proved too small, blacks were called upon and responded without rancor or regret. At war's end, the achievements were accepted and the achievers neglected; except that "neglect" inaccurately describes the reign of lynching and terror that was the black man's portion after each of the wars, including World Wars I and II.

World War II had devastated Western colonial powers. Nonwhite peoples were demanding an end to capitalist occupation and exploitation by Western nations. Communism offered a powerful alternative that both challenged and evoked great fear in this country. Paul Robeson, an international figure, by giving voice both here and abroad to what every black person knew about racism and capitalist exploitation, invested that knowledge with a legitimacy that spurred serious opposition.

And, as if that were not enough, Robeson preached the doctrine unholy to guardians of the status quo that the working classes, black and white, were not only brothers, but suffered the same exploitation, a truth quite intentionally (and all too easily) hidden from lower-class whites by appeals to racism propounded by upper-class whites from the earliest days of American history to the present. Any assumption that Robeson's right of free speech encompassed such inflammatory truths proved naive in the extreme. When he proclaimed, as he did in his autobiography, *Here I Stand*, that the enemies are the "white folks on top," and dared suggest that American blacks might not so compliantly fight for America in some future war against a non-racist country, the retaliation that followed was fierce.

Policy-makers in this country recognized and determined to eliminate this formidable black. When Robeson in 1950 demanded to know why his passport had been canceled, State Department officials said it was because he refused to sign the non-Communist affiliation oath, but they promised to return it if Robeson would sign a statement promising not to make any speeches when he was abroad. He refused.

Robeson was barred from leaving the country and denied access to concert halls and lecture platforms at home. But his message had been heard. And if far fewer rank and file Americans heeded his advice than he had hoped, far more policy-makers than have ever acknowledged it learned from Robeson that to preserve the Union and their preeminent positions in it, a twentieth century equivalent of the Emancipation Proclamation would be necessary.

In an effort to limit the effect of Robeson's speeches condemning American racism, policy-makers and the media recruited well-known blacks to refute them. . . . Among them was the baseball hero Jackie Robinson, who had benefitted from Robeson's work against discrimination in professional baseball. He testified against Robeson before the House Committee on Un-American Activities. The baseball player's prepared statement was carefully worded only to condemn as "silly" Robeson's assertion that blacks would not fight for this country. He defended Robeson's right to his personal views and acknowledged the real injustices blacks suffer.

Robeson's enemies really didn't care what Jackie Robinson said. His appearance was comment enough—especially to the press, which eagerly reported the negative in Robinson's remarks, while ignoring the more positive balance. In their turn, the leaders of the major civil rights organizations deemed it important to prove their own loyalties by condemning Robeson. Walter White, Executive Director of the NAACP, in a devastating article in *Ebony* magazine, described Robeson as a "bewildered man who is more to be pitied than damned."

Paul Robeson, while a lawyer deeply committed to civil rights, never had his name on any of the legal briefs in the school desegregation litigation that led in 1954 to the Supreme Court's decision in *Brown v. Board of Education*. Indeed, as those cases slowly made their way through the courts in the early 1950s, the government's campaign against Robeson had succeeded in portraying him as an enemy of his people and a pawn of Communist Russia. And yet, it is clear today that his strong condemnations of American racism were as effective as any of the arguments propounded by lawyers who have received credit for their roles in that landmark litigation. Robeson had stated the unthinkable. By urging blacks not to reject communism until the free world proved it offered a better deal, he enabled NAACP legal brief-writers to warn the Supreme Court that the "Survival of our country in the present international situation is inevitably tied to resolution of this domestic issue."

. . . .

By the time black protests and marches of the 1960s made *Brown* more than a symbol, Paul Robeson was on the sidelines, another in a long list of blacks sacrificed to the cause of racial equality in a land seemingly determined to destroy those who most believe in its ideals.

One wonders. What if Robeson were speaking out now? Even at the peak of his career, Paul Robeson at mid-century did not command the massive celebrity enjoyed by some well-known blacks today. A national poll found that the three most popular Americans are black: retired General Colin Powell, Masters champion Tiger Woods, who is also part Asian, and basketball great Michael Jordan. Their popularity spans across age, regional, professional, racial and political subgroups. They are better known among Democrats than President Clinton, and more popular among Republicans than House Speaker, Newt Gingrich. Powell, Woods, and Jordan are multimillionaires with income and wealth beyond anything Paul Robeson could have imagined.

Each of these men identifies with black Americans. Powell has voiced support for affirmative action while Woods has criticized the exclusionary practices of most private country clubs. Jordan makes commercials for the Negro College Fund. What if these men emulated Paul Robeson and launched campaigns castigating America for the racism that most whites refuse to acknowledge and few blacks can escape? What if they called on whites to give up their privileges and join with blacks for major social reforms needed by all? Would their celebrity-amplified voices move whites to explore the depth and breadth of racism that every black has experienced first-hand? Or, like Robeson, would the nation prefer to silence even these messengers—no matter their fame, wealth, and popularity?

. . . In his most famous stage role, Shakespeare's *Othello,* Paul Robeson says in the final stage, "I have done the state some small service. And they know it." . . .

Robeson's message to us is that in the face of adverse reaction, we must continue our protests against racial injustice. Despite the lessons of history, we hold open the door of fellowship to America's white masses when they discover, finally, that black people are not the cause and racism not the remedy for their oppression. We blacks may not save this country through such commitment, but we will save our souls, and we will have remained true to the rich testament Paul Robeson left us.

CHAPTER 3

Ethics of Lawyering

The civil rights lawyer constantly confronts ethical dilemmas: What to do when his civil rights organization wants one thing, and the client another? What to do when one's client is a militant who has broken the law and is still defiant? A law student confronts dilemmas as well. What if she aspires to a low-paying public interest job but has high educational debts to pay off? How does one acquire the courage to endanger one's high-paying corporate job if one believes one should be a whistle blower and report corporate malfeasance? Bell grapples with some of these questions as part of a broader search for a coherent philosophy of ethical lawyering. As the reader will see, Bell believes that, for a lawyer at least, the primary ethical duty is to help others, particularly one's client. He also believes that by doing good one will often do well. The person such as a whistle blower who sacrifices a job will often find that a better one comes along.

Serving Two Masters

Integration Ideals and Client Interests in School Desegregation Litigation

The espousal of educational improvement as the appropriate goal of school desegregation efforts is out of phase with the current state of the law. Largely through the efforts of civil rights lawyers, most courts have come to construe *Brown v. Board of Education* as mandating "equal educational opportunities" through school desegregation plans aimed at achieving racial balance, whether or not those plans will improve the education received by the children affected. To the extent that "instructional profit" [and not school desegregation] accurately defines the school priorities of black parents, questions of professional responsibility can no longer be ignored:

How should the term "client" be defined in school desegregation cases? . . . How should civil rights attorneys represent the often diverse interests of clients and class in school suits? Do they owe any special obligation to class members who emphasize educational quality and who probably cannot obtain counsel to advocate their divergent views? Do the political, organizational, and even philosophical complexities of school desegregation litigation justify a higher standard of professional responsibility on the part of civil rights lawyers to their clients, or more diligent oversight of the lawyer-client relationship by the bench and bar?

. . . .

Having achieved so much by courageous persistence, [civil rights lawyers] have not wavered in their determination to implement *Brown* using racial balance measures developed in hard-fought legal battles. This

Reprinted by permission of The Yale Law Journal Company and William S. Hein Company from *The Yale Law Journal*, Vol. 85, pages 470–516.

stance presents great risk for clients whose educational interests may no longer accord with the integration ideals of their attorneys. . . . But it is difficult to provide standards for the attorney and protection for the client where the source of the conflict is the attorney's ideals. The magnitude of the difficulty is more accurately gauged in a much older code that warns: "No servant can serve two masters: for either he will hate the one, and love the other; or else he will hold to one, and despise the other."[1]

School Litigation: A Behind-the-Scenes View

By the early 1930s, the NAACP, with the support of a foundation grant, had organized a concerted program of legal attacks on racial segregation. . . . The public schools were chosen because they presented a far more compelling symbol of the evils of segregation and a far more vulnerable target than segregated railroad cars, restaurants, or restrooms. . . .

. . . .

In 1955, the Supreme Court rejected the NAACP request for a general order requiring desegregation in all school districts, issued the famous "all deliberate speed" mandate, and returned the matter to the district courts. It quickly became apparent that most school districts would not comply with *Brown* voluntarily. Rather, they retained counsel and determined to resist compliance as long as possible.

By the late 1950s, the realization by black parents and local branches of the NAACP that litigation would be required, together with the snail's pace at which most of the school cases progressed, brought about a steady growth in the size of school desegregation dockets. Because of their limited resources, the NAACP and LDF (Legal Defense Fund) adopted the following general pattern for initiating school suits. A local attorney would respond to the request of an NAACP branch to address its members concerning their rights under the *Brown* decision. Those interested in joining a suit as named plaintiffs would sign retainers authorizing the local attorney and members of the NAACP staff to represent them in a school desegregation class action. . . .

. . . .

The civil rights lawyers would not settle for anything less than a desegregated system. While the situation did not arise in the early years, it was generally made clear to potential plaintiffs that the NAACP was not interested in settling the litigation in return for school board promises to provide better segregated schools. Black parents generally felt that the victory in *Brown* entitled the civil rights lawyers to determine the basis of compliance. Perpetuating segregated schools was unacceptable, and the civil rights lawyers' strong opposition to such schools had the full support of both the named plaintiffs and the class they represented. . . .

The rights vindicated in school litigation literally did not exist prior to 1954. . . . Desegregation efforts aimed at lunchrooms, beaches, transportation, and other public facilities were designed merely to gain access to those facilities. Any actual racial "mixing" had been essentially fortuitous; it was hardly part of the rights protected (to eat, travel, or swim on a nonracial basis). The strategy of school desegregation is much different. The actual presence of white children is said to be essential to the right in both its philosophical and pragmatic dimensions: blacks must gain access to white schools because "equal educational opportunity" means integrated schools, and because only school integration will make certain that black children will receive the same education as white children. This theory of school desegregation, however, fails to encompass the complexity of achieving equal educational opportunity for children to whom it so long has been denied.

. . . .

Lawyer-Client Conflicts: Sources and Rationale

Having convinced themselves that *Brown* stands for desegregation and not education, the established civil rights organizations steadfastly refuse to recognize reverses in the school desegregation campaign—reverses which, to some extent, result from their rigidity. They seem to be reluctant to evaluate objectively the high risks inherent in a continuation of current policies.

. . . Early in 1975, I was invited by representatives of Boston's black community groups to meet with them and NAACP lawyers over plans for Phase II of Boston's desegregation effort. . . . NAACP lawyers had retained experts whose proposals for the 1975–1976 school year would have required even more busing between black and lower-class white communities. The black representatives were ambivalent about the busing plans. They did not wish to back away after years of effort to desegregate Boston's schools, but they wished to place greater emphasis on upgrading the schools' educational quality, to maintain existing assignments at schools which were already integrated, and to minimize busing to the poorest and most violent white districts. . . .

. . . The NAACP lawyers assigned to the Boston case listened respectfully to the views of the black community group, but made clear that a long line of court decisions would limit the degree to which those educational priorities could be incorporated into the desegregation plan the lawyers were preparing to file. . . . Acting on the recommendations of appointed masters, Judge Garrity adopted several provisions designed to improve the quality of the notoriously poor Boston schools. But as in the Detroit and Atlanta cases, these provisions were more the product of judicial initiative than of civil rights advocacy.

The determination of NAACP officials to achieve racial balance was also tested in the Detroit school case. Having failed to obtain an interdistrict metropolitan remedy in Detroit, the NAACP set out to achieve a unitary system in a school district that was over 70 percent black. The district court rejected an NAACP plan that would require every school to reflect (within a range of 15 percent in either direction) the ratio of whites to blacks in the district as a whole, and approved a desegregation plan that emphasized educational reform rather than racial balance. The NAACP General Counsel, Nathaniel R. Jones, reportedly called the decision "an abomination" and "a rape of the constitutional rights of black children," and indicated his intention to appeal immediately.

Prior to Detroit, the most open confrontation between NAACP views of school integration and those of local blacks who favored plans oriented toward improving educational quality occurred in Atlanta. There, a group of plaintiffs became discouraged by the difficulty of achieving meaningful desegregation in a district which had gone from 32 percent black in 1952 to 82 percent black in 1974. Lawyers for the local NAACP branch worked out a compromise plan with the Atlanta School Board that called for full faculty and employee desegregation but for only limited pupil desegregation. In exchange, the school board promised to hire a number of blacks in top administrative positions, including a black superintendent of schools.

Apparently influenced by petitions signed by several thousand members of the plaintiffs' class, the federal court approved the plan. Nevertheless the national NAACP office and LDF lawyers were horrified by the compromise. The NAACP ousted the Atlanta branch president who had supported the compromise. Then, acting on behalf of some local blacks who shared their views, LDF lawyers filed an appeal in the Atlanta case.

. . . But finding that the system had achieved unitary status [a] Fifth Circuit panel upheld the plan.

. . . .

. . . *Brown* can be implemented only by the immediate racial balancing of school populations. But civil rights groups refuse to recognize what courts in Boston, Detroit, and Atlanta have now made obvious: where racial balance is not feasible because of population concentrations, political boundaries, or even educational considerations, adequate legal precedent supports court-ordered remedies that emphasize educational improvement rather than racial balance.

The plans adopted in these cases were formulated without the support and often over the objection of the NAACP and other civil rights groups. They are intended to upgrade educational quality, and like racial balance, they may have that effect. But neither the NAACP nor the court-fashioned remedies are sufficiently directed at the real evil of pre-*Brown* public schools: the state-supported subordination of blacks in every aspect of the educational process. Racial separation is only the most obvious manifestation of this subordination. Providing unequal and inadequate school resources and excluding black parents from meaningful participation in school policymaking are at least as damaging to black children as enforced separation.

Whether based on racial balance precedents or compensatory education theories, remedies that fail to attack policies of racial subordination almost guarantee that the basic evil of segregated schools will survive and flourish, even in those systems where racially balanced schools can be achieved. Low academic performance and large numbers of disciplinary and expulsion cases are only two of the predictable outcomes in integrated schools where the racial subordination of blacks reappears in, if anything, a more damaging form.

. . . Much more effective remedies for racial subordination in the schools could be obtained if the creative energies of the civil rights litigation groups could be brought into line with the needs and desires of their clients.

. . . .

Civil Rights Litigation and the Regulation of Professional Ethics

The questions of legal ethics raised by the lawyer-client relationship in civil rights litigation are not new. The Supreme Court's 1963 treatment of these issues in *NAACP v. Button*,[2] however, needs to be examined in light of the emergence of lawyer-client conflicts which are far more serious than the premature speculations of a segregationist legislature.

As the implementation of *Brown* began, Southern officials looking for every possible means to eliminate the threat of integrated schools soon realized that the NAACP's procedure for obtaining clients for litigation resembled the traditionally unethical practices of barratry and running and capping. Attempting to exploit this resemblance, a majority of Southern states enacted laws defining NAACP litigation practices as unlawful. . . . The Virginia legislature amended its criminal statutes barring running and capping to forbid the solicitation of legal business by "an agent for an individual or organization which retains a lawyer in connection with an action to which it is not a party and in which it has no pecuniary right or liability."[3] An attorney accepting employment from such an organization was subject to disbarment. . . . The [Virginia Supreme Court of Appeals] held that the statute's expanded definition of improper solicitation of legal business did not violate the Constitution in proscribing many of the legal activities of civil rights groups such as the NAACP.

The Supreme Court reversed, holding that the state statute as construed and applied abridged the First Amendment rights of NAACP members. . . . Justice Brennan, writing for the majority, placed great weight on the importance of litigation to the NAACP's civil rights program. He noted that blacks rely on the courts to gain objectives which are not available through the ballot box. . . .

The Court deemed NAACP's litigation activities "a form of political expression" protected by the First Amendment. Justice Brennan conceded that Virginia had a valid interest in regulating the traditionally illegal practices of barratry, maintenance, and champerty, but noted that the malicious intent which constituted the essence of these common law offenses was absent here. He also reasoned that because the NAACP's efforts served the public rather than a private interest, and because no monetary stakes were present, "there is no danger that the attorney will desert or subvert the paramount interests of his client to enrich himself or an outside sponsor. And the aims and interests of NAACP have not been shown

to conflict with those of its members and nonmember Negro litigants.
. . ."

To meet Virginia's criticism that the Court was creating a special law
to protect the NAACP, the majority found the NAACP's activities "constitutionally irrelevant to the ground of our decision." Even so, Justice
Douglas noted in a concurring opinion that the Virginia law prohibiting
activities by lay groups was aimed directly at NAACP activities as part "of
the general plan of massive resistance to the integration of the schools."

. . . .

Joined by Justices Clark and Stewart, Justice Harlan expressed the
view that the Virginia statute was valid. In support of his conclusion,
Harlan carefully reviewed the record and found that NAACP policy required what he considered serious departures from ethical professional
conduct. First, NAACP attorneys were required to follow policy directives promulgated by the National Board of Directors or lose their right
to compensation. Second, these directives to staff lawyers covered many
subjects relating to the form and substance of litigation. Third, the
NAACP not only advocated litigation and waited for prospective litigants
to come forward; in several instances and particularly in school cases,
"specific directions were given as to the types of prospective plaintiffs to
be sought, and staff lawyers brought blank forms to meetings for the purpose of obtaining signatures authorizing the prosecution of litigation in
the name of the signer." Fourth, the retainer forms signed by prospective
litigants sometimes did not contain the names of the attorneys retained,
and often when the forms specified certain attorneys as counsel, additional attorneys were brought into the action without the plaintiff's consent. Justice Harlan observed that several named plaintiffs had testified
that they had no personal dealings with the lawyers handling their cases
and were not aware until long after the event that suits had been filed in
their names. Taken together, Harlan felt these incidents justified the cor-
rective measures taken by the State of Virginia.

. . . .

Justice Harlan recognized that it might be in the association's interest
to maintain an all-out, frontal attack on segregation, even sacrificing
small points in some cases for the major points that might win other
cases. But, he foresaw that:

it is not impossible that after authorizing action in his behalf, a Negro
parent, concerned that a continued frontal attack could result in schools

closed for years, might prefer to wait with his fellows a longer time for good-faith efforts by the local school board than is permitted by the centrally determined policy of the NAACP. Or he might see a greater prospect of success through discussions with local school authorities than through the litigation deemed necessary by the Association. The parent, of course, is free to withdraw his authorization, but is his lawyer, retained and paid by petitioner and subject to its directions on matters of policy, able to advise the parent with that undivided allegiance that is the hallmark of the attorney-client relation? I am afraid not.[4]

The characterizations of the facts in *Button* by both the majority and the dissenters contain much that is accurate. As the majority found, the NAACP did not "solicit" litigants but rather systematically advised black parents of their rights under *Brown* and collected retainer signatures of those willing to join the proposed suits. The litigation was designed to serve the public interest rather than to enrich the litigators. Not all the plaintiffs were indigent, but few could afford to finance litigation intended to change the deep-seated racial policies of public school systems.

On the other hand, Justice Harlan was certainly correct in suggesting that the retainer process was often performed in a perfunctory manner and that plaintiffs had little contact with their attorneys. Plaintiffs frequently learned that suit had been filed and kept abreast of its progress through the public media. Although a plaintiff could withdraw from the suit at any time, he could not influence the primary goals of the litigation. Except in rare instances, the attorneys made policy decisions, often in conjunction with the organizational leadership and without consultation with the client.

. . . .

Button's recognition of First Amendment rights in the conduct of litigation led to subsequent decisions broadening the rights of other lay groups to obtain legal representation for their members. In so doing, these decisions posed new problems for the organized bar. The American Bar Association, faced with the reality of group practice which it had long resisted, has attempted to adopt guidelines for practitioners; but the applicable provisions of its new *Code of Professional Responsibility* provide only broad and uncertain guidance on the issues of control of litigation and conflict of interest as they affect civil rights lawyers.

The *Code of Professional Responsibility* again and again admonishes the lawyer "to disregard the desires of others that might impair his free judgment." But the suggestions assume the classical commercial conflict or a third-party intermediary clearly hostile to the client. Even when the *Code* seems to recognize more subtle "economic, political or social pressures," the protection civil rights clients need is not provided, and the suggested remedy, withdrawal from representation of the client, is hardly desirable if the client has no available alternatives.

The market system mentality of the drafters of the *Code* surfaces in another provision suggesting that problems of control are less likely to arise where the lawyer "is compensated directly by his client." But *Button* rejected solving the problem of control by relying on the elimination of compensation from a source other than the client. All that remains is the warning that a person or group furnishing lawyers "may be far more concerned with establishment or extension of legal principles than in the immediate protection of the rights of the lawyer's individual client."

The *Code* approach, urging the lawyer to "constantly guard against erosion of his professional freedom" and requiring that he "decline to accept direction of his professional judgment from any layman," is simply the wrong answer to the right question in civil rights offices where basic organizational policies such as the goals of school desegregation are often designed by lawyers and then adopted by the board or other leadership group. The NAACP's reliance on litigation requires that lawyers play a major role in basic policy decisions. Admonitions that the lawyer make no important decisions without consulting the client and that the client be fully informed of all relevant considerations are, of course, appropriate. But they are difficult to enforce in complex, long-term school desegregation litigation where the original plaintiffs may have left the system and the members of the class whose interests are at stake are numerous, generally uninformed, and, if aware of the issues, divided in their views.

Current ABA standards thus appear to conform with *Button* and its progeny in permitting the representation typically provided by civil rights groups. They are a serious attempt to come to grips with and provide specific guidance on the issues of outside influence and client primacy that so concerned Justice Harlan. But they provide little help where, as in school desegregation litigation, the influences of attorney and organization are mutually supportive, and both are so committed to what they perceive as the long-range good of their clients that they do not sense the growing conflict between those goals and the client's current interests. Given the cries of protest and the charges of racially motivated persecution that would probably greet any ABA effort to address this problem more specifically, it is not surprising that the conflict—which in any event will neither embarrass the profession ethically nor threaten it economically—has not received high priority.

Idealism, though perhaps rarer than greed, is harder to control. Justice Harlan accurately prophesied the excesses of derailed benevolence, but a retreat from the group representational concepts set out in *Button* would be a disaster, not an improvement. State legislatures are less likely than the ABA to draft standards that effectively guide practitioners and protect clients. Even well intentioned and carefully drawn standards might hinder rather than facilitate the always difficult task of achieving social change through legal action. And too stringent rules could encourage officials in some states to institute groundless disciplinary proceedings against lawyers in school cases, which in many areas are hardly more popular today than they were during the era of massive resistance.

Client engagement in school litigation is more likely to increase if civil rights lawyers themselves come to realize that the special status accorded them by the courts and the bar demands in return an extraordinary display of ethical sensitivity and self-restraint. The "divided allegiance" between client and employer which Justice Harlan feared would interfere with the civil rights lawyer's "full compliance with his basic professional obligation" has developed in a far more idealistic and thus a far more dangerous form. For it is more the civil rights lawyers' commitment to an integrated society than any policy directives or pressures from their employers which leads to their assumptions of client acceptance and their condemnations of all dissent.

. . . .

The Resolution of Lawyer-Client Conflicts

. . . It is essential that lawyers "lawyer" and not attempt to lead clients and class. Commitment renders restraint more, not less, difficult, and the inability of black clients to pay handsome fees for legal services can cause their lawyers, unconsciously perhaps, to adopt an attitude of "we know what's best" in determining legal strategy. Unfortunately, clients are all too willing to turn everything over to the lawyers. In school cases, perhaps more than in any other civil rights field, the attorney must be more than a litigator. The willingness to innovate, organize, and negotiate—and the ability to perform each with skill and persistence—are of crucial importance. In this process of overall representation, the apparent—and sometimes real—conflicts of interest between lawyer and client can be resolved.

Finally, commitment to an integrated society should not be allowed to interfere with the ability to represent effectively parents who favor education-oriented remedies. Those civil rights lawyers, regardless of race, whose commitment to integration is buoyed by doubts about the effectiveness of predominantly black schools should reconsider seriously the propriety of representing blacks, at least in those school cases arising in heavily minority districts.

. . . .

The tactics that worked for civil rights lawyers in the first decade of school desegregation—the careful selection and filing of class action suits seeking standardized relief in accordance with set, uncompromising national goals—are no longer unfailingly effective. In recent years, the relief sought and obtained in these suits has helped to precipitate a rise in militant white opposition and has seriously eroded carefully cultivated judicial support. Opposition to any civil rights program can be expected, but the hoped-for improvement in schooling for black children that might have justified the sacrifice and risk has proven minimal at best. It has been virtually nonexistent for the great mass of urban black children locked in all-black schools, many of which are today as separate and unequal as they were before 1954.

Political, economic, and social conditions have contributed to the loss of school desegregation momentum; but to the extent that civil rights lawyers have not recognized the shift of black parental priorities, they have sacrificed opportunities to negotiate with school boards and petition courts for the judicially enforceable educational improvements which all parents seek. The time has come for civil rights lawyers to end their single-minded commitment to racial balance, a goal which, standing alone, is increasingly inaccessible and all too often educationally impotent.

NOTES

1. Luke 16:13 (King James).
2. 371 U.S. 415 (1963).
3. Id. at 423.
4. 371 U.S. at 462.

Professor Bell Discusses
How to Live an Ethical Life

From NPR in Los Angeles, I'm Tavis Smiley.

Derrick Bell has led an awesome and interesting life. As a professor at New York University's School of Law, Bell has earned a reputation for taking tough stands on issues that frighten many so-called intellectuals into silence. That should come as no surprise, though, since he learned how to hang tough on ethical issues standing on the front lines of the civil rights movement. Bell's new book, *Ethical Ambition: Living a Life of Meaning and Worth,* is a guide of simple principles for living life in complex times. He joins us here in our LA studios to talk about it.

. . . .

SMILEY: Your book takes on a Western cultural assumption, I think, that essentially suggests that if you want to get ahead, you sometimes have to leave your morals behind. Talk about what made you want to challenge that notion.

PROFESSOR BELL: Well, that's—my life has been that, my parents. During the Depression, I could see the struggles and the risks they took in order to keep the family together. And I think some of my colleagues at Harvard Law School are very smart individuals, very committed, but they had no experience in confronting a situation as opposed to just going along with it and moving on up. And I think while it's tough, I think these situations, small at first, gaining maybe more risk and scariness as you go along, enables you, when the big crisis comes, to think through it and maybe decide—well, bring your passion. I mean, people are smart but maybe they don't bring a passion to their work, to the endeavor that

NPR Transcript with Tavis Smiley, Nov. 28, 2002. Used by permission. © NPRÆ 2002. Any unauthorized duplication is strictly prohibited.

they're involved in. And it's that passion Jeffrey Wigand probably had—the man who made *The Insider*. Remember, he was the $300,000 executive at one of the tobacco companies, but his commitment to his work wouldn't allow him to remain silent when tobacco industry heads got up in Congress, raised their right hand and swore that tobacco was not dangerous to your health. So he spoke out and, you know, he was brought down from $300,000—his wife left him—to $30,000 teaching high school chemistry. But when he was asked, "Dr. Wigand, given what you've gone through, if you knew this was gonna happen, would you have done it?" he said, "Yes, I would have. I did the right thing."

SMILEY: You've been teaching now for many, many years. What do you hear from students these days when the issue of ethics comes up?

PROFESSOR BELL: Most of the students who gravitate to my courses are the ones that are ready to pass up the $125,000 a year to start at the big law firms. They're scrambling for those few public interest jobs with public interest law firms, with the district attorney's office, with the public defender office. And so they have the commitment but they're still worried—because they hear what you say, what the world says. You can be successful or you can be ethical but you can't be both. And they look at me and say, "Well, you quit all these jobs and you're a black troublemaker and yet your career is still first. How did you do it?" And I usually would say, "I've been very fortunate." I have been very fortunate, but that wasn't what they wanted to hear. And so the book reflects my effort during my 70th year, sort of a, you know, milestone, to put together, to isolate, to identify, to articulate some of the things that were strengths to me all the way down and inspirations from parents to people like Paul Robeson, who sacrificed and went down.

SMILEY: Professor, where does one learn about ethics? Is it inherited? Is it innate? Is it something that you learn? Where does one get his or her ethics?

PROFESSOR BELL: I think development. There's this natural law or principle that we know right from wrong from the day we're born. And maybe that's right. That's a long discussion over the years, but I think that you gain it through determination and strengthening. I mean, you can't go into a gym and snatch 300 pounds. You have to go in and start with five pounds. And I think the same thing is true with ethical living. There's so much bad stuff happening around us, which is awful on the one hand and an opportunity on the other—not to do everything but to take on things that you can take on. Maybe you're writing a letter, maybe you're saying, "Hey, boss, I'm doing your work but why do you have to keep harassing me like that?" That takes a little risk but maybe the boss will say, "Oh, I didn't realize you were upset by that. I'll stop." We don't think enough, we don't value enough about the good stuff that may happen.

SMILEY: Given all of the corporate greed and malfeasance and corporate mendacity that we've seen over the last certainly year or so, I wonder whether or not you think it is time for an ethical awakening, so to speak, here in America.

PROFESSOR BELL: It's past time. The problem is that we're not going to get it from the leadership for the most part. We had ethical leaders like King, and until he was killed, he was despised more than he was revered, so that I think we can't wait for leaders. We have to, as individuals. God is within us to a certain extent, you know, and we have to justify the miracle of our existence not by driving the E class Mercedes. Nothing wrong with that but that should not be our goal. Our goal should be to justify our existence by loving God, by loving others, you see.

SMILEY: The thing I love most about this book, Professor Bell, is that in each of the chapters, you pretty much analyze the components of an ethical life. . . .

PROFESSOR BELL: Right.

SMILEY: . . . faith and passion and courage. Tell me right quick how you came across those seven basic principles, as I recall.

PROFESSOR BELL: Well, you know, there's a lot of overlap but I was trying to identify so that it would make it easier for individuals to recognize themselves in some of these. The whole thing on faith, for example. I was born, brought up in a black church. I accepted all that and kind of modified it as I grew older, got more education and what have you. But I wasn't able to answer my students who said, "You know, I think I'm Christian but I can't believe all the stuff that Christians are supposed to believe in and I don't want to pretend to believe it for fire insurance." And I would say, "Well, there are a lot of people who I know who are wonderful, ethical people and they won't go near a church." That was not what she asked me, right? So I spent a lot of time and I found out that theologians see God not as a theistic super human being up in the air but in part within us. We didn't go to church to find God. We went to church to share God, you see. So that gets at what a lot of the theologians are saying.

SMILEY: Why is it so important for people to find passion in the work that they do?

PROFESSOR BELL: You know, I tell my students, sure, it's OK to say you want to be a head of a law firm, you want to be a corporate executive, you want to make a million dollars. Nothing wrong with that, but you basically should look for a job that you would continue doing if you didn't have to work at all—the kind of work that you're passionate about and would do out of love, commitment, and passion.

SMILEY: What is the greatest challenge, as you see it, to living a life of ethical ambition?

PROFESSOR BELL: It is just trying to hold on to that goal, trying to keep a life of integrity as your primary thing, even as you're seeking success as the world measures it. It's always tough. We're not perfect but I think that that effort enables us to—as one teacher of professional ethics once had the students at the very beginning of the class write down the obituary that they hoped somebody else would write for them. He said that got them focused correctly on how they should deal with that course. I think it's good advice.

CHAPTER 4

Revisionist History

Bell offers a vision of American history that differs from the usual version one finds in civics books. Where some might see steady progress, Bell sees intermittent breakthroughs followed by crashing retrenchment. Where some find a nation committed to racial justice and equal treatment, Bell finds unstated axioms of white supremacy operating behind the scenes. But Bell does not merely assert his contrarian view. He gives his evidence for it, challenging the more orthodox minded to come to terms with his provocatively well documented interpretation. Blacks have trouble finding out this information. Scholars and teachers have an ethical duty to bring it to the fore.

An American Fairy Tale

The Income-Related Neutralization of Race Law Precedent

Bluebeard's Castle, a French fairy tale, depicts the exploits of a nobleman who married a succession of women who entered his castle, never to be heard from again. Bela Bartok composed a darkly beautiful opera about Bluebeard's fourth wife, Judith, who leaves her family to marry the rich seigneur.

Upon entering his foreboding, windowless fortress, Judith finds the walls wet, for here the sun can never enter. . . . Along the somber corridor she detects seven locked doors and urges Bluebeard to allow her to open all of them. . . . He tries to persuade her to accept him on faith, and not look behind the doors. . . .

Still insisting, Judith gains from him one key at a time. Behind the doors she discovers chambers containing Bluebeard's torture weapons, his armaments, his gold, and his jewels. One door opens to a scene of his vast land holdings, another to a beautiful flower garden. Blood, however, stains each scene.

Bluebeard declares his love for his newest wife and urges her not to unlock the seventh door. Now fearing the worst, Judith insists on opening that door. . . .

With trembling hands Judith opens the final door and encounters Bluebeard's three former wives. He has not murdered them. Rather, they are living, very beautiful, but quite pale as they advance in single file, splendidly adorned with mantles, crowns, and jewels.

. . . Despite [Judith's] pleas for mercy, Bluebeard places on [her] a mantle, crown, and jewels. Sadly, she follows her predecessors through the door which closes after her. The stage darkens. The curtain falls.

18 Suffolk U. L. Rev. 331 (1984). Used by permission.

The fairy tale . . . is far more than an amusing narrative for children. Fairy tales did not always have happy endings, but primarily reflected the harsh experiences of the peasants' lives. . . . The suffering of American blacks is not unlike the harsh life of peasants in early eighteenth century France. . . .

American society periodically produces a symbol of redemption in the wake of unspeakable cruelties to its blacks. At the national level, the symbol is usually a document with liberating potential: the Emancipation Proclamation, the post–Civil War Amendments, the Civil Rights Acts of the 1960s and, of course, the decision in *Brown v. Board of Education.* Each of these documents contained language with the potential to expunge our national Bluebeard image, the dark stain of slavery and racism. Without looking closely at the motives behind the drafting of these documents, black Americans have accepted the language for its redemptive promise and have urged its fulfillment. . . .

. . . .

As Bluebeard's wives were doomed to suffer imprisonment, blacks seem foreordained to endure one racial-based disaster after another. . . . Each reconciliation is rich with exchanged promises of freedom for blacks and forgiveness for whites. Forgiving and extending themselves in reliance on the promises of freedom, blacks discover all too late that the new relationship, while better than the one they risked so much to escape, leaves them in a different but still subordinate posture. Each time, the symbol of the new relationship ends up behind a new and more imposing door, constructed of current economic needs and secured with a racism that is no less efficient because some blacks are able to slip by the barriers of class and wealth.

Using the idiom of Bluebeard's Castle, let us examine a few of the vanquished brides of black freedom.

The Emancipation Proclamation

Abraham Lincoln's Executive Order, purporting to free the slaves in Confederate-held territory, electrified the world and ensured that the North would triumph in the Civil War. Responding to the long-sought order with unbounded enthusiasm, disloyal slaves disrupted southern work forces, destroyed property, and absconded in ever-swelling numbers. More importantly, nearly 200,000 blacks enlisted in the Union

Army and made the decisive difference for the North in many later battlefield victories.

Although the Emancipation Proclamation, bolstered by the Thirteenth
Amendment, abolished the legal claims of slave masters, it created no
substantive rights in the slaves themselves. The freedom document left
them defenseless against resubjugation under the notorious black codes,
race riots, and widespread white terror and intimidation. Congress, for
its part, never granted the much-touted Freedman's Bureau the authority
to provide reparations for the years of free labor stolen from the slaves.
When congressional resolve foundered on the economic rock of expro-
priating the plantations of Confederate whites and using the proceeds to
provide blacks with "forty acres and a mule," blacks were left with neither the money nor the means necessary for survival in a still racially hostile world.

The Post–Civil War Amendments

Radical Republicans pushed for the passage of the post–Civil War
Amendments, which were designed to secure citizenship for the former
slaves and to provide them with voting rights. Other statesmen realized
that unless they acted to legitimate the freedman's status, southerners
would use violence to force blacks back into slavery, and the economic
dispute that had precipitated the Civil War would surface again.

To avoid another conflict, Congress enacted the Thirteenth, Fourteenth, and Fifteenth Amendments and the Civil Rights Acts of 1870–
1875. Registering to vote in great numbers, blacks helped secure Republican control of the southern states and Congress. But within a decade
southern planters rendered the Thirteenth Amendment irrelevant by exer-
cising raw economic power and using naked violence to establish a share-
cropping system that provided them with the same labor benefits as slavery without the minimum obligations inherent in the slave master's role.

Although blacks had gained the right to vote, the federal government
failed to enforce the Fifteenth Amendment effectively for almost a century
after its enactment. The Fourteenth Amendment, not passable as a specific
protection for black rights, was finally enacted as a general guarantee of
life, liberty, and property for all "persons." Following a period of judicial
ambivalence, corporations were deemed persons under the amendment
and for several generations received far more judicial protection than

blacks. Indeed, blacks became the victims of judicial interpretations of the Fourteenth Amendment and of legislation construed so narrowly as to render the promised protection virtually meaningless.

The Civil Rights Acts of the 1960s

The civil rights protest movement of the early 1960s developed out of the realization that court-mandated changes in the interpretation of the Constitution would not alone bring an end to racial segregation. Responding to the moral pressure exerted by the civil rights activists, Congress enacted legislation in 1964 and 1965, and attempted in 1968 to provide enforceable protection to the newly won rights. Even the most determined pessimist could not claim that these statutes, enacted after more than a decade of great sacrifice, failed to improve the lives and status of blacks. Today, the ugly stigma of law-enforced segregated facilities no longer exists. Black children no longer must attend public schools rigidly segregated by race and deficient in educational resources. The most odious forms of racial discrimination in jobs and housing have been laid to rest. . . .

All must applaud these reforms, and yet who can claim that the racial millennium has arrived? The new civil rights laws only address instances of overt discrimination. Policies, neutral as to race and serving some arguably valid purpose, win judicial approval even though the subtle impact of their exercise once again burdens blacks, long disadvantaged by the more open forms of discrimination. Where civil rights enforcement inconveniences or even endangers the economic interests of whites, decisions in all but the most innocuous affirmative action cases sidetrack civil rights in a manner that differs more in style than in result from the white supremacist mindset that doomed the reparation plans for blacks during the First Reconstruction.

Brown v. Board of Education

In the view of some, *Brown* is the greatest Supreme Court decision of all time. Certainly, it was a freedom symbol without equal in the long struggle for racial equality. Yet, its promise of equality emanated more from its language than from its holding. As with earlier symbols, blacks read the opinion for all it was worth and hoped for the best, but the best has proven elusive. On its fiftieth anniversary, *Brown,* like its predecessors, is fading into the gloom, long before its message has been fulfilled.

As with the earlier civil rights manifestos, opposition based on economic concerns dilutes the potential of *Brown.* Good schools and decent housing remain beyond the financial reach of most of those who were the intended beneficiaries of the *Brown* decision. Color-blind hiring policies in the computer and other high-tech fields are not likely to aid children educated in inferior schools. In short, *Brown* and its judicial and legislative progeny have opened the door toward middle-class success, but have not touched those blacks still needing the modern-day equivalent of "forty acres and a mule." Today, as throughout our history, while the idea of equality causes our hopes to soar, the economic reality of our capitalist system keeps our chances low.

. . . .

We are witnessing a number of black breakthroughs that resemble the first beams of sunlight of a promising new day—black mayors, the first black Miss America, the first black astronaut's ascent into space, and after many years of effort, a federal bill making Martin Luther King, Jr.'s birthday a national holiday.

Nonetheless, we stand helplessly by and watch an increasingly grim national scene, as black people sink ever deeper into the misery of unemployment, crime, broken families, and out-of-wedlock births, all indicia of an exploited, colonized people. These multitudes are without jobs, decent homes, and adequate education. Ironically, these same black people receive the protection of more expansive civil rights laws than any of their black ancestors.

Because poor blacks remain outcasts in this country, the progress made by better-off blacks is placed in jeopardy. The gap between the economic statistics for blacks and whites is hardly greater than that which exists between upper-class blacks and their poverty-level brethren. Blacks who have and those who have not are increasingly separated by neighborhood, schooling, employment, recreation, and even place of worship. Both groups are caught in the grip of an economic segregation as structured, and as harmful, as the law-enforced segregation that plagued their lives a generation ago.

. . . .

In the version of *Bluebeard's Castle* that Charles Perrault published, Judith's relatives arrive in time and slay Bluebeard. No possibility of a similar happy ending seems to exist in my analogous use of the fairy tale to gain an understanding of American racial policy. For here, the nation is Bluebeard, a mixture of all the evil in its history with all the potential for good in its national ideals. Neither Bluebeard nor this country is able to suppress the belief that redemption may be gained without surrendering spoils obtained through even the most pernicious evil.

. . . .

Can we sense, either from history or by analogy from the fairy tale, whether the racial pattern of white symbols and black sacrifice will ever end? I can find no such hope in Bartok's version. The opera contains an early mention of Judith's family, but never says that the relatives will arrive or that they will be successful in saving her if they do. Nor does it give any reason to believe that Judith will be Bluebeard's last attempt to regain his humanity through symbolic marriage and the inhumane sacrifice of another bride.

America can be expected to offer still another freedom symbol to blacks when blacks again become insistent or when political or economic conditions indicate that such an offer will be appropriately beneficial. Blacks will again ignore the likely motivations for such a new freedom document and embrace it enthusiastically, gain from it what they can, and watch as it too, like Bluebeard's Judith, is retired to some somber chamber while the stage grows dark and the curtain falls.

Reconstruction's Racial Realities

. . . .

... For weal or for woe, the destiny of the colored race in this country is wrapped up with our own; they are to remain in our midst, and here spend their years and here bury their fathers and finally repose themselves. We may regret it. It may not be entirely compatible with our taste that they should live in our midst. We cannot help it. Our forefathers introduced them, and their destiny is to continue among us; and the practical question which now presents itself to us is as to the best mode of getting along with them.[1]

The year was 1866. Senator Howard, abolitionist, Radical Republican, and key architect of the Fourteenth Amendment, urged Radical and Conservative Republicans alike to confront the challenge posed by the presence of the former slaves "in our midst." Grudging rather than generous, conciliatory rather than crusading, Senator Howard's statement suggests sanctuary rather than equality for blacks.

The senator's candidly expressed apprehension about the prospect of blacks living free in white America continues to echo through contemporary civil rights decisions in which the measure of relief is determined less by the character of harm suffered by blacks than the degree of disadvantage the relief sought will impose on whites. These influences can be codified in what I call Rules of Race Relations Law. . . . The Fourteenth Amendment is the definitive example of my First Rule:

Racial remedies are the outward manifestations of unspoken and perhaps unconscious conclusions that such remedies—if adopted—will

23 Rutgers L.J. 261 (1992). Used by permission.

secure, advance, or at least not harm societal interests deemed important by whites in power.

In the two years it took for the necessary two-thirds of the states to ratify the Fourteenth Amendment, public support for Reconstruction measures began to wane. In less than a dozen years, it disappeared entirely. The last Northern troops were withdrawn from the South, and Congress turned to other matters. The Supreme Court invalidated some civil rights laws and, despite the Fourteenth Amendment, generally ignored state deprivations of black rights.

Because the Fourteenth Amendment's offer of federal protection against state interference with basic rights was addressed to all *persons,* corporate lawyers realized its potential as a defense against the efforts of state legislatures to protect workers from the exploitive policies of industrial growth. American business persuaded the Supreme Court to find that corporations were "persons" entitled to the Amendment's protection. As a result, for most of its early history, . . . the provision nurtured "railroads, utility companies, banks, employers of child labor, chain stores, money lenders, aliens, and a host of other groups and institutions . . . , leaving so little room for the Negro that he seemed to be the Fourteenth Amendment's forgotten man."[2]

The Fourteenth Amendment's transition from guardian of the benighted blacks to protector of propertied interests followed a well-established tradition in American racial policy. Lincoln's Emancipation Proclamation in 1863, for example, while nominally freeing the slaves, actually advanced the Northern cause in several important areas. . . . Earlier policies abolishing slavery in Northern states after the Revolutionary War had also emulated this pattern of mainly symbolic recognition of black rights that furthered rather than infringed the property interests of whites. The moral concerns abolitionists raised accompanied such pragmatic arguments as the fear of slave revolts and the need to eliminate slave competition with free white laborers.

In the aftermath of the Reconstruction era, the country and the Supreme Court accepted the facially neutral but grossly unjust "separate but equal" standard as the constitutional justification for racial segregation that served to insure the subordination of blacks. For almost a century, the policy provided an effective and, for most whites, a satisfying response to Senator Howard's suggestion that whites seek "the best mode of getting along with them."

The law's failure to protect black rights reflects my Second Rule of Race Relations Law:

The benefits to blacks of civil rights policies are mainly symbolic rather than substantive, and when the crisis that prompted their enactment ends, they will not be enforced for blacks, though, in altered interpretations, they may serve the policy needs of whites.

. . . .

. . . In dozens of cases heard in the several decades before *Brown*, blacks had been pleading in vain that state-sponsored segregation, particularly in the public schools, was incompatible with the due process and equal protection of the laws guaranteed by the Fourteenth Amendment. But the Court finally saw the light in 1954, largely because it also saw that the decision would benefit American society as a whole in terms of both foreign and domestic economic policy.

. . . .

I do not mean to discount the valuable contributions by whites for whom recognition of racial injustice and a desire to correct it is sufficient motivation. But today, as with abolition in the nineteenth century, the number of whites willing to act on morality alone is insufficient to bring about reform. From the nation's beginning and to the present day, political factors, the desire to protect property and a priority for white interests, have dictated the recognition of blacks' citizenship rights.

. . . .

. . . For black people, the scars of racial subordination cut deep and last from generation to generation. Nonetheless, and in spite of their often discouraging struggle, blacks have achieved for whites as well as themselves a wide array of individual rights now protected by the Fourteenth Amendment. . . . Civil rights precedents that improve the plight of disadvantaged whites include: the right to fairly apportioned electoral districts, the protection of freedom of speech as against powerful public figures, elimination of non-job-related criteria from civil service tests, other job qualifications, and of college admission standards, elimination of poll taxes, and the protection of criminally accused whites from trial by a jury selected on a racially discriminatory basis.

In recent years, the Supreme Court has extended the protection of an 1866 civil rights statute to white groups discriminated against because of their Jewish religion or their ethnic affiliation as Arabs. Out of these precedents I have drawn a Third Rule of Race Relations Law:

> *The injustices that so dramatically diminish the rights of blacks because of race also drastically diminish the rights of many whites, particularly those who lack money and power or are part of an unpopular minority group or movement.*

. . . .

Discrimination based on race disguises the more subtle though hardly less pernicious class-based disadvantage many whites suffer. The compulsive attention given to the whites' superior status compared with that of those blacks in the lowest socio-economic ranks obscures the far more sizeable gap between the status of most whites and those at the lofty top levels of our society. . . . Its size mandates maintenance of blacks as a subordinate group to blame for what's wrong with society and who serve as the reassuring reminders for even the lowliest whites that blacks, and not they, are at the bottom. . . .

As an intellectual matter, we can debate which interpretation of the Reconstruction Amendments most accurately reflects the intentions of those who drafted, approved, and ratified changes in our Constitution that have so influenced the direction of American law and life. . . . There is though little room to debate the failure of those Amendments and the laws and judicial decisions relying on them to alter significantly the quasi-citizenship status of those whose forebears were black. For those seeking the equality under the law promised in the texts, the barrier remains what it has always been. . . . The Reconstruction Amendments will remain a vehicle through which policy makers can further their interests by providing a modicum of relief from the most serious deprivations of rights and opportunities to racial minorities and other disadvantaged individuals and groups.

NOTES

1. 2 *Encyclopedia of the American Constitution* 760–61 (Leonard W. Levy et al. eds., 1986) (quoting statement by Senator Howard).

2. Boris I. Bittker, *The Case of the Checker-Board Ordinance: An Experiment in Race Relations*, 71 Yale L.J. 1387, 1393 (1962).

Black Faith in a Racist Land

From the beginning, this nation has prided itself on being a Christian country, but as I sat in a black church in the deep South last Sunday and listened to the congregation fervently sing the old hymn, "Amazing Grace," I thought that God's grace could be no more amazing than has been the black man's faith in the religion learned from the slave master whose religion was force, wealth and power. Having none of these, blacks were required to place their faith in God. And thus, in a nation supposedly devoted to Christianity, we find that the most despised of its people are in fact the best Christians.

From the beginning, this nation has taken pride in its dedication to the rule of law and the protection of individual rights. But black people . . . understood that those who urged respect for and compliance with the law relied themselves on force, wealth and power. And black people, having none of these, had to place their faith in the law . . . to gain their freedom and the partial measure of dignity which we enjoy today.

The history of black people's reliance on the law in their struggle for freedom and equality is little known. . . . Little is said about the duality of motive with which even minor steps on our behalf were taken, and virtually no attention is given to just how little even some of the major events changed or improved our status.

. . . We didn't learn in school that Lincoln [freed the slaves through the Emancipation Proclamation] only after all alternatives to action were gone. . . . The Civil War was begun to preserve the Union, not end slavery, and when Lincoln issued the Proclamation, it liberated only those slaves held ". . . within any State or designated part of a State, the people whereof shall then be in rebellion against the United States. . . ." The order could have no legal effect in areas not then under control of the

17 Howard L.J. 300 (1972). Used by permission.

Union forces, and it specifically excluded slaveholding areas in Virginia and West Virginia which had not joined the rebellion.

. . . .

In the South, [slaves] simply abandoned their masters by the thousands and headed for the Union lines. It was not the law, but their faith that had set them free. It was an amazing phenomenon, one fully deserving a better fate in high school history courses.

If high school history appears like a fairy tale designed to placate rather than incite the minds of young people, then what can be said in defense of the treatment black history receives in most college texts? An example is the Declaration of Independence. Most texts focus on the ringing proclamation that:

> all Men are created equal and are endowed by their Creator with certain unalienable Rights, that among these are Life, Liberty, and the Pursuit of Happiness.

But most texts neglect to mention that a first draft of the Declaration of Independence written by Thomas Jefferson criticized the King of England for having introduced slavery to these shores. That draft was scrapped at the insistence of Southern representatives in the Continental Congress.

. . . The Founding Fathers, fearing their efforts to establish a strong central government would fail because of their serious differences over the issue of slavery, determined to resolve these differences through a series of compromises, all at the expense of blacks. . . . Even the most liberal of the Founding Fathers were unable to imagine a society in which whites and Negroes would live together as fellow-citizens. As Jefferson put it:

> Nothing is more certainly written in the book of fate, than that these people are to be free; nor is it less certain that the two races, equally free, cannot live in the same government.[1]

Thus, when the Southern delegates insisted on their right to maintain slavery, the Northerners . . . conceded the issue with the result that the Constitution contained provisions enabling slave holding areas to count their slaves for purposes of determining representation, guaranteeing the right to import slaves until 1808, and providing the constitutional basis for the fugitive slave acts.

. . . .

In law school, one might hope to find more accurate information about blacks and the law. After all law is the application of legal history to current problems; but alas, those seeking an accurate chronology of the law and racial problems in law school must find it on their own. . . . Most contemporary law students are exposed to the basic "civil rights" cases and are spared the traditional cases in agency or property that compare slaves to dogs or other animals. But while the Reconstruction Amendments rate discussion, students receive little background as to how much of politics and how little of morality constitute the ingredients which led to their enactment. And they also receive little explanation of why those who pushed the Amendments into existence lost all interest in having them enforced.

We learn that it is not necessary to read the case of *Dred Scott v. Sandford*,[2] because we are told the decision was in effect repealed first by the Civil War, later by the Thirteenth Amendment and still later, by *Brown v. Board of Education*. . . . We try to keep in mind that *Dred Scott* was repealed or reversed by later events, yet we keep wondering why so many current decisions still seem to be based on the philosophy of *Dred Scott* and not that of the Thirteenth Amendment or the *Brown* decision. A reading of the majority decision in *Dred Scott* would make it all clear.

Chief Justice Taney not only says that blacks were never intended to be citizens of the United States, he proves it by referring to all the legislation and court decisions which denied the basic rights of citizenship to free blacks and the basic considerations of humanity to the slaves. . . . Taney reviewed the status of blacks not only under the federal Constitution but under state constitutions as well. He found that blacks had been brought to the country as slaves, and although they had been generally freed in Northern states, . . . even when freed, [they] had been denied the basic rights of citizenship in virtually every state. . . .

Taney found that neither the Declaration of Independence, the Articles of Confederation, nor the Constitution improved the status of blacks in this country. . . . The Naturalization Acts limited the right of becoming citizens "to aliens being free white persons." The first militia act barred non-whites, and even the charter for the new capitol at Washington provided special fines for free Negroes and mulattoes, and prescribed terms and conditions under which free blacks could reside in the City. Clearly, the treatment accorded black people by the country during the first half century of its existence amply justified Chief Justice Taney's conclusions. . . . In *Dred Scott,* the blacks were merely pawns and the crucial issues concerned not black freedom but white greed. . . .

It is true that the Civil War Amendments voided the decision in *Dred Scott* as legal doctrine, but we learned the bitter truth during Reconstruction that the North had pressured through enactment of the Thirteenth, Fourteenth and Fifteenth Amendments as much to punish the South as to liberate the Negro. As black gains slipped away in the 1870s, the Supreme Court and the lower courts confirmed what blacks had feared, that the citizenship they had been granted . . . was citizenship in name only. . . .

. . . .

The racial injustices perpetrated against blacks in every area of life during the decades that followed would fill those history texts that now expend so much space and effort in glossing over this far from commendable period of American history. Suits challenged some of the racist practices in jury discrimination, segregated housing ordinances, the white primaries, and teacher salary equalization suits; but any victories were symbolic. . . .

The decision in *Brown v. Board of Education*[3] is usually cited as the beginning of the modern era in American race relations. . . . The men who decided *Brown* were likely sincere, and even courageous, but with hindsight it becomes clear that the decision was as predictable as was the Thirteenth Amendment, and as unlikely to be enforced. . . . White America had succeeded in cleaning up its legal image, and black folk had received as they so often do in civil rights "victories" the equitable remedy of beautiful language and the promise of more substantial relief further down the line. . . .

By this time, blacks had learned that faith is fine, but the Lord helps those who help themselves. And so, beginning with Mrs. Rosa Parks in Montgomery, they began combining religion and action based on the rights they were supposed to have and found the formula produced marvelous results. . . . Blacks succeeded in effectively exposing to the nation and the world that the rights of citizenship which had been granted at least twice in less than a century remained unredeemed and, seemingly, unredeemable. . . . The nation's racial duplicity was exposed, and Southern bigots reacted as they always had, except this time television was watching. National embarrassment grew, and the nation decided to teach those Southerners a lesson. Like the 1860s, however, the commitment, which was more to racial image than to racial equality, proved short-lived. . . . Protesters in the South whose convictions had been regularly overturned by the Supreme Court soon found that for activities which earlier they were being hailed as civil rights warriors, they were now receiving fines and jail terms that stood up on appeal.

. . . .

. . . Black lawyers—particularly in the South—have always had to have courage; courage to travel to the small and hostile towns to represent unpopular clients under circumstances so tense that as Justice Thurgood Marshall used to say, one could only fold his civil rights carefully, place them in his pocket and leave them there until he was safely out of town. . . . Such experiences are unfortunately far from being rare in the history of racism in the law. They continue today, particularly in the minor courts where so much of the black lawyer's practice is located. . . . Black practitioners daily face the prospect of having to respond courteously to judges, some of whom combine in seemingly unlimited measure qualities of arrogance, ignorance and bigotry. Demeaning comments must be ignored, and objectivity is forgotten in hearings in which the outcome is clearly predetermined. . . . It is amazing . . . that so few black lawyers have succumbed to the strong temptation to respond to these judges in kind, to refuse to go along with the system of justice which is literally a farce for so many blacks. . . .

. . . .

Decisions on racial issues today do not contain the overt racism of earlier years. Rather, they reflect "institutional racism" which Anthony Downs defines as "placing or keeping persons in a position or status of inferiority by means of attitudes, actions, or institutional structures which do not use color itself as the subordinating mechanism, but instead use other mechanisms indirectly related to color.[4]" . . . Racism is present in every aspect of the administration of the American judicial system, but because the Jim Crow signs are down, it is easy to ignore the problem or to categorize it for solution under the general heading of fairness. . . .

Racism, particularly of the institutional variety, is not limited to the judicial administration process, but can be found as well in the great majority of decisions that present racial issues. [It takes the form of:]

1. An abiding, albeit seldom expressed and often unconscious, belief that blacks as a group are inferior to whites.
2. A predisposition to resolve conflicts between black injustices and the needs of the white majority in a manner that protects and promotes the latter, even if it perpetuates the former.
3. Realization (in varying degrees) of the basic inconsistency between American ideals and the status to which blacks have been relegated on the basis of race.
4. An inability to recognize that actions seemingly taken to correct racial injustices are often in fact based on the promotion or preservation of white interests.

Although many decisions may seem neutral on their face, their failure to consider the history of racism that has infested all of our institutions can give a racist impact to actions and decisions that were not motivated by a desire to discriminate.[5] . . . The hardening of attitudes toward the poor that they evince portends a more difficult time for blacks. It thus behooves all of us to be alert to these unannounced dangers and ready to expose the racial significance of cases and decisions that are silent on the racial question. . . . Black lawyers like black historians have a special obligation . . . .

. . . .

I would hope that increasing numbers of black lawyers will give serious consideration to entering the teaching profession. . . . It has many rewards, and certainly law students, black and white, will benefit from the special insights and experiences blacks have about the law. These experiences and insights are woefully lacking from virtually all of the predominantly white law schools today.

NOTES

1. Staughton Lynd, *Slavery and the Founding Fathers,* in M. Drimmer, Black History 117, 129 (1968).
2. 60 U.S. 393 (1857).
3. 347 U.S. 483 (1954).
4. Anthony Downs, *Racism in America and How to Combat It,* U.S. Comm'n on Civil Rights 5–6 (1970).
5. Haywood Burns, *Racism in American Law,* in 2 Amistad 43, 58 (1971).

CHAPTER 5

Sexuality and Romance

Romantic and sexual attractions intrigue and disrupt the lives of most people. Add race, and sometimes things become more complicated. The excerpts that follow deal with sexual orientation, interracial attraction and romance, and black men who brag about their sexual prowess. As the reader will see, Bell holds that sexuality and love are gifts that no one should squander. They can serve as sources of inspiration, support, and energy, particularly for the dispossessed.

The Entitlement

If happiness can be equated with acquisitions, Donnell B. Dancer was a very happy man. He had it all. Luxury apartment, fine car, fancy clothes galore, a bank account replenished as often as it was emptied, and a seemingly endless procession of the most stunning women all these advantages inevitably attract. Donnell—everyone called him "Donny B. D."—referred to these women, though not in their presence, as "showpieces."

As much as money and what it can buy in late-twentieth-century America, Donny also craved celebrity. After years as a so-so show business performer, he had that as well. Donny was the good-looking, jive-talking host of the syndicated television talk show, "Let It All Hang Out," which was a hit from its first week. Five afternoons a week, the show featured interviews with a steady stream of personalities, mostly black, talking about their sex lives. The plan was simple: to give his audience of middle-class housewives, college students, and people hanging out in cafés and bars every imaginable verification of all the myths about black sexuality—and then some. This was not a new idea. Several of the network talk shows had similar themes. Donny B. D. did them one better by ensuring that all his guests were either blacks talking about one or another aspect of sex or interracial couples—always a turn-on for his viewers—doing the same.

After little more than a year, he was right up there in the ratings with the top talk show hosts. Fact is, Donny considered himself better than his competitors, who sometimes presented guests who talked about something other than sex. That's why he was really miffed when that black sister Jill Nelson published an article on talk radio in the *Nation* and didn't even mention his name. Hell, his guests were dealing with all the stuff she described in her article: "mate swapping, men who beat women, fat women who are porno stars, the super size of black men's penises, transvestites, men who don't support their children, . . . people who love to have unprotected sex, . . . white women who love black men, strippers, black women who love white men."

He had meant to write and complain, but he was too busy. Plus, he was getting plenty of print from real magazines like *People* and *Jet*. Mention in those mags helped the ratings. Plus, it attracted more of the kind of guests whose stories boosted the ratings even more. Donny B. D. laughed to himself remembering the two white girls who actually got into a fist-fight on camera over which of their black boyfriends was the best lover. Actually, they were yelling, but didn't exchange blows until he brought out the boyfriend of one of them, and that boyfriend turned out to be—much to everyone's shock except his own—the man both women were boasting about. Funny, the two women went at one another, not the man. The audience ate it up.

Donny's show featured young black studs bragging about the number of "bitches"—usually teen-age girls—who had had their babies. Or young mothers who claimed that nobody cared about them, including the children's fathers, and that having babies would give some meaning to their lives. Or, people who talked about the nitty-gritty details of every imaginable love triangle, even a quadrangle or two. Or, women who explained that they had given up jobs as secretaries and beauticians because they could make more money selling their bodies. The show was as hot as the FCC would allow, and probably a lot more, particularly when Donny's male guests bragged about beating up and otherwise abusing women who still came crawling back for more of their "once in a lifetime" loving.

Donny expected the show to go on forever, or at least long enough to challenge Donahue and Oprah. That's why he was so damn mad the Monday he arrived early at his office all set to prepare for that afternoon's show, and in comes this raggedy-ass messenger with a letter from the station manager. Two sentences to tell Donny that the show has been canceled "effective immediately."

"He can't do that, can he?" Donny was screaming over the phone. His agent, upset himself, was trying to calm Donny down.

"I am afraid he can, Donny. It's in the contract. Plus, Donny, what else could they do? Half of your guests haven't shown up for two weeks, and your ratings have dropped through the basement."

"So what! It's just a little slow, man! I can keep things going with jive talk till the guests start comin' back. We need to pay them more. . . . If the network talk shows can pay big bucks, so can we if that damn station would get up off some of that money my show's been pullin' in."

Donny's agent was quiet. There was no reasoning with his client just now. The show's producers had been offering double the usual rates for appearances. There were few takers. The agent understood that all the other talk shows were having the same problem—at least, with their black guests. "I'll see what I can do, Donny. Call you back."

"Wait! Wait!" Donny shouted. "Don't hang up." The receiver clicked. "Damn him! He'll pay for that."

He slumped down in his ultradeluxe office chair and sighed audibly. His irritation had not affected his mind. He might yell, but he had not gotten where he was by being a screaming maniac. He knew as well as the agent and the station manager that something was amiss. This black sex thing was a winner. White people, going all the way back, had transferred all their most base feelings onto blacks. Out of whites' demand for dominance came all of these sexual fantasies about the blacks they dominated. And, as the ultimate mark of their oppression, many blacks accepted this racist view equating their personhood with their sexual prowess. Exclusion from many of the job and career opportunities that help define who one is contributed to the willingness of some blacks to live out society's sexual stereotypes.

Donny knew all of this, simply by growing up in a Detroit ghetto. He didn't pass judgment on it, he simply wanted to get rich from it. His father had taught him that. "A smart man doesn't just enjoy sex, he exploits it." Now, all of a sudden it seemed to be ending, at least for black people and those whites married to or otherwise having sex with them. Donny shook his head. It made no sense. But, just maybe, the thing he had been experiencing for a week or so, was happening to others—scaring them as much as it had him. And, if it was, he could sure as hell understand why they didn't want to talk about it. He certainly didn't. It was too damn upsetting, to say nothing of embarrassing.

Donny's intercom interrupted his thinking. "Mr. Dancer, it's the reporter from *Essence* magazine here to interview you. Her name is Curia, and you promised her a half hour. Shall I show her in?"

Donny hesitated. Ordinarily, he would have welcomed a story in *Essence*. With its holier-than-thou editorial policy, the magazine had been critical of shows like his. Now, he thought, what the hell? "Show her in." The way things are going, I may not be able to even buy publicity.

Ms. Curia—G. C. Curia, she said her name as she extended her hand—was the kind of black woman Donny recognized instantly and just as instantly dismissed as "too serious." Smartly dressed in a conservative navy-blue suit, briefcase in hand, the tall, dark-brown-skinned young woman with her large horn-rimmed glasses looked to be a graduate, three or four years before, from an Ivy League college determined to make it in journalism and then write the novel that would put her name on the literary map.

"Thank you for seeing me, Mr. Dancer. I just learned about your show's being canceled."

"And *Essence* sent you here to rub it in?"

"Not at all," she said, somewhat coldly. "I asked for this interview two weeks ago. But," she paused, "there may well be a connection between your show's cancellation and the S.E.T."

"The S.E. what?"

"We at the magazine working on the story have dubbed it 'S.E.T.' for Sexual Entitlement Therapy."

"So what the hell is it? And what does it have to do with my show?"

"That's what a team of reporters from *Essence, Ebony,* and *Emerge* are trying to find out. So far we know that couples began experiencing the S.E.T. a couple of weeks ago. At first, people didn't talk about it, but finally some confided in close friends, in strictest confidence. Then shocking reports began to leak out. When black women are approached for sex by husbands, boyfriends, girlfriends, or even casual pickups, many—but not all—find themselves unable to carry out their desires. The same is true when wives, unmarried women, or gay men initiate the lovemaking. That one partner is not black does not prevent the S.E.T. from striking in otherwise appropriate situations."

Donny noticed the matter-of-fact manner in which Curia spoke about this S.E.T. business. He was impressed. She was professional and articulate. "What else have you learned?" he asked.

"Well, it has proven a real stopper in abusive sexual relationships. And, as far as we know, most prostitutes and participants of both sexes in porno films have been unable to practice their profession. Virtually all unmarried teenagers are barred from having sex by the S.E.T., as are those who are H.I.V. positive, unless they or their partner is practicing safe sex. And, let me see, S.E.T. seems to have halted all rapes and coerced sex in which a black person was either the aggressor or the victim. Incest has become impossible. S.E.T. even seems to interfere with prison rape, though unfortunately not with the many other physical abuses that occur behind prison walls.

"That's not all. Gay and lesbian couples who had maintained that their sexual relationships were no more unnatural than those of heterosexual couples, gained a proof of their argument that many would have just as soon done without. In fact, until it became known that S.E.T. could affect all forms of lovemaking, homosexuals feared that a society notoriously hostile to them had come up with some new and particularly vicious technological means of gay and lesbian bashing."

Donny was listening intently. "Your magazine must love this thing, whatever it is. Why haven't the white media gotten a hold of it? Sounds like it would be the story of the year."

"Not many whites have been affected, and, Mr. Dancer, as something of an expert in this area, we thought you might have heard about it from your guests, the very black or interracial couples who would likely be having the S.E.T. experience. We haven't gotten much data on its incidence because most people don't want to talk. . . . For reasons easier to comprehend than describe, the failure or inability to have sex translates all too quickly into feelings of inadequacy—regardless of the real cause."

"You're talking like some college textbook, hon—I mean Ms. Curia. It's not true. My program was a hit because black people were more than willing to come on and put all their most intimate business dead in the street. Now, to turn down a few minutes on the tube plus a free trip here from wherever, something must be scarin' the livin' shit—excuse my French—out of these folks. So, what have you heard?"

"I have our latest findings right here." G. C. Curia opened her briefcase, ruffled through a thick pile of papers, pulled out one, and read: "Couples contemplating consensual sex who are struck by the S.E.T. have basically similar experiences. They disrobe or otherwise prepare for lovemaking. Then, just as they are 'getting it on,' as some told us who may be more versed in the act than in its articulation—"

Donny laughed, then excused himself. "A good line. I'll have to remember it. Please continue."

Curia barely smiled at the interruption. "At the crucial point all their movements toward one another meet not the softness of a human body but the flinty surface of an invisible shield that has somehow slipped between them. No matter what they do or say the shield refuses to yield.

And as they struggle, each partner hears, from nobody knows where, a gospel choir singing softly and a cappella. The melody is clear and hauntingly beautiful, but the lyrics are muffled. The baffled men and women can make out only these words of admonishment: 'You got to earn the Entitlement.'"

Donny, a veritable master of cool, almost lost it. He coughed to cover his discomfort. "I guess that's enough to scare a helluva lot of folks into takin' vows of chastity."

"That's not in our reports, but we estimate the S.E.T. has frustrated a lot of passionate people in bedrooms, hotels and motels, on living room sofas, in the backseats of cars, even on rooftops and in cellars, alleys, and hallways. Initial embarrassment all too often gives way to accusation. Accusation to anger. . . . But for the invisible shield, the anger—many women tell us—would be followed by blows. Efforts to break through the shield set off a sort of electric shock that both stings and chills any remaining sensuality. Some people try to defeat this invisible barrier by running around it, climbing over it, or crawling under it. We gather they look pretty funny, particularly given their various states of dishabille, but soon learn that a willingness to look foolish does not enable them to reach their partners to either hit them or go back to lovemaking."

"Hey, some of those couples would have made dynamite guests on my show! But is this S.E.T. thing happening to all black folks?"

"Yes and no, Mr. Dancer. It appears that all black couples hear the music, but many couples—evidently those in healthy, nonabusive relationships—experience no barriers. The gospel music serves as a pleasant background, even an enhancement of their activity. These reports add to the frustration of those visited by S.E.T., interrupting what many deem the most important part of their relationships—yes, even their lives. When they learn that other couples—most of them married or in long-term relationships—are continuing to make love without the difficulties they are having, they really get upset."

"I assume," Donny asked, "that this S.E.T. thing hits even those who fall in love at first sight?"

"Not necessarily. Our reports show that sex, even on a first date, is still possible where the lovemaking is mutually agreed to and not marked by either dominance or manipulation."

"I bet I know what the S.E.T. victims do when they learn that some people are exempt. They start blaming their partners. Right?"

"Right. Once they understand S.E.T. is not universal, many men—yes, and some women—conclude that the fault lies with their partners. The solution? Here, individuals constrained by the S.E.T. decide that the solution—"

"I know. Find a new sex partner. And it doesn't work, does it?"

"Not even for those who already had another sex partner—or partners. In this instance, having a spare or 'something on the side' almost never results in anything but more of the frustration they had already experienced with their primary sex mates. Setting out to make new conquests does not seem to work either. . . ."

Donny's tie was undone, and he was perspiring heavily. "Well, Sister Curia," he said, struggling to regain his composure, "now I know what happened to my guests, my audiences, my ratings, and my show. . . . So, what's the bottom line—blacks can't have sex until they get sainthood?"

"Not quite, Mr. Dancer. But the reporters working on this thing find, that as a result of S.E.T., sex for black people is no longer a right, as many men believed. Nor is it an obligation, as many women had concluded. Blaming racism does no good—though racism has undoubtedly contributed to stresses that lead to misbehavior. Civil rights law offers no relief for those afflicted. And, as many are learning the hard way, . . . no help is available in either medical science or in the old or new nostrums that are quickly flooding the marketplace."

"Right, right! I know damn well what won't work. Tell me what will?"

"Like it or not, Mr. Dancer, lovemaking for black people is no longer a matter of ability and appeal. It is an earned privilege, or what the staff is calling 'the Entitlement.' Sexual fulfillment has to be deserved, the result of loving treatment flowing in both directions between two people who honestly love and respect one another. The Entitlement can, we are finding, be lost by outrageous behavior and regained by a return to the fundamentals of gender equality—though the recapture is far more difficult than the loss."

"Sounds very boring!"

"Maybe to you, Mr. Dancer, but a great many women—and some men—see it as a godsend. And not all the reaction to the S.E.T. has been destructive. If this thing continues, several black civic and church organizations are planning to lobby to amend existing social welfare laws. They predict, for example, a precipitous drop in teenage pregnancies, and want to redirect the resulting savings to enhance aid for teenage mothers, including child care and educational assistance. Educators in public schools and after-school programs are considering courses to provide pre-pubescent young people with the principles of gender equality and really prepare them for the demands, as well as the rewards, of marriage. Existing black men's groups and new ones springing up are sharing their experiences, listening to family experts, and edging their way toward new understandings of their roles as men at home, on the job, and in the community. Black women's groups are providing a similar function. Some are pondering 'outreach' sessions that will bring men and women together to explore and test the new relationships.

"So, Mr. Dancer," G. C. Curia wound up, "what do you think?"

. . . .

"All this S.E.T. stuff must sound good to you, Sister Curia, and I'm not denying a lot of bad shit goes down around sex, but I don't think anybody should mess with Mother Nature. I mean, you just can't go around depriving individuals of their God-given sexuality. It's as much the right of a person as breathing and eating. Sure, you women bitch about sexism and—what do you call it?—patriarchy. O.K., O.K! But it's not right to do this just in the hope—in the hope, mind you—that black men and black women will get along better. The price is too high.

"This is the U.S. of A., sister. White folks been castrating black men, physically and mentally, since the beginning of this damn country. It ain't accidental that so many lynch mobs cut off or mutilated their black victims' sexual organs. Today the white folks do the same thing economically by cutting us out of jobs we need to support families and keep some bit of dignity. Now some supernatural force trying to be helpful has up and done the white folks' work for them.

"This S.E.T. thing is wrong. It sounds even-handed, but it operates on the basic assumption that men are sexual predators, and women compliant and submissive. I mean, sister, men ain't all that bad, and women ain't all that good! And sexual shit is far more complicated than that gospel group singing about you got to earn the Entitlement. You understand what I'm saying?"

"It is complicated," Curia acknowledged, "but it is too often abusive and exploitive as well."

"Well, even if this S.E.T. brings about an end to all sexual abuse among black people, . . . with all the stuff the conservatives are layin' on us, it makes no sense to mess with our sexuality. Plus, we black men did not invent sexism and patriarchy, so if these things are so bad, how come blacks getting punished for copying the white originators, who are going scot-free?"

"Perhaps it's because, as you admit, blacks use sex to compensate for their lack of money and power. So the problem in the black community may be more serious." . . . Curia put away her tape recorder and notepad. "Mr. Dancer, even as a fairly sheltered co-ed, I found myself in situations that would—were I willing to make them public—earn me a guest spot on your show. And these were not just ghetto studs, but middle- and upper-class college men and women, white and black, who see sex as a power thing, a get-over thing, a prelude to domination, a means of proving manhood, womanhood.

"I believe the S.E.T. you and so many black people have experienced is less about sex than it is about our survival as a people. This most drastic treatment enables us to see the need to restructure our spiritual selves, to rethink what life is all about, and to bring into harmony all the forces of our being, forces that bespeak our basic humanity and the miracle of our lives.

"Human sexuality, viewed as a God-given right—as you put it, Mr. Dancer—leads to all manner of abuse, a lot of which you had on display on your program. As a young black woman, I found it disgusting. Sex should be the reward for achieving full personhood, instead of a substitute for it. Engaging in sex without honestly caring about one's partner leads eventually, if not sooner, to despair, not bliss. It leads to exhaustion, not exaltation; to heartache, not happiness; to disappointment, not deeper affection—"

"Watch out, Jesse Jackson!" interrupted Donny. "This woman's stealing your thunder!"

Ignoring him, Curia went on. "And a political component is at work here. Our reporters found that those penalized by S.E.T. tend to be politically apathetic and socially uncaring. Evidently, only when our hearts are in play can our minds fully open to the needs of those around us and to the dangers that threaten. Your program provided a daily parade of people who are being torn apart by behavior that is misogynistic and otherwise destructive of self and of those they abuse.

. . . .

"Mr. Dancer, rather than continuing to exploit the myth of black super sexuality, why not put on a program devoted to the Sexual Entitlement Therapy phenomenon? You might well find even more listeners willing to undo the myths that have robbed them of their humanity as well as their entitlement to sexual fulfillment. Think about it!"

For once, Donny did not even try for a sassy response. "Sister, you just might have an idea there!"

Curia picked up her bag and held out her hand. "Thanks for the interview, Mr. Dancer. . . ." But she didn't head for the door. She gave Donny a sly smile and then slowly dissolved into nothingness right in front of his widening eyes.

The Last Black Hero

The bomb's explosion at the antiracism rally was intended to wreak havoc. It did. Six people died. Dozens were injured. All were members of the militant, community-based organization Quad A (the African American Activist Association). Gravely injured in the explosion was the group's founder and leader, Jason Warfield.

The bombing, far from spelling the end of Quad A—the goal of the white supremacists who carried out the attack—brought the organization thousands of new members, millions of dollars in contributions, and a national prestige that ensured their programs would be taken seriously by the media, foundations, and the nation as a whole. From being just another black leader with a small though committed following, Jason Warfield became a national hope—"a true hero for his people."

He surely looked the part; with a resonant voice and soul-stirring rhetoric that only emphasized his deep commitment to black people. More important, he lived his heroic role. He had risked his life in every imaginable protest from month-long fasts to thousand-mile marches. He had been arrested, jailed, threatened, and harassed.

Fiercely independent, Jason took enormous pride in saying and doing what he wanted, despite the opposition of whites who deplored his militant rhetoric and growing support from blacks in all sectors. . . .

In a talk-show interview made just before the bombing and frequently replayed after it, Jason said, "My goal is to see racism eliminated from America. Period. I know, though, that racism is such an important component in American life that I may not succeed. But," he added, "I am not deterred or discouraged. I plan to fight racism as long as I live."

In the same interview, Jason spoke of his earlier life. "Initially, I wanted to be a singer, serious music. My hero was Paul Robeson. People even thought I sounded a little like him. Then I read a book about his life and decided that a singing career, even if I made it"—and he laughed—"was a trap in this schizophrenic society which welcomes and admires the talent of a black person like Robeson, but rejects him for his race. That's why," he said sadly, "so many talented black people who seem to have it made start acting like such damn fools. It's not that success has gone to their heads. It's that after years of struggle to achieve in athletics or entertainment—fields that seem open to blacks—they come to see that the acclaim they receive is not for them, but for their talent. In this society they, as persons, are still 'niggers.'"

After working his way through college, Jason decided, as Paul Robeson did, to go to law school. "I worked in civil rights law for a few years. It was exciting, but I became frustrated with the law's proclivity for preserving the status quo even at the cost of continuing inequities for black people. It was too much for me."

"I understand," the interviewer inquired, "that Dr. King was another of your heroes?"

"In everything I do, I refer to King's writings, speeches, and especially his actions. He was my reason for turning to the ministry—I even went back to divinity school. King's life enabled me to realize . . . that activism more than legal precedent is the key to racial reform. You can't just talk about, meet about, and pray about racial discrimination. You have to confront it, challenge it, do battle, and then—"

"That is what *you* do," the interviewer interrupted, "but what if every black person in this country adopted your militant stance? Would racism end?"

Jason shook his head. "Universal black militance would end black people. Whites could not stand it. Even now, many whites treat a militant speech like a revolutionary conspiracy. When even a small group of blacks gather for some purpose more serious than a card party, whites get upset. Dr. King was deemed a militant black, as was Malcolm X, Medgar Evers, too many others. . . .

. . . .

"Militant black leadership," Jason continued, "is like being on a bomb squad. It requires confidence in your skills. One mistake, and you're gone! Sometimes you're gone whether or not you make a mistake."

The interviewer nodded. "But what are you saying about Quad A, given the history of black groups? I think of Marcus Garvey's 'back to Africa' movement of the 1920s, and Dr. King's Southern Christian Leadership Conference, both of which floundered after their leaders were imprisoned or killed."

"Quad A ain't no one-man band," acknowledged Jason, lapsing from his customary formal speech. "It's dangerous for black organizations to rely on a messianic leader. That's why even though Quad A started in my church, we've delegated leadership widely, so if anything happens to me, one of my deputies is capable of taking over. We won't miss a beat."

Now miraculously recovered from his injuries and scheduled to return to his leadership post in New York in a few days, Jason was no longer in physical pain. But he was suffering intense emotional distress as he considered how Quad A and black people generally would respond to an unexpected manifestation of his vaunted independence.

As he sat in his hospital room staring out at the Arizona desert, he saw the source of his emotional turmoil drive into the parking lot. Through his window high up in the sanatorium complex, he had an unobstructed view of her sky-blue Z-240 sports car ("my one extravagance until you," she had told him) turning into the parking area, hesitating at a seemingly filled row, and then whipping into what had to be the only open space in the huge lot. . . .

. . . He owed his life to Sheila's medical skill, supplemented with her almost constant care. The anguish he was feeling now was caused not by his injuries, but by the doctor who had been responsible for healing them. That anguish was compounded by the debt he owed the dedicated group of deputies who, despite dire predictions that Quad A would collapse without Jason's presence, had kept the movement together during his long convalescence. He knew they expected him to return to the racial wars unencumbered by a new love—particularly one not a member of their group. A majority of those deputies were black women. "Why not?" he had always responded when the question of their gender was raised. "They're all smart, hard-working, committed." "And," a news reporter once added, "fiercely loyal to you."

It was true. They were loyal and knew he loved and respected them as they did him. Their relationships had many dimensions, none sexual. Romance was an occasional temptation, but Jason's years in the church had taught him about the troubles that followed romance with women in a congregation. . . .

After Jason's injury, the deputies had selected Neva Brownlee as acting director. Daughter of a prominent Washington, D.C., surgeon, Neva had resigned a tenured professorship at the Howard Business School to join Quad A soon after Jason organized it. As his chief associate, her managerial and fund-raising skills, together with Jason's leadership, had made Quad A an effective force. Despite the deputies' suspicions that Jason's feeling for Neva—and hers for him—might be personal, their relationship had not developed beyond mutual respect for each other's competence.

. . . .

His doctors had requested Neva not to contact him about Quad A business during what they feared would be a long and perilous recuperation. They did not want to hurt his chances for a full recovery in the quiet of the remote Arizona sanatorium. Neva responded to her appointment as acting director by redistributing and sharing authority even more widely than had been the case under Jason's leadership. . . .

One day, while having lunch with her mother, Neva poked absentmindedly at her tuna salad as she explained that she had not heard from Jason in the more than ten months since he had left. "I don't think it's his fault—but, Mom, I must admit Jason's silence is strange. Even a few words of support and encouragement would be helpful. He must know this. It's not at all like him."

"Is that all?" her mother probed.

"Oh, Mom, not you, too! The Quad A deputies are treating me as though I've been jilted by Jason. We were working associates, friends, and that's it!"

"It's understandable. You two worked so closely together—and you do make a splendid-looking couple. No wonder some of your friends were skeptical when you told them you were joining Quad A just out of respect for the work Jason was doing."

"I guess it may have seemed that way, considering I was giving up a tenured position at a good school, selling my house, and moving myself from D.C. to New York. But, Mom, I was really excited about Quad A's potential for a new kind of civil rights organization. We look to ourselves for everything—skills, money, workers, lawyers, everything! My feelings for Jason are based on mutual respect and the strong bonds of friendship that developed over our years of shared struggle. I love my work, and I like and respect the man I work with." Neva paused, then added wryly,

"Given my romantic history, that may be about the best I can hope for in a relationship."

Her mother nodded. Both recalled Neva's disastrous marriage soon after she finished college. . . . A handsome, talented man, her husband had been immature and threatened by her intelligence. A second marriage had also ended when Neva discovered her husband engaged in an affair that had preceded her meeting him and not ended after the marriage.

"Two failed marriages in seven years told me that my work—not romance or marriage—would prove the reliable foundation in my life. Oh, I brooded about it for a time, but finally came to agree with you when you said to me one day when I was really low, 'Listen, honey, it takes an extraordinary man to be better than no man at all.' And, Mom, I think of that each time a friend's seemingly enviable relationship breaks up because the man has acted like a bully, a dog, or a fool."

"That's good advice," her mother cautioned. "But it doesn't tell me how you feel about Jason's silence. Have you tried to reach him?"

"Several times. It's impossible to get through, and he doesn't answer my letters." Neva sighed. "Well, the medical reports indicate he should be released quite soon. I'll just have to wait—and so, Mom," she smiled, "let's stop the interrogation and talk about something else."

Under other circumstances, Neva and Sheila might have been close friends. They certainly shared similar characteristics: intelligence, persistence, and commitment. Their backgrounds, though, were the exact reverse of what one might have expected. Neva, though black, was the child of professional parents who raised her in mainly white, upper-class neighborhoods. Until she entered Howard University, she had attended mainly white schools. Her interest in racial issues developed late, but finally gained priority over her business ambitions.

Sheila, on the other hand, white, and born privileged, had been raised by her mother in a succession of small apartments in Queens and the Bronx. When she was two, Sheila's wealthy father had abandoned her mother who, fiercely proud, refused to seek her husband's financial help, determining to raise Sheila alone while working in secretarial jobs. Sheila learned both how her black and Hispanic peers felt and reacted to racial discrimination, and came to understand herself the meaning of minority status. She was not ashamed to be white, but her closest friends growing up were black or Hispanic. Majoring in black studies in college reflected both her academic interests and her already developed commitment to racial issues.

With her mother's tutoring, Sheila's quick mind and compulsive study habits enabled her to transcend the uneven education available in the public schools. Aided by a series of scholarships, she resolved her dual attraction to both law and medicine by earning degrees in both professions. Medicine had proven the greater challenge, and her work with traumatic injuries at Harlem Hospital had won her both respect among her peers and a staff position at the Arizona hospital that specialized in the treatment of the seriously injured. It was there that Jason was brought and placed under her care.

Jason glanced at his watch. Sheila had left town for two weeks and promised to return at four that afternoon. It was now just a few minutes after two. Did she plan to surprise him by arriving early? Not like her. She knew as well as he what was at stake. He watched her leave the car and then walk away from his building and toward a small park that overlooked the artificial lake that provided welcome relief to the endless cactus and desert.

During the last few months when he had been able to walk again, Sheila had accompanied him to that small park on innumerable occasions. And there she had announced one evening, "You know, Jason, your recovery is going extremely well, but I'm turning over your medical care to another doctor."

At his look of hurt and surprise, she explained, "It's both unwise and unethical to have a love affair with your patient."

Jason protested, "We've talked, we've held hands, but there hasn't been any, you know—"

"There hasn't been any, and, that's the point," Sheila said. "I don't know where our relationship is going, but I can't pretend that seeing you as frequently as I do is solely for your care and treatment. Freed of my medical responsibility, I hope we can be friends, discuss all the things we share and care about, and see where it leads."

After that evening, they walked a great deal and talked daily on that park bench. As their feeling for each other grew, they found they didn't have to talk all the time but were comfortable sitting in silence, looking out over the water toward the mountains far off in the distance. Even after acknowledging their love for one another, they recognized that the social barriers to their relationship were as serious as those facing Romeo and Juliet. "But," Jason assured Sheila—and she agreed—"unlike Shakespeare's doomed lovers, we are not teenagers. We are mature adults committed to our professional missions in life."

Now Sheila sat on their bench and contemplated alone the scene they had so often shared. Seeing her even from a distance reminded him of how much he had missed her. He was tempted to go down, join her in the park, and tell her so. He hesitated. She had carved out this time to think, to prepare for his response to her proposal, made before she left town, that she return to New York with him.

"Despite our love," she had said, "I think I know all the reasons you may never ask me to marry you. It is such a hateful paradox. You have fought racial barriers imposed by whites. Yet your concern about one erected by blacks threatens our future together. I cannot and will not change what I am: a white woman. But, Jason, I reject all the privileges society has bestowed upon me because of my race, and accept willingly all the burdens of yours, including a decision that you must return to your work without me. This is presumptuous, but I want to go back with you. I think I can find work in New York, and I know I can make you happy."

Jason glanced at his watch. A quarter to four. He looked out the window. Sheila was still sitting in the park, but in a few moments she would leave and enter his building. He could almost hear her familiar knock at his door.

Jason closed his eyes and, as much in inquiry as in prayer, asked, "Lord, why was I spared? By every estimate, the bomb that exploded near the podium where I was standing should have killed me. Others died. I live. Why? Surely, I was not saved to fall in love with Sheila and make her, rather than my death, the instrument that destroys Quad A?"

. . . .

Long before receiving the anonymous letter with the photograph of Jason and Sheila seated on the park bench, their arms entwined, Neva had sensed that his long silence reflected something more than hospital policy. The picture, though grainy and blurred, clearly revealed two people very much in love. The writer of the typed note threatened to send copies of the print to the other Quad A deputies unless Neva purchased the negative at a large price which she knew would only guarantee future demands for more money.

Requesting that she not be disturbed, Neva closed her office door and for an hour allowed alternate waves of pain and rage to sweep through her. She was beyond tears. "How could you do this to me, to us, to them?" There was no answer, and she knew deep down that no answer would suffice. She recognized as well that time permitted neither grief nor rage. It would be better if Quad A's staff learned from her about the photograph and heard her deny its implications. She resolved to meet with them later today and remind them of the seriousness of Jason's injuries and that the note said the woman was his doctor. Jason hugged everybody. This embrace could have been gratitude rather than passion. She would urge them to wait until he returned to explain. She, too, would try to wait.

Late that night, Neva reviewed the long day's events with her mother.

"That was a courageous thing you did today, Neva. I'm proud of you."

"I don't deserve praise, Mom. I'm so angry, so hurt. I tried to explain that photo, but as impossible as it seems, I'm afraid that Jason, my boss, my hero—yes, someone who, if things had worked out, might have become my love—this man is going with a white woman.

"You know, Mom, we black women are always being reminded of how unworthy we are. We're never smart enough or beautiful enough or supportive, sexy, understanding, and resourceful enough to deserve a good black man."

"But, Neva," her mother protested, "suppose Jason's doctor had been black, would you feel less hurt?"

"You're damn right I would! Sure, I'd be disappointed that, after working four years with me, he chose someone else without even giving our relationship a chance, but I wouldn't feel rejected as a person."

"You shouldn't jump to conclusions about Jason that you urged Quad A's members to put aside until he returns," her mother counseled.

"Oh, he loves her all right! And he *will* bring her back here. I know Jason."

"And will you then resign?"

Neva shook her head. "I just don't know. I'm afraid Quad A won't make it without me. . . . Moreover, it would simply confirm what many in the group will think: that Jason has betrayed the organization and me.

"In fact," she continued "he may have discovered what I've been trying to get across to Quad A's deputies during the last year: that true love knows no boundaries of race and politics. For black women in particular to hold the view that we can never marry a white man is the real legacy of slavery and an unjustified restriction on choices already restricted by society's devastation of so many black men.

"If you can believe it, Mom, I've been urging more tolerance of black people who choose interracial love and marriage."

"And now Jason has given you the chance to prove you're ready to practice what you preach," her mother said. "It's a terrible choice, but one you needn't make tonight. Why not wait a few days before you decide?"

"Waiting isn't my style, Mom. And I've been working my tail off for over a year building this organization and readying it for a big push when Jason returns. Now he has put all of our efforts in jeopardy, and for what? No, Mom, I can't just wait, though Lord knows what I should do!"

"I have faith you'll do what's best, dear."

"Remember, Mom," Neva said wearily, "you warned me once that in a racist society, our black men's self-esteem is under constant attack, so that black women should be a source of strength and comfort for them."

"I continue to believe that's our responsibility."

"Perhaps," Neva said quietly. "But, Mom, how do we accept our responsibility in the face of betrayal and maintain the respect that was a basis for love in the first place?" . . .

Sheila sat staring at the lake without really seeing it. The two-week "vacation" she had told Jason she was taking to give him space to consider her marriage offer was only part of the reason for her West Coast trip. She had also been searching for a new job. Hospital officials, appalled at her so obviously having some sort of relationship with a patient, and a black one at that, had suspended her, allegedly for violating their doctor-patient regulations. She knew she had been scrupulous in her dealings with Jason while he was her patient and understood that racism was the real reason for their censure. She told them as much in her letter of resignation, an action that—as she had discovered on her trip—would not make it easier to find another position.

At this moment, though, her thoughts were on Jason and the agony her proposal was causing him. "What," she asked herself, "does a man who is decisive and fearless do when he is rendered indecisive and afraid?" She knew he was deeply concerned about the fate of Quad A, of the black community, and of his place in history. But he was, after all, Jason Warfield, the last black hero, fearless and decisive. He would marry her and make it work for him, for them. Won't he? Shouldn't he? Is he not his own man?

For a brief moment, her spirits soared on the wings of optimism and then, pierced by an arrow of reality, spiraled down to earth with a pit-of-the-stomach-jarring thud. Why had she done it? Love was the easy answer, but she was old enough to understand the thrust of the title to Tina Turner's hit song "What's Love Got to Do with It?" What, indeed? Love is more than an idle emotion. Real love connotes commitment and the acceptance of responsibility.

She had offered to marry him, she said, to give him a choice, but it was the cruelest of Hobson's choices—the kind of choice, she realized, white people give blacks all the time. "You can have this job, promotion, house, membership, provided you subordinate your thinking to ours and don't make waves on racial issues. Be acceptable and, if possible, grateful."

Her proposal was not as condescending as many; but had she been totally honest, her marriage proposal should have been, "Jason, I love you and want to marry you. In conformity with the age-old pattern of black sacrifice to serve white needs, will you risk your leadership role in Quad A and the respect you've earned in the black community in return for my love?"

Sheila shuddered and shook her head. "No!" she said aloud to the desert air. She simply would not use her love for him or his for her as the basis for perpetuating in their relationship the pattern of black sacrifice. She must give him his freedom whether he wanted it or not. Her decision made, Sheila rose wearily from the park bench and started toward the hospital. Then, eyes brimming with tears and her determination wavering, she returned to the bench and cried. Finally, she dabbed her eyes dry with her handkerchief. It was almost four o'clock. Jason was expecting her.

One of Jason's admonitions to Quad A members was to make sacrifices for the things you believe in. Well, she was giving up Jason for her belief in what? Not Quad A, whose members would never believe her love for him was real. Not even for Jason, whose terrible ambivalence had made her decision necessary. No, she was making this sacrifice for her belief that it was right. Painful but right.

The knock on his door relieved Jason's tension. Uncertain though he remained, he felt he would make the right decision.

"Come in Sheila," he called.

The door opened, and a soft voice asked "May I come in?"

"Neva, how did you get—?" Jason's voice trailed off in the shock of seeing her. He realized suddenly how much he'd missed her.

"Hello, Jason," said Neva as calmly as she could in the equal shock of seeing him after so many months. "I decided it was time to take you home, and I flew out this morning." She bit her lip, fighting to control emotions that—kept in rein since she had received the letter—now threatened to overwhelm her.

"It's great to see you." Jason was standing now.

"I'm afraid, Jason, that what some of us consider bad news travels fast." She opened her bag and brought out the blackmail letter, the grainy photograph, and a copy of the statement she had made to top Quad A members. Her hand trembling, she handed him the envelope. "I think you should take a look at these, and then whatever you want to tell me I guess I'm ready to hear."

Jason felt weaker than he had in weeks. He read both letter and statement and then held them in his hand, wondering what to say.

Neva spoke first. "Lord knows, I have tried to understand—but, Jason, how could you allow yourself to fall in love with her? Did you think what it would mean to all the black women who idolize you, who pray daily for your recovery, who view you as their model of what black men should be?"

Neva continued, seeking to answer her question. "Oh, I realize that Quad A's work is frenetic, high-energy, intense, and crisis-oriented. Here, on the other hand, the atmosphere is relaxed and calm, and the relationship with your doctor is one of dependency and intense trust and intimacy. In this setting, you were far more vulnerable to a romantic relationship."

"Neva," Jason interrupted, "you don't have to make excuses for me."

"You misunderstand. I am saying that I can imagine how any seriously injured man might fall in love with his beautiful female doctor, but, Jason, you're not just any man. You are our ideal, our hero."

"It's a title I never wanted and should not have accepted. . . . I am Jason Warfield. I am not God in heroic form come to save you. The best I can do is to try and save myself and perhaps in my struggle serve as model for you and others as you seek salvation in your own lives."

"But what kind of model are you Jason when you preach taking care of the sisters and then forsake us for a white woman? It's a departure from everything you said you stood for. I understand love is blind, but I don't see why you want to enter what will be a conflicted, uncomfortable relationship!

"Damn you for a hypocrite!" she said hotly. "Isn't it you who are always cautioning black men, 'Watch out lest the white woman come to represent a rite of passage to the status of whiteness? Because she's the model of beauty and femininity'"—Neva was mimicking Jason's deep voice, her arms folded, her legs apart in one of his characteristic stances —"'a white woman will appear to provide a black man with access to formerly restricted areas and also symbolize achievement. In particular, black men who acquire a measure of education, wealth, or status feel that dating white women is like moving out of the ghetto—a way of doing better for yourself.'"

"Just calm down, Neva," Jason said. "I feel bad about disappointing you—and the others at Quad A. But I don't have to stand here and take your abuse. Hell, I've never advocated hate for whites as a component of our black pride program. Of course, we emphasize and encourage strong black families as an essential for survival in a hostile racist society. But Quad A has never barred membership to interracial couples."

"No, Jason, but we do every damned thing we can to encourage black men"—she was mimicking him again—"'to look to the sisters,' as you said, 'and do not forsake them.' And, 'in black women,' you used to tell us, 'you will find both counsel and civility, love and support, friendship and faithfulness, probity and integrity. For the black man, the black woman is the equivalent of home.'

"There!" Neva concluded. "Just to show you what a fool I was, I memorized that homily of yours, believed it, preached it to others when —evidently—I should have been shouting it to you."

Despite herself, the tears were streaming down her face. Jason felt close to tears himself. He lowered his voice. "You didn't have to, Neva. I believed myself what I told others. I came here to get well, not to fall in love. I didn't want it to happen. To the extent that I considered entering a serious personal relationship with anyone, I guess it was with you."

It was, he realized immediately, a well-intended but ill-timed admission of his earlier interest in her.

"Now you tell me! Now you tell me!" Neva sputtered. "Is that supposed to be a compliment? Am I and other black women the Avis of sexual choice for you black men? 'Hey, black women, you are still Number Two! You will simply have to try harder!' Give me a break!"

Unable to bear looking at Jason, Neva turned and stared out the window. Her breath was coming in sharp stabs, and her nose was running. She started to open her bag for a handkerchief, then stopped. To hell with it! she thought. The last thing I care about is looking good for that—that traitor. "Is it any wonder," she said more to the desert landscape than to him, "that so many black women view black men who choose white women with deep skepticism? Is it any goddamned wonder?"

"Neva, save the black woman rhetoric. I've heard it all before. But having a bomb go off almost under your feet that kills your friends and damn near kills you can change your outlook on a lot of things. Sheila literally put me back together. I was grateful, of course, but then I realized she's quite a woman, quite a human being. I feel really alive in her presence."

Neva turned from the window and stared at Jason, hearing him but not believing the strange words coming from that familiar voice. "You betrayed us! You told us over and over these five years that Quad A's work is too important to risk a relationship with me or one of the other black deputies. But now all your concerns evaporate, become mere 'image,' after a few months of close contact with a white woman. For her, you're willing to risk destruction of your organization as well as the hopes of vast numbers of black people."

Even through her anger, Neva realized that Jason had already answered her question. She tried to calm down and made her question more general. "Jason, tell me, why do the very men black women pray for—sensitive; successful warriors for truth and community, courage and integrity—always marry white women—women whose interest in our culture just happens always to include taking our most desirable men?"

Jason felt Neva's distress and wanted to help her. "I realize this is tough for you to hear. It was tough for me. I've imagined all manner of fantasies to explain how this could have happened."

"Such as?"

"Well, you said yourself that recovering from my almost fatal injuries left me vulnerable in a way I was not back at Quad A. What if my injuries caused by the bomb blast had included blindness? What if, while I was recuperating in this remote place, Sheila had come as doctor and then become, as she has, the most important person in my life? My inability to see would not have insulated me from her warmth, her wisdom, her grace, and, after a time, her love."

Neva's sigh of dismay was close to a cry of pain. But Jason decided to continue. "Despite my oft-stated resolve to remain committed to Quad A, I might have fallen in love with Sheila's presence and then her person, without ever knowing until I regained my sight that she was not my ultimate African queen, as her melodiously throaty voice, her knowledge of black history, and her love of black culture would have led me to believe. If, in short, I had not realized Sheila was white, could I not plead some form of romantic entrapment?"

Neva sighed again and slowly shook her head. "Your deception defense won't work, Jason. In fact, it is more than a little insulting to me and to all black women. The sum of my existence is not confined to a knowledge of black history and a love of black culture. My identity cannot be so readily appropriated by *any* white woman—to the extent that even a blind black man would mistake her for me."

The silence that ensued after Neva's statement was interrupted by another knock on the door. This time Jason was sure he knew who it was. He sighed.

"Come in, Sheila."

For just an instant, Sheila was startled to see Jason had a visitor. Then she realized instinctively who the woman must be, why she was there.

Establishing her claim to Jason, she kissed him quickly on the forehead, then turned to Neva. "You must be Neva Brownlee. I've seen you on the news talking about Quad A. Welcome to Sanctus Sanatorium!" she said, trying for ease in what was clearly a thorny situation.

"So," Neva stated flatly, "you're Dr. Sheila Bainbridge."

Then, with one accord, the two women turned expectantly toward Jason. He, deep in his self-inflicted distress, hoped, for just an instant, that some undiscovered but devastating component of his injury might strike him down and remove him from this impossible predicament.

"Neva," Jason began slowly, looking at her, "I at least owe you candor. Sheila has been away for two weeks so we could each try to decide the future of what you have learned is our romance. Despite the sleazy source of your information, that romance is based on a love that is real. I am hoping we can be married soon."

As Jason looked intently at Neva, Sheila felt like an intruder eavesdropping on a conversation by her lover about their love—and thus hardly welcomed hearing either Jason's protestation of love or his decision to marry her. Deciding to follow his lead, she also addressed Neva.

"Ms. Brownlee, Jason is right. We are in love. But I have decided that I can't marry Jason—not because of his race, but because of mine. I know and think I understand how black people, and particularly black women, feel about losing one of their most able men in an interracial marriage. I'm afraid it would destroy Quad A. I simply will not do that to Jason or to black people."

Neva was furious. "Just a minute, Dr. Bainbridge! You need not play the martyr. We can survive and continue to grow whatever you and Jason do."

Sheila responded evenly, trying not to reveal her emotions. "My martyrdom, as you call it, may be as objectionable to you as your self-righteousness is to me. We both have strong attachments to the black community. And we both have suffered because of them."

"Given your knowledge of black history," Neva said "you will understand that Jason is not the first black leader who has failed to live up to the people's expectations and hopes. I doubt he'll be the last. He has, in fact, provided us with a needed, if unwanted, reminder that human heroes have feet of clay."

Neva's words hit Jason like a blow to the stomach, taking his breath, rendering him speechless. He remembered—too late—why he had determined not to get caught up in any romantic situations at Quad A. And saw as well that he had himself fallen into the interracial trap he had warned other black men to stay clear of.

"When you reveal your relationship with Dr. Bainbridge," Neva continued, turning to him, "Quad A may have a rough time for a while. They'll know her only as 'that white woman.' But if you both return and she joins you in our work, there's just a chance that Quad A can come to terms with it, just as many black families do when one of their children marries a white person. I assume, Jason, that Dr. Bainbridge has qualities —other than her race—that attract you. In time, Quad A members may recognize them as well. Since, as I understand it, she is a lawyer as well as a doctor, surely she has skills we could use."

"You can't be serious!" Sheila interjected. "Quad A certainly wouldn't accept me as a staff member."

"On the contrary, Dr. Bainbridge, that may be the only way you can gain acceptance and perhaps prove that your concern for our cause is not limited to capturing one of our best men."

"And what will you do, Neva, if we both return?" Jason asked.

Neva's control escaped her. "Isn't it a bit late in the game for you to become concerned about my welfare, Jason? After not hearing from you for a year, I assumed you didn't care how I felt as long as I kept your organization running for you. I'll do what is best for Quad A. Someone," she added, "has to give the organization priority over their personal feelings."

"You seem to forget, Ms. Brownlee," Sheila said with a hint of irritation, "I have decided not to return with Jason, and I'm certainly not going to disrupt Quad A by trying to join its staff."

"Oh, you'll return with him," said Neva. "Jason can be very persuasive when he wants to be. And I gather he wants *you*! I don't think either of us can do anything about that."

She stood and headed for the door. "I'm planning to take the late flight back to New York, I expect you'll let me know when you plan to arrive. I'll try to keep things going until—"

"Neva," Jason interrupted, "I owe you a great deal."

"Yes, Jason, you do, and I wish you didn't. I'll see you in New York."

After Neva closed the door, Sheila and Jason looked at one another for a long time.

"Well," Jason said finally, "Neva was right. Quad A needs your skills. I hope you will join our struggle."

She hesitated. "I would love to work with you and your group—if they'd have me—but I don't think I can compete with Neva. It's obvious she came to see you as much out of devotion to Quad A as out of love for you."

"You don't have to compete with her," Jason assured Sheila. "We can get married right away."

"I've never believed the law of marriage could ensure a continuance of love."

"Then I'll resign from Quad A," he said with determination.

"I know you mean that out here, where we've spent so much time together, away from the real world. But you must return to your world, the only world you know. What will happen to our relationship then? It's awfully risky, Jason."

He took her in his arms and whispered, "Life *is* a risk, Sheila—and Quad A and you and Neva and I are all part of life. We might as well face up to whatever it brings."

Holding Jason close, Sheila took a deep breath and exhaled slowly. "Neva was right. You can be very convincing. But this has been quite an ordeal," she added, moving away, "and you should get some rest. I'll come back tomorrow."

She kissed Jason, again on the forehead, but with far less confidence than she had an hour earlier.

"And you'll make our plane reservations? Jason asked.

Sheila hesitated at the door. Shaking her head in disbelief, she heard herself say, "Yes, Jason, I will make the reservations."

He sank down on the bed and for a long time simply lay there, staring at the ceiling, unseeing and numb. Both Sheila and Neva deserved better than the unheroic mess he had created by trying to do right in a situation where every choice was a snare, every decision a trap.

. . . .

He had prayed for life to continue the fight for his people's rights and well-being—a fight based on his confidence that he would intuitively know what direction to take, what policy to adopt, which to reject. Now his confidence was undermined by, of all things, an interracial romance.

Well, he thought, white folks will be pleased or, at least, relieved. Somehow, the once unthinkable act for a black man—marriage to a white woman—was taken as proof that black men in such relationships were, despite their militant rhetoric, not really dangerous. On the other hand, blacks—and particularly black women—felt generally as Neva did: betrayed.

. . . .

Jason pulled himself up, soaked a towel in cold water from the washbasin, and buried his face in its redeeming coolness. He felt better—not heroic, but better. He went to a closet and pulled out his suitcase.

As he began packing, the words of "I Don't Feel No Ways Tired" ran through his head—a favorite old gospel song, he remembered, of Neva's. Then, encouraged by its message and—strangely—by his memory of her humming it as she worked, he opened his mouth and sang:

> I don't feel no ways tired.
> I've come too far from where I started from.
> Nobody told me that the road would be easy.
> I don't believe He brought me this far, to leave me.

Shadow Song

The restaurant was in a quiet, pre-lunch-crowd mode. The staff served us quickly, and as we set to, Gwynn, my companion that evening, asked: "Want to hear a story?"

I nodded.

"For as long as I can remember, I've had a shadow. . . . When I was a girl, my shadow was my best friend. Even then, I knew no one would believe me, so I never told anyone about her. Of course, sometimes my mother would hear me talking to my shadow, and she'd tell me it wasn't nice to talk to myself.

" 'I'm not talking to myself, Mom,' I'd tell her. 'I'm talking to my shadow.' My mother would smile sweetly and say something like 'Say hello to your shadow for me, dear.'

"As I grew older, I didn't share the other girls' fascination with boys. All that incessant talk about them was boring. By then, my shadow was not as playful, more moody and withdrawn. I thought it strange, but figured I was growing up and, maybe, growing out of my shadow friend.

"The first time I lied to my girlfriends and pretended I was as interested in boys as they were, my shadow moaned loudly, moved off in a corner and just stared at me.

"It took me a long time to realize that my shadow knew that, in order to be one of the 'in' crowd, I was denying my true feelings, denying myself. Of course, for a long time I didn't know a girl had any other choice but to go out with fellows. And when I did learn about women loving other women, the names they were called and the abuse they had to take made me deny myself and my true feelings even more.

"In college and in law school, I tried hard to hide my sexual orientation, but it was tough. While most of the black women were complaining about the lack of social life, men were coming at me from all sides. That's why I hated looking like Joan Crawford. It attracted all manner of male attention—for all the wrong reasons.

"After a while, my shadow just kept its distance. It didn't speak to me. It certainly didn't play any games. It looked mournful, and it sang a refrain I recognized later as a gospel hymn. Do you know 'I'm Climbin' Up the Rough Side of the Mountain'?"

"I think all gospel lovers know it, but I bet you wish you'd never heard it."

Gwynn smiled. "No, it wasn't taunting. It was supportive in a strange kind of way, urging that I be myself."

Then she softly sang the lyrics in an astonishingly beautiful voice.

"With a voice like that, how come you didn't go for a serious concert career?"

"Well, I took lessons for several years and sang in high school productions. I recognized, though, that my talent—my voice—is a gift from God. A successful career is—as I once heard Van Cliburn say on the radio —a gift from the public. I saw too many gifted singers and actors, too, who never got the chance to display their talents. The public, as you're learning, is fickle. I decided to develop other talents whose use I had more control over."

"A good point," I agreed. "Tell me, though, choosing the law didn't provide much insulation against your fears, did it?"

"That's putting it mildly!" Gwynn laughed lightly. "It's one reason I welcomed working as your research assistant. I could hide out in your office. Plus, you treated me like a person—not a potential catch."

"But you never mentioned your confusion about your sexual identity —and we talked about everything."

"How could I? You were like a father to me, and at that point, I hadn't even told my own father. And, anyway, by that time I'd come to accept living as someone else while the real me lurked off to the side singing a gospel song. But then"—she paused, looking at me as though she expected me to know something about it—"I came out of the closet."

"When was that?"

"Shows how observant you are, Professor!" She laughed. "You were there. In fact, you were part of the reason I did it!"

At my blank look, she reminded me of the coalition of student groups that had rallied at my old law school in support of my protest against its not having on its faculty any women of color.

"At one point in the rally," Gwynn said, "a member of the Coalition of Gay and Lesbian Students spoke about the difficulties of gayness. She understood, she said, why people remained in the closet, but their invisibility came at a terrible price—self-denial. She summoned the gay and lesbian students to come forward on their own to take a stand. First, other members of the group formed a line behind the speaker. Then, slowly, other students—who had until that very moment kept their sexual orientation secret—came forward and joined hands with the COGLS members. On the spur of the moment, I pushed through the crowd and linked my arms with theirs. Everyone was moved, tears were flowing, and the students were applauding and cheering."

As she spoke, I recalled the rally and Gwynn's joining the group. "But," I said, "I thought you all were heterosexual students showing solidarity with the gay and lesbian group."

"You were probably the only one who thought that, Professor, but that's the way it should be. . . . Acknowledging that I was a lesbian lifted a great burden, one I was glad to be free of. But"—she laughed ruefully —"it brought several new ones in its place. Friends dropped out of my life as though I'd contracted some dread disease, and some of the men who'd been panting after me now barely knew my name, and few would look me in the eye. And after law school, you can't imagine the jobs I didn't get, the apartment leases that were terminated!"

Gwynn's voice broke, and she paused to sip her coffee, her hand trembling slightly as she lifted the cup. I waited until she had collected herself. "You know," she went on, "the toughest part was dealing with lots of folks in the black community, including any number of my black sisters. When whites shunned me, I considered it part of the price of being black. When my own turned their backs on me, it was tough. . . . Oh, I understand some of the psychology. Our difference enables the oppressed to become the oppressor. In fact, it is a sexual difference to which people react with a hostility based on fear, as they did this morning to your political difference. All too many black men and heterosexual black women succumb to the temptation as though we are the threat, when we need to save our energies for our true enemies."

"I would guess, Gwynn, that part of your burden is dealing with those who, with the best of intentions, try to put you back on the right and righteous path. If you're a lesbian and particularly if you're up front about it, you have an addiction—like alcoholism or gambling—and you need professional counsel and lots and lots of prayer."

Gwynn smiled wearily. "Particularly, the prayer. I've had perfect strangers come up to me and quote the Bible as proof of my sin and certain damnation."

I was well aware how dangerous the Bible can become when people view it as literal truth rather than as inspirational message. I mentioned to Gwynn an article in *Essence* magazine by Linda Villarosa, the executive editor, in which she analyzes the scriptural passages that seem to condemn homosexuality.

. . . .

"Yes," Gwynn said, her eyes shining, "Villarosa has more courage than most of us. She has not only written about her life as an African American lesbian, but actually goes out lecturing about her experiences and what she has learned. She really catches it! . . . I can't tell you how much insight and support I've gained from Villarosa, as well as from the writings of other women, like Audre Lorde, Dionne Brand, Sarah Schulman, who are willing to speak out about discrimination that, while devastating, is not—with a few exceptions—prohibited by law."

"Of course," she added, "the extension of civil rights laws to cover sexual orientation will offer little protection against the anti-lesbian hysteria of many black men."

"The federal courts aren't much help either," I ventured, "refusing, except in the most egregious cases, to do what they'll have to do eventually —acknowledge that homosexuals are an identifiable group suffering discrimination because of innate characteristics that entitle them to special protection of their basic rights."

"You seem awfully certain about that."

"That's certainly true for the present, but I think that as more and more lesbian and gay persons want to buy and sell property together, marry, have or adopt children, make wills, and carry out all the aspects of life controlled by legal rules, the law will have to recognize and encompass these transactions. It's already happening with the enactment of 'partnership laws' in many places that still refuse to recognize homosexual civil rights."

"You're only saying that, Professor, because the law abhors a vacuum. It will fill the need for our property transactions, but won't recognize our different sexual needs that give rise to those property transactions. Small comfort, I must say! And, don't forget, the few gay and lesbian civil rights statutes now on the books are under attack."

"I'm certainly not saying there's no problem, Gwynn, but it's far from hopeless. And the continuing hostility in some segments of the public is certainly no reason not to have you represent me in the suit against Congress. I may be old and out of touch, but in the more than a quarter of a century I've been teaching law, I've had a goodly number of openly gay and lesbian students. Knowing them as students and then friends has simply confirmed my conviction that sexual preference is a personal matter. Those not involved should stay out of it."

"That's fine for you, Professor. But you and I both know the world out there, particularly the black community, is not at all tolerant of gays and lesbians. Given the trouble you're facing, are you sure you want to risk taking on this issue, too?"

"Look who's talking about troubles! Here you are black, a woman, and openly lesbian, and yet you're still fighting and willing to do publicly what you did privately in that Committee of Two Dozen meeting this morning, and come to the defense of a most unpopular brother. Yes, Gwynn, I absolutely want you to represent me! You're a good lawyer and a very savvy person, just the one to have on my side. Is that clear?"

"You're a nice man, Professor, but—" Gwynn's hard look told me that she found me wanting in a certain shrewdness, as Geneva sometimes did. "If we go ahead with that lawsuit against the congressional sponsors of the Freedom of Employment Bill, I'm not sure you really know what you're in for. They have lots of clout, and people, particularly a lot of black people, will try to do you in for a little bit of money—and I do mean, relatively speaking, a little bit. So get ready for all manner of gratuitous attacks—including insinuations that we're going together, like we heard this morning—just because I stood up for you and left after they put you out. Or, some will suggest that your hiring me, a lesbian, as your lawyer proves you must be gay yourself. How are you going to respond in a press conference when one of the tabloid reporters asks you if you're gay?"

"I'd answer, 'My sexual preference is entirely my business. It has nothing to do with the issues. Let's stick to them.'

"And, as for betrayals by some blacks, Gwynn, we know what our own did to Martin Luther King when he broadened his critique to include economic injustice and the unjust war in Vietnam. Malcolm X was killed when his criticism of America's hypocrisy about race began to include what he deemed hypocrisy within the Muslim leadership. And black leaders abandoned Paul Robeson for speaking the truth about racism in the middle of the post–World War II fear of communism. . . ."

. . . .

"You said earlier that I'm a fighter. Well, I try, but it's been hard. Last night, I told my companion both that I expected there'd be a lot of hostility against you at the CTD meeting, and that I planned to stand up for you and defend you. She and I had quite an argument. . . . She can't see why I should be risking my career and our relationship all for one black man, as she put it."

"She may be right."

"She's not, and you know it. What they're trying to do to you is what this society has done—or tried to do—to every black man who has stood up for the race or for his rights since 1770 when Crispus Attucks, a runaway slave, was the first man to fall at the Boston Massacre. And every black person who hears what happened to Attucks knows it was no accident the British got him first."

. . . .

"I assume your Meredith has the scars of her lesbianism?"

"True enough. And I just took it for granted that our understanding in one important area of our lives—sex—where we're outsiders would also cover at least the main parts of another area: race. But I realized last night that Meredith can never understand what it is to be black in America."

"You're certainly right about many whites, but we both know white people who do come to understand—at least as well as some of our own."

Gwynn shook her head. "It's true," I assured her. "What you have to remember, Gwynn, is that you've brought Meredith into a life, yours, that in many ways is like taking her to another country, one where she doesn't know the language, the rituals, the customs, nothing."

. . . .

"Oh, Professor, don't side with her! Had I taken her to another country, everything would be fine. It's here at home where whites have almost no empathy for blacks as a people. Whites can deal with, even come to love individual blacks, but only if they separate the individual from the mass. 'You're different' is no compliment when you're being distinguished from your people."

"O.K., Meredith is at home, Gwynn, but it's home on the other side of the looking glass. Everything is reversed, back to front. She doesn't realize what's happening. You do. So if you love her, it's your responsibility to teach her. She can learn, as we did, the psalms of survival when home is an alien land."

Gwynn took a deep breath and let it escape very slowly. "Maybe. Maybe. I don't know. Right now, I don't care. Love is out there. My work is right here. Love in the absence of work can't survive."

"Hmm. An interesting variation on the Biblical reminder that '[f]aith without works is dead.' But doesn't Shakespeare urge that 'love is not love / Which alters when it alteration finds, / Or bends with the remover to remove'?"

"I'm too old," Gwynn protested, "for all that business about love's being 'an ever-fixed mark, / That looks on tempests and is never shaken.'" And she laughed as she capped my quote from Shakespeare's Sonnet 116. "That's denial," she went on, "and I'm too old for denial, too. Audre Lorde has written of the separation she felt from her white lover: 'Over time I came to realize that it colored our perceptions and made a difference in the ways I saw pieces of the worlds we shared.' Lorde was willing 'to deal with that difference outside of [her] relationship,' to let it be her 'own secret knowledge,' her 'own secret pain.' But I'm not!"

Gwynn smiled at last and moved her empty cup out of reach. "My shadow is me now," she said, patting herself on the chest, "and I am it." She began to hum, "'I'm com'in' up—on the rough side—of the mountain.' That's what I like to sing," she added, "when I'm trying to cope with some racial or sexual problem."

I reached out my hand to Gwynn. "You know," I said, "the rough side is the only way you can climb a mountain. On the smooth side, there are no footholds, nothing to grab on to. So, the hard way, the rough way, is the only way."

The Southern
Romance Temptation

Presenting my motion for a preliminary injunction in the school desegregation case, I know in advance that it will be rejected. The white-haired Southern judge is of the old school. He has never seen a civil rights lawyer he liked, nor heard a civil rights petition he was willing to grant. Even so, I did my best, not for the judge, but for the courtroom filled with black people. For the plaintiffs in the case and their friends and relatives, this was a rare treat. A black man bold enough to talk up to a white man— even one in robes, with real power, sitting up there high and communicating his contempt with every comment. The black people who had arrived early and were waiting outside in a long line before the courthouse opened were orderly, but I could almost feel their excitement at being a part of history, feel their approval of me, the black lawyer come all the way from New York City to represent them.

Through their formal silence in this courtroom, I could feel their support, almost hear their responses as if in church. "Yes," "Um-hum," "You tell 'em lawyer. You certainly tell 'em."

. . . Then, I saw her. No great feat, there. She would have been tough to miss. Very black with that almost translucent skin that only truly black people possess, her hair was shoulder length, also very black. "Good hair," would be the description in the black community. Her suit was a soft wool, teal I think, and maybe a bit bright, but quite in keeping with how many Southern women dress. I caught my breath and then sat down to confer with Ed Sharpe, the local lawyer on the case.

The hearing lasted all day. We put on our case with the appeal in mind. It was well we did. At hearing's end, the judge's firm rejection of our motion still ringing in my ears, I turned to leave and there she was, waiting at the courthouse door. Jeannine Henry, one of the plaintiffs, introduced her.

"Attorney Bell, I wants you to meet my cousin, Hattie Boman. She teaches school over in Green County, but took off to come over and hear you."

Ms. Boman smiled and extended her hand gracefully, palm down. I was not sure whether she expected me to shake her hand or kiss it. I took her hand.

"Thank you for coming Ms. Boman. . . ."

Hattie Boman was looking directly at me, but did not seem to hear. "Attorney Bell. You were wonderful."

Her eyes echoed the sentiment. "Well," I said, rather nervously. "The plaintiffs and lawyers are having dinner. Would you join us?"

"It's all arranged," Jeannine Henry announced. "Let's go."

A dozen of us sat at a large restaurant table eating soul food. Ms. Boman was at the end of the table away from me, but whenever I glanced in her direction, she seemed to be looking right at me. At dinner's end, I met with Ed Sharpe for a few moments assuring him that I would file the appeal papers. Then, I suggested that I had better turn in early as I had an early flight. Ed said he would drive me to the airport in the morning and drop me at the motel tonight.

"If it's O.K., Ed," Jeannine asked, "let Hattie follow you. She is spending the night at the motel and will drive back home early in the morning." Ed agreed, adding, "One of these days, we will make it safe for our pretty, black woman to drive these roads at night, but that time is not yet."

We arrived at the motel, one of the few run for blacks in the area. It was clean, but hardly distinguished. Its guests tended to stay only a few hours rather than all night. Based on experience, I tried not to stay in such places on a weekend when even those guests who wished to sleep were kept awake by the coming and going. It was mid-week and should be relatively quiet. I said goodnight to Ed, saw that Hattie Boman was checked into her room, and without a desk, spread out my pleadings on the bed in my small room.

I reviewed what needed to be done, checked to ensure I had the necessary pleadings I planned to file in the city I was heading to the next morning. I was packing everything in my briefcase when a knock came at my door.

"Yes, who is it?"

"It's Hattie Boman. May I come in for a few minutes."

I opened the door. She was still wearing her teal suit.

"I know you are busy and need to leave early, but I want to talk to you if I can."

"Of course," I said, the nervousness I felt when I met her returning. She spoke of her admiration of my work and of how she had always wanted to go to law school.

Always the advocate of legal education, I told her to sit in the only chair. I sat on the bed and launched into my standard spiel about the benefits of becoming a lawyer, the ordeal of law school, and the benefits of service as well as status and income that would follow. As in the courthouse, she did not seem to be really listening. Sighing and nodding as I talked, she moved from the chair and sat beside me on the bed.

"It sure sounds good when you say it, Attorney Bell, but on this school stuff, I'm not all that sure our children will be better off cross town in those hateful white schools, and white folks sure as hell not sendin' their kids to black schools."

"You sure know how to get me started, Hattie." And I shared my own misgivings about the real benefits of desegregated schooling for black children, especially those not really gifted. I developed this theme noticing that now Hattie was listening intently.

"If you have all these doubts, why do you keep doing it?"

"It's my job. It's what the black people want. You saw them there today."

She sighed, shook her head and sat quietly beside me.

"You don't agree with trying to desegregate the schools?" Hattie shook her head.

"It's selfish, but when you win this suit, I'm goin' to lose my job, a lot of the other black teachers too. You all up North ever think about that?"

I looked over and while she tried to hide her head with her hands, I could see she was crying. I put my arm around her.

"Hattie, we are concerned about black teachers and principals and, if we need to, we will file suit to protect their jobs."

"Then you haven't been reading the stuff we get from the National Black Teachers Association. They say black schools are closed and black teachers and principals lose their jobs soon as those school orders come down." Her sobs grew louder. "I can't say nothing around here. Folks think I don't want progress if I can keep my job. Attorney, why can't we have progress and keep our jobs too?"

Hattie asked me for my handkerchief and wiped her eyes with it.

"I'm sorry to act like this. It's not your fault, but I'm afraid of what will happen. I need my job to take care of my ailing mother. Thanks for hearing me out."

Hattie stood and I stood with her. I gave her a hug and she reached up and kissed me full on the mouth.

I drew back in surprise. "Thank you, Hattie, but I . . ."

"You are so good to comfort me. Nobody down here to give me comfort. Nobody I care about, nobody like you. You don't know me but I know you. I have managed to come over here each time you were in town, and my cousin Jeannine and I talk about you all the time. Until today, I never let her introduce me." She paused, still looking at me intently.

"Attorney Bell, I love you. I am not a loose woman. I work hard at my teaching and one day I will be a lawyer, but I just want to be with you for awhile."

"Thank you, Hattie. I'm complimented, but I am also married."

"Don't you think I know that? Your marriage is up North. You down here, right now. I don't want to mess with your marriage, but I do want to be with you. You understand?"

I recognized the non sequitur in the response, but somehow things got away from me. I have always been afraid to ask women for sex, fearing rejection if they turned me down, and complications if they acquiesced. But, on the few occasions when a woman I know and like has made her interest unmistakable even to me, refusing her seemed, somehow, ungentlemanly. Before long we were both in bed, without our clothes, and with no discussion at all about law school, school desegregation, and her fears about her job.

Time passed. Don't ask how much. Suddenly, what I had feared would happen if I did what I was now doing, happened. The heavy banging on the door sounded like the drums of doom.

"All right, You'all. It's the police. Open up in there. . . ."

I sat up in bed and froze. Hattie grabbed me and held on. She began to cry. With a crashing sound, the door splintered, then burst open. Police in riot gear poured into the room, guns drawn and aimed right at us. They were followed by media people with bright lights glaring and cameras grinding.

In the instant before they dragged us out of bed, I could see the front pages of the local papers the next day, the headlines about the civil rights attorney, so self-righteous as he tried to ruin the Southern way of life, the photographs revealing quite literally the naked corruption of this black outsider. The charge, fornication, a felony in this state. Hattie Boman would lose her job and be disgraced for life. The Northern papers might not run the story, but my wife would surely find out. She would murder me first and then file for divorce.

I awakened shaking and quickly turned on the light for reassurance. It had been a dream of the worst kind. Calming myself, I realized that the essence of the goody-goody stance I had adhered to since puberty was not morality, but built in prudence mixed with cold fear. I was not supposed to have normal, sexual urges like other men who boasted of their conquests—whether or not they were married. My upright reputation was hard-earned but due as much to good fortune as to practiced restraint.

Early Bloomers

[Eds. Derrick Bell's first wife of thirty years died of cancer in 1990. He met Janet Dewart several months later and not long after she declared her love. "Early Bloomers," Bell's poem to her, is a statement of appreciation for her love and his understanding, given his still uncertain emotional state, of the risks that she was willingly accepting.]

The essence of Spring is not new life,
but that risk of death—assumed eagerly
by those first blossoms
eagerly offering proof of Winter's end.
They break forth, more bravely than wisely,
into weather more likely freezing
than graced with unseasonable warmth.
Despite what may prove a fatal chill, they stand.
Proud sentinels on watch for a spring
they herald, but may never see.

My love is one with these first blooms.
Beautiful yet far too fragile to face
blustery winds of season's change.
How honor courage that is its own reward?
How protect those who value heart-shaped duty over safety?

Whether fortuity or fate,
those first flowers burst forth too soon,
reminding a waiting world to look beyond blowing snow
toward waving fields of bee-filled blooms:
the more fortunate but no more noble successors to these first few.

There is parallel, but no protection, for a heart too filled with love
to wait a season that might never come. She stands then
in an uncertain climate and, like early blooms,
relies on an inner warmth,
responding to an older rhythm than logic,
relishing in the simple glory of risk.

CHAPTER 6

Politics of the Academy

In the selections that follow, Bell addresses the politics of the academy and relations with fellow faculty. These excerpts show Bell struggling to come to terms with the pressures that plague minority law professors in predominantly white schools, describe the challenges of persuading his colleagues to hire more professors of color, and identify courses of action open to the minority professor at an elite school who finds himself beating his head against a stone wall. A later chapter deals with pedagogy and Bell's efforts to provide innovative instruction to his students. The chapter concludes with two letters and a Chronicle dealing with specific crises in Bell's life and career as a Harvard professor.

The Chronicle of the DeVine Gift

[Eds. Geneva recounts the following story to Professor Bell.]

It was a major law school, one of the best, but I do not remember how I came to teach there rather than at Howard, my alma mater. My offer, the first ever made to a black, had been the culmination of years of agitation by students and a few faculty members. It was now the spring of my second year. I liked teaching and writing, but I was exhausted and considered resigning, although more out of frustration than fatigue.

I had become the personal counselor and confidante of virtually all of the black students and a goodly number of the whites. The black students needed someone with whom to share their many problems, and white students, finding a faculty member willing to take time with them, were not reluctant to help keep my appointment book full. I liked the students, but it was hard to give them as much time as they needed. I also had to prepare for classes—where I was expected to give an award-winning performance each day—and serve on every committee at the law school on which minority representation was desired. In addition, every racial emergency was deemed "my problem." I admit that I wanted to help address these problems, but they all required time and energy. Only another black law teacher would fully understand what I had to do to make time for research and writing.

So, when someone knocked on my door late one afternoon as I was frantically trying to finish writing final exam questions, I was tempted to tell the caller to go away. But I didn't. And, at first, I was sorry. The tall, distinguished man who introduced himself as DeVine Taylor was neither

From Foreword: The Civil Rights Chronicles (Supreme Court 1984 Term), 99 Harv. L. Rev. 4 (1985). Copyright © 1985 by the President and Fellows of Harvard College. Reprinted by permission.

a student nor one of the black students' parents, who often dropped by when they were in town just to meet their child's only black teacher.

Mr. Taylor, unlike many parents and students, came quickly to the point. He apologized for not calling first, but explained that his visit concerned a matter requiring confidentiality. He showed me a card and other papers identifying him as the president of the DeVine Hair Products Co., a familiar name in many black homes and one of the country's most successful black businesses.

"You may also know," Mr. Taylor said, "that my company and I have not been much involved in this integration business. It seems to me that civil rights organizations are ready to throw out the good aspects of segregation along with the bad. I think we need to wake up to the built-in limits of the 'equal opportunity' that liberals are always preaching. Much of it may be a trick that will cost us what we have built up over the years without giving us anything better to take its place. Personally, I am afraid they will integrate me into bankruptcy. Even now, white companies are undercutting me in every imaginable way.

"But," he interrupted himself with a deep sigh, "that is not why I am here. You have heard of foundations that reward recipients based on their performance rather than on their proposals. Well, for some time my company has been searching for blacks who are truly committed to helping other blacks move up. We have located and helped several of these individuals over the years by providing them with what we call 'the DeVine Gift.' We know of your work and believe that you deserve to be included in that group. We want to help you to help other blacks and can spend a large amount of money in that effort. For tax and other business reasons, we cannot provide our help in cash. And we must do so anonymously."

Realizing that he was serious, I tried to respond appropriately. "Well, Mr. Taylor, I appreciate the compliment, but it is not clear how a black hair products company can be of assistance to a law teacher. Unless"— the idea came to me suddenly—"unless you can help me locate more blacks and other minorities with the qualifications needed to become a faculty member at this school."

Mr. Taylor did not look surprised. "I was a token black in a large business before I left to start my own company. I think I understand your problem exactly, and with our nationwide network of sales staff, I think we can help."

[After a few pleasantries, we shook hands and Mr. Taylor left, promising to be in touch soon.]

When I was hired, the faculty promised that although I was their first black teacher, I would not be their last. This was not to be a token hire, they assured me, but the first step toward achieving a fully integrated faculty. But subsequent applicants, including a few with better academic credentials than my own, were all found wanting in one or another respect. My frustration regarding this matter, no less than my fatigue, was what had brought me to the point of resignation prior to Mr. Taylor's visit.

With the behind-the-scenes help from the DeVine Gift, the law school hired its second black teacher during the summer, a young man with good credentials and some teaching experience at another law school. He was able to fill holes in the curriculum caused by two unexpected faculty resignations. The following year, we "discovered," again with the assistance of Mr. Taylor's network, three more minority teachers—an Hispanic man, an Asian woman, and another black woman. In addition, one of our black graduates, a law review editor, was promised a position when he completed his judicial clerkship.

We now had six minority faculty members, far more than any other major white law school. I was ecstatic, a sentiment that I soon learned many of my white colleagues did not share. . . . Had we stopped at six, perhaps nothing would have been said. But the following year, Mr. Taylor's company, with growing expertise, recruited an exceptionally able black lawyer. His academic credentials were impeccable. The top student at our competitor school, he had been a law review editor and had written a superb student note. After clerking for a federal court of appeals judge and a U.S. Supreme Court Justice, he had joined a major New York City law firm and was in line for early election to partnership. He would be our seventh minority faculty member and, based on his record, the best of all of us.

When the Dean came to see me, he talked rather aimlessly for some time before he reached the problem troubling him and, I later gathered, much of the faculty. The problem was that our faculty would soon be twenty-five percent minority. "You know, Geneva, we promised you we would become an integrated faculty, and we have kept that promise—admittedly with a lot of help from you. But I don't think we can hire anyone else for a while. I thought we might 'share the wealth' a bit by recommending your candidate to some of our sister schools whose minority hiring records are far less impressive than our own."

"Mr. Dean," I said as calmly and, I fear, as coldly as I could, "I am not interested in recruiting black teachers for other law schools. Each of the

people we have hired is good, as you have boasted many times. And I can assure you that the seventh candidate will be better than anyone now on the faculty without regard to race."

"I admit that, Geneva, but let's be realistic. This is one of the oldest and finest law schools in the country. It simply would not be the same school with a predominantly minority faculty. I thought you would understand."

"I'm no mathematician," I said, " but twenty-five percent is far from a majority. Still, it is more racial integration than you want, even though none of the minorities, excluding perhaps myself, has needed any affirmative action help to qualify for the job. I also understand, even if tardily, that you folks never expected that I would find more than a few minorities who could meet your academic qualifications; you never expected that you would have to reveal what has always been your chief qualification—a white face, preferably from an upperclass background."

To his credit, the Dean remained fairly calm throughout my tirade. "I have heard you argue that black law schools like Howard should retain mainly black faculties and student bodies, even if they have to turn away whites with better qualifications to do so. We have a similar situation; we want to retain our image as a white school just as you want Howard to retain its image as a black school."

"That is a specious argument, Dean, and you know it. Black schools have a special responsibility to aid the victims of this country's long-standing and continuing racism. Schools like this one should be grateful for the chance to change their all-white image. And if you are not grateful, I am certain the courts will give you ample reason to reconsider when this latest candidate sues you to be instated in the job he has earned and is entitled to receive."

The Dean was not surprised by my rather unprofessional threat to sue. "I have discussed this at length with some faculty members, and we realize that you may wish to test this matter in the courts. We think, however, that precedents will favor us on the issues that such a suit will raise. I do not want to be unkind. We do appreciate your recruitment efforts, Geneva, but a law school of our caliber and tradition simply cannot look like a professional basketball team."

He left my office after that parting shot, and I remember that my first reaction was rage. Then, as I slowly realized the full significance of all that had happened since I received the DeVine Gift, the tears came and kept coming. I cried and cried at the futility of it all.

Geneva seemed to relive rather than simply retell her Chronicle. She was so agitated by the time she finished that she seemed to forget I was there and began to pace the room. . . . I tried to reassure her.

"I think that most minorities feel exposed and vulnerable at predominantly white law schools. And I know that most black teachers run into faculty resistance when they seek to recruit a second nonwhite faculty member. Of course, these teachers continue to confront the qualifications hurdle; they never reach the problem you faced. Our question, however, is whether the Supreme Court would view the law school's rejection of a seventh eminently qualified minority candidate as impermissible racial discrimination. Had litigation in the case begun before your time in this Chronicle ran out?"

"That part is fuzzy. After discovering what the school really thought about its minority faculty members—something I probably knew all along, but found it necessary to repress—I resigned from the faculty. That was stupid, of course, but I felt betrayed. I had come to feel like a part of the school and to believe in my colleagues' desire to recruit more minority faculty members. The seventh candidate, as I recall, was outraged and decided to challenge his rejection in the courts. But that is all I remember."

"At first glance," I said, "the Dean's confidence in favorable precedents was not justified. Although the courts have withdrawn from their initial expansive reading of Title VII, even a conservative Court might find for your seventh minority candidate, given his superior credentials."

"Remember," Geneva cautioned, "the law school will first claim that its preference for white applicants is based on their superior qualifications. I gather the cases indicate that the employer's subjective evaluation can play a major role in decisions involving highly qualified candidates who seek professional level positions."

"That is true," I conceded. "Courts are reluctant to interfere with upper-level hiring decisions in the absence of strong proof that those decisions were based on an intent to discriminate. Judicial deference is particularly pronounced when the employment decision at issue affects the health or safety of large numbers of people. The courts, for example, have hesitated to interfere with decisions regarding the hiring of airline pilots or professionals, including university teachers. Under current law, if there are few objective hiring criteria and legitimate subjective considerations, plaintiffs will only rarely obtain a searching judicial inquiry into their allegation of discrimination in hiring."

"In other words," Geneva summarized, "this would not be an easy case even if the plaintiff were the first rather than the seventh candidate."

"I think that is right, Geneva," I replied. "To add to the gloomy prospects, the Court's handling of recent employment discrimination cases shows that it does not wish to broaden the protective scope of existing antidiscrimination laws. . . . Many of the decisions that the Court has let stand went against plaintiffs alleging discriminatory practices."

"Do you think, then," Geneva asked, "that our seventh candidate has no chance?"

"No," I answered. "The Court might surprise us if the record shows that the plaintiff's qualifications are clearly superior to those of other candidates. It would be a very compelling situation, one not likely to occur again soon, and the Supreme Court just might use this case to reach a 'contradiction-closing' decision. Such a decision would not impose an unbearable cost on either the law school or society. And, of course, minorities and liberal whites would hail a favorable decision as proof that racial justice is still available through the courts."

"So are you now ready to predict what the Supreme Court would do in this case?"

Like most law teachers, I am ready to predict judicial outcomes even before being asked, but recalling what Geneva believed was at stake, I thought it wise to review the situation more closely. "Weighing all the factors," I finally said, "the Dean's belief that his law school will prevail in court may be justified after all."

"I agree," Geneva said. "And we have not yet considered the possibility that even if the Court found that our candidate had the best paper credentials, the law school might have an alternative defense."

"That is true," I said. "The law school might argue that even if its rejection of the seventh candidate was based on race, the decision was necessary to protect its reputation and financial well-being as a 'majority institution.' The maintenance of a predominantly white faculty, the school will say, is essential to the preservation of an appropriate image, to the recruitment of faculty and students, and to the enlistment of alumni contributions. With heartfelt expressions of regret that 'the world is not a better place,' the law school will urge the Court to find that neither Title VII nor the Constitution prohibits it from discriminating against minority candidates when the percentage of minorities on the faculty exceeds that of the population at large. At the least, the school will contend that no such prohibition should apply while most of the country's law schools continue to maintain nearly all-white faculties."

"And how do you think the Court would respond to such an argument?" Geneva asked.

"Well," I answered, "given the quality of the minority faculty, courts might discount the law school's fears that it would lose status and support if one-fourth of its teaching staff were nonwhite."

Geneva did not look convinced. "I don't know," she said. "I think a part of the Dean's concern was that if I could find seven outstanding minority candidates, then I could find more—so many more that the school would eventually face the possibility of having a fifty percent minority faculty. And the courts would be concerned about the precedent set here. What, they might think, if other schools later developed similar surfeits of super-qualified minority job applicants?"

"Well," I responded, "the courts have hardly been overwhelmed with cases demanding that upper-level employers have a twenty-five to fifty percent minority work force, particularly in the college and university teaching areas. But perhaps you are right. A recent Supreme Court case having to do with skilled construction workers suggests that an employer may introduce evidence of its hiring of blacks in the past to show that an otherwise unexplained action was not racially motivated. Perhaps, then, an employer who has hired many blacks may at some point decide to cease considering them. Even if the Court did not explicitly recognize this argument, it might take the law school's situation into account, drawing an analogy to housing cases in which courts have recognized that whites usually prefer to live in predominantly white housing developments."

"I am unfamiliar with those cases," Geneva said. "Have courts approved ceilings on the number of minorities who may live in a residential area?"

"Indeed they have," I replied. "Acting on the request of housing managers trying to maintain integrated developments, courts have tailored tenant racial balance to levels consistent with the refusal of whites to live in predominantly black residential districts. . . .

"You know," I continued, "civil rights groups developed 'benign' housing quotas before most fair housing laws were enacted. But the technique has always been controversial. Professor Boris Bittker examined the legal issues in an article written in the form of three hypothetical judicial opinions that discuss the constitutionality of an ordinance designed to promote residential integration by limiting the number of blacks who may reside in any particular neighborhood. . . . The analogy is not perfect, but the 'tipping point' phenomenon in housing plans may differ little from the faculty's reaction to your seventh candidate. Both reflect a desire by whites to dominate their residential and nonresidential environments. If this is true, the arguments used to support benign racial quotas in housing may also be used to support the law school's employment decision."

. . . .

"In other words," Geneva said, "if and when the number of blacks qualified for upper-level jobs exceeds the token representation envisioned by most affirmative action programs, opposition of the character exhibited by my law school could provide the impetus for a judicial ruling that employers have done their 'fair share' of minority hiring. This rule, while imposing limits on constitutionally required racial fairness for the black elite, would devastate civil rights enforcement for all minorities. In effect, the Court would formalize and legitimize the subordinate status that is already a de facto reality."

"Indeed," I said, "affirmative action remedies have flourished because they offer more benefit to the institutions that adopt them than they do to the minorities whom they are nominally intended to serve. Initially, at least in higher education, affirmative action policies represented the response of school officials to the considerable pressures placed upon them to hire minority faculty members and enroll minority students. Rather than overhaul admissions criteria that provided easy access to offspring of the upper class and presented difficult barriers to all other applicants, officials chose to 'lower' admissions standards for minority candidates. This act of self-interested beneficence had unfortunate results. Affirmative action now amounts to remedial activity beyond that which ordinarily would be required. It sounds in *noblesse oblige*, not duty, and has overtones of charity rather than the granting of legal relief. At the same time, the affirmative action overlay on the overall admissions standards admits only a trickle of minorities. These measures are, at best, mechanisms for slightly increasing the number of minority professionals, adopted as much to advance white self-interest as to aid the ostensible beneficiaries.

"Consider one last point," I told Geneva. "Some courts have been reluctant to review academic appointments out of concern for first amendment values. . . . The law schools' lawyers will not ignore Justice Powell's *Bakke* opinion, in which he discussed admissions standards in the context of a university's constitutional right of academic freedom. He acknowledged that ethnic diversity was only one in a range of factors a university may consider in furthering the goal of a heterogeneous student body. Given the importance of faculty selection to academic freedom, courts could end up deferring to a school's determination that a successful minority recruiting effort was threatening to unbalance the ethnic diversity of its faculty."

. . . .

"You assume," Geneva said, "that any faculty would react as mine did to an apparently endless flow of outstanding minority faculty prospects. But I would wager that if the Chronicle of the DeVine Gift were presented to white law teachers in the form of a hypothetical, most would insist that their faculties would snap up the seventh candidate in an instant."

"What you are seeking," I said, "is some proof that a faculty *would* respond as yours did, and then some explanation as to *why*. The record of minority recruitment is so poor as to constitute a prima facie case that most faculties *would* reject the seventh candidate. And most black law teachers would agree. Their universal complaint is that after predominantly white faculties have hired one or two minority teachers, the faculties lose interest in recruiting minorities and indicate that they are waiting for a minority candidate with truly outstanding credentials. Indeed, as long as a faculty has one minority person, the pressure is off, and the recruitment priority simply disappears."

. . . "You would think that whites would be secure in their status-laden positions as tenured members of a prestigious law school faculty. Why, then, would they insist on a predominantly white living and working environment? Why would they reject the seventh candidate?"

"Initially," I replied, "it is important to acknowledge that white law teachers are not bigots in the red-neck, sheet-wearing sense. Certainly, no law teacher I know consciously shares Ben Franklin's dream of an ideal white society or accepts the slave owner's propaganda that blacks are an inferior species who, to use Chief Justice Taney's characterization, 'might justly and lawfully be reduced to slavery for his benefit.' Neither perception flourishes today, but the long history of belief in both undergirds a cultural sense of what Professor Manning Marable identifies as the 'ideological hegemony' of white racism. Marable asserts that all of our institutions of education and information—political and civic, religious and creative—either knowingly or unknowingly 'provide the public rationale to justify, explain, legitimize or tolerate racism.' . . . [T]he media play down potentially disruptive information on the race question; inferior schooling for black children denies them necessary information and skills; cultural and social history is rewritten so that racial conflict and class struggle are glossed over and the melting pot ideal stressed; religious dogmas such as those espoused by fundamentalist Christians divert political protest and reaffirm the conservative values on which the white middle class's traditional illusions of superiority are grounded. You will notice, Geneva, that Professor Marable does not charge that ideological hegemony is the result of a conspiracy, plotted and executed with diabolical cunning. Rather, it is sustained by a culturally ingrained response by whites to any situation in which whites are not in a clearly dominant role. It explains, for example, the 'first black' phenomenon in which each new position or role gained by a black for the first time creates concern and controversy as to whether 'they' are ready for this position, or whether whites are ready to accept a black in this position."

"Putting it that way," Geneva responded, "helps me to understand why the school's rejection of my seventh candidate hurt me without really surprising me. I had already experienced a similar rejection on a personal level. When I arrived, the white faculty members were friendly and supportive. They smiled at me a lot and offered help and advice. When they saw how much time I spent helping minority students and how I struggled with my first writing, they seemed pleased. It was patronizing, but the general opinion seemed to be that they had done well to hire me. They felt good about having lifted up one of the downtrodden. And they congratulated themselves for their affirmative action policies: Were these policies to continue for three generations, who knew what might happen?

"Then, after I became acclimated to academic life, I began receiving invitations to publish in the top law reviews, to serve on important commissions, and to lecture at other schools. At that point, I noticed that some of my once-smiling colleagues now greeted me with frowns. For them, nothing I did was right: my articles were flashy but not deep, rhetorical rather than scholarly. Even when I published an article in a major review, my colleagues gave me little credit; after all, students had selected the piece, and what did they know anyway? My popularity with students was attributed to the likelihood that I was an easy grader. The more successful I appeared, the harsher became the collective judgment of my former friends."

"I think many minority teachers have undergone similar experiences," I consoled Geneva. "Professor Richard Delgado thinks that something like 'cognitive dissonance' may explain the shift:

> At first, the white professor feels good about hiring the minority. It shows how liberal the white is, and the minority is assumed to want nothing more than to scrape by in the rarefied world they both inhabit. But the minority does not just scrape by, is not eternally grateful, and indeed starts to surpass the white professor. This is disturbing; things weren't meant to go that way. The strain between former belief and current reality is reduced by reinterpreting the current reality. The minority has a fatal flaw. Pass it on.

The value of your Chronicle, Geneva, is that it enables us to gauge the real intent and nature of affirmative action plans. Here, the stated basis for the plan's adoption—to provide a more representative faculty and student body—was pushed to a level its authors never expected it to reach. The influx of qualified minority candidates threatened, at some deep level, the white faculty member's sense of ideological hegemony and caused them to reject the seventh candidate. Even the first black or the second or the third no doubt threatens the white faculty to some extent. But it is only when we reach the seventh, or the tenth, that we are truly able to see the fear for what it is."

Strangers in Academic Paradise
Law Teachers of Color in Still-White Schools

From a distance, it might be Camelot. The castle is located high on an impressive mountain, so high that it is often invisible in the mists and clouds that abound at such altitudes. But on a sunny day, particularly after rains have cleansed the atmosphere, it is both visible and awe-inspiring. Its high battlements of white stone reflect the sunlight so brilliantly that it is difficult to tell whether the sun or the castle is the source of the light.

. . . .

It is generally believed that those who built and reside in the castle have achieved their lofty positions through their ability to serve the rulers of the land. The residents of the castle are not the rulers, but they translate the orders of the real rulers into language which, though arcane, complex, and beyond the comprehension of even intelligent persons, communicates a sense of power that engenders an awed confusion and a subtle but real coercion toward compliance. Through the manipulation of those with power, the castle's residents gained a facsimile of power. Only the truly powerful dare describe the authority of the castle's residents in that way.

. . . Those who have gained admission to the castle refer to it as *The Academy*. The academicians, as they like to be called, embrace mystique. They are high priests whose power is based less on God than on their superior intellectual gifts. Their commitment is not to the usual ambitions, desires, or even basic needs. Rather, those in the Academy maintain whenever asked, and sometimes even when no one inquires, that their dedication is to the *Life of the Mind*. Absolutely no one knows what that means.

20 U.S.F. L. Rev. 385 (1986). Used by permission.

. . . Not one Academy, but several dot the land. All are deemed great, but some are deemed greater than others. One is acknowledged by most to be the greatest of them all, and the rest claim that their academy is "almost as good." This is, of course, logically and mathematically impossible, but because those who are not members of the Academy do not understand how academic status is achieved or maintained and because members do not reveal the formula for determining status, no outsider dares question claims that, in fact, are preposterous on their face.

These lofty beings—the Academicians—perform the magical feat of training and credentialing all who practice law in the land. This is a truly marvelous accomplishment because, with few exceptions, they have little or no experience in law practice. This is not a deficiency; the Academy's rules require that no law graduate can actually practice law before passing a difficult examination. The academies refuse to assist in preparing their students for this examination, deeming such labor neither worthy of their highly tuned intellects nor a justifiable use of their valuable time.

. . . .

Actually, if the truth be known, the Academy is not well structured to teach any but the very best students, those so gifted with intelligence and compulsive work habits that they could as well learn on their own what the Academy teaches; this is precisely how many students, bright and average, prepare themselves for their chosen profession.

This, of course, is all very sad, but please do not assume that we touch here on scandal or illegality of any kind. All of what I report and so much more has been going on for a very long time. One hears grumbling, to be sure, but no one has ever alleged or proven ethical wrongdoing in regard to the operation of the nation's legal Academy.

Moreover, few within or without the Academy manifest any concern regarding what appears a monstrous contradiction. On the one hand, those who reside within the Academy believe in the free enterprise system. They worship meritocratic concepts and despise any unearned aid, save perhaps an inclination toward private charitable aid that provides modest food for the starving, basic shelter for the homeless, and a decent burial for the worthy poor. But on the other hand, the Academy itself is structured in a way that closely resembles the communism that most profess to abhor. Once academicians obtain permanent status, which most receive after a few years, their positions are guaranteed for life. They receive much higher salaries than others who teach at the graduate level, and the fringe benefits often include generous health plans and retirement benefits. . . . In other words, academicians actually receive what most communist governments can only promise. . . .

Of course, the basic rules of governance continue to work even in this unique structure. But the exercise of authority without defined responsibility often leads to arbitrary decisions based on personal principle (and prejudice), the very antithesis of objectivity, efficiency and, in many cases, fairness. Again, as with questions of status, no one lower on the social scale than the academicians dares raise the contradiction between their preachment and their practices. Those higher on the social scale do not much care; upper class spokespersons have long preached free enterprise to the masses while practicing socialism themselves.

We must marvel at the agility of academicians able to espouse an economic system that accords them rewards long promised but seldom enjoyed by adherents of a foreign and hostile ideology. And yet those in the Academy, in cooperation with their judicial and practitioner counterparts, have performed yeoman service in protecting and furthering the capitalist system which has held sway in the nation since its earliest days. Its guiding principle is that free and robust competition will bring deserved rewards to those who through innovation, perseverance, and hard work prevail in the marketplace; but it will bless all in the land with the benefits of efficiency and productivity.

Perhaps this theory was once believable, but the record of capitalism is that its efficiency and productivity come at a very high price. Its essence is exploitation, which is based on the ability of some to require many to sell their labor for less than the value of what they produce. Of course, some in the Academy will tell us that industrial capitalism represented a valuable social reform, replacing as it did the nation's earlier reliance on human slavery.

Historians advise us that even this boast belittles the role of slavery in American history. In actual fact, the nation's earliest wealth was based on slavery. The Revolutionary War, fought with slogans of freedom and equality, was funded by the economic power slavery made possible. . . .

Much has been written about this strange contradiction: the first nation to recognize and protect the individual rights of its citizens held fast virtually all those in their midst who were black in the world's most vicious slavery. . . . Those who preached freedom and liberty could do so more safely in a slave society than a free one. Slaves constituted the main labor force, and their owners could see they had no chance to threaten the system. The preachments regarding equality were not addressed to them, but to the remaining free laborers and tenant farmers who were too few in number and too poor in pocket to constitute a serious threat to the superiority of the men who assured them of their equality. . . .

This legacy should not be forgotten the next time one of the more arrogant members of the Academy suggests that minority students and teachers are simply not intellectually ready for the rigors of academic life. No response to such condescension is required beyond a brief reminder of just how ready the earliest academicians and their judicial and practitioner counterparts were to manipulate the common law to support the statutory authority of the slave system. . . .

Of course, the most important and effective support of the capitalist system was to come after the Civil War which toppled the plantation system, replacing it with industrialization, a system, as practiced throughout much of the nineteenth century, which was hardly less exploitive than slavery but which did not carry slavery's moral onus.

In this period, the academicians enjoyed perhaps their finest hour. Working brilliantly with the constitutional amendments enacted to give the former slaves citizenship and a modicum of rights—commitments that were not much honored in those days and which, in fact, remain unfulfilled today—the courts of the time interpreted the Fourteenth Amendment to extend the protection of "persons" to corporations. And as a contemporary academician has noted, the amendment for most of its history has nurtured "railroads, utility companies, banks, employers of child labor, chain stores, money lenders, aliens, and a host of other groups and institutions . . . leaving so little room for the Negro that he seemed to be the fourteenth amendment's forgotten man."[1]

When a major depression threatened to topple all, the courts at last became disenchanted with what had been the heady elixir of the *Lochner* era's rhetoric. . . . And thus it was, with members of the Academy playing important, albeit backstage, roles, a consensus developed that workers should be protected as well as exploited by a system where equality is a symbol and class-based privilege is a fact.

It must be said that the Academy is not without those fully aware of the injustices in the legal system. Many of these liberal academicians, working with civil rights and public interest litigators, strive to use the law and the test case as vehicles of social reform. But alas, whatever short term relief even their most successful efforts might bring to a few, the long-term results serve the needs of the upper classes for stability, regularity, and acceptance of the status quo by the poor. And by these means do those in the Academy who oppose the existing socio-economic structure support that structure.

. . . .

. . . Outsiders gained access (though not acceptance) to the Academy in a strange and rather frightening way. Two dozen years ago, a great upheaval took place among the colored lowlanders who asserted that discrimination based on color must be no more and that all institutions—including even the academies—that had always been white must be so no more. A strong and insistent demand called for "integration"—full and complete access by those who for so long had been excluded. This demand, it was said, could not be denied.

Those in the Academy were very sly. As it turns out, they won the integration battle by seeming to concede defeat. When those demanding change grew close and their clamor could no longer be ignored, many academies, rather than manning the ramparts, simply opened up the gates. They went forth and urged that the best of those long excluded be brought forward. When this happened, the selected ones were taken inside. The gates were closed, the clamor subsided. The former claimants celebrated, but only the most sharp-eyed observers could see any change. In the main, the Academy went on as before.

The experience of the persons of color selected as pioneers in the Academy varied over time and place. Their chronicles are incomplete and unofficial. We know of many casualties among both those who have been refused permanent status and many more among those who have received it. As the pioneers of color discovered, there is no escaping societally-imposed expectations. Either they are deemed mediocre, thereby fulfilling the comforting assumption that they are not up to the task, and previous generations of academicians were right in excluding them entirely, or the minority's work is deemed competent, in which case the person is deemed a happy exception to the general rule.

. . . .

When the discussion ends, your interlocutor will no doubt reiterate the school's commitment. And meanwhile, the standards being applied grow tighter and tighter. Those teachers of color who saw themselves as trailblazers charting the way for the many have become wandering prospectors hoping to find and save a few survivors. The tortuous way they came is covered and lost. Few are likely to follow, and those who come will have to discover new routes.

. . . .

Strangely, our status as blacks, Hispanics, Asians, and Indians is our major shield and a potentially potent point of our attacks if we will but remember who we are and how much so many sacrificed so that we could have this moment as strangers in an academic paradise. We are the minority law teachers in still white schools. That is our tragedy and also our strength.

NOTE

1. Boris Bittker, *The Case of the Checker Board Ordinance: An Experiment in Race Relations,* 71 Yale L.J. 1387, 1393 (1962).

Application of the "Tipping Point" Principle to Law Faculty Hiring Policies

It is not easy to describe the feeling of despair when the faculty rejects a qualified teacher of color who you know full well they would quickly hire were you to suffer a heart attack and drop dead. "Is it," the minority teacher wonders, "that I am doing such a good job that they see no need to hire others like myself? Or is it, rather, that my performance is so poor that they refuse to hire anyone else for fear of making another serious mistake?"

Whatever conclusion the teacher of color reaches, it is unavoidable that he or she is less a pioneer blazing a trail for those who follow than an involuntary barrier whose token presence has removed whatever onus is borne by an all-white institution. Actually, and paradoxically, if the first minority teacher's performance is very good, it will be harder rather than easier to convince the faculty to hire a second nonwhite teacher. Even this "let's not test our luck" attitude is condescending and far from a compliment.

In *The Chronicle of the DeVine Gift*,[1] a lone black teacher in a prestigious law school is weary from overwork and frustrated at her inability to find other teachers of color with qualifications acceptable to the faculty. But with recruiting help from a secret foundation, she is able to produce five highly-qualified black, Hispanic, and Asian candidates. When it appears the minority teachers may reach 25 percent of the faculty, the school calls a halt and refuses to hire an outstanding black applicant.

10 Nova L.J. 319 (1986). Used by permission.

Consider arguments the law school might use to defend its refusal to hire the minority candidate in the unlikely event that a court found the candidate of color more qualified than his white counterpart. Among these, the school argues that it features a larger percentage of minority faculty than any of its competitors, that an even greater number will alter the school's image and jeopardize its recruitment of students, faculty, and its alumni support. In effect, the law school argues, "our record of minority hiring is the best in the country and we should not be required to do more until other institutions do as much."

Public housing authorities and private apartment developers offer similar justifications for limiting the percentage of minorities in a particular residential area or apartment complex for fear that whites will see the neighborhood as "turning" or "tipping" from white to black or Hispanic. . . . The tipping theory, according to one authority,[2] "posits that every community exhibits a 'tipping point,' a specifiable numerical ratio of blacks to whites beyond which the rate of white migration out of a transitional area will increase rapidly, eventually yielding a predominantly black community."[3] Courts have approved the policy on the grounds that it furthers the national goal of integrated housing. And several legal commentators have expressed support for "anti-tipping" policies because they would "effectively prevent resegregation by keeping the number of blacks just below the point at which mass exodus is expected to occur."[4]

Anthony Downs explains the tipping point as a desire by whites for middle-class dominance.[5] White people tend to confuse ethnic and socioeconomic status because a high proportion of minorities are low-income persons. But basically, according to Downs, the middle class wishes to "protect the quality of life it has won for itself through past striving and effort."[6] In his view, the middle-class dominance goal of whites can be achieved without completely excluding minorities because "white insistence on what amounts to 'neighborhood racial dominance' does not bar the establishment of stable racially integrated areas."[7]

The parallels are not exact, but it is clear that something other than a total commitment to merit motivates law faculties when they hire and promote. Merit and tenure are contradictions. Tenure serves many functions deemed worthwhile by most teachers, but merit is hardly one of them. Any rational commitment to fielding the best possible faculty would use selection processes that turned on frequent evaluations and comparisons with all who sought the positions of those holding them.

Determining the best teacher for each position would be a formidable task. . . . Proponents of the status quo might well maintain that no quality lawyer would sacrifice opportunities in practice to teach law if his career were subject to frequent review and the possibility of interruption by a competitor found more qualified. This is a strange position coming from those who teach and often espouse the efficiencies of a free enterprise economic system. And yet it is an argument likely to prove convincing to many.

Stability and job security are strong attractions to lawyers who enter law teaching, regardless of their color. And it is not necessary to restructure the profession in order to improve the current crisis in the status of minority-race faculty members. What is essential is that faculties of mainly-white schools be honest, for the facts are:

- Traditional qualifications are useful but do not enable accurate predictions about the performance of law teaching candidates. Many highly regarded law professors, including most nonwhites, did not graduate from one of the top schools or earn the highest grades in their schools.
- Adherence to traditional qualifications and the refusal to consider success in practice and qualities of maturity, commitment, and judgment will limit the number of teachers of color in most law schools.
- Qualifications aside, law school faculty (other than those in the four traditional black schools) consider their schools as "white schools" and would resist hiring beyond a certain number of even the most qualified teachers of color.

Given these conditions, only one alternative offers itself to the current counter-productive policies of tokenism in minority hiring. Law faculties must sit down, determine just how many teachers of color they and their schools can accept or tolerate, and then work out a time schedule that calls for locating and recruiting that number of minority teachers in the shortest period that budgets will permit. Those who respond that such a procedure would constitute an unconscionable stigmatizing of non-white faculty of a character as shameful as the use of "tipping points" to determine the percentage of integration of a residential community are absolutely correct. But just as policies of controlled racial occupancy enabled a degree of housing integration in areas that otherwise would have remained all-white or become all-black, so adopting similar procedures in legal education could result in a much-needed increase in the number of truly integrated law faculties and a far more productive and humane career for all teachers of color.

. . . .

In the short run, the few schools willing to play pioneering roles in minority hiring policies will receive quite positive public attention even during this conservative era. When I was named dean of the University of Oregon Law School, the school received far more commendation than criticism from both the media and the community. . . . Admittedly, the parallels are not precise. I left Harvard Law School to become the dean at Oregon. Even on traditional criteria, I was as qualified as the other candidates. But the benefits of my presence at Oregon were not in the main based on my reputation, but on my blackness. Schools will gain similar benefits if they hire a truly representative number of teachers of color with experience and potential. The judicial deference traditionally accorded university faculty hiring and promotion decisions should insulate the school from successful litigation as long as no specific number of faculty slots are set aside on the basis of race.

In the long run, both the law school and the society will benefit from the perspective that many teachers of color have gained the hard way. . . . The presence of a nucleus of able teachers of color working within the structure of established main-line institutions of legal education, receiving help, support, and comment from white colleagues, could make a major difference in avoiding the domestic catastrophe that looms as large as that of a nuclear holocaust. And if, in the end, it fails, those who tried will at least have the satisfaction of having seen a new vision, taken risks to realize it, and failed, yet moved forward.

NOTES

1. Excerpted *supra* this chapter.

2. Note, *Tipping the Scales of Justice: A Race-Conscious Remedy for Neighborhood Transition*, 90 Yale L.J. 377, 379 (1980).

3. *See, e.g.*, Otero v. New York City Hous. Auth., 484 F.2d 1122, 1140 (2d Cir. 1973).

4. Navasky, *The Benevolent Housing Quota*, 6 How. L.J. 30 (1960). *See also*

Bruce Ackerman, *Integration for Subsidized Housing and the Question of Racial Occupancy Controls,* 26 Stan. L. Rev. 245, 308 (1974).

5. Senate Select Committee on Equal Educational Opportunity, Part 5: De Facto Segregation and Housing Discrimination 2966 (Sept. 1, 1970).

6. *Id.* at 2976.

7. Anthony Downs, Opening Up the Suburbs 98–102 (1973).

Memorandum to Harvard Law School Appointments Committee

MEMORANDUM
February 4, 1990
TO: The Appointments Committee, Harvard Law School
FROM: Derrick Bell
SUBJECT: Permanent Appointment for [Current Visitor]

This is to urge that you give the most serious consideration to a recommendation that the faculty vote [our current visitor] a permanent position that will enable her to join the faculty for the 1990–91 school year. I am aware of the policy that discourages taking such action during the year of a visitor's residence. I believe though that we must move aggressively to add women of color to this faculty, and her strengths in teaching experience and scholarly attainments and promise make her the ideal person to play the pioneering role in correcting this serious deficiency in our faculty make-up.

I wish it wasn't so, but reading [her scholarship], hearing her presentation at the plenary session on diversity at last month's AALS [Association of American Law Schools] meeting in San Francisco, and hearing from any number of women students about her WLA [Women's Law Association] dinner speech last Fall all require the conclusion that hers is a unique voice in legal scholarship. I value the work of our graduates Anita Allen (Georgetown), Kimberlé Crenshaw (U.C.L.A.), Peggy Davis (NYU), and Patricia Williams (Wisconsin). Mari Matsuda (Hawaii), is also making valuable contributions to the legal writings by women of color.

Even so, her voice is unique. In one work she urges that women of color translate their experience-based insights into legally viable text complete with footnotes. As a model of what she urges, she chooses a case, *Chambers v. Omaha Girls Club*.[1] Facts like these cause even most liberals to duck and run for cover. I must admit that when covering this case in great detail a year or so ago, I found it difficult to defend an employee who intentionally became pregnant in violation of her employer's specific and seemingly understandable rule against unwed pregnancies.

She writes that female legal scholars of color must accept the responsibility of moving society beyond its pathological view of minority women and "capture the dignity, righteous resistance, and practical endurance that are ingrained in our cultures." Citing the amazing things minority women achieve with limited resources, she urges scholars to take on the enormous task of "capturing the complexity of their legal status and of translating their concerns into those that the legal scholarly community recognizes. . . ."

Applying this call to the *Chambers* decision, the candidate advises:

A black feminist jurisprudential analysis of Chambers must seriously consider the possibility that young, single, sexually-active, fertile, and nurturing black women are viewed ominously because they have the temerity to attempt to break out of the rigid economic, social, and political categories that a racist, sexist, and class-stratified society would impose upon them.

Developing this theme, she writes:

For those who have no understanding of the historical oppression of black women and no appreciation of the diversity of their contemporary cultural practices, the outcome of the Chambers case might have a certain policy appeal, one born of sympathy for poor black youngsters and desperation about stemming "the epidemic" of teenage pregnancy that plagues them. According to such an assessment, the Club's hope that its members could be influenced by committed counselors who, by example, would prove that life offers more attractive alternatives than early pregnancy and single parenthood is at worst benign, if it is not benevolent.

But for better informed, more critical evaluators, the opinions are profoundly disturbing. Firing a young unmarried, pregnant black worker in the name of protecting other young black females from the limited options associated with early and unwed motherhood is ironic, to say the least. The Club managed to replicate the very economic hardships and social biases that, according to the district court, made the role model rule necessary in the first place. Crystal Chambers was not much older than some of the Club members and her financial and social status after being fired was probably not that much different from what the members would face if they became pregnant at an early age, without the benefit of a job or the assistance of a fully employed helpmate. On the other hand, she was in many respects better off than many teen mothers. She was in her early twenties, had a decent job, and planned her pregnancy. Chambers' condition became problematic because of the enforcement of the role model rule.

This analysis has had a profound effect on many of my students. Not every student has embraced her views or appreciated her outspoken stance on sensitive issues of race and gender, but those positions need to be heard, and we need to do whatever is necessary to retain some one with the insight and courage to voice them.

To be honest, I have assumed that as a black person, I could represent and respond to racial issues for both men and women. I now recognize that black women are uniquely vulnerable to discrimination because of their gender as well as their race. Anti-discrimination law and policy that focuses on either race or gender serves to obscure the barriers black women face. Without a clear understanding of the harm, traditional race-sex thinking fails to address real problems or remedy real needs. At this point, that recognition is not widespread.

At least some of you will remember Charles Fried's luncheon talk on affirmative action last summer. It was our visitor's first day here. I brought her to the lunch. Fried observed that under the Court's recent cases, race-based remedies were tested under the strict scrutiny test. But because policies challenged as sex discrimination had been measured by an intermediate scrutiny test, he assumed that affirmative action polices intended to remedy sex discrimination against women would also be appraised under this lesser standard. Charles suggested that this distinction between policies designed to help blacks and those intended to aid women was somewhat paradoxical. "You mean white women," she interrupted. Charles was taken aback. It was obvious that he had never realized that black women fall quite literally into a "no man's" land in race discrimination law. He was not alone. The visitor has been bringing that much-needed perspective into her classes and in informal talks with faculty during her stay here.

I understand that we have about 390 minority students in all three classes. More than half of them are women. We need minority women faculty members able by reason of experience and insight to provide in the classroom and in our formal and informal discussions the views and concerns of this group. As indicated above, minority women are not the only beneficiaries of this presence. We should give a high priority to insuring a meaningful representation of minority women. [Our distinguished visitor] is here now. We should do everything possible to insure that she stays.

NOTE

1. 629 F. Supp. 925 (D. Neb. 1986), *aff'd,* 834 F.2d 697 (8th Cir. 1987).

Letter to Robert Clark,
Dean, Harvard Law School

HARVARD LAW SCHOOL
CAMBRIDGE, MASSACHUSETTS 02138

April 9, 1990
Dean Robert Clark
G - 200

Dear Bob,

I regret that I must give you this inadequate but quite firm notice of my intention to request a leave without pay effective with the end of the current school year and continuing until a woman of color is offered and accepts a tenured position on this faculty. While addressed to you as dean, I consider this a matter of community concern and will share this letter with all regular faculty members. I hope you and they will honor my request not to share this letter with either students or the media.

During this, my 20th year of law school teaching, I have been trying to assess whether my teaching and writing have done justice to the student petitions and persistent requests for black faculty that preceded my appointment. In fairness, I think there have been successes and failures, but until now, I genuinely believed that I was keeping the faith with those students and their successors who took substantial risks so that I might be hired.

Although I have never forgotten my representational function on this faculty, I was slow to recognize that as a black man, I am not able to understand, interpret, and articulate the unique conditions and challenges black women face. While I urged the hiring of black women, I thought that as a black man, I could both comprehend and represent the needs and interests of black women. A modicum of exposure to feminist writings, particularly those by black women, and [our current visitor's] presence and effectiveness have disabused me of this unintended but no less inexcusable presumptuousness. The large role our black women students are playing in the recent diversity protests here confirms what should have been obvious to me years ago.

I wish the push for women of color on the faculty was simply a matter of seeking conformity with a currently popular social goal. It is not. As each day's newspapers reveal and a flood of studies confirm, black and Hispanic men are faring quite poorly in contemporary society. It is not fortuitous that—despite the best efforts of our admissions office—there are many more women than men of color in our student body. The disparity is larger at the college level and is most obvious at black colleges where the ratio of black women to black men is often five and six to one. We simply must do justice by our black and Hispanic women for it appears they will have to handle an ever-increasing share of the leadership role in the 1990s and beyond.

Unfortunately, I have never been able to convince this faculty to act on those racial matters of the most basic concern to me. Thus, I was not pleased but hardly surprised that not one member of the Appointments Committee responded substantively to my February 4th memorandum (copy enclosed) urging a permanent appointment for [our current visitor]. When I raised the issue during a meeting on another matter, you indicated that because of the faculty policy deferring tenure votes on visitors during the year of their residence, it would be prudent to delay consideration of [our current visitor] until next year. I understand the factors that likely motivated faculty adoption of this policy, but after giving the matter more thought, have concluded that it is both unfair and unwise to apply this policy to visitors who are members of groups not now represented or seriously under-represented on the faculty.

It is unfair because, at the very least, the policy poses the potential for lengthy delays in correcting our current non-representation of black women, Hispanics, Asians, Native Americans, gays and lesbians, and the handicapped, to cite those groups represented in the Coalition for Civil Rights. I confess that I have been as insensitive to these special diversity concerns of other groups as I have regarding those of black women.

It is unwise because visitors who are members of unrepresented groups with credentials and performance records sufficient to earn them a visit here will also be seriously sought after by other schools. Indeed, their presence here as visitors will likely help generate permanent offers from other schools. This was the case with [two other visitors] and now [our current visitor] who has a tenured offer from Michigan and a visiting offer from Stanford. It is likely that Penn, [her] home school, will not allow her to depart without offering her a strong inducement to return. Given this demand, we have a far better chance of keeping her than we have of getting her to return after visits at Michigan and Stanford, assuming she does not accept the Michigan tenure offer outright.

I imagine that if by some combination of unexpected factors, none of the six black men now on the faculty was able to teach for the next several years, all would deem our loss a crisis. It would not be difficult for you to generate a consensus that minority replacements—women as well as men—must be found and pressed into service by next September. But in terms of our students' present needs, that is precisely the position we are in with no tenured black women or other unrepresented minorities on the premises and—under the present policy—no possibility of tenure for anyone until at least the 1991–92 school year.

I realize that in hiring and promoting faculty, perhaps you and certainly a number of faculty members resist appointments based on any consideration other than academic potential as traditionally measured. The experience of the last two decades though teaches that persons of color, by utilizing their non-traditional credentials, can make valuable contributions to the school and to legal scholarship. Moreover, their presence in representative numbers enhances the school's ability to attract minority candidates with qualifications that all agree are outstanding.

Despite the progress we have made in hiring and promoting black men, I must agree with our students who are telling us that the faculty is as seriously unrepresentative now as it was before I joined it in 1969. I very much want to teach here next year and, quite frankly—despite my support for a faculty salary freeze—simply cannot afford not to teach. I do hope that this explains why I cannot in good conscience continue in a role that limits rather than expands the faculty diversity I think we all want and need.

Sincerely,

Derrick Bell

Encl.

The Final Report
Harvard's Affirmative Action Allegory

The Tragedy

Everyone in the Cambridge community knew it was a disaster the very moment it happened. . . . None who heard or saw it ever forgot the earth-shaking explosion and the huge, nuclear-like fireball. When the smoke cleared the following day, the former President's residence, 17 Quincy Street, had disappeared. A deep, smoldering crater marked the site in Harvard Yard where the building had stood.

The explosion and the all-consuming inferno claimed the lives of the President of Harvard and 198 black professors and administrators—the university's total complement of black, full-time professionals. As part of a year-long campaign to increase the number of minorities on campus, the university's Black Faculty and Administrators (the Association) had called for an all-day meeting with Harvard's President. He accepted the group's invitation, and the meeting had begun as scheduled. A much published group photograph taken during the lunch break, and intended to record those who attended, served to confirm those who died.

There were no clues as to what or who caused the explosion. Every possibility was explored: accident, terrorism, even supernatural forces. The official investigation, after months of searching, found little more than everyone knew in the first hour after the blast. A building and all within it had disappeared in a flash of fire that reduced even stone and steel to a fine, volcanic ash.

In the absence of answers, surmise served as substitute for fact. Many whites assumed that the Association was responsible: that, frustrated with their inability to increase their numbers, the blacks—or some of

87 Mich. L. Rev. 2382 (1989). Used by permission.

them—had conspired to blow up the meeting place in a bizarre murder-suicide pact. Acting on this theory, racist hate groups launched random attacks on blacks. Rumors ignited riots in inner-city areas.

In time, the victims became martyrs to the cause of racial equality. The tragedy and the ensuing racial violence with its threat of social disorder prompted renewed commitment to affirmative action enforcement by long-dormant government agencies. Civil rights groups organized protest marches. The most spectacular of these marshaled more than a million college students who walked from their campuses to Harvard for the massive memorial service held at the Harvard stadium and the surrounding grounds. The investigation did uncover information about what came to be known as "the final meeting."

The Final Meeting

The final meeting at the Quincy Street house was closed, but files from both the President's office and the offices of the co-chairs of the Association contained the meeting agenda and a proposed affirmative action plan officers planned to discuss with the President. The proposed plan was dedicated to Dr. W. E. B. Du Bois who, following his graduation from Fisk University, entered Harvard in the fall of 1888. Two years later, he graduated, *cum laude,* with a major in philosophy, one of five graduating students chosen to speak at the commencement exercises.

At Harvard, Du Bois' intellectual gifts earned him the attention of faculty members William James, George Santayana, and Albert Bushnell Hart, who became his mentors. Academic ability though did not insulate Du Bois from the racial discrimination he encountered at every turn on Harvard's campus. His years were filled with loneliness and alienation. And despite clearly superior intellectual gifts, it was inconceivable that Harvard might offer Du Bois a faculty position at his *alma mater.*

In its prologue, the Association noted that Dr. Du Bois would now find a substantial number of black students at Harvard. Spared the overt hostility that Dr. Du Bois experienced, most still encounter color-based discrimination in many subtle and debilitating forms.

The Association acknowledged that in the last two decades, Harvard has established a Department of Afro-American Studies and an Institute named to honor W. E. B. Du Bois. At the administrative level, the university adopted an affirmative action plan in 1970. The Association noted that while their numbers remain minuscule, black teachers, staff, and students have made substantial contributions to the Harvard community.

. . . .

Background to the Final Report

No records survive of the discussions that followed the opening statements. Investigators, piecing together information gained from files and interviews with victims' relatives and friends, were able to provide a clear picture of Association efforts prior to the final meeting. The Association's goal was to improve what they deemed Harvard's abysmal record of hiring African American professors and professional staff. In the 1988–89 school year, only 17 of the 957 tenured faculty (1.8%) were black. And the 2,265 tenure-line or ladder faculty positions included only 26 blacks (1.1%).

Embarrassed and deeply concerned about their minuscule representation on the nation's most prestigious campus, Association officers met with Harvard's President in an effort to identify and discuss the reasons for Harvard's poor performance in hiring and retaining black faculty and administrators. Following that session, the co-chairs and the Association's executive committee decided to meet individually with the academic deans. . . . The deans readily acknowledged both the inadequacy of black representation on faculty and staff at their schools, and the many values their schools would realize with a greater than token black presence. They uniformly expressed their willingness to support actions that might improve the numbers of blacks in teaching and staff ranks. Several deans reviewed actions they had taken or planned to increase the number of black students, faculty, and administrators, while still others gave varying reasons for the embarrassingly small numbers of blacks on their faculties: the decrease in the number of black American doctorates; the lack or inadequacy of pools from which black applicants might be drawn; the lack of openings; the lack of funds for hiring new faculty; and the difficulty in obtaining tenure. The most often heard explanation was that faculty openings required qualifications which few if any blacks hold. . . .

A generous assessment of these meetings is that the President and the academic deans were concerned about minority hiring but comfortable with existing hiring criteria. The Association saw its task as bringing the deans and their faculties to at least recognize that their frequently expressed resistance to hiring African Americans with success and experience in other than traditional academic fields contradicted both logic and past hiring patterns for both whites and blacks. The deans found little significance in the facts that:

1. African Americans have been hired and promoted at Harvard despite (for some) a lack of traditional qualifications. Many of these individuals now perform at a high level of effectiveness, a fact that does not alter the too readily expressed fear that minority candidates without traditional qualifications may not succeed.
2. Not all whites hired and tenured in accord with traditional, academic criteria perform at consistently high levels as teachers and scholars.

Notes from a planning session held by Association leaders indicate that they planned to emphasize the following barriers to increasing the percentage of black faculty and administrators at Harvard:

White Superiority: During Du Bois' years here (and likely for three-quarters of a century thereafter) the strictures of law and widely held prejudices about the superiority of whites and the inferiority of blacks barred all blacks—including those with Du Bois' academic qualifications—from any position of importance at Harvard. The inertia generated and sustained during this long exclusionary period survived the enactment of anti-discrimination laws. Whether intended or not, questions of qualifications now serve subtly the role once performed overtly by racially exclusionary policies.

Faculty Conservatism: Tenured faculty exercise the major role in hiring and promotion decisions. Almost by definition, they are conservative when it comes to admitting new members to their ranks. They take seriously their roles of guardians of Harvard's scholarly reputation. This guardianship is appropriate, but in practice it simply replicates the status quo by selecting candidates from similar backgrounds, with interests and ideology like those of current faculty members. . . .

Scholarly Compatibility: Even outstanding scholarship, if not performed in a traditional format, can disqualify a candidate seeking a position or promotion. Narrow measures of excellence harm many candidates, but tend to exclude disproportionately large numbers of blacks whose approach, voice, or conclusions may depart radically from traditional forms. As a result, the selection process favors blacks who reject or minimize their blackness, exhibit little empathy for or interest in black students, and express views on racial issues that are far removed from positions held by most blacks including—often enough—the groups who pressured for an increased minority presence.

Tokenism: While the lack of an adequate pool of blacks with traditional qualifications serves as the major excuse for little or no progress, it is apparent (from the drop in interest in minority recruitment after one or two blacks are hired) that an unconscious but no less real ceiling limits the number of blacks that will be hired in a given department—regardless of their qualifications.

The Secret Tape

A cassette tape, uncovered by police investigators during their zealous search for clues, contained recorded portions of an Association planning session. . . . The footage reveals a quite heated argument over whether the Association should sponsor a series of direct action protests.

Ramona Berrywell, a personnel officer in the graduate school, strongly supported demonstrations. According to friends, she had not been much engaged in racial issues until she was passed over for promotion three times in a ten-year period. She filed and ultimately prevailed in a long and bitter employment discrimination proceeding. Berrywell's voice came through clearly on the poor recording.

Ms. Berrywell: "I understand why you tenured faculty types are opposed to protests. You are afraid they would be undignified, and not in keeping with your image."

[Muffled response]

"Listen. Neither your titles nor your tenure can change the fact that Harvard is no less a plantation for you faculty folks than it is for black administrators who can be—and are—eased out if we do anything that is threatening to our white supervisors, including doing our jobs more competently than those we watch 'move on up' while we are expected to wave them on and satisfy ourselves with the thought: 'at least I work for Harvard.'"

[Incoherent discussion to which Ms. Berrywell responds:]

"Quality of life for blacks on this campus? We work hard and smile pretty while doing it. In return, they tolerate us, but we are not part of the family."

[Several comments of disagreement with an unidentified professor's voice coming through:] "Ramona, you're wrong. We are treated like everyone else. I don't want to be pampered."

Ms. Berrywell: "Professor, I know you have been here a long time, and you have earned far more respect than you receive. But you signed that South Africa divestment petition with the rest of us, and what response did it get us besides gross rationalizations? Can you imagine what Harvard's reaction to apartheid would be if a black minority subjugated a large, indigenous, white majority in South Africa—or anyplace else for that matter?

"We are the surviving by-products of the 1960s riots. Unless we act, Harvard will return to its comfortable, all-white status. We will get nothing we do not insist on. I promise you one major demonstration: a 24-hour vigil around Massachusetts Hall, a 9-to-5 sit-down strike in the Yard, even a 2-hour gospel sing while blocking the passage under Holyoke Center. Any of these protests will get the message across that we want promotions as well as jobs, respect as well as pay, consideration and not condescension masked behind a thin veil of civility."

Professor: "We need to stop the hypocrisy. We know and they know that very few blacks are qualified for professional teaching or staff positions at Harvard. Neither pretense nor threats will change that. Face it. If racism has been as devastating as we claim and has prevented all but a few black folks from gaining Harvard-level credentials, we need to stop demanding that they hire nonexistent people. And if despite racism, qualified blacks are begging to be hired, we need to tell the schools where they can be found and stop complaining about discrimination."

Ms. Berrywell: "But for what you call 'hypocrisy' by activists in the 1960s, Professor, neither of us would have our jobs. The pool of blacks is so small because there are so few jobs. And that won't change unless we demand that Harvard find those who can do the work and train those who have the potential.

"I know some of you fear that protests will worsen our situations, perhaps justify our dismissals, and certainly ensure that any of us who participate will never be promoted."

Professor: "Ramona, protests are not appropriate for persons in an academic setting. We will turn off the university policymakers and give them an excuse not to take us seriously. Why not continue writing the President for more aggressive enforcement of existing affirmative action regulations, and then request a meeting with him to discuss our concerns?"

Ms. Berrywell: "The President is not God. His office gives him influence, but he has little more power over tenured faculty than we have. We must give him a reason for insisting on a vigorous affirmative action effort. If we don't act, who will? Remember what Preston Wilcox, the Harlem activist, preaches: 'No one can free us but ourselves.'

"Friends, we won't live forever. If they ask in the Hereafter what did you do to help the cause of your people, don't you want to be able to say more than that you worked at Harvard University?"

[The balance of the tape was blank.]

Discovery of the President's Plan

One month after the explosion and just prior to the massive memorial service to honor all those who lost their lives in the catastrophe, a proposal turned up among the late President's papers. Scribbled comments suggested that he had planned to present the paper to the Association at some point during the final meeting. The statement read: ". . . I agree that it is time to honor our words with deeds and linking a new affirmative action program with Dr. Du Bois' name is an excellent idea. Therefore, I plan to issue a proclamation commemorating the Centennial of Dr. Du Bois' Harvard presence with a Du Bois Talented Tenth black recruitment and hiring program.

"The goal of this program is that by the Fall of 1990—the 100th anniversary of Dr. Du Bois' graduation from this institution—ten percent of Harvard's faculty and administrators should be black, Hispanic, Asian, or Native American. . . .

. . . .

"Our black students need teachers. Teachers are models as well as trainers, and while, as Du Bois and dozens of educational studies would agree, not all teachers of black students need be black . . . some representative number of faculty should be persons of color. Adopting Du Bois' Talented Tenth standard as the immediate goal for all Harvard faculty and administrative positions is both a reasonable and appropriate means of moving Harvard's affirmative action commitment beyond tokenism.

"I plan to organize the Talented Tenth program along the following lines: During the 1988–89 school year, the President's office will sponsor a search and recruitment program including necessary timetables that will enable every department to begin a vigorous campaign intended to locate and attract black, Hispanic, Asian, and Native American faculty and staff.

"During the 1989–90 school year, the recruitment efforts should enable available vacancies to be filled by persons of color until the school or unit contains no less than ten percent [minorities]. Where despite good-faith efforts vacancies cannot be filled with persons of color by the end of the 1989–90 school year, then an amount equal to the salary of the majority person hired should be used to promote a visit, fund a scholarship or fellowship, or in some other way further the Talented Tenth Centennial goal. This funding should continue each year until a minority candidate is recruited and hired. I would expect that the desired progress will be achieved without further sanctions by my administration.

. . . We must face that race has served for three centuries as an absolute bar for faculty status at Harvard. . . . My proposal responds to the need for reform that will improve rather than degrade Harvard's standards of scholarly excellence. First, by vigorous effort, vacancies can be filled by blacks who have either traditional qualifications or their equivalents. Second, where such persons cannot be found or recruited, funding equal to the salaries of those positions will be devoted to fellowships and other support that will enable promising students of color to gain the necessary credentials and experience to fill teaching and staff positions in the future, either here or at another school."

The Triumph

Read at the memorial service, the President's Plan was as effective as one would imagine. With a seldom-seen unanimity, the Harvard community made implementation of the "Talented Tenth" plan a matter of the highest priority. By the Fall 1990 deadline, the percentage of black faculty and staff reached levels double those at the time of the fatal explosion. In addition, scores of black graduate students were benefiting from the fellowship funds the plan provided. The program had captured national attention and was being emulated at colleges and universities across the country.

Finally, exactly two years after the never-explained explosion, an elegant building, the new home of the Du Bois Institute, opened on the site of the disaster, a fitting memorial to the past and a stately manifestation of a university that had merged its commitment to affirmative action with impressive accomplishments.

Making Fiction Real

Happily, the tragedy described here never occurred. But who can doubt that so great a disaster would motivate concerted action to memorialize its victims with the realization of the Talented Tenth plan. This plan would add to the luster of a great university, and might well spark a national movement. This is the leadership role appropriate to Harvard. Acceptance of that role without the motivation of grief and the need to memorialize lost colleagues would not render that role less worthy. Most of us thought that the 1954 Supreme Court decision in *Brown v. Board of Education* would close the book on racial discrimination and open a new era of opportunity that knew no color line. We were wrong. The challenge of overcoming white supremacy remains. Harvard cannot respond effectively to this challenge with a faculty whose blacks hardly constitute one percent of the total. To paraphrase Jesse Jackson, we are a better university than that.

CHAPTER 7

Nationalism, Separatism, and Self-Help

Nationalism, separatism, and self-help are major themes not only in Bell's writings but also in those of many black intellectuals. Should the black community look to whites for support, or learn to tend its own garden? When whites are the main architects of a civil rights breakthrough, is it likely to endure? How valuable are symbolic holidays and events commemorating, for example, Black History Month or Martin Luther King's birthday? Should blacks seek integration with whites, in schools, for example, or separation? What if a prominent black makes a disgraceful public statement, castigating Jews, for example? Should other blacks rush to denounce him? In the selections that follow, we see Bell's insistence that the black community play a decisive role in its own struggle, politics, education, and even economy—even in the face of white resistance.

Brown v. Board of Education and the Black History Month Syndrome

February has become the time in which we move through the series of racial pride–oriented programs which have become the now predictable agenda of Black History Month. This year, I am thinking ahead to the anniversary of the Supreme Court's precedent-making decision in *Brown v. Board of Education*. Strangely, I am not looking forward to the event with enthusiasm.

Usually, as I approach the fateful day, May 17th, I feel a rising sense of pride about a court case that the skill of black lawyers and the courage of their black clients made possible. The pride reinforces a determination to make real the Court's promise to end racial segregation in the public schools of this country. But now, my most strong determination has been diluted by still another year of mostly no progress toward a goal that once seemed so close.

Considering how many thousands of black children complete schooling without much of any improvement traceable to the *Brown* decision, my mind travels back to a time years before 1954. Then, the expectations of most working-class blacks were more limited, bordered as they were by church on Sunday and the proverbial good time on Saturday night.

A hard-driving, rhythm and blues song quite popular in black communities back in the late 1940s or early 1950s opened with the line "Have you heard the news? There's good rockin' tonight. I'm goin' to hold my baby tight as I can, tonight she'll know I'm a mighty man. Pass on the word. There's good rockin' tonight."

Ed. Week, Feb. 22, 1984, at 24; 1 BlackLetter J. 13 (1984). Used by permission.

With the heavy beat capable of luring even poor dancers like me onto the dance floor, the lyrics of "Good Rockin' Tonight" promised a good time for all. Pretty girls, and plenty of food and libation. In short, a Saturday night party not to be missed.

. . . .

"Tonight," he seemed to say, "we can do as we like," implying of course that white folks will not interfere or try to control the event. Buoyed with that unspoken thought, he boasts, tonight my girl will know "I'm a mighty man."

. . . .

In a far more formal fashion, Negro History Week, now grown to Black History Month, has served a similar function. It too serves as a brief period in which black America can parade its best, dust off its heroes, try and encourage its youth, and pretend that the annual ritual alone can make a lasting imprint on racist practices and beliefs that thrive unchecked the rest of the year.

The public schools of our nation, often with the best of intentions, have become the chief disseminators of Black History Month. Out come the dog-eared pictures of Frederick Douglass, Martin Luther King, and that ever-reassuring figure of the brilliant but humble black scientist, George Washington Carver. Films are shown, recordings of the old Negro spirituals and the newer freedom songs are played. Discussions are held, and every black in the community of any reputation at all is recruited to come to school and take part in the annual brotherhood program.

You will hear no condemnation of these programs from me. In many schools and school districts where the black population is strong, or the white school officials sensitive, Black History Month projects can be impressive affairs indeed. And even where blacks represent a small and not very powerful minority, and the condescension of whites is thick enough to cut, these programs offer some reassurance to black children and a small reminder to their white classmates that black people, or some of them, are achievers worthy of respect.

What I fear as I see civil rights groups gearing up for the anniversary is the transformation of a once powerful legal precedent into the equivalent of an annual holiday with no more implication for equal educational opportunity than that likely to come out of celebrations dutifully carried out each year for Black History Month.

On May 17, 1954, no black person who thrilled to the promise implicit in the words of the decision would have believed that it could come to such a fate. All of us said at least a silent Amen when Chief Justice Earl Warren read, "In these days it is doubtful that any child may reasonably be expected to succeed in life if he is denied the opportunity of an education. Such an opportunity," Warren warned, "where the state has undertaken to provide it, is a right which must be made available to all on equal terms."

Surely, the unconscionably bad conditions that prevailed in segregated schools prior to 1954 are mostly gone. But just as surely, the goal of an equal educational opportunity remains beyond the reach of a whole generation of colored children who need it now more than ever.

. . . .

But as we now know, the evil of segregation was not that the schools were all-black, but that the state had decreed their segregated character and, with the same power, had allocated the best of school resources to whites and given whatever remained to blacks. The wrong was the allocation system, and the evil was the racism that motivated both the allocation and the segregated schools.

The racial balance strategy was valuable, even necessary, during the first decade or so after *Brown,* when Southern school officials used every possible technique to appear to be complying with the law while, in fact, keeping the schools segregated. But as school systems in the larger districts became increasingly black, the racial balance approach to compliance with *Brown* lost force. Most whites, whatever their thoughts about school desegregation, were not willing to have their children bused from mainly white neighborhoods and enrolled in mainly black schools.

And when the Supreme Court stymied civil rights efforts to have courts order consolidation of mainly white suburban school districts with their almost all-black urban counterparts, the possibility of fulfilling *Brown's* promise via racial integration simply ended.

I have been one of the mainly unheard voices urging that the *Brown* decision required equal educational opportunity, which meant no coerced assignment of blacks by race, but also that school systems must allocate resources without discrimination and, most important, must permit blacks to be participants in all policymaking so that they can play the important role in the schooling of their children so essential to effective education.

Where this has occurred, the educational results have been encouraging, and the integration process has not suffered. For social integration, by definition, presumes the coming together of equals, an impossibility when a handful of poor black children are bused long miles from their homes to a white, middle-class school where they are subjected to color-blind policies that all too often manage to replicate the racial harm the *Brown* decision so deplored.

But in this post–civil rights era, even my less threatening approach to compliance with *Brown* receives little real support. . . .

And so as we commemorate Black History Month, we can make a mental note not to pack the paraphernalia too far back in the closet. For much of it can serve double duty on May 17th. There will be speeches and discussions, and recordings of the freedom songs will be played. But if the sound is not turned too high, and we listen carefully, at least some of us will be able to hear far off, but seemingly coming closer rather than fading, the pseudocarefree rhythms of that more basic palliative of America's black masses, "Good Rockin' Tonight."

The Real Cost of Racial Equality

Blacks . . . have lost much of their post-*Brown* enthusiasm for racial integration as a goal in itself. Increasingly, their emphasis has shifted to building political power, increasing job opportunities, strengthening existing school structures, and improving housing conditions in black areas. They are exerting pressure on government agencies to enforce existing laws, petitioning to broaden already-accepted precedents, and organizing for action within the black community.

The goals blacks now see as crucial do not lend themselves to direct action protests as did the integration of lunch counters and waiting rooms. More importantly, black people are less willing today than they were in the past to base efforts to lessen racial injustice solely on appeals to white guilt. Such appeals require a posture of supplication that is futile, for we have learned that guilt *per se* is an inadequate lever with which to pry loose existing racial structures that protect vested economic and class interests.

Moreover, growing numbers of whites are refusing to cease practices beneficial to them until they are required to do so. That is a normal, if regrettable, human reaction. It is surprising only when it manifests itself in those whites who, before the problems of racism and remediation reached their northern doorsteps, were so outraged and outspoken in denouncing overt segregation in the south.

. . . .

How about protest as a self-help tool for blacks? It is interesting how many white liberals bemoan the death of the civil rights movement; they equate it with the glorious days when they could jet-ride South and walk arm-in-arm "with Martin and the others" through the streets of some dusty southern town and sing the songs that equated freedom and

1 Civ. Lib. Rev. 79 (1974). Used by permission.

brotherhood, suggesting that the time for both was at hand. Those were indeed glorious days and courageous deeds, and there is simply no way of calculating how many black lives were saved because whites went South to march with the protesters, bringing with them the national news media and the country's concern. But the civil rights movement did not end because the marches stopped or the leaders began squabbling. (Leaders are always squabbling, and integration has taught blacks that whites squabble as much as or more than they do.) Conditions and deeds changed, so tactics and methods had to change. The civil rights movement in its broadest sense—that is, the determination of blacks to continue opposing the racism that fills their lives—has not changed at all.

Even so, protest leaders face a dilemma. Protests that are clearly protected by the First Amendment (such as picketing in front of Mayor Daley's office on a downtown Chicago street) are so unlikely to gain attention or encourage change that few people want to participate in them. Protests that are peaceful, but done in an innovative way (such as picketing in front of Mayor Daley's home), are likely to draw hostile crowds that justify police interference. This is precisely what happened to a protest march led by comedian Dick Gregory. The Supreme Court reversed the Gregory group's disorderly conduct convictions on procedural grounds. But in a strong concurring opinion, Justices Hugo Black and William O. Douglas made it quite clear that if its statutes were properly framed, the city had the authority to halt even peaceful picketing in places where it will disturb the tranquility of residential areas or the peace and quiet required to carry on the functions of courts, libraries, schools, and hospitals.

Protests are neither dead nor unavailing. Harvard's black students proved this in protesting the school's failure to take any responsibility for the activities in South Africa of American corporations whose stock Harvard owned. But it is difficult to mount effective protests that are not disruptive. Willingness to go to jail or be expelled as a result of a protest demonstration is simply not strong among blacks today. Some may see this as a sign of growing weariness. Others may discern increasing wisdom.

Pessimism Tempered by Faith

The racism discernible today is more often than not subtle and institutional rather than overt. One finds it in a number of areas: welfare, public health, child care, prison reform, the administration of criminal justice. To the black trapped by it, however, subtle racism is no less a handicap than overt racism. Commitments to racial fairness issue freely but when a program designed to compensate for past discrimination poses a threat to white interests, that program sparks self-righteous opposition as contrary to law, fairness, and the American Way.

Somehow, the integration ideal has become a matter of community uplift rather than an entitlement guaranteed blacks under the Constitution. Rather than a legally-supported mechanism that a long-suppressed minority can deploy to gain equal opportunities, integration often serves, like slavery and segregation, as one more device by which the majority can maintain control over blacks.

Time for the Teachers
Putting Educators Back into the Brown *Remedy*

Looking back on my part in the campaign for school desegregation, I fear that too many of us embraced that goal with our hearts and ignored the pragmatic considerations that might have become apparent had we approached the whole matter with our heads.

Experience taught us little, and that learning we ignored. The Emancipation Proclamation was supposed to free the slaves. By its very terms, limiting coverage to those slaves resident in states still under Confederate rule and thus beyond Union authority—we learned—it did not. The Civil War Amendments aimed to release the former slaves from a new, more vicious servitude, but when the interests of the nation turned elsewhere, the laws based on those Amendments were not enforced or, when enforced, were declared unconstitutional.

In approving the "separate but equal" doctrine, the Supreme Court mandated that segregated facilities for blacks must be equal.[1] As we learned, only the "separate" part of segregation policy was taken seriously and rigorously enforced. The equality portion of the social formula came into play only when the disparities shocked the white conscience, which on this issue was a well-insulated measuring device indeed. Out of these experiences, we concluded that black children would never get an equal education unless desegregation came to public schools.

. . . .

Our poor judgment was perhaps understandable. It had taken two decades of dedicated legal work by civil rights lawyers and their black

52 J. Negro Ed. 290 (1983). Used by permission.

clients to convince the Court that limiting an entire people to separate areas of every imaginable public facility violated equal protection.

. . . .

But having acknowledged what every black parent knew about schools segregated by law, the Court did little more for the next decade than warn those engaged in massive resistance that they must obey the order of the federal courts. . . . Then, in response to widespread noncompliance by school boards, civil rights lawyers and their supporting organizations came to condemn every school whose population was black, viewing all-black as synonymous with segregated. Such schools, we argued, were both educationally bad and morally evil.

The goal, to racially balance every school in every system, became all-encompassing. Civil rights lawyers went so far as to argue that racially balanced schools were preferable even if the black children were doing less well academically than they had in segregated facilities.

When, usually after long years of effort, a school system was desegregated, we characterized the continuing discrimination in the school as "second-generation" segregation problems. Closer examination revealed these difficulties as simply new means of continuing the old regime: whites get what they need, and blacks get whatever is left.

Even when courts struck down gross jim-crowlike schemes, which included maintaining segregated classes within "integrated schools" and assigning students by "ability grouping," we were slow to recognize how effectively black children could be denied the equal education opportunity despite compliance with court orders prohibiting the maintenance of all-black schools.

. . . .

. . . Equal educational opportunity will not [arrive] for scores of poor minority children through traditional desegregation orders calling for remedies that rely on racial balance in school assignments. Lawyers and lawsuits will play a role, but it will be now what, perhaps, it should have been all along: a supporting role to the lead of black educators.

Reliance on the Teachers

Of all the lawyers who labored on the school cases that led to the victory in *Brown v. Board of Education,* only a handful have published their thoughts on the outcomes of that momentous decision, and none has been more thoughtful and honest in their reappraisal than the former NAACP general counsel, and now a Federal district court judge, Robert L. Carter. . . . Carter served as a chief legal strategist under Thurgood Marshall in the decade-long court battles that led up to the *Brown* decision. He played a major role in organizing and presenting the social scientist testimony that served as important support for vital aspects of the *Brown* opinion.

In preparing the attack on the "separate but equal" standard, Carter urged the use of social scientists because until the *Brown* decision was handed down, "we had neither sought nor received any guidance from professional educators as to what equal education might connote to them in terms of their educational responsibilities." He admits that he felt no need for such guidance "because of our conviction that equal education meant integrated education. . . ."[2]

The conviction was soundly based on bitter experience. White school officials had concocted every conceivable way to manifest contempt for their "separate but equal" obligations, and the sad evidence of that contempt, from deteriorating school buildings and raggedy school buses, to dog-eared obsolete texts handed down by the white schools, to too large classes taught by underpaid teaching staffs, all left bitter memories that for many blacks could be erased only by the enrollment of black students in previously all-white schools.

For many blacks, school desegregation became as much a penalty to be inflicted on white parents as a remedy to further the educational needs of black children. And, whatever the motivation, as Judge Carter writes, "Northern and Southern white liberals and blacks looked upon racial segregation by law as *the primary* race relations evil in this country." [Moreover,] "It was not until *Brown I* was decided that blacks were able to understand that the fundamental vice was not legally enforced *racial segregation* itself; that this was a mere by-product, a symptom of the greater and more pernicious disease—white supremacy."

Judge Carter's statement . . . should have marked the long-overdue loss of civil rights innocence. It did not. The romantic notion that integration is the means to as well as the greatly sought end to the long struggle with racism continues to find favor with middle-class liberals of both races.

Happily, many black educators, though not invited to participate in school desegregation strategizing, have made impressive strides in developing techniques to increase, sometimes dramatically, the level of learning in black schools. It is significant that their success with black children in all-black school settings has generally received more attention from the white media than from civil rights policymakers still committed to the school integration ideal.

. . . .

In-depth studies of how black inner-city schools achieve success with children who were almost guaranteed scholastic failure have been few. Until recently both educators and their funding sources have given most of their attention to schools desegregated on the racial balance model. Ron Edmond's work indicates that dozens of inner-city public schools are performing well, indicating that the periodic news stories about effective black schools are more than exotic but nonreplicable phenomena.[3]

. . . .

The common element among successful black schools was a strong principal willing to give priority to his or her vision of education even over policy directions coming from the central administration. To buck the system, the principal must have the strong support of the parents and the community, support that can come only if the school makes measurable progress with the students. . . .

Teachers at the effective schools were also mavericks. Like the principals to whom they were quite loyal, they have won the support of parents, and they don't worry about personal promotion. They agreed with the principals that their top priority is high achievement. To bring this about, they risked violating union contracts to spend non-class time tutoring pupils, and they worked before and after school to reinforce skills for students who needed extra help. They also made important decisions about instruction, materials, and student placement and programs.

Many principals and teachers share the belief that black and poor children can learn. . . . Unfortunately, no magic formulas are in sight. . . .

Effective school policies include: publication of and prompt enforcement of school rules and penalties; daily principal visits to classrooms and rigorous supervision of staff; meaningful parent participation in the school program; close monitoring of students' progress; criterion-referenced tests to determine reading groups; teaching assignments determined on the basis of expertise, not preference; highly structured, self-contained classrooms tempered with affection and consideration; using effective teaching materials not approved by the board, especially phonics, mathematics word problems, and black history, culture, and literature.

Reconciliation

In an old rhythm and blues song, the lyric chides a less than faithful lover with the message: "I may not be the one you want, but I sure am the one you need." In our romantic infatuation with racial balance remedies, we have over the years not sought suggestions from black teachers for fear they might take the form of self-serving testimony designed to protect their jobs rather than advance the schooling needs of our children.

It turns out that black teachers might have been interested in doing both. . . . Only the pursuit of school integration as something akin to a romantic object could have blinded us to the truth that court decisions do not of their own effect equal educational opportunity. School desegregation processes carried out so as to permit school boards to discharge black teachers and humble black administrators who were invariably reduced to assistant status, often with no real duties, represented no achievement for either us who "won" such cases, nor for the black children we were trying to serve.

. . . .

Educators and social scientists are now compiling the instances of success and analyzing the growing number of studies of effective schools in ghetto areas. Much of this literature has grown out of the disenchantment with racial balance remedies, particularly in large urban areas that are all-black. Additionally, the new studies are a response to the widely-held view that education cannot compensate for social status or family background.

Whatever the situation in 1955, when civil rights lawyers and courts began the long road toward compliance with the *Brown* decision, plenty of evidence now shows that all-black schools can educate effectively. Millions of minority children attend all-minority schools in urban areas so dense that desegregation by the racial balance model is politically and demographically impossible. . . .

In short, the time is ripe for the successors to Robert L. Carter to adopt the educationally-oriented school desegregation strategy that now in hindsight he wishes he had placed in effect in 1955.

NOTES

1. Plessy v. Ferguson, 163 U.S. 537 (1896).

2. Robert L. Carter, *A Reassessment of* Brown v. Board, in Shades of *Brown*: New Perspectives on School Desegregation 23 (Derrick A. Bell ed., New York: Teachers College Press, 1980).

3. Ron Edmonds, *Effective Education for Minority Pupils*; Brown *Confounded or Confirmed,* in Bell, Shades of *Brown, supra,* at 108.

The Chronicle of the Slave Scrolls

[Geneva recounts the following story to Professor Bell:]

From my cabin window I look out on the full moon, and the ghosts of my forefathers rise and fall with the undulating waves. Across these same waters how many years ago they came! What were the inchoate mutterings locked tight within the circle of their hearts? In the deep, heavy darkness of the foul-smelling hold of the ship, where they could not see the sky, nor hear the night noises, nor feel the warm compassion of the tribe, they held their breath against the agony.

O my fathers, what was it like to be stripped of all supports of life save the beating of the heart and the ebb and flow of fetid air in the lungs? In a strange moment, when you suddenly caught your breath, did some intimation from the future give to your spirits a hymn of promise? In the darkness did you hear the silent feet of your children beating a melody of freedom to words which you would never know, in a land in which your bones would be warmed again in the depths of the cold earth in which you will sleep unknown, unrealized, and alone?[1]

As Christians are drawn to the Holy Land, so I was one day called to the West Coast of Africa. In frustration and growing despair, I had abandoned my civil rights practice and found refuge in religion. After several years of study and missionary endeavor, I became the minister of a black church in Atlanta. A short time later, I decided to make a pilgrimage to Ghana. On my last evening there, I found the revelation for which I had come and for which, indeed, I had been searching all of my life.

On that evening I walked along a wide, desolate beach, and as the sun fell slowly beyond the waves, its light cast a multicolored splendor across

From Foreword: The Civil Rights Chronicles (Supreme Court 1984 Term), 99 Harv. L. Rev. 4 (1985). Copyright © 1985 by the President and Fellows of Harvard College. Reprinted by permission.

the sky. Even the gray sand was transformed into palettes of rich pastel color. As I marveled at this display, I saw the model ship, only a few inches away, almost buried in the sand beneath my feet. Perhaps two feet long, it was a likeness of those the slave traders had used to transport African captives to America, and from its worn appearance I could tell that it had been submerged in sand for quite some time. Held up against the fading light, the ship evoked in me renewed sympathy for those whose first contact with western civilization had signaled the onset of despair and misery.

Later that evening in my hotel room, I examined the vessel more closely and found that I could open it by removing a wooden plug stuck deep into its stern. With some difficulty, I managed to withdraw the plug. Inside the ship's hold I found three tightly rolled parchment scrolls. Contained on the scrolls and written in an antiquated English dialect were the answers to the questions: "How does the human spirit accommodate itself to desolation? How did they? What tools of the spirit were in their hands with which to cut a path through the wilderness of their despair?" The authors of the scrolls, like the authors of the spirituals, would probably never be known. But the miracle of their existence rendered unimportant the uncertainty of their origins. Just as the spirituals had enabled the slaves to survive, so the scrolls would enable their descendants to overcome.

I returned home to my church in Atlanta and began teaching the message of the slave scrolls. . . . After a few weeks of intense study in "healing groups" of twenty-five people or so, the members of the congregation began to shed the marks of racial oppression. The scrolls contained no magic potion or charm, no religious creed, and no political philosophy. They simply taught the readily available but seldom read history of slavery in America. That history is gory and brutal, filled with more murder, mutilation, and rape than most of us can imagine or easily comprehend.

But the humanity of our ancestors survived, as the spirituals prove. In the healing-group sessions, black people discovered this proud survival and experienced the secular equivalent of being "born again." Those who completed the healing-group process began to wear four-inch-wide metal bands on their right wrists to help them remember what their forebears had endured. Blacks left the healing groups fired with a determination to achieve at levels that would forever justify the faith of the slaves who hoped when there was no basis for hope. If revenge was a component of their drive, it was not the retaliatory "we will get them," but the competitive "we will show them."

Word spread quickly, and soon the congregation grew beyond the confines of our small church. The members of my congregation became missionaries, traversing the country to teach black people what we had learned. They led healing sessions in public auditoriums, parks, street corners—wherever they could. Excitement in black communities grew, but, with the exception of a few black newspapers, the media initially ignored the movement, viewing the slave scrolls as just another charlatan scheme designed to prey on the superstitions and fears of ignorant and gullible black folk.

Within a year, the marks of historic oppression—crime, addiction, self-hate—slowly began to fade, and increasing numbers of blacks became gripped by a fierce desire to excel. Unemployed blacks who could find jobs did so. Those who could not gain employment worked as volunteers. All manner of community enterprises sprang up and flourished. Black churches became social aid centers, and blacks who had taken themselves off the public assistance rolls began sending small repayment checks to welfare agencies. Black family life rebounded as the number of divorces and out-of-wedlock births diminished. Blacks excelled in the public schools and attended newly opened community classes held in converted taverns and poolhalls. They learned the truth about their slave history and prepared themselves for future leadership roles. In short, black people became what white people boasted their parents from the old country had been.

Understandably, a great many white people, after initially experiencing a rather patronizing surprise, became alarmed over what struck them as the abnormal numbers of blacks surpassing whites in business, industry, and education. It was, some whites felt, neither right nor fair—even un-American—for a minority group to succeed so greatly. White employers and educational institutions disbanded their affirmative action programs; many imposed explicit ceilings on the number of black candidates they would hire or admit. More immediately, many whites became severely disaffected by the increasingly wide-spread evidence of blacks' economic and political gains and carried out violent attacks against adherents of the healing movement. At several publicly held healing sessions, groups of whites pelted blacks with insults and projectiles; in one highly publicized incident, white attacks resulted in a violent melee in which several persons were killed. In other incidents, several blacks who *wore the four-inch-wide wrist bands in public received brutal beatings. These events spurred both the media and law enforcement officials to engage in a frantic search for evidence of wrongdoing or subversive activity on the part of blacks, but no such evidence was found.*

Finally, a popular television minister found in "American morality" what no one had yet discovered in law: an answer to the "black success" problem. In a now-famous sermon, the minister told his fundamentalist audience: "Success that is the result of self-help is the work of God." But, he claimed, the preaching of racial hatred was subversive. The slave scrolls, he asserted, created hostility between the races by teaching blacks about the evils of a system wiped out more than a century ago. The minister warned that unless the scrolls were banished, their teachings would prove as pernicious as those of Nazism and the Ku Klux Klan. Ideologies based on racial hatred, he asserted, should have no place in a country committed to interracial brotherhood.

The minister's sermon provided the key to action. Despite the opposition of blacks and civil libertarians, virtually every state enacted what were called Racial Toleration Laws. These measures severely restricted —and, in some states, banned outright—public teaching that promoted racial hatred by focusing on the past strife between blacks and whites. Penalties were severe for leading or participating in unauthorized public healing sessions, or for publicly wearing what the law termed "symbols of racial hatred." State officials enforced these laws with vigor, severely hampering the ability of blacks to carry out their healing campaign. Whites whose fears were not allayed by the government's actions organized volunteer citizens groups to help rid their communities of those whose teachings would destroy the moral fabric of American society.

The rest is almost too painful to tell. Whites perverted the law; many still resorted to violence. Like their forebears in the Reconstruction era, blacks tried to hold on. For longer than was perhaps wise, black people resisted, but the campaign to suppress those who wore the distinctive bracelets proved too strong. Black enterprise proved no match for the true basis of majoritarian democracy: white economic and military power. Nor were the courts of much help. Our best lawyers' challenges to the Racial Toleration Laws were to no avail.

For the black community, the teachings of the slave scrolls proved the equivalent of a bridge too far. Soon, the need to survive dictated peacemaking efforts—a prelude to a return to the past. My church, which had become the symbol of what by then was called the "Slave Scrolls Move-ment," undertook so-called "negotiations" with the white community. In fact, we had no choice but to surrender all. We returned the scrolls to the hallowed model ship. Then, at a massive service held in accordance with the surrender terms, thousands of black people renounced the lessons of the healing groups. We removed and destroyed our bracelets, and watched with silent tears as the ship and the slave scrolls were burned.

"That is quite a story," I told Geneva. "But it is one I imagine many whites and more than a few blacks will dismiss as highly implausible."

"You, too?"

"No, Geneva," I said quickly. "The history of Reconstruction reads quite like your Slave Scrolls Chronicle. The newly freed blacks made im-pressive educational and political gains during that brief period, despite the failure of the national government to provide meaningful reparations. But their very success served to deepen and intensify the hostility of southern whites."

"The Chronicle," Geneva said, "mirrors black history in one other im-portant way. White society has often persecuted black leaders and groups who have placed a high priority on ridding blacks of their slave mental-ity. Take, for example, the fate of the Marcus Garvey movement early in this century, or the more recent experiences of the black Muslims, Paul Robeson, W. E. B. Du Bois, Martin Luther King, and Malcolm X. Their calls for black communities to organize for mutual protection and bene-fit gained them many followers but engendered crushing enmity among whites. Malcolm X was primarily interested in the 'decolonization of the black mind—the awakening of a proud, bold, impolite new conscious-ness of color and everything that color means in white America.' It was that threshold task of decolonization that the slave scrolls achieved."

"But if the blacks in the Chronicle had become decolonized," I asked, "why did they give up all that they had achieved?"

Geneva said simply, "Think about it. The Chronicle suggests that black people long ago learned how to survive in white society. Blacks learned that too much success in competition with whites for things like money and power threatens black survival. But in a society where success is so important, a deliberate decision not to succeed creates a spiritual vacuum. Just as some poor whites relieve their frustration by feeding on the myth of their superiority, many blacks engage in self-destructive and antisocial behavior as an outlet for their despair. The teachings in the slave scrolls caused black people to forget their basic survival lesson, and the enmity of whites made it necessary for them to learn it anew. The public ceremony in which they renounced the teachings of the slave scrolls was a symbolic surrender of their rediscovered sense of their true worth. It marked the end of their rekindled expectations that black people can gain acceptance in America by becoming super-achievers. Once again, they discovered that success is an option usually reserved only for whites."

NOTE

1. This passage is excerpted, in edited form, from Howard Thurman, *On Viewing the Coast of Africa,* in For the Inward Journey: The Writings of Howard Thurman 199 (A. Thurman ed. 1984).

Shadowboxing
Blacks, Jews, and Games Scapegoats Play

I was working in my office at the law school on a late summer afternoon when someone knocked on my door. Thinking it a faculty member or someone from the administrative staff, I invited the person to come in. The door opened and I looked up to see a somewhat seedily dressed black man standing there.

"Are you the professor who publishes those stories with Geneva Crenshaw?"

"Yes," I said, thinking the fellow had purchased one of our books and wanted an autograph. I was wrong.

"My name's Nat T. I'm looking for Geneva Crenshaw. Where can I find her?" He remained standing at the door. Noting the anger in his voice, I got up and walked over to him.

"Mr. T, I take your question as a compliment, but I assure you that Geneva Crenshaw is a purely fictional character, a representation of many black women I have known and learned from during my life."

He would have none of it. "Man, don't put me off. I know she's real. And I also know she understands how this country works to keep us down."

"Are you a writer?"

He laughed. "No, man, but I can read. That woman is wasting her time trying to convince you of the obvious. When we get together, we are going to organize black folks as never before. You wouldn't understand, so just give me Geneva Crenshaw's address or her phone number."

Reprinted by permission from *Afrolantica Legacies* 81 by Derrick Bell, Chicago, Illinois: Third World Press, 1998.

Nat T's intensity made me nervous. I wasn't sure whether he was mentally disturbed or just scarily purposeful.

"Look, Professor," he went on. "Don't get me wrong. I'm not a nut. Fact is, ten years ago, I was a law student, going to a fancy law school just like this one. They flunked me out after my first year. The all-white faculty didn't like my black nationalist views.

"Well, I'm sorry," I said with a touch of unintended sarcasm, "but if you talked about a revolution instead of contracts and property, your teachers probably weren't impressed."

Nat T was not amused. "I was a good student," he retorted. "I worked hard. They decided I was too militant. I only wanted to understand how the law was able to preach justice and still keep my people down. I wanted maybe to teach others some day. They told me I would never make a good law teacher with my attitude. Nor a lawyer, either. It's the story of my life. I have the brains, I work hard, but I lose jobs because I don't have the right 'attitude,' meaning I don't walk a racial tight rope trying to be myself and still not threaten white folks."

"Law schools grade exams anonymously to prevent bias of that character," I suggested. He just looked at me as though I was the most pathetically naive person he had ever met. I decided not to push the point.

"After they flunked me out and refused to give me another chance," he said, "my life kind of fell apart. I had always wanted to be a lawyer, a sort of legal Malcolm X. He was my hero. When I couldn't find a decent job with my undergraduate degree, my wife took our son and headed back to the West Coast where she had a job offer. On the way they were both killed in an auto crash."

"That's awful," I replied cautiously. "And you connect her tragic accident with your treatment by the law school?"

"Wouldn't you? That and the hostility of a society that brings us down and keeps us down. Professor, it's time we give back in kind the harm done to us because we are black."

"An eye for an eye," I responded, "is neither moral nor, for the most part, has it been how black people have responded to racist oppression."

"And look where we are as a result, or," and he looked hard at me, "where most of us are. Black people need to live by a rule of racial retaliation."

"Racial what?" I asked incredulously.

"Racial retaliation," he repeated. "In a society that has actively practiced racism since its inception, it's no surprise that except for some feeble, hard to enforce, anti-discrimination laws, whites can discriminate against blacks just for the hell of it. We don't respond in kind, and so they keep on doing it."

"Well," I conceded with some relief that he had switched his anger from me to the system. "I can hardly disagree with your assessment, but —"

"Professor, whites should know that their acts of discrimination have broad ramifications. They need to exercise due care in the light of this knowledge, and they should be held to full account for actions that are likely to set in motion devastating racial reactions."

"It's an interesting variation on standard court law, Mr. T, but not one the law and those who enforce it will take kindly to."

Nat T responded angrily. "You teach the law, Professor, but you sure as hell don't understand it. The law is what the society wants it to be. Why do you think the law, including the U.S. Constitution, condoned slavery for all those years? Certainly not because it was right and moral. Slavery was profitable—the only morality this damn country cares about. When did slavery end? It ended when the big profits started going[, not to plantation owners but] to factory owners exploiting white wage slaves most of whom felt superior to blacks. We were left out. Well, no more. When white society sees blacks have stopped killing one another and turned their rage on the real causes of their desperation, whites will change and not one second before."

"With all your anger," I ventured, "you have a lot more faith than I do that this society will do other than strike back with a massive display of firepower."

Nat T ignored me and began describing in more detail than I really cared to hear how he was going to organize the black community and build an effective retaliatory force. He obviously had given the matter of revolution a great deal of thought.

He sensed what I was thinking. "You still think I'm crazy. But see, Professor, we've all been crazy to rely all these years on whites ever treating us decently unless they see something in it for them. Well, rather than moan about it, I'm going to show them that not treating us well is going to be very, very costly. They're putting all the young black men they can find in prison, and for as long as they can. But the brothers will get out someday with plenty of rage, no chance for a job, and no obligation to a society that has shut them out. I'm going to recruit them into a quiet force. No loud blustering about what we are going to do like the so-called militant black groups of the 1960s. We will simply do what is called for and fade back into the woodwork."

At that point, I had heard enough. I told Nat T that I really had to get back to work. He raised several more questions about Geneva Crenshaw: where did she work? When had I last seen her? When did I expect to see her again?

"I am sorry. She exists only in my imagination."

He shook his head. "Man, don't you understand? In denying Geneva Crenshaw's existence, you are denying your existence. There is no hope for you, man. No hope."

Nat T turned to leave and then turned back and faced me squarely.

"I'm going, but I'm telling you, right now. I am coming back."

"Oh?" I remarked dubiously.

"Yes," he responded with that same seriousness. "Once I find Geneva Crenshaw and get our revolution started, one of my first missions will be to return and blow your head off."

Unnerved, I tried not to show it but merely questioned his priorities. "You know," I told him, "in order to reach my office, you will have to pass the offices of several of my white colleagues."

"I know that," he replied, "but the revolution must first deal with all you black tokens. As agents of the enemy, you are a danger. You do more damage with your token jobs than the real enemy."

"So," I said, feeling my anger rise, "your racial retaliation theory will begin at home?"

"It will begin with the enemy," he responded. Then, as suddenly and resolutely as he'd come, he left.

I closed the door, returned to my desk, and tried to pull myself together. Feeling some ambivalence, I reached for the phone, my hand shaking, dialed the campus police and reported the incident. Then I heard my office door opening and, startled, looked up fearing it was Nat T again. Instead, it was Ben Hirsch, a member of the faculty, and visibly angry.

"Bell. Was that black guy, who just passed me in the hall, visiting you?"

I felt irritation replace my fears. "Believe it or not, Ben, not every black person in this building is here to visit me even though, despite my best efforts, I remain one of only three persons of color on this faculty."

Ignoring my criticism, Ben blurted out. "I asked him where he was going and he called me a white S.O.B. Said it was none of my damn business. Pushed me aside and walked out of the building. I called campus police. I keep telling the dean we need better security around this place. As it is, anybody can walk in here."

"Meaning, Ben, any black can walk in here and get upset when you question him about his business, a process I would guess you don't do with any of the dozens of whites who walk through here all the time. Am I right?"

"O.K., I get your point, but still it's upsetting—accosted in your own building."

"The building is open to the public." Angry as well as shaken, I sat down wearily at my desk. Hirsch, slim, intense, rather nerdy looking, just stood there until I waved him to a chair. He was far from the person I wanted to be with at that moment. We seldom talk. He's a staunch supporter of Israel where he travels frequently and consults with the government. He seems to be active in every Jewish cause. And since he visited the death camps in Poland, Majdonek, Treblinka, and Auschwitz, his commitment to Judaism has become a personal crusade, one I gather that annoys others on the heavily Jewish faculty who are embarrassed by Hirsch's super-Jewish posturing.

. . . .

To break the uneasy silence, I told him of Nat's visit.

"Oh," he replied. "That's serious. Did you call the police?"

I nodded.

"A bad scene, Bell. Now you know why I and other Jews get so upset and respond so heatedly when Louis Farrakhan and other black nationalists attack us."

"Somehow, Ben, I don't see the connection between my run-in with Nat T and the full-throttle rage of virtually every Jewish group and most individual Jews when one black leader makes comments they deem anti-Semitic."

"Well, look at you. Still shaken. And why not? A threat like you received, filled with so much venom. It's very distressing. You don't like threats. Jews don't like threats."

"Wait just a damn minute, Ben. To my knowledge, Minister Farrakhan has never threatened to kill any Jews."

Undeterred by my rising anger, Ben pressed his point. "Not directly. Both his threats and Nat T's are for the future, but you surely cannot deny that your automatic response to Nat T's future threat was immediate defense and then counter attack. You called the police. Right?"

"O.K., I did and felt some guilt for hoping they would get him and put him away."

"But you didn't feel sufficient sympathy for the cruel hand that fate had dealt him to simply ignore his threat on your life."

"Not at that moment, I didn't. I admit it, but it was crazy. I mean what charges could I bring? A threat to kill me at some time in the future? Technically, Nat T's threat was an assault, but in the context of crime in today's world, who would take it seriously? I would have come to my senses at some point which is more than a lot of Jews seem able to do in the face, not of threats, but of simply verbal criticism and abuse by Minister Louis Farrakhan, and his now deposed spokesperson, Khalid Muhammad."

"Well, Nat T's threats, and Farrakhan's, while only those of individuals, remind us of group hostility in the society aimed at you as a successful black and me as a Jew."

"Ben, not only don't I see a connection between my reaction to Nat T's threat and the overreaction of Jews whenever a black says something negative about your group, I really resent your effort to compare the two situations."

"That's because you don't want to see it. Look, the Jewish reaction is quite similar to yours against Nat T. Jews are saying, 'After all we have been through, why should we have to be subjected to gratuitous insults by demagogues seeking to use hate tactics to gain power at our expense?' We know the tactic and have been victimized by it over the centuries. But no more. The place to draw the 'never again' line is right here."

"Ben, give me a break. The Jewish response to what they consider anti-Semitic attacks makes my call for police action seem mild in comparison —but no less futile. Full-page ads and dozens of opinion columns have castigated the Nation of Islam. The U.S. Senate has voted on a resolution condemning Muhammed's speeches. And to what end? The Nation of Islam spokespersons are glorying in levels of public attention and acclaim from their followers that they could not have purchased with love or money.

"And remember when some Jewish groups supported an effort to remove Professor Leonard Jeffries from his teaching post at CUNY, charging him with antisemitism. The matter wound up in the courts." . . .

. . . .

"O.K., Bell, let me try another tack. I think Nat T's threat was particularly upsetting because at some level it reminded you of the broad range of hostility in the society aimed at blacks, and particularly at successful blacks by some black militants. Your reaction to Nat T was not only to what he said but also to what he symbolized. He served as a reminder that he is neither alone nor entirely inaccurate in viewing successful blacks as the enemy—no matter how hard someone like you works for the progress of all blacks. Am I right?"

"No, Ben. Success for blacks means you are treated with suspicion by some blacks and become a threat to some whites. It's the price of 'moving on up.' Given the growing gap in income opportunity among blacks, it's a wonder that even more blacks like Nat T do not believe that blacks with some status have gained it at their expense and are thus their enemy. As economic conditions worsen for poorer blacks, the numbers of those who share Nat T's opinion will increase. I am sorry, Ben, I don't see any comparison between the Catch-22 plight of successful blacks and that of Jews."

"I didn't say the situations are exactly the same."

"Because you can't. . . . I called the police, Ben. I didn't run around trying to get other down-and-out blacks to denounce Nat T for threatening me. That would be stupid. And it is equally stupid when Jews demand that I denounce something Farrakhan has said. Stupid and, I will say it, racist."

"There is that overused word again."

"Overused? Hardly. Look, Ben, do any of those Jews who demand that black spokespersons drop everything and denounce the rantings of a few blacks have any sense of what is happening to black people in this society?"

"You're surely not going to blame the plight of blacks on Jews?"

"No, though those neoconservative Jewish scholars who have bad-mouthed affirmative action to death are certainly responsible for some of the distress. As, I might add, are a great many Jews who don't agree with the attacks but don't challenge them, thereby providing a silent acquiescence.

"Oh, I understand the determination when Jews say 'Never again.' Fair enough, but while they are demanding a public rebuttal to every anti-Jewish statement some black makes, blacks are being eliminated by a more subtle but no less deadly holocaust."

Ben started to protest. I wouldn't stop to hear it. "I know. Many Jews feel they have an exclusive right to that word. But listen. If the nation's policies toward blacks were revised to require weekly, random round-ups of several hundred blacks who were then taken to a secluded place and shot, that policy would be more dramatic, but hardly different in result than the policies now in effect, and about which most of us feel powerless to change. Nat T knows this, and he views me as a danger precisely because he believes I don't see or, rather, don't want to acknowledge this quiet holocaust."

Ben started for the door, shaking his head. "I understand your position and I think you understand mine. At some rather basic level of abstraction we will have to agree to disagree."

"Fine with me, Ben. I just wish more Jews would keep in mind what Professor Delores Aldridge said, namely that 'both Jews and blacks occupy a somewhat precarious position in American society and culture. Neither group has the power to determine the destiny of the other. They both warily monitor the mood of the White American mainstream.' Then she adds: 'Allies do not have to be good friends.' In my view, that means a basic respect, including a willingness to view the entirety of an ally's performance, not judge and condemn based on a few sound bites."

. . . .

Ben extended his hand. "I really have to go. I hope it works out at the police station." He closed the door quietly as he left.

Gathering my papers, I came across a quote and made a mental note to send it to Ben. In an effort to avoid the fate of all societal scapegoats, Albert Vorspan and David Saperstein, two leaders of the Reform movement, wrote in their book, *Tough Choices: Jewish Perspectives on Social Justice*:

> We can find no safety in turning inward upon ourselves, severing our links with the general community. We can find safety only if we help America deal not only with the symptoms—hatred, rage, bigotry—but with the root problems of our society—slums, powerlessness, decay of our cities, and unemployment, which spawn the evils of bigotry and conflict. Our task as Jews must go beyond the defensive job of countering the attacks of anti-Semitism to helping bring about a just and peaceful society.

Why, I wondered, can't statements like that get the public attention the conservative Jews are able to command with their latest blast against affirmative action and welfare mothers? Heading for the door, I knew the answer. It was more than a question. It was the problem.

CHAPTER 8

Price of Racial Remedies

Occasionally, in a spasm of conscience, society decides to make things right for blacks and redress a lingering injustice. When it does so, the change to a new regime will entail costs. Someone's settled expectations will be disrupted. Others will find things more difficult or at least unfamiliar. One recurring theme in Bell's work is that society imposes these costs on the black beneficiaries themselves—or on lower-class, blue-collar whites like Allen Bakke who are least able to afford them. Bell here addresses white resistance to affirmative action; what can happen to a black scholar who is ahead of his time (and dies an early death); and the pain of being a black child bused to a white school.

The Freedom of Employment Act

Civil rights proponents fought valiantly, but in vain to forestall the enactment of the Freedom of Employment Act. The President, whose election the previous year was partly based on his pledge to push for the legislation, quickly signed the measure. The law, according to its preamble, would allay growing racial hostility by eliminating unfair policies enacted in a misguided effort to remedy racial discrimination that had mostly disappeared with the advent of civil rights laws three decades earlier.

In summary, the act bans all affirmative action programs, including preferential recruitment, hiring, promotions or other employment policies, practices, rules and regulations based in whole or in part on race or ethnicity. The act assumes that all persons who, because of their race or ethnicity, were actual or potential beneficiaries of affirmative action policies obtained the positions they now hold unfairly. Under the act, such positions are rendered "vulnerable to challenge" by individuals (job challengers) not eligible for affirmative action preferences and presumed harmed by them.

If any such challenger can show that he or she had superior training or experience at the time the job was filled, the presumed affirmative action beneficiary holding the position must, upon formal demand, vacate the position within thirty days. Judicial review, after the exhaustion of extensive administrative remedies, is available, but the cost must be borne by the suspect job holder. Jobholders who lose such challenges are liable for damages in the amount of job salary from the date thirty days after the challenge was filed.

"Stop right there, Geneva Crenshaw. Given my difficulties in the past with your unorthodox racial beliefs, I don't know why I asked you to help

From Derrick Bell, "The Freedom of Employment Act," *The Nation*, May 23, 1994, at 708. Reprinted by permission.

me prepare an essay commemorating the fortieth anniversary of the Supreme Court's 1954 decision in *Brown v. Board of Education.*"

"Why indeed," Geneva responded, ready as ever to challenge what she considered my out-of-touch civil rights views. "What is there to commemorate about a four-decades-old decision that, like Lincoln's Emancipation Proclamation, promised more than it could deliver, and brought results only because so many blacks and liberal whites treated its symbols as real and gave them substance in countless nonviolent protests and endless lawsuits? Now, what we hailed as *Brown*'s new nondiscriminatory legal standard has been twisted into a more subtle barrier to racial equality, one that is hardly less pernicious than the separate but equal standard that it replaced."

"Geneva. I share your disappointments with *Brown,* but surely you are not predicting that its shortcomings are going to lead to this Freedom of Employment Act, possibly the most repressive legislation I've ever heard of. With the possible exception of a few superstars in sports, entertainment and science, it will place at risk every job held by a nonwhite. Whites can challenge our jobs under a law that unrelentingly stacks the deck in their favor. Within a few months, this law would drop middle-class blacks who don't run their own businesses right into poverty, alongside the one-third of blacks who are already struggling in the economic basement."

As some of you know, Geneva holds strange, unnerving views about racial issues, gained during the long period she spent in a coma following a car crash while she was a civil rights lawyer in the South. She gained, as well, other extraordinary abilities—including the faculty of appearing and disappearing at will—that she accepts as normal and that I never question because, to tell the truth, I am not sure I really want to know the source of her mysterious, otherworldly gifts.

"Why would Congress pass such a bill, Geneva, and why on earth would the President sign it?"

"Considering the current economic and political problems the nation is facing and refusing even to acknowledge—much less address—why not? If Jesse Helms, a conservative on many issues other than race, could overcome the substantial lead of former Charlotte Mayor Harvey Gantt, a black man, and get re-elected to the Senate by using an infamous television ad citing affirmative action as the reason whites did not get jobs, why couldn't a President be elected on a similar campaign?

"I see your point, Geneva, but you surely don't expect me to publish a piece predicting that when your new law takes effect later this year, most blacks will find their jobs in jeopardy."

"Their jobs are already in jeopardy, as they should know from the contraction in the labor market that continues even as the economy improves. And you are right, many will lose their jobs when this act takes effect. But most of them will work again," Geneva assured me.

"Well, that's a relief. In other words, the bill is less drastic than you described it."

"Au contraire, mon ami. The act is much more drastic—as you would have learned had you not interrupted me. Another provision states that all those who held or were eligible to hold affirmative action positions are, upon surrender of those positions, required to find work within thirty days, or be subject to induction into a national work force."

"Sort of like the Civilian Conservation Corps of the 1930s?" I ventured.

"More like the military services," Geneva replied. "All those found physically and mentally able must go. The terms of service are for three years, except that failing to locate a job within thirty days of mustering out results in automatic extensions of service for another three years. Oh yes, the government, at its discretion, can assign inducted workers to civilian employers with labor-intensive work deemed in the public interest."

"Like environmental clean-up operations," I suggested.

"Yes, but also farming—particularly harvests of fruits and vegetable—mining, reforestation projects and the maintenance of parks and other public facilities."

"Even as a hypothetical, Geneva, your Freedom of Employment Act is scary. Dick Gregory, commenting on the thousands of blacks without jobs, joked that slavery, with all its evils, was at least a full employment act for black people. It sounds like someone was taking Gregory seriously."

"Slaves work without pay," Geneva reminded me. "Inducted workers will receive the minimum wage, and, while deemed on duty at all times, they will normally work eight-hour days and will receive room, board and recreational facilities at no cost. Charges that the law violates the Thirteenth Amendment's indentured servitude prohibition will not slow congressional enactment . . . , and they likely will not work in the courts.

"Why do you look so concerned?" Geneva asked. "Aren't you the author who has been writing—with some persistent prompting from me—about the permanence of racism, which makes a Freedom of Employment Act not only possible but quite probable—and quite soon?"

I ignored her question and tried another tack. "Assuming that you are reading the future accurately, won't my revelation of this monstrous measure provide our enemies with a plan that they might not come up with on their own?"

"Just the opposite. By spelling it out, you delegitimize this particular plan. But opponents will devise other schemes, though, some likely even more devastating. My Freedom of Employment Act is a hypothetical warning of what can become all too real.

"Listen" she continued. "I have to leave for a while. Think about the act and how to counter it."

I could tell Geneva was annoyed. She didn't bother to use the door. She just vanished—a habit she knows irritates me.

. . . .

Geneva was back, having entered my study as mysteriously as she had departed. ". . . The fact is, all too many blacks—and whites as well—are trying to support themselves at minimum wage levels right now, and without the room-and-board benefits the new law would provide for inducted workers. But a possibly effective argument is quite like the one used by many whites who opposed slavery. The law, by providing subsidized work for blacks and Latinos, will take the jobs of thousands of whites. This fear was crucial to the ending of slavery in the Northern states after the Revolutionary War. It also led many Midwestern and Western states to bar not only slavery but all black people as well. They were protecting white men's jobs."

"So," Geneva continued, "the argument may still work. My only concern is that if black people rely so heavily on the courts, other approaches will suffer a loss of energies and resources. For example, if thousands of blacks declare that they will not allow themselves to be inducted or, if inducted, they will refuse to work, the plan may fail."

"Many blacks may also die," I said. "You didn't mention it, but I am sure the new law has adequate provisions for court-martial-type proceedings for those who disobey orders, or leave their post."

"It does," Geneva said, "but the harshness of the act, its obvious hostility not only to affirmative action but to blacks and Latinos as a group, could serve as a much-needed wakeup call reminding all of us that the racial policies of the past three centuries have not really changed as we approach a new millennium."

"So, Geneva, you view your Freedom of Employment Act as something of a blessing for the victims of racial discrimination."

"Blessing? Hardly. It is a disaster, just as slavery was. But perhaps a law that forces us to face up to any imprisonment by the history of racial subordination in America will enable us to recognize—as our enslaved forebears had no choice but to recognize—our true condition. Acknowledging where we are is the prerequisite to understanding that the history of black people in this country is less a story of success than of survival through an unending struggle that guarantees a triumph of the spirit even as we suffer defeat after defeat."

Diversity's Distractions

Had I not been litigating, teaching, and writing about the difficulties of providing effective schooling for black and other children of color for most of my 45-year career, I might have joined civil rights advocates' expressions of satisfaction and relief with the Supreme Court's 5-4 approval of Michigan Law School's admissions program in *Grutter v. Bollinger*.[1] These are difficult times for those working for racial equity, and there is value in declaring victory after a years-long litigation. I fear, though, that further events—even in the short term—will render this latest civil rights victory, like so many before it, hard to distinguish from defeat.

The Court rejected the undergraduate admissions plan, *Gratz v. Bollinger*,[2] finding that the policy "that automatically grants 20 points, or one-fifth of the points needed to guarantee admission to every single underrepresented minority applicant solely because of race, is not narrowly tailored to achieve the interest in educational diversity that respondents claim justifies their program."[3] To the surprise of many, Justice Sandra Day O'Connor provided the swing vote in the law school case and wrote the majority opinion. She described the law school's admission process as a "highly individualized, holistic review of each applicant's file, giving serious consideration to all the ways an applicant might contribute to a diverse educational environment." In this process, she found that race counts as a factor, but is not used in a "mechanical way."[4]

Justice O'Connor generally votes with the Court's four conservative justices to defeat race conscious policies intended to remedy the continuing effects of past discrimination. Here, though, her vote gave new life to Justice Powell's opinion in the *Bakke* case.[5] Written 25 years ago, Powell's position that college admissions policies could, if carefully consid-

103 Colum. L. Rev. 1622 (2003). Used by permission.

ered, use race to ensure diversity in the classroom has been the source of both determined litigation and unrelenting controversy.

. . . .

Read together, the two Michigan decisions provide a definitive example of my interest-convergence theory. . . . Michigan lawyers and their civil rights allies shifted the focus from remediation for past discrimination to the value of diversity to the schools and to society. In support, they lined up 64 *amicus* briefs that represent more than 300 organizations, including academics, labor unions, Fortune 500 companies, and retired military and civilian defense officials. The friend of the court briefs all maintained that a racially diverse, well-educated work force is essential to the success of their operations.

Thus, it was diversity in the classroom, the work floor, and the military, not the need to address past and continuing racial barriers, that won the day. Once again, blacks and Hispanics are the fortuitous beneficiaries of a ruling motivated by other interests. . . .

. . . .

The narrowness of this ruling in the law school case and its vulnerability in future litigation comes into glaring relief in the *Grutter* dissents. Chief Justice Rehnquist, writing for himself and the three dissenters, denied that the diversity position met the Court's tough standards set in earlier cases. He contends that the majority departed from the close scrutiny given other affirmative action cases and that its review of the Michigan Law School's admission policies was "unprecedented in its deference." Rejecting the school's contention that it sought a "critical mass" of minority students so that they would not feel isolated or spokespersons for their race, he noted that year after year, a far larger percentage of African American students gained admission than either Hispanics or Native Americans. He concludes that "the Law School has managed its admissions program, not to achieve a 'critical mass,' but to extend offers of admission to members of selected minority groups in proportion to their statistical representation in the applicant pool. But this is precisely the type of racial balancing that the Court itself calls 'patently unconstitutional.'"[6]

In a lengthy opinion in the same case, Justice Clarence Thomas declares his unswerving opposition to affirmative action in all its forms, dismisses diversity as a "faddish slogan of the cognoscenti," and insists that "blacks can achieve in every avenue of American life without the meddling of university administrators."[7]

Justice Thomas opens his opinion dramatically with a short quote from a speech Frederick Douglass delivered to the Massachusetts Anti-Slavery meeting in January, 1865. There, Douglass told the audience that the colored people simply want justice. Thomas quotes a portion of that speech in which Douglass says:

> The American people have always been anxious to know what they shall do with us. . . . I have had but one answer from the beginning. Do nothing with us! Your doing with us has already played the mischief with us. Do nothing with us! If the apples will not remain on the tree of their own strength, if they are worm-eaten at the core, if they are early ripe and disposed to fall, let them fall! . . . And if the negro cannot stand on his own legs, let him fall also. All I ask is, give him a chance to stand on his own legs! Let him alone! . . . [Y]our interference is doing him positive injury.[8]

Justice Thomas follows the quote by stating that: "Like Douglass, I believe blacks can achieve in every avenue of American life without the meddling of university administrators."[9] . . .

Yet, Frederick Douglass saw clearly 150 years ago what Justice Thomas and so many affirmative action opponents ignore today: the continuing efficacy of racism. . . . Justice Thomas, though, misreads Frederick Douglass' position in a more important regard. While he would strike down all admissions practices that consider race either directly or indirectly, Thomas acknowledges the role of legacy admits and standardized test results that play so important role in the admissions process. Dissenting in the law school case, he writes:

> [T]here is much to be said for the view that the use of tests and other measures to "predict" academic performance is a poor substitute for a system that gives every applicant a chance to prove he can succeed in the study of law. The rallying cry that in the absence of racial discrimination in admissions there would be a true meritocracy ignores the fact that the entire process is poisoned by numerous exceptions to "merit." . . . For example, in the national debate on racial discrimination in higher education admissions, much has been made of the fact that elite institutions utilize a so-called "legacy" preference to give the children of alumni an advantage in admissions. This, and other, exceptions to a "true" meri-

tocracy give the lie to protestations that merit admissions are in fact the order of the day at the Nation's universities.[10]

Justice Thomas, though, does not believe the Equal Protection Clause flatly prohibits standardized tests or "unseemly legacy preferences or many other kinds of arbitrary admissions procedures." And yet, these are precisely the kinds of restrictions that Douglass maintained did not let a black person "stand on his own legs." . . . Studies show that such tests are notoriously poor predictors of performance either in school or after, but they measure quite accurately the incomes of the applicants' parents. Because many schools receive so many more applications than positions, and because our society is fascinated or intimidated by "hard figures," the standardized tests are in common use even though they privilege applicants from well-to-do families, alumni children, and those born into celebrity.

In short, these qualifications are means of advantaging privileged applicants in ways more subtle but hardly less confining than the apprenticeship status General Banks imposed on the recently freed slaves. Justice Thomas reads Douglass' words, but misses that great man's spirit and his unwavering dedication to uplifting his people. Douglass recognized that the Constitution and the country were born in slavery, but he believed they contained an essence sufficient to make all free. Douglass would not construct no-exit rationales that rendered all use of race invalid and that barred minorities as surely as any Jim Crow law. . . .

Justice Scalia, dissenting in the law school case, predicts that the two decisions "seem perversely designed to prolong the controversy and the litigation." Reviewing some of that possible litigation, Scalia says, "I do not look forward to any of these cases. The Constitution proscribes government discrimination on the basis of race, and state provided education is no exception."[11]

Justice Souter, dissenting in the undergraduate case, highlights the confusion between the two decisions that will likely lead to the litigation that Justice Scalia fears. He points out that with the exception of granting minority applicants 20 points, each undergraduate application is viewed holistically—just as in the law school policy that a majority of the Court approved. Souter notes that nonminority students may receive 20 points for athletic ability, socioeconomic disadvantage, attendance at a socioeconomically disadvantaged or predominantly minority high school. At the provost's discretion, they may also receive 10 points for being residents of Michigan, 6 points for being residents of an underrepresented Michigan county, and among other matters, 5 for leadership and service. If holistic review is the new talisman, colleges will be quick to seize on it, while their detractors search for ways to challenge their sincerity.

. . . .

How predictable, then, that only a few weeks after the Court decided the Michigan cases, Ward Connelly, who led successful campaigns to ban racial and ethnic preferences in California and Washington State, announced that he and other affirmative action foes would launch a similar campaign in Michigan and other states.

NOTES

1. Grutter v. Bollinger, 123 S. Ct. 2325, 2343 (2003).
2. Gratz v. Bollinger, 123 S. Ct. 2411, 2427 (2003).
3. *Id.*
4. Grutter v. Bollinger, 123 S. Ct. 2325, 2343 (2003).
5. Regents of the University of California v. Bakke, 438 U.S. 265 (1978).
6. 123 S. Ct. at 2325.
7. 123 S. Ct. at 2352.
8. *Id.* at 2325.
9. *Id.*
10. 123 S. Ct. 2359–2360.
11. 123 S. Ct. 2325.

A Tragedy of Timing

The biblical maxim about a time to live and a time to die is accurate without providing the reassurance of truth. For life is seldom too long, and death, coming too soon, always brings the special sadness of tragedy. But beyond the usual feeling of loss, the death of Clarence Clyde Ferguson, Jr., is tragic in ways that some who knew him well will intuitively understand without any certainty that they can communicate to those for whom an explanation is required.

. . . .

Law teacher, scholar, and dean, government official, ambassador, and United Nations representative, Clyde Ferguson worked in these and many other areas with impressive effectiveness. He thought deeply, spoke elegantly, counseled wisely, and fit well the role of the urbane, sophisticated professional at ease anywhere in the world in which he travelled widely.

But the loss of Professor Ferguson at age fifty-nine is tragic in the special sense that while he did much, he was a victim of racial timing, destined never to play out his full potential or exhibit the full range of his talents. Clyde lived during a time of racial transition when the possibility of equal opportunity brought to blacks who sought it more frustration than fulfillment.

. . . .

Clyde Ferguson was a model of what W. E. B. Du Bois described as the Talented Tenth. He was extremely able and seemed committed to the proposition that recognition and acceptance could come for blacks in this society through the exhibition of superior talent. Nevertheless, his career, as brilliant as it was, displayed a certain pattern.

19 Harv. C.R.-C.L. L. Rev. 277 (1984). Copyright © 1984 by the President and Fellows of Harvard College. Used by permission.

An outstanding law teacher in the 1950s, Ferguson entered the field of legal education too soon to make possible an appointment to the faculty of a major school. He was dean of the Howard Law School in the 1960s when predominantly white schools would not consider a black for such a position. His impressive career in the diplomatic field came before the government was ready to appoint blacks to the most important posts. And his hope that his government performance would lead to a well-deserved federal court judgeship evaporated when his political party moved swiftly to the right and conservative power brokers intensified their determination to exclude from important appointments even faithful party members of color.

He was finally invited to join the Harvard Law faculty, but he was not the first black on that faculty,[1] as he deserved to be and would have been, but for the perversity of the racial time clock. His performance as a teacher and a member of numerous committees was in keeping with his talents. In many ways, however, Clyde Ferguson at Harvard was the Satchel Paige of legal education—still able to throw the fastball and keep up with the opposition, but with too few years left to set the records which would have reflected his full talents.

Perhaps all of these near misses would have been eased but for the untimely death of his wife in the late 1960s, depriving him of the wonderful support she provided and leaving him to raise three daughters alone. But in our hearts many of us know that the tragedy of Clyde Ferguson's life that perhaps hastened his death was his constant conflict with racial timing decreed not by God but by his fellow human beings.

NOTE

1. I was the first black professor to whom Harvard Law School gave tenure.

Minority Admissions and the Usual Price of Racial Remedies

An implicit, often unacknowledged stumbling block lies in the way of our society's approach to racial remedies. The central issue in remedying past discrimination commonly has been conceived in the following terms: "Conceding that blacks have been harmed by slavery, or segregation, or discrimination, which groups of whites should pay the price or suffer the disadvantage attending relief?" This question, which focuses on the cost to whites of racial remedies rather than on the necessity of relief for minorities, obviously has been framed by whites for discussion with other whites. Their attitude is not unlike that of parents who, in the old days, might have hushed a protesting offspring with a curt, "Keep quiet. We are talking about you, not to you."

The exclusion of minorities from meaningful participation in the *Bakke* litigation and, for that matter, from much of the scholarly debate over the case, was more polite, but no less firm.[1] Minority interests were not represented on either side of the counsel table as the *Bakke* case wound its way through the courts. Allan Bakke's counsel opposed the interests of minorities; attorneys for the University of California Board of Regents, except perhaps by comparison with Mr. Bakke's position, could hardly claim to speak for them, either. Indeed, the Regents took the *Bakke* case to the Supreme Court over the vehement protests of virtually every minority rights group in the country.[2] Those groups, after reviewing the unfavorable lower court decisions, which were based on the inadequate record developed by the Regents, concluded that Supreme Court review might prove an invitation to disaster.[3] Minority representatives earlier

67 Cal. L. Rev. 3 (1979). © by the *California Law Review*. Reprinted from the *California Law Review* by permission of the Regents of the University of California, Berkeley.

had urged the California Supreme Court to remand the case for a new trial so that "the real parties in interest" could intervene and present evidence to flesh out a "wholly inadequate and almost non-existent" record.[4] Undaunted, counsel for both parties stipulated that the case be heard on the pleadings, declarations, interrogatories, and the deposition of the University of California at Davis medical school admissions officer. On appeal, the Regents' attorney sacrificed one issue after another in order to facilitate Supreme Court review of the constitutionality of the Davis admissions program.[5]

Minority representatives, potentially and properly the star players in the drama, found themselves relegated to the wings trying to make themselves heard through the always problematic prompting of *amicus* briefs. That communications medium was rendered particularly ineffective because over 150 groups filed more than 50 statements of their widely divergent views.

If minority groups had appeared directly in the *Bakke* case, they would have brought a sorely needed realism to litigation that proceeded more like a law school exam or an exercise in moral philosophy than a matter of paramount importance to black citizens striving for real citizenship. . . . Minority groups were prepared to argue that the Davis medical school had discriminated against minority applicants in the past—when the school opened in 1968, for example, no blacks or Chicanos were admitted, and only two blacks and Chicanos were admitted in 1969. If the case had been remanded for a full trial, impressive evidence would have shown that the Medical College Admission Test (MCAT) is not a valid indicator of minority performance in medical school, and that Davis therefore was justified in attempting to compensate for the test's antiminority bias.[6] A record of this character would have made a much stronger case for minority admissions and might well have resulted in a far more favorable decision than the one the Regents obtained. . . . For example, Justice Powell did not find anything in the record negating the educational justification for traditional admissions criteria, such as grades and MCAT scores, that have a serious and disparate impact on minority applicants.

The absence of minority representation in *Bakke* continued an old precedent. When the Founding Fathers wrangled over whether slavery should receive protection under the new government's fundamental law, black slaves were neither represented nor heard. Indeed, nonrepresentation of minority interests has been the unacknowledged rule in almost every national debate over who should bear the cost of remedial measures designed to rectify racial discrimination. Not surprisingly, then, racial remedies for blacks have tended to benefit whites, while the ostensible beneficiaries were left to pay the costs.

Faced with social and political pressures to increase the minuscule number of minority students, colleges and professional schools typically opted to use minority racial status as a positive admissions factor. The alternative route, the reformulation of admission standards, was generally rejected as "drastic and academically injurious."[7]

Certainly, racially neutral admissions programs, as mandated by the California Supreme Court, or multitrack admissions criteria, urged by Justice Douglas, might prove an administrative nightmare. But the chosen solution—simply recognizing minority exceptions to traditional admissions standards based on grades and test scores—has served to validate and reinforce traditional policies while enveloping minority applicants in a cloud of suspected incompetency. . . . Although the debate over the validity of traditional admissions criteria continues, mounting evidence shows that grades and test scores cannot predict success in the practice of law or medicine. . . . Minority students admitted under a dual admissions policy can succeed, but to do so they must carry a heavy and undeserved burden of inferiority.

Some critics of preferential admissions maintain that this stigma is too high a price for minorities to pay. Society concedes its guilt, but denies its liability. Even the term "affirmative action," which encompasses minority admissions programs, connotes the undertaking of remedial activity beyond what normally would be required. It sounds in *noblesse oblige,* not legal duty, and suggests the giving of charity rather than the granting of relief. The recipient class may request benefits, but is not entitled to receive them as a matter of legally enforceable right.

The presence of racism in policies intended to remedy racism is not generally recognized. Rather, as in the minority admissions debate, issues of cost and cost assessment disappear from view in complex and ultimately confusing legal discussion about the appropriate equal protection standard to apply to remedial measures embodying racial classifications. In *Bakke,* the Court clouded the matter further by burdening the nondiscriminatory admonition of Title VI of the Civil Rights Act of 1964 with a meaning not considered by Congress. It could have clarified the real issue by more attention to history and less reliance on legal precedent or moral philosophy.

. . . .

Viewed in historical perspective, Allan Bakke and his supporters are far from unique. Few among them would argue that the inferior social, economic, and political position of blacks in this country happened entirely by accident, and some would acknowledge that the inferior status of blacks conferred a relative advantage on whites. But Bakke's supporters resist any policy that appears to require that whites pay for racial wrongs that they did not themselves commit. The similar opposition to nineteenth century emancipation efforts supports a prediction that blacks, in one way or another, will pay most of the price for those affirmative action programs that survive the *Bakke* decision.

   . . . .

The Price and the Prize in Minority Admissions Policies

College and professional school affirmative action seemed a sensible response to mounting racial tensions caused by the failure of the civil rights movement to effect more substantive improvement in black opportunities and status. Special policies and processes enabled minorities, few of whom could expect to meet regular academic and financial requirements, to gain admission to elite schools.

Those regular admissions requirements, of course, posed a serious barrier to lower-class whites as well as to minorities. But as history enabled us to predict, the attacks from upwardly striving whites like Marco DeFunis and Allan Bakke focused neither on the exclusionary effect of the general admissions process nor on the most-favored-status it provided well-to-do applicants. Rather, their challenge took aim at the relatively minuscule number of seats set aside for minorities to ameliorate the harmful effects of past discrimination.

Certainly, the open use of racial classifications to identify the socially and economically disadvantaged left these programs legally vulnerable. But the reasons why special treatment for minority applicants upset working- and middle-class whites so much more than preferences for applicants whose parents are faculty members, alumni, or major contributors cannot be explained solely by the broad protection against racial classifications offered by the Fourteenth Amendment. Had Bakke's supporters succeeded in invalidating any consideration of race in the admissions process, they would have thwarted minority admissions programs without in any way countering the white, upper-class bias that permeates the admissions decisions of almost all colleges and professional schools.

The self-defeating nature of this strategy is evident. One would imagine that only a perverse form of racial paranoia can explain white opposition to racial remedies that, history teaches us, benefit whites more than blacks. For example, the generation-long struggle over school desegregation that began with the *Brown* decision has brought far more attention to the plight oi the public schools—and far more money and resources to improve their quality—than would ever have occurred had blacks not made the effort to achieve an "equal educational opportunity." Today, public schools are improved, but remain mainly segregated and unequal.

In the voting area, the federal courts for years refused to interfere with gerrymandered legislative districts that gave disproportionate political power to sparsely populated rural areas at the expense of urban districts. The successful black challenge to a blatantly discriminatory redistricting of Tuskegee, Alabama broke the Supreme Court's resistance to entering the "political thicket"; the "one man-one vote" cases soon followed. But these precedents have proven far more useful in correcting disparities in voting districts based on population than in ending those that aim to dilute the potential voting strength of blacks.

Consider also the development of student due process rights in school disciplinary proceedings, which grew out of black-sponsored litigation to protect student protesters from retaliatory suspension or expulsion.[8] These precedents have provided little protection to black students who are being expelled from desegregated schools in large numbers for a variety of suspect school violations. On the other hand, middle-class white students, better able to afford the lawyers and experts necessary to enforce due process, have deployed the new rights with impressive effect. Again, blacks have made the breakthrough under the banner of racial remediation, but the victory inures primarily to whites.

As suggested earlier, this process is recurring in the college admissions setting—special admissions criteria have expanded to encompass disadvantaged but promising white applicants. The open admissions program in New York City's university system, to cite one highly publicized example, came about as a result of minority pressure, but it is lower-middle-class whites who have been the chief beneficiaries.[9] In the more sensitive area of professional school admissions, affirmative action litigation and the spectre of future lawsuits probably encouraged some schools to give more emphasis to social and economic disadvantage and less to race.

Paradoxically, we cannot expect that opposition to minority admissions will disappear as colleges and professional schools expand their criteria to include whites whose promise is not reflected in grades and test scores. Working-class and upwardly striving middle-class whites perceive correctly that the share of educational opportunities available to their children is limited. That share, they believe, is threatened by programs designed to help minorities. Their belief gains force from the conviction that blacks are not supposed to get ahead of whites, and the realization that poor whites are powerless to alter the plain advantages in educational opportunity available to the upper classes.

Thus, the pattern of cost burden on black progress is not likely to end soon. It is the result of entrenched beliefs about the relative importance of white and black humanity. . . . Blacks progress only when the white majority perceives that progress is a clear benefit to whites, or at least not a serious threat. Black advancement requires major effort and sacrifice by blacks to change policies that likely have oppressed some whites as well as blacks. When the policy changes are effected, whites usually will prove the primary beneficiaries, and blacks will have paid the major cost. It is not the happiest prospect imaginable, but it outlines the route that minorities must take in reforming social injustices that frequently are not limited to one racial or ethnic group. The minority admissions issue is simply one leg of what remains a very long journey.

NOTES

1. In one case, Justice Powell cited ten law review articles, all of which were written by well-known white professors. See 438 U.S. 265, 279 n.25.

2. *See, e.g.,* Brief of Amicus Curiae, The National Conference of Black Lawyers (NCBL), Regents of the University of California v. Bakke, 98 S. Ct. 2733 (1978).

3. *Id.* at 1.

4. Petition of National Association for the Advancement of Colored People for Leave to File Amicus Curiae on Petition for Rehearing and Brief, Bakke v. Regents of the University of California, 18 Cal. 3d 34, 553 P.2d 1152, 132 Cal. Rptr. 680 (1976), *aff'd in part, rev'd in part,* 98 S. Ct. 2733 (1978).

5. Professor Ralph Smith details the jettisoned issues and lost opportunities as well as the efforts by minority groups to discourage taking the case to the Supreme Court. *See* Smith, *Reflections on a Landmark: Some Preliminary Ob-*

servations on the Development and Significance of Regents of the University of California v. Allan Bakke, 21 HOW. L.J. 72, 77–79 (1978).

6. ASSOCIATION OF AMERICAN MEDICAL COLLEGES, THE MCAT AND SUCCESS IN MEDICAL SCHOOL, *reprinted in* Petition of NAACP, *supra* note 4, app. B, at 4. The report states that "the 'black' group can 'succeed' in medical school with lower MCAT scores than the 'white' group, where success is narrowly defined as uninterrupted progress through the first two years in medical school."

7. Brief for Sanford H. Kadish, Dean of the School of Law, University of California, Berkeley; Pierre R. Loiseaux, Dean of the School of Law, University of California, Davis; William D. Warren, Dean of the School of Law, University of California, Los Angeles; Marvin J. Anderson, Dean of Hastings College of the Law, University of California, as Amici Curiae, On Petition for a Writ of Certiorari to the Supreme Court of California at 5.

8. *See, e.g.,* Tinker v. Des Moines Independent Community School Dist., 393 U.S. 503 (1989); Dixon v. Alabama Bd. of Educ., 294 F.2d 150 (5th Cir. 1961).

9. *See* Weiss, *Open Admission Found of Benefit to Whites, Too,* N.Y. TIMES, Dec. 29, 1978, pt. B, at 1, col. 8.

The Chronicle of the Sacrificed Black Schoolchildren

All the black school-age children were gone. They had simply disappeared.

No one in authority could tell the frantic parents more than they already knew. It had been one of those early September days that retain the warmth of summer after shedding that season's oppressive humidity. Prodded perhaps by the moderate weather, the pall of hateful racial invective that had enveloped the long desegregation battle lifted on what was to be the first day of a new school year. . . . Plaintiffs' lawyers had insisted on what one called a "full measure" of racial balance, while the school board and the white community resisted, often bitterly, every departure from the previous school structure.

Now it seemed all for nothing. The black students, every one of them, had vanished on the way to school. Children who had left home on foot never appeared. Buses that had pulled away from their last stop loaded with black children had arrived empty, as had the cars driven by parents or car pools. Even parents taking young children by the hand for their first day in kindergarten, or in pre-school, had looked down and found their hands empty, the children suddenly gone.

You can imagine the response. The media barrage, the parents' anger and grief, the suspects arrested and released, politicians' demands for action, analysts' assessments, and then the inevitably receding hullabaloo. Predictable statements were issued, predictable actions taken, but there were no answers, no leads, no black children.

Give them credit. At first, the white people, both in town and around the country, were generous in their support and sincere in the sympathy

From *And We Are Not Saved* by Derrick Bell 102 (1987). Copyright © 1987 by Basic Books, Inc. Reprinted by permission of Basic Books, a member of Perseus Books, L.L.C.

they extended to the black parents. It was some time before anyone mentioned publicly what, early on, many had whispered privately: that while the loss was tragic, perhaps it was all for the best. Except in scruffy white neighborhoods, "all for the best" never quite escalated to "good riddance."

Eventually it might have. After all, statistics showed the life chances for most of the poor children were not bright. School dropouts at an early age; no skills; no jobs; too early parenthood; too much exposure to crime, alcohol, drugs. And the city had resisted meaningful school desegregation for so long that it was now possible to learn from the experience of other districts that integrating the schools would not automatically insulate poor black children from the risks of ghetto life.

Even after delaying school desegregation for several years, many white parents bitterly opposed the now-unneeded plan on the ground that "their schools" might have to have a 50 percent enrollment of black children to enable the school system to achieve racial balance, the primary goal of the desegregation plan and its civil rights sponsors. So high a percentage of black children, these parents charged, would destroy academic standards, generate discipline problems, and place white children in physical danger. But under all the specifics lay resentment and the sense of lost status. Their schools would no longer be mainly white—a racial status whites equated with educational quality, even when the schools were far from academically impressive.

Black parents had differed about the value of sending their children to what had been considered white schools. Few of these parents were happy that their children were scheduled, under the desegregation plan, to do most of the bus riding—often to schools located substantial distances from their homes. Some parents felt that it was the only way to secure a high quality education because whites would never give black schools a fair share of school funds, and as some black parents observed: "Green follows white."

Others, particularly those whose children were enrolled in the W. E. B. Du Bois School—an all-black, outstanding school with a national reputation—were unhappy. Du Bois's parents had intervened in the suit to oppose the desegregation plan as it applied to their school. Their petition read:

> This school is the fruit of our frustration. It is as well a monument of love for our children. Our persistence built the Du Bois School over the

system's opposition. It is a harbor of learning for our children, and a model of black excellence for the nation. We urge that our school be emulated and not emasculated. The admission of whites will alter and undermine the fragile balance that enables the effective schooling black children need to survive societal hostility.

We want our children to attend the Du Bois School. Coercing their attendance at so-called desegregated schools will deny, not ensure, their right to an equal educational opportunity. The board cannot remedy the wrongs done in the past by an assignment policy that is a constitutional evil no less harmful than requiring black children to attend segregated schools. The remedy for inferior black schools that some seek from the courts we have achieved for ourselves. Do not take away our educational victory and leave us "rights" we neither need nor want.

The district court denied the Du Bois School's petition. Under the desegregation plan, two-thirds of the Du Bois students were to be transferred to white schools located at the end of long bus rides, to be replaced by white children whose parents volunteered to enroll them in an outstanding school.

In fact, Du Bois School patrons were more fortunate than many parents whose children were enrolled in black schools that were slowly improving but lacked the Du Bois School's showy academic performance. Most of these schools were slated for closure or conversion into warehouses or other administrative use. Under a variety of rationales, the board failed to reassign any of the principals of the closed black schools to similar positions in integrated schools.

Schools in white areas that would have been closed because of declining enrollment gained a reprieve under the school-desegregation plan. The older schools were extensively rehabilitated, and the school board obtained approval for several new schools, all to be built in mainly white areas—the board said—the better to ensure that they would remain academically stable and racially integrated.

Then, in the wake of the black students' disappearance, came a new shock. The superintendent called a special press conference to make the announcement. More than 55 percent of the public school population had been black students, and because state funding of the schools was based on average daily attendance figures, the school system faced a serious deficit during the current year.

The system's financial crisis, the superintendent explained, contained several additional components:

Teacher Salaries. Insisting that desegregation would bring special stresses and strains, the teacher's union had won substantial pay raises, as well as expensive in-service training programs. The district had hired and trained a whole corps of teacher aides to assist teachers with their administrative chores. Many newly hired teachers and all the aides would have to be released.

School Buses. To transport students under the desegregation plan, the board had ordered one hundred buses and hired an equal number of new drivers. The buses, the superintendent reported, could be returned. Many had made only one trip; but the new drivers, mechanics, service personnel, and many of the existing drivers would have to be laid off.

School Construction. Contracts for rehabilitation of old schools and for planning and building new schools had placed the board millions of dollars in debt. The superintendent said that hundreds of otherwise idle construction workers were to have been employed, as well as architectural firms and landscape designers. Additional millions had been earmarked for equipment and furniture suppliers, book publishers, and curriculum specialists. Some of these contracts could be canceled but not without substantial damage to the local economy.

Lost Federal Funds. After the courts ordered desegregation, the board applied for and received commitments for several million dollars in federal desegregation funds. These grants were now canceled.

Lost State Funds. Under the court order, the state was obligated to subsidize costs of desegregation; and, the superintendent admitted, these appropriations, as well as the federal grants, had been designated to do "double duty": that is, while furthering school-desegregation efforts, the money would also improve the quality of education throughout the system by hiring guidance counselors and sufficient new teachers to lower the teacher-pupil ratio.

Tax Rates. Conceding that the board had won several increases in local tax rates during the desegregation process, the superintendent warned that, unless the public agreed to double the current rate, the public schools would not survive.

Annexations. Over the last several years, the city had annexed several unincorporated areas in order to bring hundreds of additional white students into the public school system and slow the steady increase in the percentage of black students. Now the costs of serving these students added greatly to the financially strapped system.

Attorney Fees. Civil rights attorneys had come under heavy criticism after it came out that the court had awarded them $300,000 in attorney fees for their handling of the case, stretching back over the prior five years. Now the superintendent conceded that the board had paid a local law firm over $2,000,000 for defending the board in court for the same period.

Following the school superintendent's announcement, the mayor met with city officials and prepared an equally lengthy list of economic gains that would have taken place had the school-desegregation order gone into effect. The president of the local chamber of commerce did the same. The message was clear. While the desegregation debate had focused on whether black children would benefit from busing and attendance at racially balanced schools, the figures put beyond dispute that virtually every white person in the city would benefit directly or indirectly from the desegregation plan that most had opposed.

Armed with this information, local government appropriated a large sum to conduct a massive search for the missing black children. For a time, searchers held out hope, but eventually abandoned the quest. The children were never found, their abductors never apprehended. Gradually, all in the community came to realize the tragedy's lamentable lesson. In the monumental school desegregation struggle, the intended beneficiaries had been forgotten long before they were lost.

CHAPTER 9

Pedagogy

An innovative and popular teacher, Bell has long been interested in pedagogy and the art of teaching. Some of his writings center on the special challenges facing black students in white schools, or on the role of teachers, curricular planners, school boards, and textbook writers in presenting black history. Others concern themselves with classroom dynamics and with how to structure courses so as to secure the greatest degree of student engagement and participation. Should white (or black) teachers shy away from discussing sensitive topics, such as slavery? Bell says no, but offers advice on how to approach these barbed subjects. He also encourages teachers and administrators to endorse humanistic values in their teaching and not aim for an unobtainable objectivity.

Humanity in Legal Education

[Eds. Writing prior to assuming his position as Dean of the University of Oregon Law School in 1980, Professor Bell explains that what is needed in legal education is ethical training, better fiscal support for programs, and more effective teaching methods.]

Legal education has become an increasingly complex and expensive business. This is due, in part, to modern pedagogy's return to the idea that students learn to practice best by practicing. Most nineteenth-century lawyers were trained in law offices, rather than in the law schools. Clinical courses, in which students assist clients or prepare for practice through simulation, lead the way to the future by emulation of the past. While these offerings excite all but the most dedicated disciples of Christopher Columbus Langdell, they must irritate critics of ever-increasing law school budgets, who conclude that we have replicated the nineteenth-century clerkship but at a much higher cost.

The purpose of these reforms is more than the transformation of law schools into vocational institutes. Experiments reveal that able and diligent lay persons with no law school training can pass bar exams with no more preparation than that provided by a good bar review course. Indeed, that bar review courses not only exist but flourish should give those of us in academia pause about the value of our efforts.

Teaching legal skills then, as challenging and difficult as this may be, cannot be the sole justification for a law school. Our highest responsibility is to change lay people into professionals. The process by which we accomplish such a change must also strengthen character, increase sensitivity to humanitarian concerns, and deepen moral values. Too often law schools have done just the opposite.

59 Or. L. Rev. 243 (1980). Used by permission.

Lawyers need conscience as well as craft. To borrow an old but picturesque phrase, skilled lawyers without conscience are like loose guns on a sinking ship, their very presence so disconcerting that they wreak damage whether or not they hit anything. It is said that teaching morality is not possible, or that it is not the function of a law school. That may be true. But even so, law school faculty and administrators must instill ethical values in students through coursework and by example. Lawyers must have the courage to apply conscience, as well as competence, in each situation they face. This courage must be taught, nurtured, and practiced on a daily basis if it is to serve reliably in times of crisis.

Roger Fisher, a former colleague at Harvard, begins his course in Professional Responsibility by suggesting that each student prepare his or her obituary as they hope it will be written after their death. Fisher claims that this exercise creates the correct frame of mind for studying the Canons of Legal Ethics. It seems to me that it also provides a valid perspective for living a worthwhile life. We need more such reminders that law school should prepare us for service, and that our professional and personal success must come through that service.

. . . .

The real shame of political and corporate scandals is not that officials should prove susceptible to a patently risky temptation. It is rather that the free enterprise system leads so many people to believe that today's promises of power and big money, no matter how empty, are an acceptable trade for integrity. . . . I am convinced that those lawyers who best serve their clients are those who maintain a close check on the condition of their souls. . . . I hope to emulate that aspect of leadership.

No law school can produce lawyers able to meet this challenge if it lacks the financial resources necessary to attract high-level faculty members and to develop new programs better-suited to its students. . . . Promising students, white and minority, should not be forced to choose schools based on financial aid packages alone. Faculty should be able to lure some of these students as research assistants. The faculty themselves should have research leaves, and paid research time during the summer months.

Schools need all that and more if graduates are to be proud of the education they have received. The selection of the right school is a momentous decision, immutable once graduation is past. Any alumnus can testify about the many occasions during a professional career when a lawyer is identified with his or her alma mater. The identifications are more satisfying when alumni can refer to the school with pride.

That pride is more justified where graduates have made and honored a commitment to give back to the school at least as much as it has given them. If these have been satisfying years, this commitment should be easy. If they were not, the commitment is necessary to help make the school in the future those things it has not been in the past. Schools should perform a role and deserve the support of all those connected with the profession, alumni and non-alumni alike.

Brown v. Board of Education served as a signal to all Americans that the ideals of equality and educational opportunity must not be simply preached on the Fourth of July, but should be practiced throughout the year. It was a great decision because it was right—more importantly because the Court, one of our major institutions, placed itself at substantial risk to proclaim that truth. The Court's decision has not eliminated injustice, racial or otherwise, but this nation has come closer to that goal than many thought would ever be possible.

Despite my qualifications and experience, the Oregon Law School faculty by offering me this job also took a risk, and thereby conveyed their signal that the spirit of *Brown* survives. The student body has concurred in that signal in many ways which have been both complimentary and reassuring to me. It would not have been easy to turn away from the challenge they have offered. I have always been attracted to individuals and institutions willing to take risks.

My appointment is in keeping with my predecessor Eugene Scoles' remark, made in this journal when he assumed the deanship twelve years ago: "A law school must be a place where things are tried."[1] Then Dean Scoles warned that not all experiments succeed, but that risk of failure is the prerequisite for any success. Dedication, hard work, and the willingness to take appropriate risks have resulted in a law school that has served its state well and should guide it through the difficulties and challenges of the future.

NOTE

1. Scoles, *Challenge and Response in Legal Education,* 48 OR. L. REV. 129, 140 (1968).

The Law Student as Slave

Several years ago, I considered teaching a course on the law of slavery. In trying to ascertain student interest, I asked a black student whether he might consider enrolling. "No sir," he replied. "I don't need a course to teach me that the law of slavery was a whip."

Complex issues of law grew out of the Constitution's recognition of property in human beings, of course, but the violence of the gun and the lash was the essential force that enabled white men to reduce blacks to little more than commodities. . . . Failure to obey all orders would result in immediate death or punishments from which death would seem a welcome release.

Survival as a slave meant more than compliance with all orders; it also required the adoption of a servile demeanor that conveyed to the master a sense of total subordination. Indeed, slaves found it worthwhile to exhibit behavior that indicated they were not worthy of better than they received, that they were shiftless, without either cares or feelings, and were suitable subjects for a life of endless toil.

Under this slave mentality, the victims' hatred of the master could actually be transformed into an unthinking regard and respect. . . .

. . . Under slavery, that many blacks escaped and in other ways rebelled against the system is truly amazing. But for most, the strong drive was to survive and hope for a better day, if not in this life, then in heaven.

By this point, I hope you begin to see some relationship between the total physical domination of a people that accompanied slavery and the more subtle, though still effective, subordination of self that occurs in legal education.

. . . Law students are threatened with neither death nor the whip, but modern society has imposed quite effective facsimiles in the form of the

11 Student Lawyer, Oct. 1982, at 18. Used by permission.

competitiveness needed to get into law school, the ambition and determination to do well, and the sense that success will be aided by an accepting attitude toward whatever does or doesn't happen to you during the process of learning law.

The goal is to get a degree, to avoid all confrontations with persons in authority, and to defer service activities and good works until you are well established in your practice. Of course, in most cases the avoidance and deferment become a life-time pattern that, as with the slaves, continues naturally and without thought long after the original motivation is forgotten.

Your fear is not of death but of failure. Your chains are forged not of iron, but of the magnetic force of money, status, and professional recognition and acclaim. These fetters can be as effective a restraint on liberty as was the slave's desire to live and avoid the lash. But wealth and recognition are not the modern equivalent of the freedom sought so fervently by African slaves. Meaningful survival—as slaves like Nat Turner, Harriet Tubman, Gabriel Prosser, and Frederick Douglass learned—requires risk, confrontation, and revolt.

. . . Here and now I call on law students to lead a revolution that is much overdue and sorely needed.

The subjugated people who must be freed are not the benighted and beleaguered citizens of some exploited Third World country. They are not the millions around the world living under what superpatriots in this society call godless communism. Rather, they are the students of the law schools in this country.

The time has come to stop ignoring your subjugated state, to stop rationalizing the pain and suffering you are experiencing, and to recognize that law school need not be a degrading and educationally inefficient three-year period of travail. It need not be a confusing, traumatic, and overwhelmingly boring gauntlet to be traversed, in pain, by all those who seek the keys to the law and law practice.

And, most important, learning to think like a lawyer need not and should not mean that you must stop thinking, acting, and feeling like a human being.

Why should you want to revolt against law school? Let me count the ways:

1. Law students are not getting their money's worth.

With its reliance on large classes, instructed by relatively small faculties via the casebook and Socratic teaching methods, with student achievement measured by the sudden-death final exam, a law school is the most cost-effective and profitable enterprise in a university. . . .

. . . But academic entities are most resistant when outside agencies threaten sources of funding, and because law faculties are better paid than their colleagues in other parts of the universities—a fact those colleagues never tire of mentioning—law school administrators are at a disadvantage when they seek an accounting of law school tuitions and a more fair apportionment of university funds. Reform is delayed and forgotten because law students continue paying their term bills without complaint.

2. Law school teaching is inadequate.

Law schools are the only professional training institutions I know of in which many of the teachers have little or no actual experience in doing what they are supposed to be teaching their students to do: practice law. When they select faculty members, law schools give priority to applicants who attended nationally known schools, earned high grades, edited the law review, and held prestigious judicial clerkships. There is no closer correlation between such qualifications and effective teaching than between the bar exam and good lawyering.

Most law schools provide no instruction in teaching, and at many schools teachers who do so poorly that they receive devastating student evaluations are allowed to proceed unsupervised until their tenure review. And tenure will likely be granted to a promising scholar even if his or her teaching is quite poor.

3. Law school tenure is a barrier to effective education.

Faculty tenure at the law school level is a contradiction in terms that serves neither students nor teachers. If we in law teaching insist that market forces require that we earn at least close to what our counterparts in private practice earn, why the need for job protection? Perhaps the comfort of job security has encouraged some professors to undertake long-term scholarly projects that are controversial or that bring no immediate remuneration, but that security could also be the reason so many law teachers publish so little after they receive tenure.

Certainly it is too late in the game to claim that tenure protects academic freedom. Few who stray too far from academic orthodoxy receive appointments—much less tenure. Even those with tenure receive little protection if their words or actions—inside the classroom or out—depart too far from the economic and social norms.

I recognize that the debate over the value of tenure is far from settled. But whatever its value as status, as security, and as the crucial support for academic freedom, tenure is the antithesis of the meritocracy so much proclaimed during the recent years of affirmative action.

Where is the merit of a system that fills a faculty with people who, having at some time in the past satisfied their colleagues as to their teaching ability and scholarly enterprise, are thereby entitled to hold their chairs until retirement or death?

. . . .

4. Law school endangers human values.

Law school curricula are woefully inadequate in preparing students to live as competent, caring professionals for whom integrity in the face of temptation and service beyond the call of the canons of ethics are the cornerstones of their careers and lives. That many lawyers' accomplishments reflect commitment to these ideals is a tribute to their characters; law schools can take little credit.

This last point, of course, is the most serious indictment of law schools and represents the greatest challenge to law students.

Somehow in the process of teaching, we in the law schools manage to dehumanize our students. . . .

. . . .

It is not enough that law school is not as bad as it used to be. *The Paper Chase* is not a fit model against which you can measure your law school's functioning or by which you can determine the present state of your academic subordination. Teachers often say with sly satisfaction that students are the worst consumers in the world. The less they get for their money, the happier they are. But such teachers mistake for consumer apathy what is a pathetic acceptance of an overpoweringly oppressive system that seems beyond students' abilities to change. . . .

Law students cannot look to those of us in the teaching profession for salvation. We are like the slave masters of an earlier time, part of the problem. For just as slave-owners prior to the Civil War could claim that such property in people was an economic necessity, so law teachers and administrators today can state, and quite convincingly, that budgetary realities and educational traditions determine how today's legal education is organized. . . . The law schools in America will not provide their students with the quality of education they need and deserve if they are not forced to do so. Upon that point one may speak with a dogmatism that all history justifies.

Law students would do well to borrow the battle cry of Harlem activist Preston Wilcox: "Nobody can free you but yourselves." Your time in the purgatory of law school is brief, the difficulty in bringing about real change is great, and the risks of too vigorously pushing to alter the status quo are quite real. But the damage you and all other law students suffer by not challenging the current system "generates a feeling of inferiority as to their status in the community that may affect their hearts and minds in a way unlikely ever to be undone." The insertion of Chief Justice Earl Warren's famous lines from *Brown v. Board of Education* is both intentional and appropriate.

Law students are understandably concerned that all of their work, sacrifice, and trauma will provide no more than the barrier of a bar exam and no job opportunities.

The gruesome statistics are well known. In legal education, as in most other aspects of our society, the principles of the free market simply do not work. Many forces push undergraduates toward law school: the dismal job prospects in the traditional liberal and fine arts graduate programs, desire for independence accompanying professional status, the flexibility law offers those who have no specific career goals, and even—in some cases—idealism.

. . . .

In reaction—and not surprisingly—law students have tended to become more conformist, more supportive of the status quo, more determined to accept rather than challenge. The protest/reform era of decades ago has almost vanished from our halls, replaced by a fierce and often inhumane competitiveness that manifests itself not simply in better class attendance and more filled seats in the law library, but in taking liberties with exam rules and paper requirements, and even stealing or defacing library books so as to gain an advantage over classmates.

. . . Students are not willing to protest too loudly or vigorously the failure of most schools to make more than token curriculum reform, or to depart from traditional hiring practices except in [token ways]. . . .

No law student strikes that I know of have demanded that teachers reserve a reasonable number of hours per week for out-of-class student contact, or that they base final grades on more than one long final exam. Women petition for more women teachers with growing success, while blacks continue urging that more black teachers be hired with steadily diminishing success, but few insist that all teachers be hired on the basis of standards that include a keen interest in students and a commitment to teach based on both a knowledge of the subject matter and actual and impressive experience in practicing what he or she intends to teach.

. . . I can assure you that little reform of significance can take place until you demand that it does. The obstacles are many, the personal risks are real, and the chances for meaningful victories are not great. But as many blacks have learned (and their obstacles to inclusion in this society make your law school challenges seem almost petty), an important form of liberation comes from attacking the status quo, confronting the obstacles, and taking a stand against injustices.

As the slavery experience has shown, the subordination of a group can have fearful and long-term consequences. The marks of oppression are real and tend to be indelible. Freedom can come only through struggle, confrontation, and a fierce belief that your integrity and freedom are more important than success as this world measures it.

It is time to free yourselves, move your law schools toward liberation, and thereby increase the chances that you and the lawyers who follow you will have the courage as well as the skill to provide this country the leaders we so desperately need—leaders for whom the bottom line is not dollars earned but personal integrity and public service.

Pedagogical Process
Active Classroom and Text as Resource

Over the years, I have found that student interest and learning are enhanced if they are actively engaged in the learning and teaching process. An analogy to driving a car, or riding a bicycle, may not be exact, but as with skills requiring coordination of many faculties, understanding and advocacy of constitutional issues improve greatly with practice.
. . . .

The design of Constitutional Law, as I teach it, is the antithesis of the traditional inculcation of "passivity as the norm" so common in legal education. In my experience—and as my students frequently have told me—students do vastly more work, and learn more from, an engaged teaching methodology that requires them to perform very much like the lawyers they will soon become. The demands on individual students mimic, in many ways, the world of practice and require that they assume substantial personal responsibility for their professional education. Law students gracefully rise to the challenge and meet it with a competence that might surprise some educators.

My text's substantial departure from the norm in Constitutional casebooks supports "learning by doing" simulations, mimicking the kind of process that an attorney, researching an unfamiliar area of law, might employ to investigate prior decisions. In practice, lawyers are called to research and to write; to comprehend legal arguments; to guess at the probable effect of and interaction between judicial, statutory, legal, and policy arguments in court; to argue, persuade, and debate; to work cooperatively with colleagues; and for some, to judge those arguments and decide cases and issues of law. This is as true in the practice of Constitutional

Constitutional Conflicts xlviii (1997). Used by permission.

Law as in any other area. Once their research skills are in place, most students are aware that they have the capacity to learn, relatively quickly, whatever they need or want to know regarding any legal question.

Students often discover that they are drawn to teaching while they are in law school, but few at that time experience the responsibility for conveying the substance and debates pertaining to a given topic to other students. Some are drawn to scholarly debate, embark on careers which contribute to the intellectual life of the profession, and go on to teach. As these students argue a contested question of law in a manner sufficiently persuasive to sway their peers, they master areas of Constitutional Law in much the same way as does a teacher: well enough clearly to explain the concept to a law student. This early experience of the demands of teaching is helpful both to students who already know they may want to teach, and to alert those who would make excellent teachers but have not yet considered teaching as a career option. The value of the process is not limited, however, to those specific few who will enter teaching.

The process I employ in the classroom is a model rather than a rigid formula. It could be altered to fit class size and student and teacher inclination. The key is to replace a basically passive procedure, consisting of assigned reading and lecture listening, with one requiring active engagement, similar to the multiple aspects of practice, teaching, and judicial functions. For all the pressures of the legal curriculum, students give every indication of welcoming responsibility, opportunity, and challenge. For myself, I find that I learn from my students' fresh encounters with the Constitution, as we look at new questions and question old answers. Potentially, such a procedure allows us to approach the Paulo Freire ideal: that students become teachers and teachers become learners.

One Approach

For my part, I alter and try to improve the course each time I teach it. Most recently, 80 students and I met for three hours, twice a week. Prior to the first meeting, students reviewed all the hypothetical cases and, following a selection process, each was assigned both as an "advocate," who would brief and argue one case, and a "co-chief justice" on a different case. I placed these selections in a "class docket" that served as a course syllabus. After the first few introductory classes, each class featured the argument, discussion, and decision of one of the hypothetical cases. The advocates for each side prepared and submitted a four to six page brief setting out their arguments and supporting authority. These were reproduced and distributed to the class at least one period prior to the scheduled argument.

I began each class with a fifteen- to twenty-minute overview of the subject matter. Then, I turned the class/court over to the co-chief justices who called on each advocate for a five- to ten-minute uninterrupted summary of their arguments. The advocates then responded to questions from the co-chief justices and the rest of the class (associate chief justices). During this process that usually lasted for about an hour, I injected comments and questions intended to insure coverage and to raise perspectives the students had not raised in their questioning. The class almost always asked more questions than time permitted. At some point, the questioning moved to a general discussion about how the case should be decided and why. The latter process was intended to resemble the Supreme Court's conferences. Toward the end of the class . . . each of the associate justices turned in an "opinion sheet" indicating how each voted along with a summary of the reasons for that vote. The written votes are placed in an associate's file maintained for each student. Only students who have been present for the argument and conference can submit written votes. Copies of the written votes are provided for the co-chief justices who prepare a summary opinion reviewing the factors that influenced the class vote and quoting apt portions of individual students' opinion sheets. These summary opinions are subsequently reproduced and distributed to the class.

Within a few weeks following each hypo presentation, the co-chief justices who heard the case prepared a final exam question covering the subject matter of their hypo. The question could be a variation of the hypothetical facts or might be an entirely new question covering the appropriate subject area. By the end of the course, we had a packet of final exam questions equal to the number of hypotheticals presented. Each student received one of these packets and I reviewed each of the questions during the final class sessions. During the final class, each student learned for the first time which of the exam questions to answer. I assigned them at random, taking care not to give a student a question based on the one he or she argued or helped write. Students had one hour on an open book basis to write an answer to the question received. At the conclusion of the exam, I collected the answers identified only by the student's exam number, sorted them, and gave them to the chief justice teams who wrote the questions. These teams then spent an hour or more reviewing the answers and writing comments on them. I read both the answer and the comments.

To determine student grades, I averaged each student's hypo presentation, final exam grade, the quality of the daily opinion papers, and the work as a team preparing the summary opinion memo and the final exam question. In addition to a grade, I prepared a two to three page memorandum for each student reviewing and commenting on their work in the course. This process is time-consuming, but the classes are always interesting, and the memo-writing, while laborious, is not as burdensome as grading final exams.

Final Words

Again, the course procedure deviates markedly from a number of law school teaching norms. It does not assume that the teacher is all-knowing and thus should occupy center stage in the classroom. Rather, by decoupling several traditional aspects of legal instruction, it frees the student to learn to analyze and perform independently. The instability and malleability of constitutional law doctrine render certainty a myth and *stare decisis* a fiction. The teacher can guide students through the precedential confusion, but primarily must impart, through experience, the knowledge that each student is competent to do so. I find that this guidance is most effective as the students seek to find their own way through the thicket of conflicting rules and multi-opinioned decisions. While students must grasp the concepts key to the making of a Constitutional argument, it is quite clear that because Supreme Court decisions defy even the most skilled efforts to explain or harmonize as neutral, or objective, interpretations of the Constitutional text—in itself a dubious exercise—the important point, the one each student should retain long after the case names fade from memory, is to understand that rather than a revered relic bequeathed by the Founding Fathers to be kept under glass and occasionally dusted, the Constitution is a living document, one locus of battle over the shape of our society, where differing prescriptive and proscriptive visions compete, over what is, what should be, and what will be.

For many students, the task-oriented circle process brings some of the participation-based excitement of moot court into the classroom. Students often, entering the classroom on the first day of Constitutional Law, and sensing that Con Law is in some way unique, feel a strong sense of anticipation. This course is likely to be, they have been told, the high point of their legal educations, where they will study and wrestle with the cases defining the legal conceptual foundations of our nation. As Con Law traditionally is taught, that anticipation is disappointed. For most the traditional exercise has been dusty dry, and none but the most resolute and rare of law students see the possibility of testing today's unresolved dilemmas on the battlefield of Constitutional Law as a project in which they themselves could engage.

As I teach Con Law, students spend long hours haggling over the facts in cases they are writing and practicing the arguments that they must present before their peers. The quality of case presentation varies, but my classes are far more exciting when students participate in this way than when I stand before them and try to "convey the word." In fact, students are far more ready to listen to my views after they have struggled with their own cases. Certainly, whether they adopt or reject my views, they are deeply engaged: they have experienced the Constitution as a living document, one with contested meaning, greatly influenced by historical context, a vehicle capable of conveying and sustaining a moral vision.

As to final exams, I have always believed that much of the learning potential in law school final exams is wasted on the teacher. The real learning comes in writing the exam questions. Indeed, it is impossible to write a decent question without a fairly good knowledge of the material. Students studying to take exams written by the teacher certainly hone their knowledge of the subject, but it is a passive-defensive process (what is the s.o.b. going to hit us with). When, on the other hand, students, working with others, write an exam question, they are actively engaged in shaping the facts and the issues. They are motivated to do their best in formulating a question that some of their classmates must answer. They realize that while they will grade the answers, their classmates will be judging them as well. Taking responsibility for a job well done can take precedence over grades when we provide a structure that makes this possible.

Students seldom grade other students at the law school level. Competition for good grades, it is assumed, will over-power honesty and integrity. That has not been my experience. Student circles usually spend long hours discussing the relative merits of the answers they are grading. Their comments are usually right on target and far more detailed than students usually receive from even the most conscientious teacher. In my overall grading, I usually comment on the comments, but I seldom have to correct statements that are either wrong or wrong-headed. Students are also a bit astounded to find that they cannot bring themselves to recommend an undeserved "A" for an exam paper: they prepared the question, have an idea of what would comprise an excellent response, and differentiate between better and worse with sudden understanding that grading, while no science, is also not entirely random. . . . Con Law courses, while often large, are taught far more like seminars where students usually receive more individual attention and do better work on papers than they might on a traditional final exam. I provide each student with a multi-page memorandum summarizing performance on each course component. My grades are usually higher than the guidelines recommend, but I have copies of my memos to explain the reason for those grades.

For most students, grades become a secondary consideration to the benefits they gain from learning constitutional law on a participatory basis. It is said of a great teacher that "he taught as a learner, led as a follower, and so set the feet of many in the way of life." That is quite a model. It moves me to close with the admission that more important than teaching structure or technique or writing style or jurisprudential philosophy is the effort of all successful teachers who succeed in communicating not only subject but self.

We all know that the memorable teachers in our lives hold that status even though we do not recall a single thing they taught us. Rather, we remember them as enviable individuals who spurred us to learn on our own both the subject matter and ourselves. In the law school curriculum, few courses are better suited than constitutional law as vehicles for the accomplishment of this transference.

Victims as Heroes

A Minority Perspective on Constitutional Law

Recently, a black student sought my help in his and several classmates' efforts to persuade a first-year property teacher to include a component on the significance of slavery to the development of American property law. The teacher, recalling past complaints when he offered a slaves-as-property course segment, was reluctant to assent to the students' request. I begged off intervening, citing the traditional discretion that faculty members exercise in regard to the content of their colleagues' courses.

Actually, the students have a point, although it is one more appropriately addressed to constitutional law scholars than to those who teach the first-year property course. For it was in the wearying negotiations that led to our Constitution that the framers' idealism regarding the worth of the individual collided with their more pressing, pragmatic concern for the protection of vested property and political status based on wealth. It was a dilemma that would arise repeatedly in our history and that would usually be resolved according to the framers' response to the slavery dispute. As if tacitly recognizing the impossibility, within a slave economy, of a government that would protect life, liberty, *and* property, they chose to protect property interests, even when that decision necessitated the legally sanctioned enslavement of roughly 20 percent of the population.

Jurists, scholars, and others engaged in giving contemporary meaning to constitutional provisions readily acknowledge the presence of racial considerations in the original structure of the document. All agree that

The United States Constitution: Roots, Rights, and Responsibilities 163 (A. E. Dick Howard ed., 1992). Used by permission.

the slavery compromises reached between delegates from Southern and Northern states became the sine qua non without which no federal government would have been possible. Those compromises served to protect the property interests of slaveowners at the cost of freedom for blacks, and to leave in place an inherent contradiction that the nation's basic legal document still retains.

What if one supposed that the slavery compromises of 1787 were merely an unhappy decision made under the pressure of the crisis of events and influenced by then-prevailing beliefs that (1) slavery was on the decline and would soon disappear of its own accord and (2) Africans were a different and inferior breed of beings. In that case the loyalty to property interests, even when it meant retention of a slave system, would have been fathomable, if not fully forgivable, and certainly no less sad. But the slavery compromises were too extensive to be dismissed as an oversight. The insistence of Southern delegates on protection of their slave property was far too vigorous to suggest that the institution would soon be abandoned. And the antislavery statements by slaves and white abolitionists alike were too forceful to suggest that the slavery compromises were the product of men who did not know the moral ramifications of what they did.[1]

The compromise of 1787 is much more than history. It is the original and still-definitive illustration of the ongoing struggle between individual rights reform and the maintenance of the socioeconomic status quo. . . . It is not the case that, like slavery itself, the country could not have come into being without the race-based compromises placed in the Constitution. It is simply that—as it happened—the economic benefits of slavery and the political compromises of black rights were thought to be essential to the growth and development of the nation.

. . . .

The decision was foreordained, predictable, and possessed of compelling logical force for the framers. Even Gouverneur Morris, the Convention's most outspoken opponent of slavery, had understood that "life and liberty were generally said to be of more value, than property, [but] an accurate, view of the matter would nevertheless prove that property was the main object of Society."[2] Chief Justice Roger B. Taney missed the point. It was not, as he proclaimed in *Dred Scott*, that the Constitution's commitment to individual liberty was not intended for Africans, but that the constitutional injunctions went to those who owned property—a qualification that excluded many whites as well as most blacks.

The Protection of Property in a Post-Revolutionary World

To the framers, the subordination of black rights in 1787 was acceptable, if not particularly welcome (as indicated by their celebrated refusal to "stain" the Constitution with the words "slave" or "slavery"). But at that time, Northerners as well as Southerners reaped the profits of slavery. Only avid (and mostly ignored) abolitionists and unrepresented (and mostly mute) slaves could decry the compromise that the framers were too ashamed to admit having made. But by 1857 the economic battle lines were plain. The differences between planters and businessmen, obscured seventy years earlier by shared vulnerability to the same dangers, could no longer be settled by the involuntary sacrifice of black rights. Justice Taney's conclusion that blacks had no rights that whites were bound to respect—a view rather clearly reflecting the prevailing belief of his time, and of the framers—was shocking less because it sought formally to remove all blacks from the ambit of constitutional protection than because it attempted to place the Supreme Court on one side of the fiercely contested issues of economic and political power that were propelling the nation toward civil war.

But after the Civil War amendments had been enacted and then cast aside, constitutional jurisprudence, while condemning Taney's opinion regarding the rights of blacks vis-à-vis whites, nevertheless fell in line with his conclusion. For the next seventy years, the Civil War amendments stood as definitive illustrations of the vulnerability of even constitutional provisions intended to protect the basic rights of blacks when those rights threatened the property and political interests of whites. With few exceptions, the Court's decisions in racial cases were marked by hostility and hypocrisy.

During the same era, the constitutional protections initially promoted to shield former slaves were transformed into the major legal bulwarks for corporate growth and the exploitation of working-class whites. . . . Compare *Lochner v. New York*[3] with *Plessy v. Ferguson*,[4] decided only eight years earlier, upholding the state's police power to segregate blacks on the basis of race, even though such segregation must, of necessity, interfere with the liberties of facilities' owners to use their property as they see fit. The Fourteenth Amendment, the Court insisted, did not guarantee "social equality" between the races.

Both opinions are quite similar in the Court's use of Fourteenth Amendment fictions: the economic liberty of bakers in *Lochner,* the political equality of blacks in *Plessy.* And both protected existing property and political arrangements, while ignoring the disadvantages to the powerless attributable to those relationships. In both decisions, Justice Harlan railed in dissent against the majority's refusal to recognize what they all knew: the injustice of declaring the law's formal equality in a grossly unequal world.

In *Lochner,* Harlan was morally right, but . . . he did not—as Justice Holmes did in his dissent—directly attack the Court's adoption of the laissez-faire economic philosophy that underlay the *Lochner*-era cases. In *Plessy,* though, Harlan urged—this time in line with that philosophy— that the state's segregation laws violated Fourteenth Amendment prohibitions by interfering with the personal liberty of citizens. He predicted, accurately enough, that segregation laws would signal the subordination by race of all blacks and would "permit the seeds of race hate to be planted under the sanction of law."[5] . . .

In his dissent, Harlan wrote: "Our Constitution is color-blind, and neither knows nor tolerates classes among citizens."[6] That now famous platitude was even more of a fiction than those upon which the majority relied. . . . In effect, the majority refused to take from whites the vested advantages of their whiteness, which included, in those days, the right not to associate with blacks in public facilities.

. . . The Court's "hands-off" attitude on segregation legislation that overrode principles of free association, occupational liberty, freedom of contract, and property rights was actually at odds with the freewheeling, laissez-faire constitutionalism of that era. Focus on the corporate charter did not obscure that fact. But in a period of rampant Negrophobia, seemingly supported by Social Darwinism, few beyond the justice Harlans and, of course, the blacks themselves were much concerned with judicial findings that state-sponsored restraints could further individual freedoms.

Justice Harlan failed to tell us how a color-blind Constitution could be expected to provide even the most basic protection to blacks in a country where, according to his own prideful admission in the same paragraph, the "white race deems itself to be the dominant race in this country." "And so it is," Harlan continued, "in prestige, in achievements, in education, in wealth and in power. So, I doubt not, it will continue to be for all time, if it remains true to its great heritage and holds fast to the principles of constitutional liberty."[7]

For the fact is that the general belief as to which race is dominant in the society has helped motivate—and justify—the many compromises in which the interests of blacks are bartered and sometime sacrificed to further accords between groups of whites. Over time, beliefs in white dominance, reinforced by policies that subordinate black interests to those of whites, have led—as the plaintiff in *Plessy* contended—to an unrecognized but no less viable property right in whiteness, an entitlement to those advantages gained over blacks by virtue of a white identity. . . . Ironically, now the passwords for gaining judicial recognition of the still viable white property right include "higher entrance scores," "seniority," and "neighborhood schools." And Justice Harlan's bold—if unrealistic—reminder that our Constitution is color-blind has become, in our time, the major argument of those who oppose all affirmative action remedies. . . .

Further examples could be cited, but the illustrations already given should help broaden recognition of the intricate relationship of race and political and social reform. Discrimination based on race provides a dramatic focus that reveals more subtle, though hardly less pernicious, disadvantages suffered by many whites. By looking carefully at black history, and the struggle for opportunity and dignity, one can also see there the history of most whites. Compulsive fascination with the difference in status between blacks and whites obscures the far more sizable gap between the status of most whites and that of the few who occupy the highest echelons of our society.

. . . .

Thus, in the long effort to gain equality through integration, blacks have learned that white America will accommodate the interests of blacks and other racial minorities when and *only* when those interests converge with those of whites. . . .

. . . The availability of constitutional protection for the society's disadvantaged—blacks, women, the poor, homosexuals, and the mentally and physically disabled—is not actually determined by the quantity of harm alleged or of liability proved. Social reform remedies, judicial and legislative, are instead the outward manifestations of unspoken and perhaps unconscious policy conclusions that the remedies, if granted, will secure, advance, or at least not harm societal interests deemed important by the middle and upper classes.

It is for this reason that racial and social justice—or their appearance—may from time to time be counted among the interests deemed important by the courts and by society's policymakers. Of course, in every reform movement since abolition, some individuals found the principles of justice and equality sufficient motivation. But, as with abolition, the number who will act on morality alone is insufficient to bring about the desired reform.

. . . .

Perhaps we may achieve our goal more readily if those of us teaching and writing about the Constitution begin more often to view it through the eyes of those whose only property was faith, who tried, and who continue to try, despite all the obstacles, to elevate that faith into constitutional protections of life and liberty, regardless of property, for all.

NOTES

1. WILLIAM M. WIECEK, THE SOURCES OF ANTISLAVERY CONSTITUTIONALISM IN AMERICA: 1760–1848, at 42–43 (1997).

2. 1 MAX FARRAND ED., THE RECORDS OF THE FEDERAL CONVENTION OF 1787, at 533 (1991).

3. 198 U.S. 45 (1905).

4. 163 U.S. 537 (1896).

5. 163 U.S. 537, 560 (1896).

6. 163 U.S. 537, 559 (1896).

7. 163 U.S. 537, 559 (1896).

CHAPTER 10

Racial Standing

Who has standing to speak for blacks? Can a white lead the black cause? And what of blacks who criticize black radicals and innovators? Are they traitors? Should they at least remain silent so as not to wash dirty linen in public? If a black accepts a high-visibility position in a white institution is he or she just a token who legitimizes a probably racist institution, or may he or she do some good by working from within? What should the civil rights community do about conservative blacks who embrace individualism, disavow affirmative action, and reassure whites by preaching that racism is dead and anyone can make it in America? Bell addresses these and similar topics having to do with role, courage, and misplaced passion.

The Law of Racial Standing

Minister Louis Farrakhan is back on national television. Yes, Farrakhan is back, and we bourgeois black folk will need to be ready because white America views this man as a big problem that can be solved—evidently —by making what is threatening for them a problem for us.

Personally, I am glad to see Farrakhan's return after about a two year absence from the national T.V. scene. Very smart and super-articulate, he is perhaps the best living example of a black man ready, willing, and able to "tell it like it is" regarding who is responsible for racism in this country.

. . . .

It does not matter whether you agree with me or not, each of you is going to have to deal with Minister Farrakhan. Or, more specifically, all of us have to deal with the media, colleagues at work, and friends any-place—many of whom will want our view (critical if possible) of Far-rakhan. . . .

. . . .

For many people, Minister Farrakhan is a black David going one-on-one against the Philistines that bestride the land, abusing their power and generally messing over black folk. But when Farrakhan issues his chal-lenge, no Goliath comes forth. Rather, some of the Philistines come run-ning, not to Farrakhan, but to any black person they can find, asking: "Did you hear what that man said about us? What are *you* going to do about it?"

Now, I have been asking myself: why must I do something about Min-ister Farrakhan? Those he condemns are not without power, not without money, not without guns. A sad history serves as proof that they know how to use all three. Why me?

2 Yale J. L. & Liberation 117 (1991). Used by permission.

"Oh," I am told, "that man is hurting your cause." But the cause of black people has been under attack for three hundred years, not by one black man, but by the dominant white society. The suggestion that our current plight would improve if Farrakhan would just shut up is both naive and insulting. It also reveals more about those who would silence him than they likely want uncovered.

Remember when, a few years ago, Farrakhan was scheduled to speak in, I think, Madison Square Garden in New York City. The then mayor ordered his black staffers not to go, but to speak out and denounce Farrakhan. Some did as they were told. Others, to their credit, refused to condemn and did attend. Again I ask, why them? Why me? Why us?

My friends, I think I have the answer and so does every lawyer in this room. The answer is in the law of standing. More specifically, the answer is in what I want to call "The Law of Racial Standing."

The standing doctrine requires the party who invokes the court's authority "to show that she personally has suffered some actual or threatened injury as a result of the putatively illegal conduct of the defendant," and that the injury "fairly can be traced to the challenged action" and "is likely to be redressed by a favorable decision."

A third year student who co-taught my civil rights seminar last Fall pointed me toward this special extra-legal form of standing. She noted that while the law grants litigants standing based on their having sufficient personal interest and stake in the issue to justify judicial cognizance, black people (while they may be able to get into court) are denied standing-type legitimacy when they discuss real world experiences with racism or attempt to give a favorable evaluation of another person of color's work. Our statements are deemed "special pleading" and thus not entitled to serious weight. If one of us recommends a person of color for a position or for a promotion the response will all too often contain the scarcely concealed question, "Who else likes this person?" We know *who* "who else" is.

When, as my first lawyering job, I went to work at the Justice Department back in 1957, there were only two or three black lawyers there. One of them, Maceo Hubbard, had been there for years and taught me a lot that I had not learned in law school. "When white folks ask you for an evaluation of another black," Maceo warned me, "you have to remember one thing. However carefully you can say it, you can hurt the brother, but you can't help him."

From this, one exception follows to the lack of standing rule. You guessed it. The exception occurs when blacks disparage blacks whose actions are upsetting whites. Suddenly, our statements are given greater value than they are worth. Thus, Thomas Sowell and Walter Williams gained national celebrity as experts on race based upon their willingness to minimize the effects of racism on the lowly status of blacks. That most blacks dispute these assessments is mostly ignored.

Similarly, when my colleague Randy Kennedy suggested that minority scholars have no special legitimacy in writing about race, and that their scholarship, measured by traditional standards, is flawed, his criticism was given enormous attention. "Even Randy Kennedy says their writing is bad." If Randy had written a piece lauding critical race writing, his article would have gained little attention. In fact, Randy has written a half-dozen fine articles giving white folks Hell. None of them has been covered by the *New York Times*.

. . . .

. . . When Lee Iacocca lauds Chrysler cars, we take his words with a grain of salt. But if he were to criticize Chrysler, it would be front-page news. Any laudatory statement by a person affiliated with a product or institution is viewed as to some extent, puffing. Criticism or whistle-blowing by an insider, on the other hand, wins immediate attention.

The problem is that a people's petitions protesting racism are a far cry from a company's product-enhancing puffery. Not only do listeners discount our complaints, they deem us untrustworthy in matters regarding race. . . . Unlike whites, we cannot be objective on matters of race and will favor our own regardless. It is that deep-seated belief that fuels a continuing effort—despite all manner of Supreme Court decisions intended to curb the practice—to keep black people off juries in cases involving race. Black judges hearing racial cases are eyed suspiciously and, sometimes, asked to recuse themselves in favor of a white judge without those making their request even being aware of the paradox in their motions.

But criticism of blacks doing or saying things upsetting to whites when that criticism comes from other blacks is welcomed with a special glee reflective of a character trait that, were it not so common, would be diagnosed as schizophrenia. Our critical comments are often distorted and, when the need arises, our criticism is magnified to censor, or our condemnation used to damage or destroy careers. In the case of Minister Farrakhan, those who don't like what he says want to use our criticism to isolate, separate, and silence him, not in the eyes of his followers, but in the minds of whites who believe that the threat he represents will dissipate by our responding to their plaintive plea: "Tell us it ain't so."

Consider the double standard here. One need not agree at all with Farrakhan's statement about Judaism being a gutter religion to understand that Israel has sought to hide many deeds against black Africans, black Jews, and the Palestinians under the cloak of religion. Moreover, when Farrakhan attempts to explain that his statement was aimed at Israel as a state and not Judaism as a religion, his explanation is rejected out-of-hand. The attitude seems to be: "You said it, and thus you must be condemned for all time."

The Reverend Jesse Jackson has experienced a similar "lifetime renunciation," notwithstanding his frequent and fervent apologies for his regrettable "Hymie" and "Hymie town" remarks made during his 1984 presidential campaign. I understand why a group is upset by what it deems racial or religious insults, but I doubt that I am alone in understanding why blacks who lack any real power in this society are not forgiven, while whites, including those at the highest levels of power, are pardoned. For example, many Jewish spokespeople complained bitterly when President Reagan went to Bitburg, but they do not continue to harass him everywhere he goes. No one denounced him as anti-Semitic for going. More significantly, neither President Bush nor whites who support him are called on to condemn Reagan in order to prove that they are not anti-Semitic.

One need not agree with Farrakhan that African Americans need to separate from this country to understand that, after three hundred years of trying and not yet having the acceptance in this country that non–English speaking white immigrants have on their first day on this soil, we need to be thinking (if not yet doing) something other than singing "We Shall Overcome." Whatever his rhetorical transgressions, Minister Farrakhan and his church are giving the most disadvantaged black people reason to hope when most of the country and more than a few of us have written them off. His television hosts have given him credit for cleaning up a neighborhood in Washington, and yet they question his motives for accomplishing what few government officials have even seriously tried.

I am troubled that some Jews view Farrakhan as anti-Semitic, even if they are wrong. But I am infinitely more disturbed by my helplessness in the face of the not-so-gentle genocide going on in our inner cities. If Farrakhan, whatever his views, is able to bring inspiration to a people who have every reason for despair; if he has the ability to back up his fiery rhetoric with grass roots projects that restore pride and safety to neighborhoods the nation has written off, then I am for Farrakhan.

When some of his advisors told President Lincoln that he should relieve General Grant of his command because of heavy drinking, Lincoln noted that Grant was the only Union Army leader able to win battles. Rather than chastise Grant, Lincoln ordered a keg of liquor sent to each of his generals. Lincoln was not advocating alcoholism, he was trying to win a war. Similarly, when we support Minister Farrakhan or at least refuse to criticize him publicly, we are not endorsing insensitive remarks, we are trying not to harm his effort to save a people. That people is ourselves.

I notice that those whites so anxious for me to "do something" about Farrakhan are not usually those who are themselves doing anything about the racism he condemns. Of course, I recognize that Farrakhan's statements can be hurtful to many whites who are doing a great deal to fight racism and alleviate its devastation. I think it correct that Farrakhan is not talking about such individuals but about the group to which they belong and the power that all members of that group—good and bad— are able to exercise over all of us in this society because we are black and they are white.

. . . .

We must be extremely sensitive to the dangers of our criticism. And, we must be candid and cautious about the rewards this society bestows on those blacks willing to denigrate a troublesome black. To the extent we deem it necessary, we can air our criticisms in private or in group sessions. Someday, such caution may be unnecessary, but that day is not yet. . . .

We know that poverty and joblessness are the major causes of inner-city despair. But when blacks suggest racism as a major cause of the problem, society remains determined to blame black victims. Even data from respected white sources are ignored when they do not conform to the comforting image. A recent study published in the prestigious *New England Journal of Medicine* found that in a recent period black men in Harlem were less likely to reach the age of 65 than men in Bangladesh. In the period studied, 2,421 people died needlessly—that is 800 a year more beyond the number that would have died if Harlem shared the health of the nation. Twenty-two percent of the excess deaths were due to homicide and drug abuse, but most were due to undetected cancer, strokes, and heart attacks due to high blood pressure.

You did not hear about this study? I am not surprised. Media coverage was scant. In contrast, an article in the same issue questioning the value of oat bran in controlling cholesterol received splashy coverage everywhere. Ralph Ellison's much acclaimed novel, *Invisible Man,* depicted a category of human beings whose suffering was so thoroughly ignored that they might as well not have existed. The only change in the thirty-eight years since that novel appeared is that the number of those suffering and ignored has increased.

. . . .

When we sought relief against discriminatory policies that were not racist on their face, like civil service tests, college admission standards, and trade union qualifications, but that, as administered, excluded blacks, many whites screamed foul and "reverse discrimination." That is why so many whites who profess to support civil rights oppose affirmative action and other remedies that may disadvantage so-called "innocent whites." None of this is new, but when blacks articulate the obvious, the old racial standing problem serves as an automatic jamming device so that our message never gets through.

As I say, Minister Farrakhan understands all of this and has decided that the only way to be heard over the racial standing barrier is to place the blame for racism where it belongs. Using language that is direct, blunt, even abrasive, he forthrightly charges those who do evil under the racial structure that protects them and persecutes us, that uplifts them regardless of merit, and downgrades us regardless of worth. If he is sometimes outrageous, who here will say that his words are more dangerous or more damaging than the outrages our people constantly suffer?

. . . .

Most of us work hard. We earned what we have and deserve to have a fine dinner in a beautiful setting, and to anticipate an evening of dancing at the end of a tough week. But if enjoyment is not sin, neither is a straight-talking Muslim minister who is willing to say what many of us think, while challenging the very foundations of the racism without which I am not sure this country can function.

. . . .

Thurgood Marshall

The news of Thurgood Marshall's death made page-one headlines throughout the nation. A flood of eulogies portrayed Marshall's life and accomplishments in superlatives usually reserved for heads of state. No one who scanned these obituaries could doubt that the nation had lost one of its most notable citizens.

Hosts of dignitaries, headed by the President of the United States, came to honor Marshall at his funeral in Washington's National Cathedral. Mourners from every level of society came to pay their respects to this lawyer, son of a Pullman porter, who for almost a quarter of a century as a Supreme Court Justice continued to speak for the disadvantaged. . . .

But . . . I believe that Justice Marshall would not have wanted these deceptive illusions embellished in eulogy; he recognized the vast difference between dedication to racial reform and the realization of improvement in the status of black people. Indeed, he was disdainful of the value of "role models" like himself in a society that deems racial tokenism both progress and proof that personal failings, and not racism, explain the meager achievements of so many blacks.

Several years ago, Justice Marshall returned to speak at his alma mater, Howard University. Refusing to indulge in the usual admonishments to hard work and sacrifice as the guarantors of success, he spoke candidly, and caustically, about the limited achievements of the civil rights movement:

> Today we have reached the point where people say, "We've come a long way." But so have other people come a long way. . . . Has the gap gotten smaller? It's getting bigger. . . . People say we are better off today. Better than what?

68 NYU L. Rev. 212 (1993). Used by permission.

I am amazed at people who say that, "the poorest Negro kid in the South is better off than the kid in South Africa." So what! We are not in South Africa. We are here. People tell me, "You ought to go around the country and show yourself to Negroes; and give them inspiration." For what? Negro kids are not fools. They know when you tell them there is a possibility that someday you'll have a chance to be the o-n-l-y Negro on the Supreme Court, those odds aren't too good.[1]

Marshall's audience of budding black professionals at Howard likely recognized with him that racial tokenism was of little value to young people, and a poor measure of the inadequate gains made in the struggle for equality to which he had dedicated his life. Of course, Thurgood Marshall, like it or not, was a model to black lawyers and law students across the country. I remember in the early 1960s, traveling across the South and working with those few black lawyers who, despite economic and physical risks, were willing to represent black people in civil rights cases. Thurgood Marshall was their hero. Thurgood knew most of these lawyers personally and had worked with them over many years. They all respected him as a great lawyer, as a good friend, and as living proof that black lawyers were capable of successfully handling important cases.

Many of these lawyers strategically placed a framed photograph of Marshall on their office wall, where clients could not miss seeing it. Burdened by the enduring stereotype of the black lawyer as an incompetent Calhoon of Amos and Andy programs, they hoped that Marshall's picture would help them to allay, if not eliminate, this unfortunate image.

. . . .

Though he denied it, many felt that Marshall left the Court an embittered man, having witnessed the dismantling of many precedents he had fought long and hard to establish. . . . But a likely greater source of bitterness was the mistaken faith that he and his colleagues in the civil rights movement had placed in the law. That blind faith all too often served to betray our clients, as well as the many other black people who relied on our counsel and pinned their hopes on our professional skill and commitment.

In retrospect, it is apparent that we placed our advocacy in the service of our integrationist ideals, ignoring in the process our personal knowledge of racism's resiliency. We viewed segregation as the prime barrier to black advancement, realizing too late that once segregation was vanquished by our sustained efforts, it would be replaced by "race-neutral" standards, a more sophisticated and even more invidious vehicle for maintaining white dominance.

Consider, for example, the strict scrutiny standard in equal protection analysis. Designed to protect discrete and insular minorities from majoritarian tyranny, the Supreme Court now interprets it to protect members of the majority against modest policies intended to remedy past injustices. Such reversals in legal doctrine, combined with the devastating incidence of poverty, unemployment, crime, and family destruction among blacks, are occurring despite, and not because of, the committed efforts of civil rights lawyers. And yet, we urged the use of law and litigation as the major means to end racial discrimination. We did so in good faith, but with an inadequate understanding of the limits of law and the pervasive role of racism in our society.

If Marshall was bitter at the close of his Supreme Court tenure, the source of that bitterness was not a group of conservative whites appointed to the Court during a conservative political era. Instead, I think he recognized that, despite a lifetime of struggle and accomplishments that ensure him a major place in American history, he—like many of us who tried to emulate him—had relied on the law only to discover that the system had transformed the rights for which we advocated into doctrines of neutrally imposed oppression.

Yet Marshall's recognition led him not to despair, but to call for continued struggle. In what was one of his last major speeches, Marshall said, "The battle for racial and economic justice is not yet won; indeed, it has barely begun."[2] Whatever his bitterness, he was still the pragmatic advocate.

Justice Marshall also warned against seeking sanctuary in the suburbs. "We cannot play ostrich. Democracy cannot flourish amid fear. Liberty cannot bloom amid hate. Justice cannot take root amid rage."[3] Rather, Marshall urged continued confrontation with the evils he had fought all of his professional life. No promise of victory here, no guarantee of success. He called us to seek the sense of salvation inherent in struggle for struggle's sake:

> We must go against the prevailing wind. We must dissent from . . . in-
> difference. We must dissent from . . . apathy. We must dissent from the
> fear, the hatred and the mistrust. We must dissent from a government
> that has left its young without jobs, education, or hope. We must dissent
> from the poverty of vision and the absence of moral leadership. We must

dissent because America can do better, because America has no choice but to do better.[4]

NOTES

1. Justice Thurgood Marshall, speech at Howard University (Nov. 18, 1978), *in* THE BARRISTER, Jan. 15, 1979, at 1, *reprinted in* DERRICK BELL, AND WE ARE NOT SAVED: THE ELUSIVE QUEST FOR RACIAL JUSTICE 63 (1987).

2. CARL T. ROWAN, DREAM MAKERS, DREAM BREAKERS: THE WORLD OF JUSTICE THURGOOD MARSHALL 453 (1993).

3. *Id.*

4. *Id.* at 454.

The Racism Is Permanent Thesis

Courageous Revelation or
Unconscious Denial of Racial Genocide

Based on a review of three hundred years of American history, I found a pattern of racial subordination that led me to conclude in *Faces at the Bottom of the Well* that racism is not going to go away. Rather, racism is an integral, permanent, and indestructible component of this society. Because this is true, not only will we not overcome in the sense that all of us believed so fervently in the 1960s, black people will never achieve full equality with whites. At best, we can hope for what I have called temporary "peaks of progress," short-lived periods of improved conditions that last a few years until white dominance once again reasserts itself . . . .
    . . . .

For white people who both deny racism and see a heavy dose of the Horatio Alger myth as the answer to blacks' problems, how sweet it must be when a black person stands in a public place and condemns as slothful and unambitious those blacks who are not making it. Whites eagerly embrace black conservatives' homilies to self-help, however grossly unrealistic such messages are in an economy where millions, white as well as black, are unemployed and, more important, where racial discrimination in the workplace is as vicious as (if less obvious than) it was when employers posted signs "no negras need apply." . . . We must reassess our cause and our approach to it. The simplistic repetition of time-worn slogans simply will not do. As a popular colloquialism puts it, it is time to "get real" about race and the persistence of racism in America.

To make such an assessment—to plan for the future by reviewing the experiences of the past—we must ask whether the formidable hurdles we

22 Capital U. L. Rev. 571 (1993). Used by permission.

now face in the elusive quest for racial equality are simply challenges to our commitment, whether they are the latest variation of the old hymn "One More River to Cross"? Or, as we once again gear up to meet the challenges posed by these unexpected new setbacks, are we ignoring a current message with implications for the future which history has already taught us about the past?

Such assessment is hard to make. On the one hand, contemporary color barriers are certainly less visible as a result of our successful effort to strip the law's endorsement from the hated Jim Crow signs. Today one can travel for thousands of miles across this country and never see a public facility designated as "Colored" or "white." Indeed, the very absence of visible signs of discrimination creates an atmosphere of racial neutrality and encourages whites to believe that racism is a thing of the past. On the other hand, the general use of so-called neutral standards to continue exclusionary practices reduces the effectiveness of traditional civil rights laws, while rendering discriminatory actions more oppressive than ever. Racial bias in the pre-*Brown* era was stark, open, unalloyed with hypocrisy and blank-faced lies. . . . Today, because bias lurks hidden in unofficial practices and "neutral" standards, we must wrestle with whether race or some individual failing has cost us the job, denied us the promotion, or prompted our rejection as tenants for an apartment. Either conclusion breeds frustration and alienation and a rage we dare not show to others or admit to ourselves.

. . . .

Careful examination reveals a pattern to seemingly arbitrary racial actions. When whites perceive that it will be profitable or at least cost-free to serve, hire, admit, or otherwise deal with blacks on a nondiscriminatory basis, they do so. When they fear—accurately or not—a loss, inconvenience, or upset to themselves or other whites, discriminatory conduct usually follows. . . . This difficulty, when combined with lackluster enforcement, explains why discrimination in employment and in the housing market, for example, continues to prevail more than two decades after enactment of the Equal Employment Opportunity Act of 1965 and the Fair Housing Act of 1968.

. . . .

The "them against us" racial ploy—always a potent force in economic bad times—is working again today. Whites, as disadvantaged by high status entrance requirements as blacks, fight to end affirmative action policies that, by eliminating class-based entrance requirements and requiring widespread advertising of jobs, have likely helped far more whites than blacks. And today millions of Americans, white as well as black, suffer the same unemployment, high-cost health care, inadequate housing, mediocre education, and unhealthy environment. The gap in national incomes between the rich and the poor approaches Third-World proportions. Yet conservative white politicians, without addressing any of these problems appeal to needy whites to identify on the basis of their shared skin color, and urge them to close ranks against the Willie Hortons, racial quotas, or affirmative action. . . . The mass of whites will accept large disparities in economic opportunity in respect to other whites as long as they have a priority over blacks and other people of color for access to the few opportunities available. . . .

. . . .

Black people are the magical faces at the bottom of society's well. Even the poorest whites, those who must live their lives only a few levels above, gain their self-esteem by gazing down on us. Surely, they must know that their deliverance depends on letting down their ropes. Only by working together is escape possible. Over time, many reach out, but most simply watch, mesmerized into maintaining their unspoken commitment to keeping us where we are, at whatever cost to them or to us.

. . . .

. . . On an average day in America, one of every four African American men, ages twenty through twenty-nine, was either in prison, jail, on probation, or on parole. . . . Other studies show that in the country's largest fifty-six cities, fifty-one percent of non-white males will be arrested and charged with a felony and acquire a criminal record. This figure does not include misdemeanor arrests, which make up the largest share of arrests and booking into jails nationally.

Last year, a study in Washington D.C. estimated that, minimally, seventy percent of the young black men living in D.C. would be arrested and jailed at least once before reaching age thirty-five. The lifetime risk was between eighty percent and ninety percent. What these figures mean for employment opportunities is too obvious and painful to spell out in detail.

The new president has promised to create more jobs, but how do you create laboring and semi-skilled jobs at decent wages in an economy where such jobs are disappearing because of technology, export to foreign countries, or are occupied by the hundreds of thousands of legal and illegal immigrants willing to work for sub-standard wages? Taken together, these factors, magnified by a harder to prove but no less pernicious racism, provide a formula for a not so gentle genocide of a great many African Americans.

But, you may ask, what of the thousands of black professionals and others able to work, earn, and live middle-class lives? Surely, they are beyond the dangers of ghetto life. Talent and hard work surely have taken them beyond the snares of discrimination? This widely held assumption, though, is punctured by talking to seemingly successful blacks as they speak of the barriers they had to survive in order to achieve a success more fragile than even they like to think.

Despite their undeniable progress, no African Americans are insulated from incidents of racial discrimination. Our careers, even our lives, are threatened because of our color. Whatever our status, we are feared because we might be one of "them." Success, then, neither insulates us from mis-identification by wary whites, nor does it ease our pain when we consider the plight of our less fortunate brethren who struggle for existence in what some social scientists call the "underclass."

. . . .

The charade of colored complicity in their conquered condition is made more believable because some blacks through enterprise, good fortune, and yes, sometimes the support of white progressives, have achieved a success that many believe all blacks could attain—if they just worked hard, were lucky, or both. "You made it despite being black and subject to discrimination," the question goes, "so why can't the rest of 'them' do the same?" For those who pose it, the question carries its own conclusion. . . .

. . . .

I have worked my whole professional life in the struggle against racism. My challenge is now to tell the truth about racism without causing disabling despair. For some of us who bear the burdens of racial subordination, any truth—no matter how dire—is uplifting. For others, it may be reassuring to remember Paulo Freire's words: "Freedom is acquired by conquest, not by gift. It must be pursued constantly and responsibly. Freedom is not an ideal located outside of . . . [the individual]; nor is it an idea which becomes myth. It is rather the indispensable condition for the quest for human completion. . . ."[1]

In a similar vein, Frantz Fanon conceded that,

> I as a man of color do not have the right to hope that in the white man there will be a crystallization of guilt toward the past of my race. . . . My

life [as a Negro] is caught in the last of existence. . . . I find myself suddenly in the world and I recognize that I have one right alone: that of demanding humane behavior from the other. One duty alone: that of not renouncing my freedom through my choices.[2]

Fanon argued two seemingly irreconcilable points: On the one hand, he believed racist structures to be permanently embedded in the psychology, economy, society, and culture of the modern world—so much so that he expressed the belief that a true culture cannot come to life under present conditions.[3] But, on the other hand, he urged people of color to resist psychologically the inheritance into which they had come. He insisted, despite pages of evidence suggesting the inviolability of the racial order, that "I should constantly remind myself that the real leap consists in introducing invention into existence. For the world through which I travel, I am endlessly creating myself."

NOTES

1. Paulo Freire, Pedagogy of the Oppressed 31 (1989).
2. Frantz Fanon, Black Skins, White Masks 228–29 (1967).
3. *Id.* at 187.

Getting Beyond a
Property in Race

I am honored to be here, but I would be far happier were I sitting out there with you listening to the person originally invited to give this lecture. The Honorable A. Leon Higginbotham quite literally gave his life last December in the struggle in which he was often heard but too infrequently heeded. Now he has joined Dr. Martin Luther King, Jr., Malcolm X, and W. E. B. Du Bois in that uniquely American racial Valhalla, a place where each is accorded in death a place of high honor usually reserved for those who have achieved rather than failed to accomplish the goals for which in life they worked so hard.

. . . .

Higginbotham, like King, was determined to speak the truth about race as he saw it. . . . On the bench he defied racial stereotypes. For many years after I began teaching in 1969, Leon was one of the few federal judges to whom I could refer black students with the assurance that their clerkship applications would receive serious consideration—even if they were not at the top of their classes and editors of their law review. Yet, his list of former clerks reads like a who's who of people of color. Many owe their careers to a model and mentor who was not afraid of ignoring tradition in the furtherance of justice.

Leon Higginbotham was a race man. In addition to his duties as judge and law teacher, he labored for several years to compile his pathbreaking *In the Matter of Color.*[1] The first book-length publication that treated the body of case law dealing with slavery in a systematic, scholarly fashion, this volume reminded the legal academy that major precedents in con-

---

1 Wash. U. J.L. & Pol'y 27 (1999). Used by permission.

tract, property, wills, and criminal law dealt with slavery, an unhappy fact of American legal history and one that holds contemporary significance.

Judge Higginbotham excelled in every aspect of law as practitioner, jurist, teacher, and scholar, and yet his lofty status did not alter his willingness to speak out strongly for the civil rights cause as he did on many occasions. Following a major address to black historians in the early 1970s, officials of a white union defending an employment discrimination case before him filed a motion asking him to recuse himself. The motion referred to the speech to support a charge that Higginbotham was a black civil rights advocate and thus could not objectively preside over their case. Far from intimidated by the allegations, Higginbotham responded at length and in the strongest terms both refused to recuse himself and condemned the subconscious but widely held view that only white judges could decide racial issues fairly.[2]

Of course, many know Higginbotham from his public condemnations of the Clarence Thomas appointment to the Supreme Court.[3] He did so knowing that many of his judicial colleagues viewed his hard-hitting remarks as inappropriate, intemperate, and out of place. Higginbotham's criticism did not prevent Justice Thomas from gaining a seat on the Court, and, to date with few exceptions, Justice Thomas has voted in a manner that justifies Higginbotham's warning.

One may say that I am too harsh and that Justice Thomas can cast only one vote on a conservative Court. However, that response reminds me of what my late wife Jewel would say when I complained that some conduct of mine was no different than that of other men. She would reply quietly, "I did not marry those other men." Whether he likes it or not, Justice Thomas is one of us, and in a society in which we remain the subordinate other, what he does affects us in a way that the votes of others on the Court do not.

There is, though, a basis for consolation. The vehemence of Higginbotham's critiques has frustrated the expectation of those who appointed Thomas. They had hoped his conservative positions could be cited as reflecting the views of at least a percentage of the black community. However, Justice Thomas speaks only for himself. Even so, it is distressing to realize that Justice Thurgood Marshall's successor on the Supreme Court seems to personify a path to success for minorities that an unfortunate number have chosen. If we ignore the continuing perversity of racism and act as though the law is fair and color-blind, those who grant positions and prestige will reward conformity with these rose-colored assumptions.

. . . .

The historic pattern of finding members of the victim class willing to extoll the system while blaming their own for their miserable state is neither a new nor a fortuitous phenomenon. Robert L. Allen's book, *Black Awakening in Capitalist America*,[4] reminds us that what we deem as progress, measured by the number of blacks who have moved into management-level positions, is quite similar to developments in colonial Africa and India. The colonizing countries maintained their control by establishing class divisions within the ranks of the indigenous peoples. A few able (and safe) individuals were permitted to move up in the ranks where they served as false symbols of what was possible for the subordinated masses. In this and less enviable ways, these individuals provided a semblance of legitimacy to the colonial rule that it clearly did not deserve.

In similar fashion, Allen views black America as a domestic colony of white America. Colonial rule is predicated upon "an alliance between the occupying power and indigenous forces of conservatism and tradition."[5] Allen finds aspects of this policy in [much of America's racial history]. . . .

. . . .

What happens for those minorities less fortunate than ourselves? In ways that none of us is prepared to recognize, we unintentionally can make things worse instead of better for minorities who have been excluded from the programs that have helped us gain skills and acceptable credentials. Enjoying our positions and the occasional opportunity to do good, we are pointed out to the majority of blacks who are still without work or trapped in low-wage, dead-end jobs. We want to serve as models for the disadvantaged, but as scholars, judges, and practitioners we are for many whites living proof that no color bar operates today.

. . . .

. . . The ideology of whiteness continues to oppress whites as well as blacks making whites settle for despair in politics and anguish in the daily grind of life. Segregation solidified because working-class whites insisted that they needed government reassurance that despite their lowly economic condition they were better than blacks. As historian C. Vann Woodward concluded after studying this period, "Political democracy for the white man and racial discrimination for the black were often products of the same dynamics."[6] Jim Crow laws were intended "to bolster the creed of white supremacy in the bosom of a white man working for a black man's wages."[7] . . .

. . . .

Today, few whites would openly espouse racial superiority as the cause of any animosity they may feel toward blacks. Indeed, most whites vigorously deny that they are racist or prejudiced against black people. It is true that since Dr. King was killed and civil rights policies motivated by the riots that followed his death were enacted, many whites now work with, live near, and are friendly to black people. What many do not recognize, however, is that racism is not simply open bigotry. As Beverly Daniel Tatum explains in her book, *Why Are All the Black Kids Sitting Together in the Cafeteria?* racism is a system of advantage that benefits all whites whether or not they seek it.[8] This system is far more than personal ideology based on racial prejudice; it includes cultural messages and institutional policies that advantage whites and disadvantage people of color. Tatum explains, "Racial prejudice when combined with social power—access to social, cultural, and economic resources and decision-making—leads to the institutionalization of racist policies and practices."[9]

. . . .

At the end of his life, Dr. King increasingly saw through the camouflage of race to the hidden divisions of class. Poverty, illiteracy, and joblessness know no color line save the one imposed by those whites seeking some comfort in their own low status. King hoped the Poor People's March and his efforts on behalf of the garbage collectors in Memphis would shift the focus of civil rights to where perhaps it should have been all along. Were he alive today I think he would still be trying to convey the message that too few whites would want to hear or heed about the benefits and the costs of their racism. In other words, he would continue trying to tell them what we blacks all know but are unable to communicate across the color line of this still color-conscious citizenry that prefers reassurance rather than reality from black speakers.

One wonders if law and litigation can further social change. The answer based on my experience is that sometimes it can but not for long. At times the nation's often-stated ideals are so glaringly compromised that the courts respond out of idealism, to avoid embarrassment, or to prevent injustice from worsening. As a result, decisions come down that alleviate the most serious of racial abuses for blacks. . . . The precedents then take on lives of their own, often enlarging the scope or quality of rights for whites to a greater extent than they did for those intended as the initial beneficiaries.

In reviewing the positive influence of these cases initially intended to curb serious racial wrongs, one realizes that the quest for black rights has served well the cause of full citizenship generally. This theme was a major thrust of a speech Judge Higginbotham presented in 1987 at the hundredth anniversary dinner of the *Harvard Law Review*. Held at the Boston Harvard Club, it was a very posh, black-tie affair. Those who invited the judge must have expected something unique for the occasion, and the judge did not disappoint. In a speech that lasted well over an hour, Higginbotham reviewed in great detail the failings of Harvard graduates on the high Court both in practice and in scholarship. He said he did so not to embarrass anyone, although embarrassment was likely not the strongest emotion his listeners felt that night. Rather, he concluded in words that reflected his beliefs and stood as a worthwhile standard for those who would follow in his footsteps. "In my opinion, lawyers must be the visionaries in our society. We must be the nation's legal architects who renovate the palace of justice and redesign the landscape of opportunity in our nation."

. . . Each lawyer's vision of society and his or her dedication to the dignity of individuals will affect the quality of life in our country in ways that mere technical skill in drafting a document, constructing a statute, writing a brief, or authoring a law review article can never approach. If lawyers are to play the important social and moral roles that I believe we can and should, then we must begin by recognizing that our nation's basic human problems have not arisen because the legal profession misunderstood Blackstone, the *Bluebook,* the *Uniform Commercial Code,* or the *Federal Rules of Evidence.* Poverty, hatred, malnutrition, inadequate health care and housing, corruption in government, and the failures of our public school system continue to haunt us today because those in power often have lacked personal morality or have failed to act according to the values that they have professed to hold. . . . Critical moral and human values cannot arrive through even the most meticulous reading of opinions or statutes. Each lawyer must consciously and constantly assess his or her values and goals in forging rules of law for the future.

NOTES

1. A. LEON HIGGINBOTHAM, JR., IN THE MATTER OF COLOR: RACE AND THE AMERICAN LEGAL PROCESS: THE COLONIAL PERIOD (1978).

2. Commonwealth of Pennsylvania and Raymond Williams v. Local Union

542, International Union of Operating Engineers, 388 F. Supp. 155, 181 (E.D. Pa. 1974).

3. *See, e.g., An Open Letter to Justice Clarence Thomas from a Federal Judicial Colleague,* 140 U. PA. L. REV. 1005 (1992); *Justice Clarence Thomas in Retrospect,* 45 HASTINGS L.J. 1405 (1994).

4. ROBERT L. ALLEN, BLACK AWAKENING IN CAPITALIST AMERICA: AN ANALYTICAL HISTORY (1969).

5. *Id.*

6. C. VANN WOODWARD, THE STRANGE CAREER OF JIM CROW (1955).

7. *Id.* at 68–77.

8. BEVERLY DANIEL TATUM, "WHY ARE ALL THE BLACK KIDS SITTING TOGETHER IN THE CAFETERIA?" AND OTHER CONVERSATIONS ABOUT RACE 7 (1997).

9. *Id.* at 7–8.

The Black Sedition Papers

[Eds. Shortly after one of Harvard sociology professor Orlando Patterson's criticisms of blacks appeared in print, Professor Bell received the following letter from a friend.]

Dear Professor:

No one in authority is willing to acknowledge that the studies are underway. The sponsors as well as their funding sources are unknown. The purpose of the studies, if persistent rumors are accurate, is so controversial that secrecy is understandable—if hardly more justifiable. According to my sources, social instability in the black community is alarming policy-makers at the highest levels. All concede that blacks have survived hundreds of years of societal hostility and, in the process, have exhibited amazing resilience in the face of oppressive racial policies ranging from slavery to segregation.

Today, however, many blacks are experiencing unprecedented and precipitous declines that pose a national security risk. To meet this danger, the nation has so increased penalties for criminal conduct that an ever increasing number of blacks are either in prison or are enmeshed in the criminal justice system. Even so, the leaders of this project believe the society must be prepared to accept measures that circumvent due process and other constitutional safeguards.

The genesis of this racial crisis can be summarized easily. The ending of legally enforced segregation led many blacks to assume that desegregation laws would be enforced with the same vigor as their segregation predecessors. They were not. Indeed, much to the

Reprinted by permission from *Afrolantica Legacies* 137 by Derrick Bell. Chicago, IL: Third World Press, 1998.

consternation of those who had worked long and hard for their enactment, civil rights laws intended to protect blacks from discriminatory practices now bar programs intended to remedy decades of
discrimination.

In addition, long-established stabilizing forces in the black community weakened as better-prepared blacks moved into mainly
white work sites, schools, neighborhoods—even churches. Massive
unemployment, referred to euphemistically as "down-sizing," has
decimated black and white workers, but the impact on black families and communities has been particularly devastating. . . .

Given these developments, the secret project leaders decided to
quietly commission a series of "black sedition papers." These papers will record the effects on blacks of late twentieth-century economic, political, and social disadvantage. Under the ground rules,
the papers are to focus on black pathology, describing it in detail
and condemning those afflicted with it. Whenever possible, the
studies will endorse self-help solutions criticizing blacks for not
thinking of and adopting these solutions themselves.

Except as asides, the studies do not place any responsibility on
the society's racism for the black pathologies under examination.
Investigators are urged not to "muddy the waters" by suggesting
that black conduct is in any significant degree the result of environmental forces including, particularly, white racism. Comparisons
of negative behaviors of blacks with similar conduct by other oppressed groups is frowned on. On the other hand, writers are encouraged to make uncomplimentary comparisons between black
failure and the greater success of other disadvantaged peoples.
West Indian immigrants are a favored comparison group. Successes
by Asians, Hispanics, and Jews are also welcomed.

The project gathers studies by a diverse array of individuals and
groups. Black social scientists, though, are preferred for reasons
that seem to elude those blacks who are selected. The public's responses to these "black papers" are carefully followed and
recorded. It is important that if the racial crisis worsens and au-
thoritarian measures are called for, the public will be prepared.

Sincerely,
D.M.S., Ph.D.

. . .

I cannot say for a fact that Professor Orlando Patterson's *Blacklash* article is one of the "black sedition papers." To confirm my suspicions, I tried to contact my friend to find out more about these papers. He had not mentioned any of the scholars the secret project commissioned to write for them. And, yet, in trying to understand why Patterson would write a paper that so distorts black history and contemporary black distress, it is reasonable to raise questions and, perhaps, hope for answers. Consider:

Even the title is accusatory. "Backlash," in contemporary usage, often refers to the strong negative reaction by whites to civil rights remedies they think go too far. *Blacklash* suggests that blacks are turning against one another and thus are primarily responsible for growing opposition to civil rights in general and blacks in particular. In fact, racial policies in this country have very little to do with black "worthiness" and everything to do with the perception of what will best serve white interests. Justice Clarence Thomas' appointment fit the Republican political agenda. That being the case, it was irrelevant that he lacked the usual qualifications for the Supreme Court, and additionally was accused of conduct that fits the fearsome black male stereotype.

On the other hand, virtually no political support addresses the roots of black crime even though fear of it has helped elect presidents. Crime also serves as sufficient justification for massive funding programs for prison contractors and operators. . . . Professor Patterson's failure to address this basic reality is fatal to a paper that—whatever his intentions—will harm more black folks than it will help.

Patterson, using the Anita Hill–Clarence Thomas debacle—a topic he has explored before—weaves a destructive image of the relationship between black men and women in a society where, he claims, blacks have gained "final acceptance . . . as integral—even if still greatly disadvantaged—members of the society." He explains that the Hill-Thomas hearings were symbolic of blacks as accepted members of society. Patterson says that Anita Hill and Clarence Thomas are more importantly a man and woman who just happen to be black. And the relationship or lack of it that existed between them is no different than the relationship that exists between white males and females.

It is tempting to join Professor Patterson in reaching for any slight evidence that the increasingly heavy burden of racism is easing, but the hearings were not that. I think it safe to say that most black people in America—with the exception of Professor Patterson—were constantly and painfully aware of the race of the two protagonists and many of their witnesses. Had Anita Hill been white and Clarence Thomas' wife black, the questioning of both—and likely the outcome of the hearings—would have been very, very different.

In the gender debate the hearings generated, Anita Hill, Patterson claims, was a symbolic figure for white women as well as black women. Here, his racial optimism ignores black history. Campaigns for racial justice have often served as a vehicle for other groups to further their own advances. And though those groups make progress toward their goals due to black people, they continue to hold racist views. In the beginning of the women's suffrage movement, women and blacks fought side by side. Frederick Douglass and Susan B. Anthony often campaigned together for legislation that would give both groups access to the ballot. But, when it appeared that black men would receive the right to vote before white women, Anthony and other white women quickly dropped all ties with blacks. Some early feminists even went so far as to insinuate to white men that black people were not human and, thus, not deserving of the ballot. . . .

On the dubious evidence of the Thomas-Hill hearings, Patterson envisions an American landscapes swept clean of the "culture of slavery" though he concedes that "its legacies are still very much with us." Asserting that blacks are no longer outsiders concentrating on getting in, Patterson writes that we must focus on the top of the "internal racial agenda . . . the crisis-ridden problem of gender relations between African American men and women." *Blacklash* is filled with "there is racism, but" statements that acknowledge the racist source of the problems Patterson describes, but he refuses to find them the prime factor in the behavioral patterns he deplores. Instead, Patterson points to black women in general and black feminists in particular as the cause of a crisis, one he asserts would be more obvious if black feminists were not obscuring our understanding of gender relations by insisting that they bear a double burden based on race and gender.

Patterson believes that close examination of the life experiences and social relationships of the two sexes within white dominant society reveals that African American men, not women, are at the bottom of the well. In order to invalidate the "double burden theory" of African American women, Patterson depicts a grim picture for African American men and an encouraging one for African American women. He states that in some instances, black women are in better economic position than white women by historically tracing the black woman's ability to gain entry into the dominant white world. This entry, Patterson feels, allowed black women a chance to experience "finer things in life" and an opportunity to develop relationships with their white counterparts.

Patterson cites statistics showing higher education attainment and income for African American females as compared to black males to support his position that the life chances of black males are worse than those of their female counterparts. Furthermore, Patterson argues that the economic status of black women is not only better than that of their male counterparts, but also that white men do not find them attractive as women. This unattractiveness, Patterson claims, shields black women from sexual oppression by white men. Therefore black women, Patterson states, exist in a small crevice, better than white women, not higher than white men, but sufficiently better "that black professional men tend to get crushed."

. . . .

Patterson then claims that after slavery a black woman's ability to pass accelerated because she performed work as a domestic, nanny, nurse or clerk. These positions, he states, allowed black women "greater access to the wider dominant white world." Service sector employment brought black and white women together to share close relationships. Unfortunately, black men, due to their sex and inability to bear children, could not pass into the white world, nor could they obtain employment which would allow a relationship to grow between them and their white counterparts.

The evidence contrary to this position is enormous. . . . Black women seeking careers in law teaching will also wish to differ with Patterson. Studies show they have had a disproportionately hard time gaining entry into law school faculties, compared with black men. Their numbers on faculties at Harvard University are ludicrously small, a fact that Patterson overlooks out of either misplaced loyalty or an acceptance of the Harvard line that "we simply can't find any who are qualified." According to one study, Harvard University, which features only 80 blacks of 4,842 faculty members (1.7%), will require until the year 2072 to reach the national average of black faculty (4.5%), if it continues at its present pace—five new, black faculty members in seven years. At present, no more than two or three of the tenured blacks at Harvard are women.

Even in the marketplace, black women face disadvantages. A survey of new car dealer pricing practices revealed that black women are charged more for the same vehicle than either white men and women, and more than black men.

Given the widely held belief that competitive market forces will eliminate racial and gender discrimination, and that such discrimination will occur only in markets in which racial or gender animus distorts competition, the car dealer study reveals double-bind bias with a special vengeance. My point here is not to engage in a battle of studies, but to illustrate that the assumption that black women have an easier time in this society than black men cannot be proved. Its assertion as gospel is divisive in a gender setting already beset with external pressures due to a racism Patterson would have us believe is no longer a primary factor.

. . . .

One cannot doubt that black men are in crisis, with more in prison than in college. Nor can one doubt that some employers see black women as capable of better fulfilling affirmative action obligations because they occupy dual positions as blacks and women. The debate, though, should not focus on whether black men or black women suffer most. Rather, our efforts should focus on why black men are suffering a genocide-like demise from the work-force, from the family and, increasingly, from life itself. . . . It is only when we observe the black man and woman in unison rather than individually, that we can fully understand the plight of African Americans.

. . . .

No one will disagree with Professor Patterson when he asserts that black people must assist ourselves. Such urging, though, coming from one writing from the safe haven of the academy harms rather than helps when it charges that a segment of our community is without morals, values, and feelings as though these all too obvious deficits occurred without an external cause or that they can be corrected without a reversal of social policies that now sustain conditions and motivate behaviors that we all deplore. Shifting the root cause from a hostile society to black women is both inaccurate in fact and counterproductive to the self-help goal Patterson espouses. The only predictable result is reinforcement of a belief in even some liberal whites that blacks are genetically predisposed to antisocial life patterns. Secure in this unspoken view, policy-making whites are freed of any obligation for even thinking about, much less funding, expensive new programs of social reconstruction.

At this point, I planned to end my critique by urging Professor Patterson and other academics to remember that we not only enjoy a degree of academic freedom that protects our writings from retaliatory censure, but also brings them a degree of attention far greater than anything the masses we profess to speak for can equal. Given our representative role for the black community, whether we want it or not, it is appropriate that when discussing racial issues, we adopt a basic precept of physicians: "First, do no harm."

After all, when we attack those responsible for and profiting from racism's continued virulence, those we accuse are not without either the power or the will to respond. But when we aim our assaults at a people whose dire predicament is without precedent in a history that includes 200 years of slavery, then we are under an ethical obligation to consider our positions in the light of the likely use of our words by those who despise and are quite willing to see dead a segment of our people who— after all—look like us, however different they may act. As Cornel West made clear in reporting an incident with New York taxis that most of us have experienced, our looks for many whites are conclusive—regardless of our educational, cultural, and even financial attainments.

Must we then remain silent about serious shortcomings and self-defeating activities in black communities? Of course not. We need no black Daniel Moynihans bemoaning that they have been crucified on a cross of truth about ghetto pathologies. But Moynihan's critics were not afraid of the truth. . . . Inclusion of causes as well as effects is essential to counteract the presumption of unworthiness that translates the failings of a subordinated people into self-caused fault rather than an externally-imposed fate.

After completing my response, I received a message from my academic friend investigating Black Sedition Papers. Again, I share his letter with you.

Dear Professor:

I received your message. I have two pieces of information that you will be interested in. First, I can confirm your suspicions. Professor Orlando Patterson's *Blacklash* article is considered a Black Sedition Paper. It will be quietly circulated to policymakers as evidence of both the hopelessness of the black condition and of blacks' inability or unwillingness to take the strong, moral steps needed to continue as productive members of the society. I found no evidence that anyone commissioned Patterson to write this paper, or paid him anything to write it. Indeed, I found no evidence that he is even aware of how his paper will be used.

Second, I have learned that the Black Sedition Paper files contain a number of writings that are as unremittingly harsh in their assessments of whites and racism as you claim Professor Patterson is heartless in his assessment of black people. This group of quite militant papers actually supplements their more conservative counterparts. It is expected that, when it is time to invoke them, the militant and conservative papers together will be used to convince a larger spectrum of the white population of the need for draconian measures against all blacks.

I understand that the militant files contain a number of your writings.

Sincerely,
D.M.S.

Wanted

A White Leader Able
to Free Whites of Racism

My title does not promise new legal strategies but instead calls for new leadership in the fight against racism—to be more specific, new white leadership. Many whites of course believe in and work for racial equality, but for the most part, they are not well known. We are not likely to see them on the *Lehrer News Hour* or *Meet the Press*. The leaders I seek and that this country needs must be well-known, able to be heard and with the power or charisma to be taken seriously.

Let me say quickly, emphatically, and somewhat sadly that the leadership role we need cannot be filled by a black person. We know from the Reverend Jesse Jackson's runs for the presidency that an articulate black can gain support across racial lines when advocating a range of social programs for those who, as Reverend Jackson phrased it, "take the early bus." When dealing directly with race, however, any black's message will be dismissed at best as special pleading and at worst as racial condemnation.

. . . .

What we need is a white leader who is both able to be heard and courageous enough to deliver a three-point message about race. First, race in America is not a black but a white problem. Second, racism might never be overcome and might play a permanent role in the American social structure. Third, even if eradicating racism is an impossible goal, the fight for tolerance and equality carries an inherent value.

. . . .

While it is beyond denial that blacks have borne the heavy burden of "the other" in our society, the barriers that racial discrimination places on blacks should not be the focus of the leader's statements, or of discussions among whites. Rather, the dialogue must focus on the cost which that burden exacts from whites. I am not referring to the moral or ethical cost, however high those costs might be. Rather, the white leader that I call for must demonstrate to other whites the economic harms, social disadvantages, and lost opportunities that white people have suffered and continue to suffer as a result of the pervasive and corrosive effects of social neglect which are linked directly to institutionalized racial inequality.

The leader will ask all whites to consider why the United States, the world's richest nation by a wide margin, lags behind any number of less affluent countries in health care, housing, education, child care, and protection for the aged. I speak not just of wealthy western European nations; Canada and even Cuba far exceed the United States in protecting all citizens against such destroyers of life as pestilence, poverty, and ignorance. The leader I seek would force whites to acknowledge that racial separation in this country plays a major role in maintaining the discrepancy between total wealth on the one hand and the unequal distribution of such basic necessities as shelter and education on the other.

Economist Robert L. Heilbroner observed years ago that while blacks suffer from social neglect in America in disproportionate numbers, merging the issues of race and economic neglect serves to rationalize the policies of inaction that have characterized so much of the American response to need. Many perceive programs to improve slums as intended to "subsidize" blacks and proposals to improve prison conditions are seen as measures to coddle black criminals. A list of such perceptions could continue *ad infinitum*. All too often, "the fear and resentment of [blacks] takes precedence over the social problem itself. The result, unfortunately, is that the entire society suffers from the results of a failure to correct social evils whose ill effects refuse to obey the rules of segregation."[1]

While on a trip last week I picked up a local paper in which I found a letter to the editor arguing that we should stop coddling drug dealers. Give them a quick trial and, if found guilty, execute them. Sadly, such sentiments are common. Any white leader, in order to emancipate whites from their racial pathologies, must ask: what fuels the fear that manifests itself in the fact that the United States is the only major country that retains the death penalty? Not only do we retain it, we extend it to more crimes at every opportunity. Simultaneously we dismantle legal services for the poor, which provide the only means of legal defense for many facing the death penalty.

Why is it that our Congress refuses to enact meaningful gun control laws, even as we witness a series of attacks on our schools, businesses, and even churches, perpetrated by whites, including young students, armed with an array of lethal weapons, that kill scores of innocent, unarmed persons? Could deepset racial fears be the real barrier to joining the rest of the civilized world in abolishing the death penalty and controlling the purchase and possession of guns? How was president Clinton able to replace a deeply flawed welfare system with a draconian series of measures by calling for an "end [to] welfare as we know it," a slogan with racist overtones which overlooked that most persons on welfare are white, and that the real recipients of government largesse are not the poor but corporations, banks, and other major entities in our economic system? The white leader this nation needs, though likely does not want, will force whites to confront these issues.

This discussion may lead to an understanding that a major barrier to much-needed social reform is the unacknowledged, but very real, fear and resentment of blacks. Powerful entities in our society harness this deepseated fear and resentment to convince a great many white people to think and act in ways that contradict their own best interests. Fear and resentment of blacks led many whites in North Carolina to reelect Jesse Helms to the Senate over Harvey Gantt; now it is Helms who blocks the appointments of even highly qualified individuals and advocates that the United States withdraw from the United Nations.

Helms is highly conservative and supports economic measures that advantage the rich while burdening the lives of poorer whites—the very constituents that provide Helms with his electoral victories. And Helms is not alone. The leadership of both the House of Representatives and the Senate hold their powerful positions in substantial part because, like Helms, they convinced whites that if elected, they would preserve the racial status quo. Having done so, congressional leaders can ignore the nation's need for health care, environmental reform, effective schools, and a decent minimum wage. They need not acknowledge the growing gap in wealth and income. Congressional leaders can protect the interests that fill their campaign coffers with millions of dollars in legal, but nonetheless immoral, bribes.

This confusion of race and self-interest dates back to early colonial times, when plantation owners convinced working class whites to support slavery even though they could never compete with those that could afford slaves. Slave holders appealed to working class whites by urging that their shared whiteness compelled the two groups to unite against the threat of slave revolts or escapes. The strategy worked. Poor whites vented their frustrations by hating the slaves rather than their masters, who held both black slave and free white in economic bondage. While slavery ended, the economic disjuncture, camouflaged by racial division, continued unabated.

During the latter half of the nineteenth century, a shared feeling of racial superiority to blacks was one of the few things that united the huge influx of European immigrants, who themselves were brutally exploited by the mine and factory owners for whom they toiled long hours under wretched conditions for subsistence wages. Of course, many of these immigrants were far more recent arrivals than the blacks that they mocked. The racially derogatory minstrel shows of that period helped immigrants acculturate and assimilate by inculcating a nationalism the common theme of which was the disparagement and disadvantaging of blacks. Immigrants focused on maintaining racial oppression, rather than uniting across racial lines to resist the exploitation and deprivation which respects no color line, then or now.

The ideology of whiteness continues to oppress whites as well as blacks. Whites employ whiteness to make whites settle for despair in politics and anguish in the daily grind of life. Somehow, whites have observed that a majority of America's population is white and that most power is held by whites and interpreted these facts as meaning that, as whites, they are privileged and entitled to preference over people of color. Over time, these views have solidified into a kind of property—a property right in whiteness. The law recognizes and protects this property right just as it safeguards other forms of property. . . . Maintaining their political advantage over blacks, though, requires that whites not identify with blacks even regarding matters that transcend skin color. To give continued meaning to their whiteness, whites must identify with the whites at the top of the economic heap, not with blacks, with whom most whites hold so much in common save their skin color.

Personal experience provides just one example of how this self-inflicted, racial disadvantaging works in practice. Not long ago, I met a young man attending a law school at which most of the students were from white, working-class families. Most were the first in their families to attend law school and, like this young man, most opposed affirmative action. This student, who felt he had made it on his own, told me that, while there had been racial discrimination in the past, we had to move on. In his view "everyone, including black people, must make it on merit. That is the 'American Way.'"

In response, I suggested that, while he seemed quite able, he would have a hard time getting hired at large corporate law firms, which prefer to hire students from Ivy League schools. Many of the students at these schools come from upper-class families. They aren't any smarter than he is; they were just born into wealthier families. Was that fair? My question stopped him cold. His eyes glazed over. Obviously, he had never considered the class disadvantage he suffered. After several moments, he said with a shrug, "Well, those are the breaks."

In other words, any time a black got a job that this particular student had sought, he suspected preferential, and therefore unfair, treatment. If a white who benefited from being born into an upper-class family got the job, however, the student did not presume the same unfairness. . . . This attitude, which is widespread, explains much of the opposition to affirmative action in college admissions, while legacy admits—children of alumni, faculty, or large contributors—remain unscathed, even though more spaces are taken by such students than by those for whom race is a factor. And the alumni children, as an aggregate, do not possess better academic credentials than the minority students.

And one need not possess prophetic power to predict that if the law student is turned down for the job he seeks in favor of a person of color, he will harbor suspicions and resentment that unfair, race-based hiring policies motivated the decision. Some employers may build on these suspicions by suggesting, usually untruthfully, that they had to give the job to a black candidate. Politicians and some employers are altogether too ready to suggest that the understandable job anxieties of whites are the fault of programs intended to remedy longstanding discrimination against blacks. . . .

Such deepset suspicions must not sidetrack the white leader into the routes most racial discussion generally follow—namely about blacks, our intelligence, our morality, our entitlement to rights, and all the other issues that usually monopolize American race discussions. Rather, this leader must keep the spotlight focused where the discussion belongs and where it should have been all along: on whites. This much-needed dialogue should not turn on who is or is not racist. That debate leads to rancor, not reconciliation. As Beverly Tatum points out in her book, *Why Are All the Black Kids Sitting Together in the Cafeteria?* racism is a system of privilege, based on color, that advantages all whites regardless of whether they seek such advantage.

If race is not a black but a white problem the white leader we need will have to ask the nation's whites two questions. First, if blackness does not mean subordination then what does it really mean to be white, not as a matter of appropriate respect and pride in cultural heritage, but as a social and economic fact of life in these United States? Second, do whites in this country have enough love and respect for one another to remain a stable society without using blacks as a societal glue?

When whites discuss race, optimism usually trumps reality. "These things take time" is a ready response to troubling instances of continued racial discrimination. "Well," others say, "the answer is intermarriage, so that one day all Americans will be a pleasing shade of year-round tan." The leadership I seek, though, will understand, and be willing to speak plainly about, the barriers to moving beyond reliance on an outgroup for social stability. Those barriers are monumental in a nation where whites of widely divergent stations make common cause through their unspoken pact to maintain a system of presumptions and priorities based on race—a system that enables some blacks who combine talent, hard work, and good fortune to advance, but keeps a great many on the bottom. No other aspect of social functioning has retained its viability and its value to general stability from the very beginning of the American experience to the present day.[2]

. . . .

You might think that combating racism requires not a charismatic white leader but a truly extraordinary educational campaign. That is, given a true understanding of the harm racial discrimination inflicts on blacks, whites might find it easy, or easier, to abandon racism. Education leads to enlightenment. Enlightenment opens the way for empathy. Empathy foreshadows reform.

But, however much individuals might deplore it from time to time, the harm done by racial discrimination is an open secret, which everyone has agreed on. Whites might recognize, at some level of consciousness, that they, the oppressors, are among the oppressed, but nonetheless conclude (like my law student) that "those are the breaks." Although difficult for me to imagine, being white in this country means you represent the norm and that you need not think about race all the time, and almost never about racism. Certainly racism is not something that most whites could conceptualize as constantly disadvantaging their own lives.

The problem, though, may extend beyond these forms of racial thoughtlessness. Just as I know that all whites benefit from racism, I know that not all whites are evil or guilty in any normative sense. Consequently, I wonder whether factors more fundamental even than white racism, more essential than good government to a civilized society, cause the plight of black people in this country. While some racial reforms stem from financial considerations, disaster, threat, guilt, love, and, yes, even education, a primary barrier to racial reform may nullify all these.

I wonder whether here, as seems the case in many other societies, the melding of millions of individuals into a nation requires that some within it must be sacrificed, killed, or kept in misery so that the rest, who share the guilt for this monstrous wrong, can forge out of their guilt the qualities of forbearance and tolerance that are essential to group survival and growth. If so, who in the legal system plays the more important role: the prosecutors who are the instruments of the sacrifices mandated by a social physics we do not understand, or the defendants, whose efforts are destined to fail but who, by those efforts, serve to camouflage from society the bitter reality of those sacrifices and, alas, from themselves as well?

If racism forges the bonds that maintain a stable society, perhaps its value is greater than generally realized. In addition to providing a comforting sop to the poor and a convenient scapegoat for politicians, it connects all whites in a knowing but unspoken alliance. . . . As paradoxical as it seems, viewing racism as an amalgam of guilt, responsibility, and power, all of which are generally known but never acknowledged, may explain why educational programs undertaken by the leader I seek are destined to fail.

. . . .

In a society that worships success, it will be tough for even the most effective leader to convince this country's whites that value—a kind of spiritual salvation, really—inheres in undertaking causes for which the chance of victory, as conventionally defined, is remote. The outstanding white leader I seek may come, but I would hope that no one would await such a leader's arrival. Others have not been waiting; the crusade to diminish race as a basis of privilege and priority is already underway. Many white, antiracist groups are organizing and enacting plans to reduce the dangers, and disadvantages, of using whiteness as a measure of worth—

a normative standard. A national network of groups who call themselves "Race Traitors" reject loyalty to whiteness in favor of loyalty to humanity. Thus, if a white person tells a racist joke or story in a group of whites, a member of this group would say: "Oh, you must have told that story in front of me because you assume I am white. I am actually black and just look white. And let me tell you why I found that story offensive."

Other whites are both recognizing and rejecting the privileges of whiteness. At each instance of special treatment, they ask, "Would you have done this were I not white?" Whites, by refusing to accept without question the privileges of whiteness, begin the process of destabilizing that construction which society relies on to preserve the current system of racial subordination. One of my students had an experience that reflects her awareness. She wrote:

> On the days when I work, I often take papers down to Manhattan Family Court. I don't dress up just to drop papers off, so last Wednesday I headed down to the courthouse in jeans and a plaid flannel shirt. I also don't carry identification marking me as the employee of an attorney—identification which would allow me to skip the metal detector and go right into the court house. While I could make some sort of badge, I never remember to do so. So last Wednesday I was in line waiting to go through the metal detector. I was the only white person in the line, and I was at the very end of the line. I was dressed considerably worse than most of the other people in the line.
>
> Nevertheless, one of the security guards spotted me, left the metal detector, came back to the end of the line and asked me why I was going in. I replied that I worked for the Family Law Center, but didn't have a badge. He smiled and waved me through. My whiteness was my badge, whether I actively asserted it or not.

For those whites who are concerned but not sure they are ready to tackle the existing system, courses and workshops can help overcome the indoctrination caused by pervasive racism. Trained persons can help whites understand and recognize the stages they must undergo to rid themselves of a sense of guilt or denial rooted in being white. Ultimately, whites must replace long-held and often destructive myths with an acceptance of whiteness as an important part of oneself, and develop a realistically positive view of what it means to be white.

. . . .

It is a paradoxical source of inspiration for whites, but perhaps those of you who can admit that we are all imprisoned by the history of racial subordination in America can accept, as slaves had no choice but to accept, our fate. Thus, by acknowledging the power of racism, we do not legitimize it or surrender to it. Rather, we can only discredit racism if we can accurately pinpoint it. Racism lies at the center, not the periphery; in the permanent, not in the fleeting; in the real lives of black and white people, not in the sentimental caverns of the mind.

NOTES

1. Robert L. Heilbroner, *The Roots of Social Neglect in the United States,* in Is LAW DEAD? 288, 296 (Eugene V. Rostow ed., 1971).

2. JENNIFER HOCHSCHILD, THE NEW AMERICAN DILEMMA 5 (1984).

CHAPTER 11

Racism as Meanness

Some white behavior toward blacks seems to have little rhyme or reason, serving neither to advance white economic self-interest nor to solidify some white privilege, but rather to evince simple meanness. Do some whites take pleasure in inflicting pain on the downtrodden? Is racial sadism, for some, a trait of human character? Or is blaming and reviling blacks a convenient excuse or scapegoat for white failings and guilt? These selections delve into the dark recesses of the racist mind in search of answers. Most of Bell's writings analyze racial dynamics in materialist terms. These are among his few writings that examine racism's psychological dimensions.

Meanness as Racial Ideology
The Port Chicago Mutiny

His interest sparked by a faded 1945 pamphlet, Robert Allen wrote *The Port Chicago Mutiny* over a period of ten years. . . . He overcame obstacles including hard-to-obtain records, lost and reluctant interviewees, and a general lack of interest in an unfortunate incident that, after all, had occurred almost fifty years ago while America was locked into a war that threatened its survival. . . . While the events Allen investigated occurred more than a decade before the Supreme Court declared government-sanctioned racial segregation unconstitutional, the racial attitudes and policies that led to a largely forgotten disaster in a small California town provide a standard for comparing current racial events, some of which are less dramatic but no less damaging. At the least, the chronicle provides another perspective on the intricacies of racial prejudice in the United States.

In 1944, during the height of World War II, the U.S. Navy loaded thousands of tons of ammunition onto Liberty ships from a dock in Port Chicago, a small town near San Francisco. At this dock, unlike other similar West Coast sites, the Navy did not use civilian stevedores but assigned this backbreaking and highly dangerous labor to black sailors laboring under the direction of white officers who were far more concerned about setting records for tonnage loaded than about safety procedures or the welfare of their men.

Trained to serve at sea, the sailors received no instruction in the handling of ammunition. Joe Small, one of the black sailors assigned to the loading group and later indicted as a leader of the mutiny, operated a

Review of *The Port Chicago Mutiny* by Robert Allen, 88 Mich. L. Rev. 1689 (1990). Used by permission.

winch that lifted nets filled with bombs and artillery shells from the docks to the holds of the ships. . . . Small was aware of the danger. . . .

Weeks before the explosion, the longshoremen's union reportedly warned the Navy of a disaster if it continued to use untrained seamen to load ammunition. The union, for example, would not allow a winch operator like Joe Small to handle ammunition unless he had years of experience with other cargo. The Navy ignored the warning and rejected union offers to send experienced longshoremen to train Navy recruits in safety practices (p. 120).

Understandably, morale among the black sailors was low. They were far from the war zone and yet assigned to very dangerous work performed under the constant pushing of white officers. They enjoyed little chance for promotion and virtually no recreational facilities. The town of Port Chicago was not friendly to blacks, nor did the military provide transportation from the base to Oakland or to San Francisco. The men expressed their opposition in varying ways. Occasionally, a man might go AWOL or simply refuse to work. Others, over time, came to discount the risks or simply accept what they could not change. Some, like Joe Small, challenged the officers regarding the risk of an explosion. The officers denied that concussion alone would explode the bombs and assured the men that the bombs were harmless with their detonator caps removed.

On July 17, 1944, what many feared, happened:

> [A]n explosion with a force equal to that of the bomb dropped on Hiroshima nearly leveled . . . Port Chicago. Two military cargo ships loaded with ammunition and the entire Port Chicago waterfront were vaporized by the blast. . . . Three hundred and twenty men lost their lives. Two hundred and two of them were black. It was the worst home-front disaster of World War II.[1]

Following the disaster, the Navy denied the surviving black sailors the thirty-day leave it allowed the white survivors. After only a few weeks, the black men were ordered back to work at another port nearby, where the conditions were just as unsafe as those that had prevailed at Port Chicago. When more than 200 black sailors refused, they were marched to a barge and held under guard for several days. Eventually, fifty men were singled out for court-martial, charged with mutiny, and convicted. By year's end, they were serving prison sentences ranging from eight to fifteen years.

. . . The uniqueness of the story comes from interviews with the survivors, principally Joe Small. In the wake of the explosion, and advised that transfers to other work, including combat, would not be granted, many of the men decided that they did not want to load ammunition any more. As one of them put it:

> I just said: No, I ain't going back on that damn thing [shiploading]. Why don't they get some whiteys and put them down there. I said hell, I'm a gunneryman. They taught me how to fire guns; I'm supposed to be on a ship. Now they got me working as a stevedore. And I'm not getting stevedore's pay. [p. 76]

Several of the men approached Small for advice. They respected him and viewed him as their informal leader. Small made it clear that he would not return to loading ammunition, though he was ready to do other work. The work stoppage that precipitated the arrests and charges was not planned. . . .

. . . During the stoppage, the base chaplain, oblivious of the incongruity both in his words and in the Navy's treatment of these black sailors, tried to appeal to their race pride. He told the men that "they were letting down the loyal men of their race and their friends as well" (p. 81). When efforts to shame the men failed, officers ordered them individually back to work. The 258 men out of 328 who continued to express an unwillingness to handle ammunition were confined to a barge tied to a pier. In the meantime, civilian contract stevedores were hurriedly hired to load the ships. Like captives in the hold of a slave ship, the men were confined in the crowded barge for three days. . . .

Following another demand that the men choose either to work or to face a court-martial for mutiny and a possible death sentence, fifty continued to refuse and were placed in the brig. All 258 men, both those who chose work and received summary court-martials and those who still refused, were interrogated intensively for the next three weeks—without benefit of counsel—in an effort to build a case against those, like Small, who steadfastly refused to load ammunition.

A few days after the work stoppage, the Navy sought to defuse racial discrimination charges by introducing a personnel rotation system so that black sailors would not be retained indefinitely at the munitions loading docks. In addition, a contingent of white enlisted men was sent to work at Port Chicago. Had the Navy responded to the black sailors' concerns with these actions initially, the black seamen would not have refused to work, and no court-martial would have been necessary.

The military formally charged the fifty with mutiny in September 1944. The Navy encouraged press coverage, perhaps, Allen suggests, both to counter claims that it would be a kangaroo court and to intimidate other dissident sailors. The trial lasted more than a month, but after only 80 minutes of deliberation, all fifty of the defendants were found guilty of mutiny. Thurgood Marshall, then counsel to the NAACP, who observed the trial, noted that this averaged out to about a minute-and-a-half of deliberation for each defendant. All were sentenced to fifteen years in prison with reductions to twelve years for some not deemed ringleaders. Even the 208 men who agreed to work after initially joining the work stoppage were given summary court-martials resulting in bad-conduct discharges and forfeiture of three months' pay. . . .

The NAACP, other civil rights groups, and the black media had taken a strong interest in the case. They pressured government officials and launched a media campaign that met with some success after the Japanese surrendered in August 1945 and war hysteria subsided. The following month, sentences were reduced to two to three years with credit for time already served.

The Port Chicago men were released from prison but not from the Navy. They were divided into small groups and sent to the South Pacific for a probationary period. . . . The men were finally discharged under honorable conditions but the mutiny convictions still stand. . . .

After returning home, Small married and raised a family despite experiencing a good deal of discrimination in civilian life. He remains philosophical about the disaster, tragedy, and hardship he has encountered over the years. He carries no grudges against the Navy. . . . Small proudly told Allen that one of his sons was entering the Navy, adding "I wouldn't want him to go into any service except the Navy" (p. 143).

Reading *The Port Chicago Mutiny* my thoughts returned to a question a black student once raised in my civil rights course. Obviously agitated by the class's lengthy discussion of racial discrimination, a student raised his hand and asked dramatically, "Professor Bell, would you please tell me just one thing. Why are white folks so mean?"

My student's question [does not lend itself to an answer that is simple,] sufficient, or satisfying. . . . For the Port Chicago tragedy is, at bottom, a portrait of racial meanness. It is a tragedy precisely because it was far more illustrative of the norm than the accidental in the history of American racial justice.

As it pertains to blacks in wartime, the American norm has always been ambivalence: an illogical oscillation between valuing blacks as comrades-in-arms in a crisis and a deeply felt need not to permit blacks to escape from their subordinate place. Meanness then is that quality of racism that is the equivalent of "piling on" in football or "kicking a man when he is down" in street fighting. That is, both analogies acknowledge a struggle and that one side, though prevailing, is moved to humiliate the opponent, to inflict an unneeded blow to remove all doubt as to "who is boss."

The racial meanness phenomenon is certainly not limited to the military. Indeed, as conditions for blacks in civilian life continue to deteriorate, it may be that the military services are something of an equality haven for blacks. But consider the meanness component in the Supreme Court's recent civil rights rulings. For example, Brenda Patterson sought relief under a civil rights statute guaranteeing blacks the same right to "make and enforce contracts . . . as is enjoyed by white citizens." A majority of the Court denied relief because the statutory language "prohibits discrimination only in the making and enforcement of contracts."[2] Thus, the statute does not reach "conduct by the employer after the contract relation has been established, including . . . imposition of discriminatory working conditions."[3] Thus construed, the statute that even in its most liberal reading had made only a small dent in the hard shell of employment discrimination assumed a status best described as ludicrous.

Inconsistency is also a form of racial meanness when it denies civil rights petitioners relief on a rationale Professor Kenneth Karst has deemed "'Heads, we win; tails, you lose.'" Karst notes that "when majoritarian politics produces an affirmative action program" like the layoff scheme in *Wygant v. Jackson Board of Education* or the set-aside plan in *City of Richmond v. J. A. Croson Co.*, challengers have argued with increasing effectiveness that the plans abandon the "principle of 'individual merit' in favor of a group remedy."[4] But when blacks show disparate impact to support charges that a policy is discriminatory despite its facial neutrality, the Court expresses a "slippery-slope" type fear that relief would be unlimited, much as it did in *Washington v. Davis.* Seemingly traumatized by this fear, the Court rejects impressive evidence of discriminatory motive, while suggesting that group harms should be remedied by majoritarian politics.

In the past, one of the best defenses against racial meanness was a black person like Joe Small. Reading *The Port Chicago Mutiny*, I wondered: In a society where black people willing to confront racial discrimination in a defiant way are treated as dangerous and subversive, what combination of circumstances produces an individual with Joe Small's pride and self-assurance? In the military and in civilian life, Small always stood up for his rights and, often enough, paid a price for his refusal to buckle under. And yet, he harbored no bitterness, proudly telling Robert Allen that his son was enlisting in the Navy. Whatever the source of Small's strengths, one wonders whether they would be sufficient were he growing up in an inner-city area today.

For those of us active in the civil rights movement, it is difficult to concede that the segregation era—with all its hardships—was less harsh than life for poor and working class blacks in this post-*Brown* period. Unlike the Supreme Court reviewing the statistics in the *McCleskey v. Kemp* death penalty case, we cannot ignore the steadily worsening statistics of black poverty, unemployment, broken homes, drug abuse, and violent crime. Thus, while Robert Allen recounts a fifty-year-old racial "mutiny" that never was, both social indicators and common sense enable a prediction that, without major reforms, future racial rebellions will not be just fabrications manifesting the meanness of racist whites. Rather, they will be the predictable consequences of that meanness, and will not likely be deterred because the charges of mutiny are accurate.

NOTES

1. This vivid description is from the book's dust jacket.

2. Patterson v. McLean Credit Union, 109 S. Ct. 2363, 2372 (1989).

3. *See also* City of Richmond v. J. A. Croson Co., 109 S. Ct. 706 (1989) (Court, using strict scrutiny test, invalidated a municipal setaside plan that required prime contractors to subcontract to minority subcontractors at least 30% of the dollar amount of each city contract awarded).

4. Kenneth Karst, *Belonging to America* 158 (1989).

Racial Libel as American Ritual

In contemporary times, Arthur Jensen, Richard Herrnstein, and others have maintained that differences in average scores on standardized tests are proof of the intellectual inferiority of blacks. *The Bell Curve*[1] is perhaps the best marketed of a long line of publications that defame blacks as a means of comforting white anxieties about "place," and convincing them that, given their genetic inferiority, taking a hard line against blacks is appropriate as well as satisfying. The viability and value of this libel are particularly useful in shifting blame, particularly in bad economic times, from those responsible for failed policies to the nation's traditional scapegoats—black people.

Despite their seeming civility, these books' defamatory object is the same. Dinesh D'Souza's *The End of Racism*[2] is almost apologetic in its condemnation of blacks. Eschewing a hateful tone apparently gives these works a legitimacy as well as a marketability that more blatant purveyors of racial hate must envy. Literally dozens of magazines and newspapers published reviews of *The Bell Curve* and *The End of Racism*. True, most reviewers were quite critical, but they did review the books and treated them as serious works, not instances of group libel. In the book promotion business, getting reviewed is more important than whether or not the review is favorable. . . . Right-wing publications, not surprisingly, found much of value in the book. . . .

Taking the opposite and—for them—surprising view, economist Glenn Loury and entrepreneur Robert Woodson, two black men whose opposition to affirmative action and other traditional civil rights remedies have made them popular guests on television, so objected to *The End of Racism* that they publicly canceled their affiliation with the American Enterprise Institute where D'Souza is a fellow. In their view, the book

36 Washburn L.J. 1 (1996). Used by permission.

justifies racism by presenting a false and malicious portrait of black social pathologies in America. . . .

. . . .

Attention not only sells books, but in a society that values celebrity over competence and scandal over substance, D'Souza has proven particularly adept in an increasingly crowded field of individuals anxious to provide what activist Julian Bond views as a "pseudo-scientific and ahistorical confirmation that whites are, after all, superior to blacks and that racism—once considered an embarrassing evil—has vanished." Attacks on racism by writers like Cornel West, Julian Bond maintains, cannot "compete with the apologies for racism written by Charles Murray and Dinesh D'Souza." These writers "offer whites a release from guilt and absolution of any responsibility for the cause of the present-day condition of blacks or for its cure."[3]

Their surface plausibility makes D'Souza's arguments irresistible to whites who feel bogged down in the bottomless swamp of racial issues—whites looking for a rescue rope of rationalities to pull them to a safe, secure position. D'Souza offers them that rope.

Bond continues:

No one is responsible for black poverty except the black poor—so no one (certainly not the taxpayers) is responsible for setting it right. Discrimination doesn't exist, so we don't need the pesky anti-discrimination laws or affirmative action anymore. Black people occupy lower income, occupational and educational rungs on society's ladder because of self-inflicted pathologies, not historical and present-day discrimination. Whites don't want to work or live or go to school with them, not because of color prejudice but because of class differences. What a relief! What a country!

After 300 years, it is easy to see the temptations that move so many in this country to take comfort in specious racial assertions rather than join the search for solutions to conditions that devastate and debilitate whites as well as blacks. But this relief comes at a very high cost, rendering many whites unable to recognize their own need—their own disadvantage.

Surely, they must see that the effort to ignore black poverty obscures and desensitizes them to the truth that two-thirds of teenage mothers and two-thirds of welfare recipients are white. It is well known that the rate of drug use by pregnant women is not significantly different across race and class lines, and that drug use in general is as prevalent in the suburbs as in the ghettos. And yet, as novelist Ishmael Reed says, "in the popular imagination blacks are blamed for all these activities, in the manner that Jews took the rap for the black plague, even in countries with little or no Jewish population."[4]

Today, the country's black plague is an economic rather than a physical illness. But, as with the plague, the toll among those who are victims of the down-sizing mania is large and growing. Fear runs rampant among the potential victims, whose jobs and income could go at any time. Meanwhile, those elected to address the uncertainty and fear are worsening an already dangerous condition by ignoring the crisis or shifting attention to relative irrelevancies.

The deficit is high and Congress wants to reduce it by cutting social programs that serve the needy while increasing the defense budget and other forms of corporate welfare. The income and wealth gap grows greater, but the budget cutters are anxious to pass tax cuts that will further benefit the already well-off.

Affirmative action has been transformed from a modest effort to give corporations, institutions, and government agencies a semblance of compliance with equal opportunity standards, into a synonym for the selection of blacks less qualified than rejected whites. . . .

. . . .

The California Board of Regents insisted that it was their commitment to merit and not political opportunism that led them to ban affirmative action in the admissions process. Now, thanks to the *Los Angeles Times,* we learn that: "Special consideration in admissions for the rich and well-connected has been part of the UCLA culture for years, extending beyond University of California regents and state politicians to include friends and relatives of local political figures, university officials and major donors."[5] Does anyone want to risk that similar practices were not going on at other California colleges?

So much for merit.

Now that it is politically unpopular, most institutions that employ affirmative action do so privately, often while condemning it in public. The conservative *New Republic* reported with some glee that the even more conservative *Washington Times,* which editorially condemns affirmative action as "race-based quotas," in fact, sponsors minority intern programs and works hard to keep blacks on its staff.[6] Note how racial hypocrisy is usually a part of the racial libel mix.

. . . .

[Eds. Bell next reviews a number of "racial hoax" crimes, in which white people blame blacks for a crime a white committed, and continues as follows:]

These culprits used the white public's fear of and antipathy toward black people in their failed efforts to mask their nefarious acts. Of course, the hoaxes gain plausibility because black crime is real. Blacks are the principal victims of crimes committed by blacks, but whites (because of racial myths and libels) are so fearful of black crime that some whites view it as a perfect cover to even the most heinous crime. The society, similarly self-deceived, refuses to concede that the so-called war on crime is an expensive failure precisely because it is a response to the fears rather than to the causes.

Building more prisons and filling them (more than a million black men at last count) is no answer to the racial discrimination–caused poverty and hopelessness that underlie so much violent crime. And failure to deal with the cause leads to an inability to separate the real from the myth regarding the danger.

It is only surprising that given their exclusion from traditional paths of upward mobility, more black men do not choose crime as their means of "making it" in a society that equates wealth and power with success—regardless of how obtained. For a growing number though, no other apparent choice lies before them. Increasingly, then, the myth of black crime becomes a self-fulfilling prophecy.

. . . .

We should not be surprised if this, the centennial of the *Plessy v. Ferguson* decision, is allowed to pass unheralded by the major media. And predictably, most comments about a case most Americans would prefer to forget will be cushioned in reminders that fifty-eight years later in 1954, the Court in *Brown v. Board of Education* declared the "separate but equal" doctrine unconstitutional. The *Brown* decision, though, was less the long-sought remedy for *Plessy* than a reinforcement of a more basic, two-part principle of this country's racial policies.

Part One: The society is always willing to sacrifice the rights of black people in order to protect important economic or political interests of whites. The *Plessy v. Ferguson* decision represents a prime example of

Part One, less because it gave segregation the status of constitutional law than because it sacrificed black rights in order to gain the support of whites for policies that harmed a great many white people.

Part Two: The law recognizes the rights of black people only when this serves some economic or political interest of greater importance to whites. Lincoln's reluctant issuance of the Emancipation Proclamation to help the faltering effort to save the Union was an example of Part Two in action. Similarly, after World War II, the United States, now the world leader in efforts to win the allegiance of mostly non-white, third-world nations, discovered that practicing Jim Crow at home made it tough to advocate democracy abroad. The *Brown* decision, by promising to close the gap between the country's ideals and its practices, provided an immediate boost to America's foreign policy efforts. Here was Part Two of the racial policy principle at work.

But while the Jim Crow signs came down after prolonged battles in the courts and on the streets, the society quickly devised means to limit the substantive value of the pro–civil rights decisions and the new civil rights laws enacted during the 1960s. Disenchantment set in when whites began to recognize that racial equality for blacks meant more than condemning the use of fire hoses and police dogs on peacefully protesting children in a deep-South town. It meant, as well, taking steps to correct for decades when blacks were excluded, remedies that sometimes required whites to surrender their expectations of privileges and priorities long available simply because they were white.

. . . .

Even in modern times, blacks who have spoken out against racism have faced retaliation: Marcus Garvey, W. E. B. Du Bois, Paul Robeson, Martin Luther King, Jr., Malcolm X, the Black Panthers, and the Nation of Islam. Just as the nation pays homage to dead black leaders it feared and harassed during their lifetimes, so it wraps a veil of righteousness around past racial protests and black initiatives that it condemned at the time. This includes the sit-ins, the Freedom Rides, marches, boycotts, and even the great 1963 March on Washington.

The pattern of fearful criticism repeated itself during the 1995 Million Man March, organized by Nation of Islam leader, Louis Farrakhan. In one of the largest and most remarkable gatherings in the nation's history, at least a million black men traveled to Washington D.C. at their own expense and on Monday, a work day. Detractors ask, of what value was it? But no one who was there, including a goodly number of black women and whites, will ever forget the feeling of brotherhood that was almost tangible throughout that massive, peaceful gathering. . . .

Some black men, such as Roger Wilkins and Judge Leon Higginbotham, did not come to the March and have spoken out about their reservations. That the media have been enthusiastically publishing their concerns should not detract from their sincerity. I was concerned about the seeming sexism in aiming the call at black men. Minister Farrakhan, and some of his followers, have made statements that are seen as homophobic and anti-Semitic. As it turned out, none of these fears materialized at the March. Nevertheless, I can understand why some blacks chose not to associate themselves because of what they might call "reverse racial libel."

For my part, though, I applied my personal "Senator Fulbright Principle of Individual Differentiation." J. William Fulbright, who represented Arkansas in the U.S. Senate from 1945 to 1974, was an outstanding and quite forward-looking foreign policy expert. On the other hand, he voted against every civil rights bill that came before the Senate. When I pointed this out to those who hailed his foreign policy contributions, they lectured me: "Bell, you must not forget. This man is a great asset to the country. But in order to get elected in Arkansas, he has to oppose antidiscrimination legislation. It is simply a fact of political life."

Over the years, I have had to apply the Fulbright Principle of Individual Differentiation to countless numbers of otherwise impressive white leaders whose skills and wisdom falter when it comes to racial issues. I have had to acknowledge their contributions and tolerate their civil rights shortcomings. I see no reason why I should take a more rigid stance with respect to Louis Farrakhan. And, that so many whites (and some blacks) insist on condemning him for some of what he has said and ignoring what he has done makes me even more reluctant to depart from my Fulbright Principle.

. . . .

The racial libel so many Americans view as a comforting cure is actually an addictive habit that masks the increasing jeopardy of both its victims and perpetrators. Thus, it appears that black people will again be condemned to suffer because of economic conditions we did not create. African Americans are bearing the brunt of unemployment, but we are also the focus of the rage of the many whites who, fearful for their own jobs and future well-being, are all too easily convinced that the threat to both is our black presence rather than the real villain: corporate greed.

And what of the future? At the least, we will need impressive well-springs of faith to withstand a fate that could bring current levels of hostility to the point of major violence and bloodshed. It would not be the first time that black people were hunted down and massacred in the streets or cremated in their homes set ablaze by angry, white mobs. Given this environment of black blame, the traditional sources of relief—the courts and the political process—are not likely to prove useful in the present crisis. They are, of course, still worthy of attention and effort, but they have proved woefully inadequate to protect our lives, much less our rights.

. . . .

Even if blacks achieve a new unity, nothing in the annals of this country justifies a prediction that our efforts will alter the destructive course of a nation where, as W. E. B. Du Bois observed, "the real allegiance is to reducing all the nation's resources to dusky dollars."[7] In pursuit of that goal, native Americans were virtually wiped out, millions of Africans were enslaved, Asians and Mexicans were exploited, and millions of working-class whites have spent much of their lives in labor only a few steps less onerous than slavery.

. . . .

Our future is dire, and yet one of the late James Cleveland's favorite gospel hymns contains an uplifting message, one echoing the resilience and faith that enabled our forebears to survive storms as severe as those that lie ahead for us and this alien land of ours:

> I don't feel no ways tired,
> I've come too far from where I started from,
> Nobody told me the road would be easy,
> I don't believe He's brought me this far to leave me.[8]

NOTES

1. RICHARD J. HERRNSTEIN & CHARLES MURRAY, THE BELL CURVE: INTELLIGENCE AND CLASS STRUCTURE IN AMERICAN LIFE (1994).

2. DINESH D'SOUZA, THE END OF RACISM (1995).

3. Julian Bond, *Letter to the Editor,* WASH. POST, Sept. 30, 1995, at A21.

4. Ishmael Reed, *Crime, Drugs & the Media: The Black Pathology Biz,* in UNCIVIL WAR: RACE, CIVIL RIGHTS & THE NATION: 1865–1995, at 27 (Peter Rothberg ed., 1995).

5. Ralph Frammolino et al., *UCLA Eased Entry Rules for the Rich, Well-Connected,* L.A. TIMES, Mar. 21, 1996, at 1.

6. Andy Lamey, *Do As I Say,* NEW REPUBLIC, June 26, 1995, at 14.

7. Attributed to W. E. B. Du Bois.

8. JAMES CLEVELAND, I DON'T FEEL NO WAYS TIRED, ON REV. JAMES CLEVELAND: A TRIBUTE TO THE KING (Malaco, MAL 1991).

Fear of Black Crime
Is Political Tool

We are shocked but we should not be surprised by the revelation that Charles Stuart, and not a black male attacker, robbed and killed his pregnant wife. Stuart used the white public's fear of black people and antipathy toward them to mask his heinous act. His reliance on race as a diversionary tactic has a long history.

Politicians, from precinct captains to presidents, have exploited fear of black people and the specter of black crime as an effective tactic to win elections and to avoid the need to address serious issues once in office. Stuart's story stands as the latest in a long line of instances in which a negative report about blacks was accepted without scrutiny because it reinforced deeply held stereotypes about black behavior.

The fear of black crime is, of course, not all based on myth. Black men in Boston, as in most urban areas, commit a disproportionately large percentage of all violent crime. Stuart's hoax was plausible because black crime is real. No less real is the poverty and hopelessness that underlie so much violent crime. It is only surprising that, given their exclusion from traditional paths of upward mobility, more black men do not choose crime as their means of "making it" in a society that equates wealth and power with success.

The grim statistics of black crime will not yield to police patrols that assume every black male in Boston's minority neighborhoods is a dangerous suspect. Police crackdowns, like the campaign to restore the death penalty in states that abandoned it, and the much publicized war on drugs, are all policies of racial diversion. They are less dramatic than

L.A. Daily J., Jan. 1, 1990, at 6. Copyright 1990 Daily Journal Corp. Reprinted by permission.

Charles Stuart's connivance but hardly less destructive for whites and blacks alike.

With attention focused on the nation's Willie Hortons, no one seems to notice the socially debilitating and potentially dangerous and widening income gap between the wealthy and the poor. . . .

Conservative policy makers find it relatively easy to shift the white public's attention from the lack of opportunity and the uneven distribution of wealth to the latent fears about blacks moving too fast—fears that, these days, are couched in anti–affirmative action language. Whites at every level share racial fears and stereotypes to some degree. Opponents of social reform are able to transform this unconscious Caucasian consensus into policies that undermine civil rights efforts.

Diversions using race pose a dual-edged danger. First, they prompt whites to oppose schooling, housing, employment, health and other effective crime-fighting policies, even when they would provide services whites need as much as blacks. Second, in this racially paranoid environment, blacks find it almost impossible to climb out of poverty, and even blacks who were doing well 10 years ago now find themselves slipping downward toward poverty.

A long-running debate rages, of course, about whether discrimination and disadvantage account for black crime or whether the tragic statistics result from inherent inadequacies of black people. This discussion is able to survive all manner of black achievements. It is a classic example of racial diversion. In the heated contentions about why blacks fail, and, in particular, why so many black men turn to crime, few take the time to consider what combination of societal factors drove a middle class white man to murder his pregnant wife.

Charles Stuart was not burdened by the racial prejudice that discourages and ultimately destroys so many African Americans. He was a white man who, from the perspective of poor blacks, had everything that so many of them turn to crime to get. The nature of his crime makes Stuart a special case, but his bold effort to shift the blame for his deed is in an American tradition that virtually defines the evil that is racism.

CHAPTER 12

Popular Democracy

Most anti-minority measures, such as miscegenation laws, have come about through the majoritarian legislative process, or else by judicial (e.g., Dred Scott v. Sandford) or executive (e.g., Japanese internment) action. With increasing frequency, however, the voters themselves, by referendum or other form of direct popular democracy, enact a measure that falls harshly on an outsider group. Courts have been reluctant to interfere with these forms of plebiscite. What can minorities do when it is the public itself that votes to eliminate affirmative action or immigration rights? In a country committed to majority rule and convinced that democracy —rule by the people—can do no wrong, one must come to terms with the possibility that the majority may tyrannize a small group. The two pieces that follow analyze, but do not solve, this problem.

The Referendum
Democracy's Barrier to Racial Equality

Provisions for referendums demonstrate devotion to democracy, not to bias, discrimination, or prejudice.　　　—Justice Hugo Black

. . . .

When Justice Black hailed referendum provisions as devotion to democracy and not proof of "bias, discrimination, or prejudice," his was not simply a rhetorical flourish. The statement embodied a central principle of his 1971 majority opinion in *James v. Valtierra*.[1] In that case, black and Mexican-American indigents had challenged Article 34 of the California constitution, which required prior approval in a local referendum before a state public body could develop a federally financed low-rent housing project. They argued that Article 34 unreasonably discriminated, explicitly against the poor and implicitly against minority groups, because it mandated special voter approval for low-income housing. . . .

. . . Noting that mandatory referenda were required by California law for other actions, albeit not connected with housing, Black viewed the referendum as a legitimate vehicle for ensuring "that all the people of a community will have a voice in a decision which may lead to large expenditures of local governmental funds for increased public services and to lower tax revenues." . . . The *Valtierra* majority not only refused to subject Article 34 to "exacting judicial scrutiny," because wealth was not a suspect state classification, but also failed to subject it to even a token

54 Wash. L. Rev. 1 (1978). Used by permission.

357

review for a rational relationship between the means employed and its ostensible purpose. . . .

. . . .

. . . The decision can be explained only by a deep-seated faith in the sanctity of referenda results, even when they seriously disadvantage minorities and the poor. As long as the disadvantage to minorities is not intentionally racial and arguably furthers a reasonable interest, judicial intervention is not forthcoming.

Justice Black's assertion that referenda demonstrate devotion to democracy was not completely unexpected. His commitment to the referendum had been amply demonstrated in earlier decisions and he has since bequeathed his faith to a solid majority of the Court, whose devotion to the referendum presents a serious danger to the civil rights of minority groups.

. . . .

Despite the broad reading given Title VII of the Civil Rights Act of 1964 and the impressive efforts of legal scholars, the Supreme Court, in reviewing equal protection challenges, has refused to disfavor laws and policies that are not overtly discriminatory even though those laws and policies disproportionately disadvantage the members of racial minorities. The question then is whether, in the practice of popular sovereignty, lurk unacknowledged aspects of racial discrimination or some other basis, such as a serious danger to our legislative form of government, which entitle minority groups to special protection when their interests are placed at risk. . . .

. . . .

The high priority many whites give to maintaining racial superiority will undoubtedly find expression at the ballot box. Throughout this country's history, politicians have succumbed to the temptation to wage a campaign appealing to the desire of whites to dominate blacks. More recently, however, the growing black vote has begun to have an impact and even effected "Road to Damascus" conversions on more than a few political Pauls, some of whom even claim "born again" experiences during midterm. This impact may be subverted if voting majorities may enact controversial legislation directly.

Public officials, even those elected on more or less overtly racist campaigns, may prove responsive to minority pressures for civil rights measures once in office or, at least, be open to the negotiation and give-and-take that constitutes much of the political process. Thus, legislators may vote for, or executive officials may sign, a civil rights or social reform bill with full knowledge that a majority of their constituents oppose it. They are in the spotlight and do not wish publicly to advocate racism; they cannot openly attribute their opposition to "racist constituents." The more neutral reasons for opposition are often inadequate in the face of serious racial injustices, particularly those posing threats not confined to the minority community.

When the legislative process is turned back to the citizenry . . . few of the concerns that can transform the "conservative" politician into a "moderate" public official are likely to affect the individual voter's decision. No political factors counsel restraint on racial passions emanating from longheld and little considered beliefs and fears. Far from being the pure path to democracy that Justice Black proclaimed, direct democracy, carried out in the privacy of the voting booth, has diminished the ability of minority groups to participate in the democratic process. Ironically, because it enables the voters' racial beliefs and fears to be recorded and tabulated in their pure form, the referendum has proven a most effective facilitator of that bias, discrimination, and prejudice which has marred American democracy from its earliest day.

. . . .

Direct legislation, the creation of progressives of another era, poses more danger today to social progress than the problems of governmental unresponsiveness it was intended to cure. This is not to suggest that we ought to ignore the defects and disappointments of the representative system which today, as in the past, have spurred public recourse to direct legislation. All too often, both Congress and the President become targets and, one fears, the captives of powerful business interests. It is also undeniable that representatives may vote on bills which they do not understand or concerning which they have been improperly influenced.

Nevertheless, our distrust and dissatisfaction with public officials should not so quickly lead us to conclude that increased reliance on direct democracy will avoid those evils. Supporters of minority rights must be concerned that both the initiative and the referendum often serve those opposed to reform. It is clear, for example, that direct legislation enables residents of homogenous middle-class communities to prevent unwanted development—especially development that portends increased size or heterogeneity of population.

Today, direct democracy finds only infrequent use to curb abuses in government or otherwise to control elected officials. Rather, intense interest mobilizes when the issues are seemingly clear-cut and often emotional matters such as liquor, gun control, pollution, pornography, or race. Complicated taxation problems and matters of governmental structure, on the other hand, typically evoke little voter response.

The emotionally charged atmosphere often surrounding referenda and initiatives can easily reduce the care with which the voters consider the matters submitted to them. Tumultuous, media-oriented campaigns . . . are not conducive to careful thinking and voting. . . . Appeals to prejudice, oversimplification of the issues, and exploitation of legitimate concerns by promising simplistic solutions to complex problems often characterize referendum and initiative campaigns. Of course, politicians, too, may offer quick cure-alls to gain electoral support and may spend millions on election campaigns that are as likely to obfuscate as to elucidate the issues. But we vote politicians into office, not into law. Once in office, they may become well-informed, responsible representatives; at the least, their excesses will confront the checks and balances of the political process.

. . . .

The Court's failure to review more closely the many opportunities for misrepresentation, financial abuse, and outright fraud can only encourage campaigners to appeal to prejudice. The record of recent ballot legislation reflects all too accurately the conservative, even intolerant, attitudes citizens display when given the chance to vote their fears and prejudices, especially when exposed to expensive media campaigns. The security of minority rights and the value of racial equality which those rights affirm are endangered by the possibility of popular repeal.

. . . .

The threat persists largely because the Supreme Court, for the most part, refuses to alter or strike down laws which, although neutral in form, function to promote racial discrimination. The courts should at least recognize that the initiative and referendum may operate as a nonracial facade covering distinctly discriminatory measures. Moreover, lower-class whites will often support referenda advancing middle-class values, to the detriment of their own economic interests, in order to secure their racial status. Thus, referenda and initiatives expose blacks to harm not only because referenda serve to enact racially hostile measures, but also because blacks are isolated from their class allies and thus suffer diminished electoral strength.

. . . .

The same danger to the republican process which was present in the multi-district cases is present here. The danger is twofold. First, in a particular referendum on a particular issue, a matter extremely harmful to minority interests but only moderately beneficial to nonminority interests may be passed; the ballot does not easily register intensity of interest as the legislative process does. Second, the initiative and referendum processes in general prevent meaningful participation by minority groups. As more legislation comes about through direct ballot, minorities are increasingly excluded from participating in decisions affecting the entire society. Of what value is it to protect an individual's right to vote for elected officials if the important decisions are made in referenda rather than in the legislature?

. . . .

Surely, . . . our [system of] representative government can prevent an electoral majority from subverting minority gains achieved through participation in representative government. Precedent provides the means to prevent the majority from abusing its power to uproot those protections against discrimination, without which minority group members are as effectively prevented from meaningful participation in the electoral process as they earlier were by poll taxes and literacy tests.

Justice Black's declaration that referenda demonstrate devotion to democracy rather than to bias, discrimination, or prejudice is in fact almost the opposite of the truth when the issue submitted to the voters suggests, even subtly, that majority interests can be furthered by the sacrifice of minority rights. The failure to recognize the special dangers to minority groups in the referendum process is evidenced in a reluctance to acknowledge either that there are minorities in society or that there is racism. Of course, both exist, and neither is likely to disappear in the near future. For ours is a heterogeneous society. Ample reason counsels that we give serious consideration to the founding fathers' cautious approach to direct democracy. They were closer than we to those basic structural arrangements by which individual rights in a free society must be protected against the tyranny of the majority. Slavery has had permanent impact on American life. Among its effects are racial antagonism and a false sense of racial superiority for the great mass of whites which, if not curable, should at least be contained by a judicial preference for the representative mode of government, where its worst tendencies toward prejudice will be chastened in legislative debate and public scrutiny and diluted by political compromise.

. . .

[Eds. After Bell published this article and the next one, the Supreme Court invalidated a Colorado anti-gay initiative in *Romer v. Evans* and the Ninth Circuit struck down large portions of a California anti-immigrant measure, Proposition 187.]

NOTE

1. 402 U.S. 137, 141 (1971).

California's Proposition 209

A Temporary Diversion on the Road to Racial Disaster

Less than a month ago my long-time friend, Chief District Judge Thelton Henderson, gave supporters of California's affirmative action programs a most welcome Christmas present. He followed up the temporary restraining order he issued shortly after the voters approved Proposition 209 with a preliminary injunction, the appeal of which through the courts would seem to frustrate the goals of this anti–affirmative action initiative for some time.

Almost reflexively, I join the applause for Judge Henderson's courageous decision. Jubilation by affirmative action supporters, though, should be restrained. For, as I suggest in my title, the decision, like the affirmative action programs it seeks to protect, may prove only a temporary diversion on the road to racial disaster.

. . . .

I want to say quite clearly that I am a product of affirmative action. I am not stupid and I work hard and would likely have had a worthwhile career without affirmative action. But that career would almost certainly not have been as a law teacher and legal writer. I absolutely would not have become a full professor at the Harvard Law School. Without the Harvard imprimatur, my unorthodox writings filled with allegory exploring the depths of racism in the law and the society would likely not have been published and, if published, would not have been taken seriously.

Did I merit the opportunities affirmative action provided me? Did my Harvard appointment deny some better qualified white man the position

30 Loy. L.A. L. Rev. 1447 (1997). Used by permission.

I filled? Such questions, though hotly debated, are totally disconnected from reality. Let's face it. The much-extolled word "merit" has only a serendipitous connection with success. If we as a society truly valued merit, we would not have the President we have, and the make-up of our leadership in every area would be far different—and certainly far better —than it is. Indeed, outside the affirmative action debate, you virtually never hear the word. We simply assume it while making decisions on an array of factors in which ability is more a fortuity than a sought-for goal. In short, merit serves as the phony pennant of color-blindness, used as justification for opposition to affirmative action.

If merit is really the concern, why don't the various anti–affirmative action measures ban legacy admits? Studies show that those admitted to California's colleges because a parent is an alum show credentials quite like those of minority candidates. Actually, if merit were really a concern, we would ban the use of SATs and other standardized tests. They all pre-dict performance to some degree, but they predict even more accurately the socio-economic status of the parents of those taking the tests. We maintain these so-called objective measures of academic potential be-cause they identify and advantage those applicants from the upper classes. When they don't, as when too many Asians in California started out-performing too many whites, serious discussion begins of altering the weight given in the admissions process, for example reducing the value assigned to math scores where many Asian Americans excelled, while en-hancing the value of the reading scores where Asians did less well.

Christopher Jencks supervised a classic study in an effort to ascertain the qualities that led individuals to enjoy success in their jobs and ca-reers.[1] The three qualities that turned up again and again were not native intelligence, academic achievement, or ability. Rather, what counted most were connections, family and otherwise, personality, and luck. For me, affirmative action made possible the connections, and luck made affir-mative action popular just when I needed it. . . .

. . . Slightly over one hundred years ago, the Supreme Court decided *Plessy v. Ferguson*,[2] upholding the widespread practice of racially segre-gating blacks in virtually every aspect of public life. Mandatory segrega-tion, the Court ruled, was valid and, as for the protections guaranteed under the Equal Protection Clause, the Court found it sufficient if the fa-cilities provided blacks were "equal, but separate."

. . . The Court, of course, had not set out on its own to repeal the Civil War Amendments and the supporting statutes enacted during the brief

Reconstruction period. Rather, it spoke for the majority of whites who, whether pro- or anti-slavery could not envision blacks as other than an inferior people whose labor was exploited, whose cultural contributions were ridiculed and then stolen, and whose very presence provided whites of vastly different positions on the social ladder with a shared sense of superiority. For the mass of European immigrants, the inculcation of a common racism was a major vehicle for their acculturation and assimilation.

. . . .

In the early 1970s, a great many corporations, government agencies, and educational institutions decided that affirmative action programs were a relatively inexpensive response to the urban rebellions, particularly those sparked by Martin Luther King's assassination. Without really altering patterns of hiring, admitting, and promoting that privileged well-off or well-connected whites, minority admission or hiring policies were designed to bring some blacks, Hispanics, and women into previously all-white and mostly male domains. Some of these programs worked better than others, while they all served the interests of the sponsoring institutions as much as they did those of minorities.

But as the job market tightened and anxiety about their future well-being increased, more and more whites opposed these programs. Politicians at every level were quite willing to win elections by blaming the nation's malaise on affirmative action programs. Given the nation's history of scapegoating serious economic problems on blacks and other minority groups, it is not surprising that polls reveal that a majority of whites, particularly white men, are rather easily convinced that their well-being is eroding, not because of policy decisions by corporate heads and their elected representatives, but by blacks who, they believe, use racial discrimination as an ever-ready excuse for demanding preferences while disdaining performance. As they did in the latter part of the nineteenth century, Supreme Court decisions in the area of civil rights in general and affirmative action in particular have swung into line with public opposition —so much so that strict scrutiny has become useless to deal with continuing racial discrimination and has become a tool for undoing modest efforts to counteract that discrimination. . . .

. . . The spirit of *Plessy*'s separate but equal standard is revived in the Court's willingness to employ disingenuous terms to disguise its continued willingness to sacrifice black rights to further white interests.

. . . .

It is Judge Henderson's failure to acknowledge these recurring patterns of involuntary sacrifice of minority interests to allay or deflect other concerns that gives his Proposition 209 opinion its cut flower quality: beautiful to look at but of likely limited longevity. . . . [Eds. Bell proved right. The Ninth Circuit quickly overturned the injunction.]

. . . .

The growing reliance on automation, the deportation of jobs to third-world countries, and the importation of cheap, foreign labor all have worsened the unemployment problem. Yet only Secretary of Labor Robert Reich was willing to point an accusatory finger at the nation's largest corporations whose downsizing tactics are ruining the lives of millions in order to retain or even enhance profit levels. As a result, growing numbers of skilled workers, both white collar and blue collar, executives, and professionals are out of jobs.

Job anxiety is now sufficiently severe that even the politicians are having trouble blaming it all on affirmative action. Advocates report that their inability to correct misimpressions was a major factor in Proposition 209's passage. . . . What this means is that anti–affirmative action thinking is so deeply fixed in the minds of many that, while its open advocacy is no longer a guarantee of election, the support of affirmative action may be an invitation to defeat.

. . . .

I admit that I might have ruled as [Judge Henderson] did for reasons concerning the courts and their functioning unknown to me that justify his action. But unless these factors were very strong, I would have written an opinion that indicated the relevance of earlier referendum cases. Reluctantly, I would then express doubt as to their continued viability after the Court's recent cases that make it easy for whites to challenge remedies for racial injustice and make it almost impossible to design effective remedies relying on racial classifications that, in the absence of overt discrimination, can withstand the "strict scrutiny" test.

I would lament the Supreme Court's retreat on civil rights in general and affirmative action in particular. I would review in detail all the reasons that affirmative action is an appropriate remedy for discriminatory policies, both those of the past and those that are continuing, and I would survey the damage to minorities but more particularly to whites if the state abandons affirmative action policies.

I would review the economic factors that led so many whites and some minorities to support Proposition 209, and I would review the history of such economic scapegoating. I would observe affirmative action has increased, point out in detail how much more affirmative action has helped whites and the society's image than it has minorities, and how, without it, the losses blacks are experiencing at every turn will be increased with adverse costs and consequences to everyone.

And having painted as bleak a picture of a future without affirmative action as I could, I would then deny the preliminary injunction and set the case for trial. Given my support for affirmative action, my decision might disappoint my friends and delight my enemies. . . . It happened to Martin Luther King, Jr., when he expanded his program from civil rights to jobs and poverty and then to the Vietnam War. I am not Dr. King but like him, I am willing to state the conclusions that my experience have led me to reach.

. . . .

Here, then, lies the challenge of Proposition 209 and all the other dangers we who are minorities in power, money, and race face during these turbulent times. We respond against overwhelming odds because we know that doing nothing will only worsen, not improve, our condition. We rise and take risks with the knowledge that, win or lose, we are on the side that we believe is right.

[Eds. Shortly after Bell wrote, the federal courts reversed Judge Henderson—although not for Bell's reasons—spelling the end of affirmative action in California.]

NOTES

1. See Christopher Jencks et al., Inequality: A Reassessment of the Effect of Family and Schooling in America 8–14 (1972).
2. 163 U.S. 537 (1896).

CHAPTER 13

Race and Class

Some believe that racism is dead, or that discrimination on the basis of class is much more serious. For Bell, the two forms of discrimination are intimately connected: The situation is not either-or. Much of racial discrimination rests on an economic base—it is a means of securing class advantage. It is also a means by which elite whites secure the cooperation of down-and-out working class whites, who might otherwise join forces with struggling blacks against the corporate forces that oppress them both.

Affirmative action, special admissions, and other reforms born of the civil rights movement often end up benefiting whites more than they benefit blacks, while, according to Bell, both black radicals and sell-outs play directly into white hands. And why is society relatively willing to grant small civil rights concessions to blacks and other minorities from time to time, but so reluctant to recognize economic rights (such as the right to food) that would benefit all the poor without regard to color? Bell shows how heeding the race-class connection enables the reformer to keep his eye on the prize.

Racism

A Major Source of Property and Wealth Inequality in America

Rural Town Gas Station—Deep South in the Mid-1960s

It is dusk, the end of a hot summer day. A half-dozen or so working class, white, "good ole' boys" are grouped around a bench in front of a run-down, two-pump gas station. An outdoor phone hangs limply from the wall. A faded sign over the station garage reads: Moultree's Oil, Gas, Repairs. Dressed in bib overalls and plaid shirts or in khaki pants and undershirts, the men are horsing around, drinking beer, and chiding a teenager, BUDDY, *who refuses to drink with them.*

MOULTREE

(The owner of the gas station, an older man, and a figure of authority, points his beer at the boy.)

Com'on, Buddy boy. Jus' 'cause you finish high school and hopin' to go to that raggedyass state college over in Greenville, don' mean you can't join us with one of these beers.

BUDDY

(Hangs his head, obviously not wanting to argue.)

This Coke is jus' fine.

GROUP

(The others hoot at the remark. They joke about the benefits of not finishing school and boast about how little schooling each has.)

ANDY

(Fat redneck, beer-belly, a troublemaker and proud of it, looks at Moultree.)

34 Ind. L. Rev. 1261 (2001). Used by permission. And from *Gospel Choirs* 103 by Derrick Bell. Copyright © 1996 by Derrick Bell. Reprinted by permission of Basic Books, a member of Perseus Books, L.L.C.

Guess you ain' tol' him, Moultree. Don' drink wit' the boys and you cain't work at Moultree's. . . . Don't work at Moultree's and you cain't afford to go to college.

J.T.

(*Tall, relatively slender in comparison with the others. Grimaces to show he doesn't like Andy's comment.*)

You wrong on both counts, Andy. My baby brother wants to work, but he got one of thos' whatcha call 'em, scholarships. An' it ain't at no state college. It's Ole Miss.

BUDDY

(*Frowns at his brother. Where he hopes to go to college was supposed to stay in the family until everything was worked out.*)

GROUP

(*Surprised and impressed by the news, they are also envious and even more anxious to cut Buddy down to size.*)

MOULTREE

(*In a dominating, almost threatening tone.*)

You better off at State, boy. Ole Miss ain't Ole Miss no more now the Feds done forced that nigger, James Meredith, in there. Looks like white men can't have nothin' to 'emselves no more. Watch what I say, niggers goin' take over the whole damn state.

GROUP

(*Make faces expressing disgust and declare, cursing, that they are not going to let it happen.*)

J.T.

(*With vehemence, not wanting to be on the wrong side of this issue.*)

You right there, Clem. Mama an' Daddy wranglin' over this thing ever since Buddy got the letter. Daddy say no chile o' his'n goin' to no school that takes in niggers. Mama let him talk, but my money say, Buddy goin' to Ole Miss.

TODD

(*The elder of the group, with little hair, fewer teeth, perched on a barrel.*)

I tell you. Our Negras was happy 'till them Northern do-gooders come down here stirrin' 'em up. My granpappy tol me same thing happened after the Confederacy. Northern do-gooders swarm in here like flies on horseshit, gave our darkies all manner o' big ideas. They got tired, after while. Left on their own—though we helped some git on back where they come from. Then we scared the niggers back into shape. Happen before, it'll happen again. Mark my word!

ANDY

Damn right, Todd. Way it suppos' to be. White man take what he want. Niggers get the leftovers. Fair and square how I sees it.

BUDDY

(*Looks hard at Andy, then at the rest of the group. He speaks in a low voice but with some feeling.*)

Been readin' a lot and thinkin' a lot. Sure, we whites kin have what we want long as what we want's is drinkin' beer in the heat and dust 'round a two-pump station out in the country. That, and keepin' niggers down. None of us got much of nothin' worthwhile. Meantime, the fat cats runnin' the companies and gettin' themselves elected to high office livin' better 'n we ever dream. When we goin' to get smart?

J.T.

(*Embarrassed at his brother's remarks that distance him from the only group he knows.*)

We goin' to get real smart after you finis' college, Buddy. You goin' smart us up real good. Right, boys?

GROUP

(*Laughs long and hard at Buddy's expense. Buddy lapses back into silence, staring at the Coke bottle in his hand.*)

TODD

(*Looks at Buddy hard. He is serious, not laughing.*)

Naw, J.T. He ain't gonna smart us up. White boys like Buddy go to college, get in line for good-payin' jobs, marry them trophy women with long hair, hands ain't never been in no soapsuds. Buddy go to college, won't have no time for the likes of us. Soon be one of them fat cats, treatin' us like we niggers. He too young to know. We ain't got no choice. Got to treat the darkies bad so they can't forget that they's on the bottom —not us.

(*All eyes turn at the sound of a deep-throated engine. A classic, beat-up Jaguar roadster pulls up to the outdoor phone. Eyes harden as* GENEVA CRENSHAW, *a very tall black woman, emerges from the car. Striking in a two-piece white linen suit she exudes a cool elegance even in the heat of the early evening. Ignoring the hostile stares of the white men, she walks quickly to the phone, deposits several coins, and dials.*)

Sanctuary of Small Rural Black Church

The REVEREND BARNES, *a large black man with a clerical collar, is leading twenty-five or so black men and women who, their voices fervent but ragged, are singing a hymn. In an office off to the side, a telephone rings. The Reverend Barnes gestures to the group to continue singing and goes to answer the phone, frowning in worry.*

REV BARNES

Hello. Reverend Barnes here. (*Recognizing the caller, he is relieved, though still anxious.*) Thank God, Lawyer Crenshaw! You O.K.? We been gettin' a mite worried. I hope you're still comin' to our meetin'. With folks bein' fired, havin' their loans canceled and all, we need the kind of reassurance only you can bring us.

Gas Station

All the men are still staring as Geneva speaks on the phone.

MOULTREE

(*Both sneering and taunting, his Southern drawl exaggerated.*) Boys, what you gawkin' at couldn't be seen in my day. Any blacks dare let the sun set on 'em in this town not be alive next mornin'. My daddy didn't let 'em light on this station 'ceptin' to clean up. He likely turnin' in his grave to see good white men standin' by while this uppity black bitch from up North showin' off her damned fancy car roun' down hyar stirrin' up our niggers.

GENEVA

(*Returns cold stare of white men staring at her.*) Don't worry, Reverend Barnes. The trial back in Jackson lasted all day, but I am on my way. Tell your people I'll be there in thirty minutes. No, Attorney Bell was not able to come with me. I'm alone, but after two years down here, I know my way around. Any of these rednecks try to cause me trouble, my car is fast enough to get me out of it. (*Geneva hangs up the phone, walks swiftly back to her car, gets in, and drives away from the station.*)

Two-Lane Highway

It is getting dark enough for headlights, and the Jaguar's rear lights gleam as Geneva speeds down a road cutting, arrow-straight, through cotton fields on both sides. A cloud of dust rises in her wake.

Gas Station

The rednecks stare after the car, cursing.
MOULTREE
(*His tone even more provocative.*) Hey, J.T., you done spent the whole damn summer fittin' that big Chrysler engine in that half-ass pickup of yourn. Les' give that nigger bitch a lil' scare. I got a ten-dollar bill say you cain't catch that fancy-ass, furrin sports car o' hers!
J.T.
(*Eagerly accepting challenge.*) Get your damn money ready, Moultree! Come on Buddy! You my witness.
Buddy hangs back, but J.T. grabs him by the arm and pulls him toward the pickup truck parked beside the station garage. The truck looks powerful, with raised suspension, oversize tires, spotlights mounted above the cab; a rifle is suspended above the bench seat. J.T. shoves Buddy into the passenger seat and sprints around to the other side. When J.T. turns the ignition switch, the engine roars to life. He shifts into gear, spins his wheels creating a shower of gravel, and tears off.

Highway Chase

As J.T. starts down the two-lane highway after Geneva, he can hardly see the Jaguar's tail lights. But soon his souped-up truck begins to close the distance between them.
Spotting the pickup's headlights in her rearview mirror, Geneva increases her speed. The speedometer moves up to 90, then to 95. Even so, the truck's lights loom larger, closer. Realizing that she can't outrun the truck, she slows and allows it to come within 150 feet. Then she hits the brakes and, whipping the steering wheel hard to the left, does a 180-degree spin to speed back past the truck heading in the opposite direction.

J.T.

(*In the pickup, muttering curses.*) Bitch must think she haulin' moonshine. Buddy, let's show her we do haul moonshine.

Buddy, his eyes wide with fear, remains silent. J.T. executes the same 180-degree skid turn and continues the chase.

GENEVA

(*Watching the pickup lights close in behind her, bites her lip in concentration and speaks coolly to herself.*) Geneva, chile, you are going the wrong way to reach Reverend Barnes's church, and those rednecks are gaining on you. It is time to poop or get off the pot!

Hitting her brakes, Geneva again spins her car in the opposite direction. She pushes hard on the accelerator, but this time swerves into the middle of the two-lane road, and shoots toward the truck, straddling the white line.

J.T.

(*Seeing Geneva's car heading toward him, recognizes immediately that she is challenging him. "Chicken" is just his kind of game. He pushes the gas pedal to the floor.*) My pickup'll squash that crazy black bitch like a bug!

BUDDY

(*Terrified.*) No, no, J.T.!

At the last instant, he reaches over and yanks the steering wheel to the right. Although his maneuver avoids a head-on crash, the truck side-swipes the Jaguar. The car veers off the road and falls, turning over and over, down the steep bank of a levee. At the same time, the pickup has careened off the road in the other direction. It plows into a tree and explodes in a ball of flames.

Recalling Geneva's courage humbled me. . . . When she aimed her Jaguar down the center of that country road and pushed the gas pedal to the floorboard, she was challenging not only the big pickup that had been harassing her, but also the systematic intimidation of blacks that was a key component of white dominance. Her action—risky, even suicidal—conveyed a powerful message to whites accustomed to deference from blacks: "Whatever the costs, we won't take it any more."

Geneva knew . . . that those black folks waiting at that church had taken some very large risks in a state long noted for its willingness to use violence to preserve its way of life. . . . Geneva could not encourage the people she represented if she personally compromised or exhibited cowardice in the face of intimidation no worse than what they faced daily as they sought what she had assured them was their right to vote, to send their children to desegregated schools, their right to live . . . without being afraid of white people every day of their lives. . . .

What if all black folks adopted Geneva's attitude? What if they, too, were to refuse to "take low" when whites demand subordination—or else? Would racism end, and quite quickly? Or, would we all be killed—also quite quickly?

A Holiday for Dr. King

The Significance of Symbols
in the Black Freedom Struggle

In New York City a few weeks ago I hailed a taxi for the long ride to the airport. Settling down in the back seat, I glanced at the driver's name tag and said, . . . "I can't believe your name is Jesse B. Semple."

"That's been my name all my life, and I'm not about to change it."

"You know," I said, ignoring his belligerent response, "that's a pretty famous name. Langston Hughes regaled millions of black people over many years with his short essays about conversations with a streetwise Harlem black named Jesse B. Simple. Hughes always called him 'Simple.' I think he published five or six books filled with those Simple stories, as they came to be known."[1]

"Who you telling," the driver injected. . . . "My mother loved Langston Hughes. Our family name was Semple, and it was a natural to name me Jesse B. If you know the character, you also know why I am not sorry about the name."

"Simple had plenty of 'mother wit' and 'street smarts,'" I conceded.

"I've read all of the Langston Hughes books," Semple said, "but that was years ago. Nowadays, I'm too busy trying to make ends meet."

"Things are tough for black folks," I agreed, "but we have come a long way. For just one example, can you believe a national holiday for Dr. Martin Luther King. Who would have thought we could ever get them to do it."

"Do what," Jesse B. Semple responded, obviously unimpressed. "A holiday is just the latest gimmick white folks have come up with to keep dumb blacks satisfied. It's an updated version of the glass trinkets and combs they used in Africa a few centuries ago."

"It's not the same," I responded. "The country has only a few national holidays celebrating individuals. And now thanks to the persistence of thousands of people, Dr. King's birthday is one of them. As the old folks used to say," I added expansively, "'black folks use to not have show, but we sho got show now.'"

"You wrong, man," Semple said disgustedly. "All we got is symbols." He paused to ensure that I got his point, then continued: "From the Emancipation Proclamation on, the Man been handing you a bunch of bogus freedom checks that he never intends to honor. He makes you work, plead, and pray for them, and then when he has you either groveling or threatening to tear his damn head off, he lets you have them as though they were some kinda special gift. As a matter of fact, regardless of how great the need is, he only gives *you* when it will do *him* the most good.

"And before you can cash them in," Semple added, warming to his subject, "the Man has called the bank and stopped payment, or otherwise made them useless, except, of course, as symbols.

"You know Langston Hughes," Semple lectured me, "but you need to read your black history, man. Get into some John Hope Franklin, Loren Miller, Lerone Bennett, and Vincent Harding. Or," he added, "if you don't believe black historians, try Leon Litwack, Eugene Genovese, and even C. Vann Woodward. They will all tell you that is how it has been, and that is how it is now."

"I do read," I responded somewhat guardedly, not prepared for a confrontation with a literate cab driver and wondering how I always get pushed into the position of defending white America. "My history tells me that the black race has come a long way from slavery and segregation to now, when we not only have laws protecting our rights, but a holiday recognizing one of our greatest leaders. We have—"

"What you have, man, is a hard-won symbol with a lot of token blacks boring us working folks to death with their speeches about what a great life Dr. King lived, with not near enough reminders of how he died. Which, as I assume you know, is how Malcolm, Medgar Evers, and probably Whitney Young and George Wylie died. And God knows how many other blacks because they had the gumption to tell the truth about the conditions for blacks in this country and then come down off the speaker's stand and actually try to do something to improve those conditions."

Semple could have added black leaders stretching back to Nat Turner, and including Marcus Garvey, Paul Robeson, and W. E. B. Du Bois, all killed or driven into exile because they posed a real or imagined threat to the white power structure. . . .

While I was musing, Semple continued to preach, his voice louder, his tone more strident than ever.

"What you have, or will have is a holiday for one black man, great as he was, when more black people are out of work now than at any time since slavery. More black families are headed by females than ever before, and more than half the black babies now being born are to unwed mothers, many of them teenage dropouts at that. Tell me where is anything in those statistics to celebrate, and tell me how a holiday for Dr. King is going to help all the poor, uneducated, unemployed, and undernourished blacks all over this still racist land."

Under this onslaught, I decided to change tactics. Semple was certainly right, but I didn't have to lose an argument on this subject.

"I know, as the poet says, that life for blacks ain't been no crystal stair. But we need some victories to keep our spirits up, and the King holiday is one, even if acknowledged by a President who claimed it was neither necessary nor justified. As the old folks would put it, 'We ain't what we going to be, but thank God, we ain't what we was.'"

"Brother," Semple replied quietly and with deadly seriousness, "for someone dressed like you are related to the Brooks Brothers, you need to get off quoting the old folks and open your eyes to what is going down right around you in the here and now."

Semple stopped talking and concentrated on driving through 125th Street. I looked out the window and saw more evidence on Harlem's main thoroughfare than I needed of the points he was making all too well.

. . . .

Today, we are witness to an increasingly grim national scene of an exploited, colonized people without jobs, decent homes, and viable educations. Their options are few, their reasons for hope virtually nonexistent. Yet all blacks are covered by more laws protecting them against racially discriminatory treatment than any of their black ancestors.

The masses of poor blacks today have legal rights that are worthless and unmet economic needs that threaten life itself. They lack the schooling, skills, or financial resources needed to survive, much less succeed, in a society where manhood is measured by job and worth by income. They, like Harriet Tubman, remain "strangers in a strange land." Because poor blacks remain outcasts in this country, the greater opportunities better-off blacks enjoy are diluted by their poverty, diminished by their despair.

The cab negotiated the traffic of East Harlem streets. The neighborhoods reflected poverty in Spanish, but radiated a vitality lacking in the black ghetto, causing me to wonder, not for the first time, whether even these non–English speaking immigrants would make it in America before poor blacks managed an escape from their current misery.

"You're right. It is pretty depressing, Mr. Semple," I said, breaking the long silence.

"It is and it ain't," Semple replied thoughtfully. "The fact is that we been living on symbols for a long time. Religious symbols, freedom symbols, legal symbols, and now holiday symbols. They are all but worthless at the bank, but sometimes black folks don't try to cash them in. They put them in their pockets and feel rich and, more important, they act rich. That is how we ended slavery and gave some meaning to that 1954 decision by the Supreme Court that promised a lot, but gave us 'all deliberate speed,' which would have translated into not a damned thing if Dr. King in Montgomery, the freedom riders in Birmingham and Jackson, and those college students in North Carolina had not proved to us that segregation would not work unless black folks went along with it."

"But," I added quickly, "the Montgomery boycott and the sit-in protesters needed the law to get them out of jail and to enforce the Supreme Court's desegregation standards. Even Dr. King said society needed both. . . ."[2]

. . . .

"You sound as much in love with laws as you are with holidays," observed Semple. "Why can't our black bourgeoisie get some love for ordinary black folks?"

"I think that's unfair," I retorted somewhat heatedly. "You don't know what contributions I have made, and many other successful or bourgeois blacks, as you call us, have given much to the black cause."

"Cool down, brother," Semple said. "I don't mean any offense. The fact is that you scotch and soda black folks hurt us drylongso[3] blacks simply by being successful. The white folks see you doing your thing, making money, latching on to all kind of fancy titles, some of which even have a little authority behind them, and generally 'moving on up.' They conclude right off that discrimination is over and that if the rest of us got up off our dead asses, dropped the welfare tit, stopped having illegitimate babies, and found jobs, we would all be just like you."

. . . .

"Are you suggesting," trying to end our discussion on a harmonious note as the cab neared my terminal, "that until white folks get smart, black folks will never be free? That we must continue the work Dr. King started with his Poor People's March and somehow forge a coalition of minorities and the poor that will finally explode the white supremacy myth that has divided blacks and whites for the benefit of the ruling classes since the earliest days of slavery?"

"Preston Wilcox is a Harlem leader," Semple said, seeming to ignore my rhetorical question. "He always says 'No one can free us but ourselves.' I believe that. And maybe it is as true for whites as it is for blacks. But for them to accept it, they will have to give up the symbol which they think is more important than life itself."

I did not have to ask him what that symbol was. Paying my fare and taking my bags, we shook hands.

. . . .

"By the way," he said, "take this clipping. It's a piece out of the National Urban League's annual report, *The State of Black America*. This guy makes my point almost as well as I can."

An hour later, my plane was heading west and in true workaholic fashion, I had my briefcase opened and papers spread over two seats. But my mind was still on my conversation with Jesse B. Semple. I glanced at the last few pages of the Urban League article he had given me. They were heavily underlined and I smiled, recognizing an article I had written which Semple's stamp of approval gave a validity I richly prized.

On the pages Semple had marked, I suggested that blacks have never been the special favorites of the laws. Rather, we have been the involuntary sacrifices in compromises between differing groups of white men, and the beneficiaries of pro–civil rights actions taken primarily to protect or further white interests. The Emancipation Proclamation and the *Brown* decision are only two of the more dramatic instances when blacks, through courageous self-help, gave substance and movement to the empty and often hypocritical symbolism that characterizes so much of civil rights policy.

But the worsening condition of so many black Americans, recorded annually in the Urban League reports, presents a challenge to blacks able to advance and perhaps prosper under the aegis of laws that we ignore at our peril. We recognize, despite improved status, that the removal of racial classifications does not insure equal opportunity, and the doctrine of equality, undefined and tailored to idealistic hopes rather than realistic assessments, can pose an unneeded barrier to still-needed racial remediation. Racism remains a principal feature of the country's economic and political structure, and will remain a barrier to opportunity for blacks until remedies encompass as well the masses of whites whose subordinate status in society is less dramatic than that of blacks but no less real. Coalitions founder when whites, particularly working class whites, are mesmerized by the race question which, as in the post-Reconstruction period, remains "an everlasting, overshadowing problem that served to hamper the progress of poor whites and prevent them from becoming realistic in social, economic, and political matters."[4]

. . . .

Martin Luther King suggested a cure for this race-based class suicide. He urged the country to adopt a broad-based and gigantic Bill of Rights for the Disadvantaged, similar to the GI Bill of Rights enacted without opposition or controversy for war veterans. He said the bill's benefits should not go to blacks alone, because poor whites, too, were the derivative victims of slavery.[5]

These sentiments are now twenty years old. Much has changed. A general social reform bill to eliminate poverty and disadvantage now seems as far away as the stars. But if blacks retain their belief in the symbols of freedom, and at least some whites come to see beyond the destructive symbol of racism, anything could happen.

On that point, I think even Jesse B. Semple would agree.

NOTES

1. *See, e.g.,* LANGSTON HUGHES, THE BEST OF SIMPLE (1961).
2. M. KING, JR., WHY WE CAN'T WAIT (1964).
3. A colloquial term in the black community decades ago. It means ordinary,

nothing special. *See* J. GWALTNEY, DRYLONGSO: A SELF-PORTRAIT OF BLACK AMERICA (1980). *Id.* at xix.

4. J. FRANKLIN, FROM SLAVERY TO FREEDOM 272 (4th ed. 1974) (quoting Watson, *The Negro in the South, in* S. CARMICHAEL & C. HAMILTON, BLACK POWER, THE POLITICS OF LIBERATION IN AMERICA 68 (1967)).

5. MARTIN LUTHER KING, JR., WHY WE CAN'T WAIT 138 (1964).

Trying to Teach the White Folks

Bong! Bong!

"With the sound of our sacred Liberty Bell calling us to freedom's task, this is the Biff Rightwing Show—the home of thinking conservatives. We don't pander: we ponder. We don't condemn commie-afflicted critics: we celebrate our conservative goals. Welcome, all you Yessirrees out there!"

Biff paused for the cheers and whistles of the studio audience, mainly middle-aged white males.

"Our guest this evening," he went on, "is an African American law professor known as a liberal. He's got some ideas we conservatives consider crazy and some that raise questions worthy of debate. Let's get right into it."

Biff Rightwing looked down at me from behind his wide desk. I was seated on a too soft couch situated in "Tonight Show" fashion—an arrangement better suited to supplication than to fair debate. "Professor, you're a black man who has obviously made it big, despite having been born and raised in relatively humble circumstances. Early in your career, you handled literally hundreds of school desegregation cases in Southern courts. You've been a government civil rights lawyer, a tenured professor at the Harvard Law School, and dean of the Oregon Law School, where most of the faculty and students were white. In fact, in a more innocent time, blacks and whites would hail you as a credit to your race.

"So, given your impressive attainments, our viewers want to know why you, of all people, would write a book asserting that racism in America is permanent? The thesis of *Faces at the Bottom of the Well*—and get this, Yessirrees!—is that black people 'will never gain full equality [but only] temporary "peaks of progress," short-lived victories that slide into

irrelevance as racial patterns adapt in ways that maintain white dominance.' Isn't that more nonsense than you've heard in a long time, Yessirrees?"

"Yessirree!" erupted from the studio audience. "Yessirree!"

Then they let loose a chorus of boos, all directed at me. It wasn't easy
to stand calmly before that sea of white faces, all angry. The lone black
man in the audience didn't seem to have a seat but strutted up and down
the aisles urging the crowd on. He was wearing a black cowboy suit complete with bright red boots and a ten-gallon white hat. Watching him, I
shook my head. It is not unknown for subordinated people to try to
please members of the dominant group, but this guy was ridiculous—and
sad. I wondered, though, about myself. Is it, at some level, any less sad to
be trying to teach whites who are obviously uninterested in hearing, much
less learning, anything contrary to their deeply held racial views?

When the audience quieted, I interjected: "Biff, my conclusion disturbs
me as much as it irritates you—and your audience. But current events, as
well as over three hundred years of American history, support it."

"Pardon me, Professor, but let's stop leaning on history. Let's look at
now. Let's look at *you*. You're a walking rebuttal of your thesis. If life was
as bad for blacks as you claim, then none of you would have risen beyond
being janitors, maids, and shoeshine boys."

"That assumption of yours, Biff, is one most whites are all too ready
to make on the slender evidence of a few blacks who, in your self-serving,
myopic view, have made it."

"Hey, Professor, you're evidence to the contrary whether you like it or
not! You are black. You have undoubtedly faced your share of the so-
called racial discrimination you liberals keep complaining about. And
yet, through ability and hard work, you have made it. Tell me, Professor,
why can't all blacks do as you have done?"

"Sure, Biff, I've worked hard, but I'm also one of the blacks this society permits to move beyond the barriers that bar uncounted others whose
talents and ambitions are equal to mine, but who have encountered one
closed door after another. I grew up in a stable family and in a community that was relatively safe and supportive. My mother didn't have to
work and could stay in touch with my teachers. And every one I knew
pushed me toward college—not as a possibility, but as foregone certainty."

Predictably, Biff Rightwing shook his head. "My advice to those kids
is to look at you and go out and do the same.

"Now, I want to get to that story in your book—*The Space Traders*—where a majority of Americans agree to trade away all our black people for gold and other goodies. Isn't this racial libel—or, more accurately, *racist* libel?"

"The First Amendment protects your right to call me and my writing anything you like, Biff. But that does not alter either the role of racism or the general understanding most black people hold about its importance to America. I lecture to many groups across the country. And when I ask whether my audience believes this country would indeed accept such a trade, virtually all blacks in the audience immediately raise their hands in agreement."

"Those must be some of the same people who cheer when Louis Farrakhan says hateful things about the Jews and other white people."

"Why not ask the Reverend Farrakhan to come on your show and explain his remarks, Biff? I'm sure he can defend them far better than I can."

"So," he went on, ignoring both my suggestion and my obvious irritation, "you want us to believe that the great majority of black people actually believe America would send them off into space for a mess of pottage?"

"I run into blacks all the time who tell me in all earnestness that were my *Space Traders* story real, they would volunteer to go. 'Better risk the unknown in space than face the certainty of racial discrimination here at home,' they say. Those statements shake me, Biff. They should shake you and those millions in your audience whose patriotism and commitment to this country's well-being you boast about so often."

"They don't shake me or my viewers. Are you shaking, Yessirrees?"

"Nosirree! Nosirree! Nosirree!" Their chant lasted until someone off-camera shushed them.

His audience's reaction stirred Rightwing up to a sort of religious fervor. "Any blacks who don't like it here are free to leave without waiting for the assistance of people from outer space. And ain't it a shame? Those blacks who tell you they're so disgusted with this country that they're ready to voluntarily leave—get this, Yessirrees!—they're still here waiting for *assistance*—there's that word again!—this time not from hard-working taxpayers, but from fictional beings from another galaxy."

"The shame is your willingness, Biff, to characterize and condemn what you don't know—"

"And how do the whites in your audiences," he interrupted, "feel about your assessment of the role of racism?"

"Some agree with me. Some don't. But when I ask them to raise their hands to signify whether a majority of whites living in their community would vote for the Space Traders' offer, most of them—however reluctantly—raise their hands."

"Not a very scientific poll, Professor."

"Perhaps not, but I bet even more of your viewers would vote for the Trade."

"And why not? Why in hell not?" Biff turned up his righteous rage button. "My viewers are red-blooded American patriots, Professor. And many of us are sick of your people's bellyaching even as you are committing most of the violent crime and receiving more than your share of welfare payments. You'd rather be coddled by wishy-washy liberals than carry your fair share of taxes and the other duties of citizenship. Considering all the trouble you folks cause, I'd be surprised if even thirty percent would vote against the Trade."

"O.K., Biff, according to you the audience and most whites would favor the Trade. It's not that they hate blacks. It's because black people take jobs from whites, live on government largesse, and commit crimes. Now, suppose the Space Traders were offering to trade for gold and other goodies, as you put it, not black people but the top executives of America's Fortune-500 corporations? Let's say that the Space Traders identified some two thousand of these CEOs as responsible for the loss of two million jobs in this country. That these CEOs had sent millions of jobs to third-world countries to get cheap labor and are importing thousands of foreign workers—skilled as well as unskilled—to this country to replace American workers."

"Well, that's ridiculous, and I would—"

"Let me finish, Biff. Suppose, in addition, that the Space Traders show how many of these corporations are firing hundreds of thousands of workers, many with years of loyal service, and all this so-called downsizing is not to cut costs but to enhance profits. And not only that, but these corporations are raking off billions of dollars in government grants and tax benefits, and much of the resulting profit goes to them or the top 1 percent of the population who now hold over 40 percent of the wealth. So, Biff, with those facts in mind, do you think your audience—or Americans generally, for that matter—wouldn't vote to trade away those CEOs?"

Biff saw quickly that my question aimed to reveal what his program and its corporate sponsors wanted to conceal beneath a nonstop attack on minorities, welfare, immigrants, and gays. Ignoring the thrust of my question, he used it to attack.

"That question should get you tried for sedition, Professor. Can you be seriously suggesting that the finest business minds in this great nation of ours are deliberately sucking up the profits of our productivity and keeping it for them and theirs while throwing most hardworking Americans the financial equivalent of a bone?"

"I couldn't have said it better myself, Biff."

"You are attacking the American free enterprise system. Shame, Professor! I know you have some radical notions, but now I see you want to resurrect the totalitarian socialism that died in Eastern Europe, and install it in America."

"But, Biff, what's all the government's support of business and the rich if not socialism? The question is what will the rest of us have when all the good jobs are gone and the government has shut down the relatively few programs that aid the working class while increasing aid to the already well-off? Where will your viewers be after the corporations bring the third-world home?"

"That's hogwash, and you know it! All talk shows are not alike. Don't confuse me with certain simple-minded hosts like that comedian Rush Limbaugh. I and my audience don't try to think and sit with the same portion of our anatomy!"

"Fine, Biff, so why not ask your listeners to tell us how they'd vote."

Biff turned to the studio audience. "What do you think, Yessirrees? Would you trade away America's finest business leaders in return for a year without taxes?"

"No, never!" Again, the lone black man was leading the charge, his "No!" distinct above all the others.

"Give me a show of hands," Biff invited, "for anyone who'd be willing to send our corporate leaders off to an unknown fate."

Not one hand went up. Biff looked triumphant. Here, before my eyes, ideology was winning over self-interest. Trying to teach the white folks never looked so difficult. "Well, Professor, what do you say about that vote?"

"I'd say don't start spending your bonus from your corporate sponsors yet, Biff. A group's willingness to vote against a hypothetical case is no guarantee of how they'll vote when they finally wake up and realize that their jobs and futures are being undermined not by supposedly slothful colored people but by greedy corporate leaders. At that point, they may not be willing to sit quietly while corporate leaders are traded off, even for a year without taxes. At that point, they'll more likely want to tear them limb from limb!"

. . . "Let me ask you something different, Professor. Why do you write these racist stories? They stir up some whites and likely rile blacks into either committing more crimes or giving up on trying to make it in this great country. . . . Blacks who are down should look for example and assistance to those who have made it or are moving up—you, for instance. And those who are making it should spend more time reaching back to help up their brethren and less time either complaining about racism or —as reported in some of your magazines, like *Ebony* and *Jet*—spending enormous sums on luxury cars, fabulous homes, and ski weekends at resorts that cater to rich celebrities and charge accordingly."

. . . .

"I'm not here, Biff, to defend the few blacks whose excesses the media love to report to whites looking for an excuse not to worry about the plight of most blacks. My aim is to enlighten whites about facts the media are not interested in reporting: about the financial contributions and volunteer efforts of thousands of black people who are quietly and impressively lending their skill, experience, and encouragement to the less fortunate."

Biff all but jumped over his desk. "They need to work harder, Professor. Black crime is on the increase. About half our prison population is black, a high percentage of black births are out of wedlock, and most of those children will live in single-parent homes. Where is it going to end?"

"These are all serious problems, Biff, but black people represent only about 12 percent of this country's population. I ask you the question that *New Republic* editor Michael Lind posed: Why do you 'treat the genuine pathologies of the ghetto . . . as the major problems facing a country with uncontrollable trade and fiscal deficits, a low savings rate, an obsolete military strategy, an anachronistic and corrupt electoral system, the worst primary education in the First World, and the bulk of its population facing long-term economic decline?' Don't you think these issues would make some difference to how your audience—and America— would vote if Space Traders offered to take in trade those Fortune-500 CEOs?"

Biff looked as though I had stomped hard on his toe. His weekly program never touches on any of those problems unless he can blame them on someone or something else: the trade deficits on immigration, for example; or military problems on homosexuals; low voter turnouts on citizen apathy; educational failure on the absence of prayer in the schools; or America's economic decline on the loss of moral values. Now Biff repeated this litany, and his awful sincerity showed me just how deeply entrenched all these false notions about blacks are.

Before I could answer him, he announced that after a break for commercials we would hear an update on the Fortune-500 vote.

"And don't go away, folks," he advised. "I want you to join me in questioning our professor about why he published in *The Nation*—an ultraliberal journal if there ever was one—an article that suggests we pass a federal law to eliminate affirmative action, oust blacks from jobs they obtain under that policy, and draft them into federal service at minimum pay if they can't get new jobs on their own. Was he just expressing some personal frustration at what he sees as the rock-and-the-hard-place dilemma of blacks? Or have we caught an outspokenly liberal black man with his pants down?"

. . . .

. . . Rightwing—who had avoided making conversation, even eye contact, during the break—got the "on air" sign.

"Biff Rightwing with you, again, folks, with an update on the Fortune-500 executive trade Professor Bell proposed. Of the first five hundred persons voting, four hundred and fifty would reject the trade and only fifty would accept it. Any comment, Professor?"

"Just that those rejecting such a trade ought to start reading the business pages of their local newspapers, with their almost daily reports of thousands of workers losing their jobs while the salaries and perks of top executives go up and up."

Ignoring my response and promising another update soon, Biff turned to my *Nation* article. "Your Freedom of Employment Act is a conservative's dream, Professor. It's also, I'd imagine, a nightmare for civil rights supporters. One of my producers even feels that this piece shows you to be not only conservative but as much opposed to affirmative action and as supportive of involuntary work programs as some other black academics we've invited to the show. And she is not alone. The papers report that Republican congressmen have turned your supposedly hypothetical act into a bill they're planning to rush through before you liberal types can do anything about it. What do you say about that?"

"They're making a serious mistake, Biff. A law like mine would not only seriously harm hardworking black people everywhere, but arouse them to a new wave of protests."

"All that 1960s 'take to the streets' stuff sounds far beyond the capabilities of a people as downtrodden as you claim black people are. Suppose, Professor, that, instead of pushing all this Doomsday-style rhetoric, you joined some of the more thoughtful, independent-minded blacks who urge an end of affirmative action as a racially divisive policy that rewards unqualified blacks and penalizes qualified whites. Wouldn't the demise of racial preferences ease the current racial hostility among whites?"

"You may refuse to acknowledge it, Biff, but you know as well as I do that opposition to affirmative action is a way for whites to manifest their own justifiable fears about the jobs they're losing by the millions—not to blacks, but to technology, to third-world workers in other countries, to legal and illegal immigrants, and to the corporate mania for downsizing. Actually, many whites need affirmative action as much as blacks do. And influential media personalities like you need to tell your viewers the truth instead of forever pandering to their worst tendencies. They need protection against class discrimination that now gives preferences to those whites who may have inferior skills but get the jobs and promotions because of their contacts and credentials."

Bong! Bong!

Biff was clearly glad to be rescued by a viewer calling in. "Sam Storm in Macon, Georgia, you're on the air."

"Evenin', Biff. I want to know why you have a lifelong racial troublemaker on your show? Why, he's made a pile of money stirrin' up our good niggers, jus' like he did when he was down here workin' to mix the races in our schools. Now, he's fomentin' class warfare. Can't see why you givin' him free air time on your show to do it."

"See, Professor, what some of my listeners think about your views and my decision to honor your First Amendment right to speak out about them! Is Sam right? Are you trying to foment class warfare?"

"I neither foment nor urge, Biff. Law teachers are seldom rabble rousers—"

"And, if you were, Professor," he cut in, "I can assure you that white Americans don't resent what you call class privilege. If they're working class, they strive to send their children to college to gain through hard work some of the advantages you see as exploitive. It is that attitude that has made America what it is. Some black people preach this form of self-advancement: Thomas Sowell, Shelby Steele, Justice Clarence Thomas, many others. Are they wrong?"

"More obsolete than wrong. Blacks, like most people, believe in work and self-advancement. But the economy over the last twenty to thirty years has denied more and more blacks the jobs that would lead to self-sufficiency, much less advancement."

"I thought your point was that whites are also suffering because of the lost jobs."

"That *is* my point, Biff. In our society, work plays a threefold role. It provides us money to pay our bills. It is also the measure of a person's place in the world and the foundation for one's self-esteem. Without employment, all three suffer profoundly. But today the number of skilled workers—both white collar and blue collar, executives and professionals—who have lost their jobs and see little hope of replacing them has risen steeply. Where—as you yourself asked a while ago—is it going to end?"

Bong! Bong!

"We have another caller, but first an update. Seven hundred and fifty people now oppose trading the Fortune-500 executives and only seventy favor it."

"Maybe some of your viewers are reading the business pages, after all," I said. "Those seventy are almost ten percent of the total."

"Sounds more like you bribed some of your friends to watch the show and they've alerted their liberal networks."

Bong! Bong!

"O.K., let's go to John Luwanski in Milwaukee. You're on, John."

"My brother-in-law lost out on a job because the company said affirmative action rules required them to hire a black applicant, even though the black had less experience. Is that what you call fair, Professor?"

"It's no less fair than giving the job to some white who's a friend of the employer. And—as you and I both know—that kind of thing goes on all the time. Or, it's no less fair than giving the job to a white woman, and white women are the principal beneficiaries of affirmative action programs."

I took the opportunity to slip in a comment about how employers use affirmative action as a convenient excuse offered to whites they don't want to hire for other reasons. "And, John, even if you don't want to believe that employers lie, aren't you concerned about the growing unemployment for *all* Americans? As I said earlier, corporate America's shifting thousands and thousands of jobs out of the country to take advantage of low wage rates, or using computers and other technology to eliminate jobs, or simply letting many workers go and requiring those who remain to pick up the slack by working longer for the same pay."

"Don't companies have to do all those things to compete, Professor, to prevent foreign corporations from taking our business?"

"Unfortunately, John, corporations are increasingly multinational. 'We' and 'they' have lost their meaning. A corporation has no allegiance to its employees, or even to its product. A corporation's only allegiance is to its profit. And the easiest way to enhance that is to lay off thousands of workers.

"But, John," I went on, "you're not off-base regarding the challenge facing corporations competing in a world undergoing drastic changes. In *The End of Work*, Jeremy Rifkin asserts that manufacturing and much of the service sector are undergoing a transformation as profound as the one the agricultural sector experienced at the beginning of the century, when machines boosted production, displacing millions of farmers. We are, according to Rifkin, 'already well into a shift from reliance on large numbers of relatively unskilled workers to a time when industry and even service work will be performed by a small, highly skilled group of workers who utilize automation in the production of goods and the delivery of services.'"

Biff had been twitching in irritation. When I paused, he exploded. "What a crapehanger, you are, Professor! Tell me, does this Jeremy Rifkin share your view that the U.S. of A. is headed down the tubes?"

"Not at all. And I agree with him. These developments don't have to mean a grim future. The gains from this new technology revolution could be shared broadly, among all the people, through a shorter workweek and new opportunities for work on socially useful projects. But Rifkin warns that the first step in any such sweeping reforms must be the acknowledgment, by those who represent us and those who set business policy, that private-sector jobs are no longer the centerpiece of our economic and social life. If we are to have a good and productive future, we will need strong, courageous, and humane government action to ensure jobs for all—perhaps with a thirty-hour week, so that our citizens enjoy more time for leisure pursuits, for furthering their education, and for volunteering to help those in need and their communities."

. . . .

"Come on, Professor! The free enterprise system has brought this country unparalleled prosperity. Why not stay on the horse that has proved itself?"

"Because, Biff, history has taught us that if the free enterprise horse is left to run without the strong hand of government to control it, it will destroy all. That nearly happened in the early 1930s—but the New Deal programs, while far from perfect, not only kept the country from 'going down the tubes,' as you put it, but provided us with much-needed stability and confidence. Similarly, after the Second World War, it was government that provided the G.I. Bill, federal home loans, and a myriad of other programs that helped to move us from a wartime to a prosperous peacetime economy. You keep saying I'm a radical, Biff, but in this time of great economic change, we need government again to keep people employed so that we can hold families together, sustain communities, and, in general, attend to the basic needs of all our citizens."

"I still say, Professor, the free market can do all these things better, cheaper, and without your misguided altruism."

"This isn't altruism, Biff, it's a way of ensuring that everyone, not just those who can pay for them, has access to the prerequisites for effective competition. Corporations, under the pressure of market forces, focus on profits in the short term and take no responsibility for any devastation— whether in terms of jobs, or the economy, or the ecology—that results from their single-minded obsession with profits. Effecting a balance between profit and growth, and stability and security, is the role of government."

"Holy cow! It sounds like the old socialism to me."

"But, isn't socialism what many in the top ten percent of our income and wealth groups are enjoying, those whose interests and lavish lifestyles receive protection from the parties and politicians to whom they contribute so generously? I'm just asking that every American have the chance to share in that life—as is certainly possible in the current technological revolution. I'm afraid, Biff, that if we don't plan for everyone's welfare, America will inevitably become a third-world nation."

"A bit extreme, isn't it, Professor?"

"No. The United States is already becoming a third-world economy. Twenty years ago, America led the world in terms of worker wages and benefits. Now we are in twelfth place, with wages, health care, vacation time, parental leave, and educational opportunity lagging behind much of the industrialized world. In addition, twenty-two percent of our children live in poverty, five million kids go hungry, and two million Americans lack permanent shelter or sleep on the streets. Food stamps are a necessity for ten percent of American families to put food on the table, and tens of millions more survive on bare subsistence, from paycheck to paycheck."

Bong! Bong!

CHAPTER 14

Survival Strategies

What is the proper balance between optimism and despair? For the civil rights advocate, things never seem to change for the better—at least not for long. How, then, keep one's chin up? These five selections ask whether, with effort, blacks' civil rights fortunes are apt to improve, and what one is to do if the deck seems, as it often does, stacked against one. One theme that emerges from these selections, indeed from Bell's writing as a whole, is the redemptive power of truth, no matter how terrible. For blacks at least, learning their civil rights history and the appalling cascade of wrongs the white race has visited on them over the years can, paradoxically, prove liberating. It shows that their present low estate is not the product of laziness or inherent inferiority but the result of a kind of racial plunder by one group or another. Psychic survival may come from the simple reminder that one is doing one's best in the face of terrible odds.

Redemption Deferred
Back to the Space Traders

We passed through that curtain of darkness into a vast enclosure, a realm of light. Above us, around us, glowed and pulsated all the colors of the rainbow, dazzling my eyes, softening my grim expectations. From somewhere over our heads, a hidden voice spoke.

"Raise your arms and clap your hands."

This was no longer the clone of Ronald Reagan's voice, with which the Space Traders had opened and conducted their negotiations with the United States. This was a black voice, warm and resonant. Whether a man's voice or a woman's, I couldn't tell.

As we raised our arms in response to the command, the manacles and chains that bound our hands together and us to one another, fell off with a fearsome clattering.

"Look down!" Again, the voice, sounding now even more familiar, a harmonious blending of Ossie Davis and Ruby Dee.

Obeying again, we found at our feet a folded piece of beautifully woven cloth. We understood that we were to pick it up. As we did, each unfolded into a soft robe, which we put on to wrap around our near-nakedness.

"Take a deep breath," came the voice, "and stand perfectly still." The soft colors surrounding us coalesced into a brilliant flash of light. Behind me I heard Geneva's soft voice, "Keep the faith, friend!" Then, darkness.

I stood in place with everyone else, neither awake nor asleep, bound but immobilized, relaxed yet not lethargic, unable to act yet clear of mind. I knew that time was passing, but had no idea how much. I wondered, By

From *Gospel Choirs* 17 by Derrick Bell. Copyright © 1996 by Derrick Bell. Reprinted by permission of Basic Books, a member of Perseus Books, L.L.C.

what means—what miracle, really—have the Space Traders suspended our vital functions for the long journey back to their home star?

After unimaginable, immeasurable time, the light flashed a second time, and again the hidden voice spoke.

"Attention, African Americans! It is now two months since we took off from your United States of America. Ahead of us lies still a long journey, but circumstances have made it necessary for us to share with you immediately our motivations and our plans.

"We have been studying Earth and its peoples for a long time, particularly the experiment with democracy in your United States of America, and even more particularly the blot upon that experiment: the refusal to grant you full human rights along with its white citizens. We have watched your long travail, from the first slaves kidnapped into the country in your year 1619, to its crass and despicable acceptance of our offer to trade you for gold and other gifts. That proved the truth of our observations: that white people consider you—as they considered you from the beginning—no more than their property, to be sold to the highest bidder.

"Ours is, as you have guessed, a society technologically advanced beyond yours. Yet astute as we have been, we have somehow lacked an element that you might call 'human.'

"Although we have been able to make analogues of your voices and expressions, we find we cannot re-create your robust warmth and humor or the emotional and spiritual strength whereby you have sustained that humanity through all your travails. We cannot, that is, re-create your ability to transcend suffering—to sing through it, as you yourselves might say.

"For despite our advanced technology, our people suffer, and we have lacked the means to relieve them. Or, we lacked them until, again after observing America, we thought that perhaps if we offered it enough of the wealth it seems to treasure beyond all else, it might be persuaded to part with the human treasure you and your people constitute.

"We hoped to bring you back to our home star, to be settlers there, to mingle with our citizens as equals and full partners in our development and growth.

"And so we devised ships to carry us through space to Earth and to America. When your country accepted our offer, we were amazed. We now have another reason for amazement.

"We have been, in these two months, monitoring the thoughts of each of you for any sign of illness or serious distress. And we find that many of you are inexplicably longing to return to the land that you call home, even though it practices the most pernicious racism anywhere in the universe—and even though it easily banished you against your will, sent you off to an unknown fate.

"It is perhaps indicative of our emotional ignorance that we assumed you would be glad of the opportunity to leave America, to make a new start in our world. But since it is imperative to our plan that you enter our society voluntarily, we are going to ask you to vote on whether you wish to do so or return to the land that has sheltered you so ambiguously these hundreds of years. If you decide on the latter, we will try to negotiate for your return.

"Before you vote, we must tell you what has been going on there in these two months. America traded you for resources that should, with prudent management, have solved its problems and ensured its prosperity for at least a century to come. Even in this brief time, however, these resources have been almost completely dissipated in a series of fraudulent corporate and government transactions. Now the economy is in shambles, the stock market has all but collapsed, and more than half the population is unemployed. The politicians, grown accustomed to using race to divert attention from their incompetence and corruption, are hard-pressed to create a scapegoat to replace you.

"Furthermore, America's acceptance of the Trade has evoked the scorn and enmity of the other nations of the world. Having listened for so long to America's self-righteous preaching of rights and liberties for all, and then witnessed its willingness to trade away one tenth of its people for what they call 'blood money,' they are now hooting at it for its hypocrisy and moral corruption. The United Nations are moving to oust it from the Security Council, and many countries have severed all ties.

"We wonder whether, knowing all this, you will wish to return to such a home. But before we ask you to vote, we understand that two of you wish to speak. First, Gleason Golightly, once an adviser to your president. We know that many of you have condemned Golightly for his espousal of conservative causes and even more when, prior to the American vote on the Space Trade, he urged you to try to trick whites into voting against it by telling them that you, having learned that our star was an idyllic land, wanted to come with us. Golightly, applying his long study of white behavior, was convinced that whites would do anything to keep black people from gaining a benefit barred to them. Many of you, seeing his strategy as betrayal, rejected it; but, in fact, he was sincere, and his was the only ploy that might have worked. Mr. Golightly!"

"Despite our past differences," Golightly began, "we now find ourselves literally in the same boat. Because we are black, our history in America has been one of suffering and sacrifice, persecution and exploitation. Yet is it not precisely that history that draws us back to our homes and the homes of our forebears? To continue on with the Space Traders would be to abandon a civilization we have helped create, and for what? For a strange world in which we can never be more than outsiders, inferior by any measure to beings who control technology beyond even the wildest imaginings of our science fiction writers?

"Yes, life in America was hard for African Americans. But as we all also know, my friends, America, whether whites liked it or not, is our land, too. For better or worse, it is our home. Our roots are there. Our work is there. There we have lived our lives, and there we have engaged in the struggle for our dignity, a struggle that—win or lose—is our true destiny. I dare to say what you are thinking: 'Space Traders, we appreciate all that you want to do, but *we* want to go home!'"

A murmuring broke out in the darkness of a multitude of voices: some approving, some uncertain.

"And now," said the hidden voice, "you will hear from one who is among you by circumstances strange beyond even our knowledge. After you have heard her, we will ask you to vote. Geneva Crenshaw!"

"Mr. Golightly," said Geneva, "urges us to return home—but home, I ask you, to what? Given the turmoil there, as reported by the Space Traders, the nation's leaders might well accept us back as a diversion from their current crisis. They might even promise the racial justice so long denied us and those who came before us. Whatever those promises, we will have heard them all before. Whatever the words, they will be as empty as all the other pledges of equality made to us since the Emancipation Proclamation.

"At each previous promise, at each new commitment to full equality, we hailed a new day—only to find that the change was cosmetic, not serious; more show than real reform. All of these pledges have come to be one means or another to keep us enslaved without chains.

"No, four hundred years is enough to convince me that America will never change—indeed, is incapable of change. Think of all the times we have bailed out white America. As slaves, our forebears provided the labor for the wealth that funded the Revolutionary War. In the Civil War, black soldiers, many of them only months away from slavery, made the difference between victory and defeat. In war and in peace, we have stood faithful, we have been patriots. But we have never understood that the essence of racism was the hope that we who were black would not exist. . . .

"Now, thanks to the Space Traders, they have their wish. Mark my words, if we succumb to Mr. Golightly's entreaty to return, we will find —likely before the welcome parties are over—that the nation will heap on our shoulders the troubles it has created for itself during our absence. Again, four hundred years of subordinate status is enough! Let us continue with the Space Traders!"

A stirring in the darkness was quickly stilled by Golightly's voice.

"I wish," he said, his voice breaking, "I wish I could guarantee that if we return, life will be different, that racism will be but a memory, and that we will, in the words of our anthem, '[l]ift every voice and sing,' till earth and heaven 'ring, ring with the harmonies of liberty.' But I cannot make such a promise. Nor would I have us vote to return on the fragile hope that America has learned anything from its double squandering: not only of the treasure the Space Traders brought them but of the human treasure of ourselves.

"I see our eviction from America as a cruel repetition of the abduction of our African ancestors. Let us not forget that those forebears suffered slavery and segregation but survived. . . . Do we not owe it to our forebears, to our children, to ourselves to return to America, not as a further gift to an uncaring nation, but as a proof that we can—by the example our ancestors set us—wring out of present danger a life of commitment and service to one another and our brother and sister Americans of any color?"

I had to give it to him, Golightly was eloquent. Geneva, too, must have felt the power of his speech, as was evident in her response.

"Mr. Golightly speaks eloquently as the representative of a compassionate, humane people ever ready to forget and forgive. But we must be honest here. We are also a people whom trials and tribulations have rendered averse to risks, all too willing to accept the devil we know rather than take on the unknown, perhaps worse danger. It is this aversion that confounds the Space Traders and confuses us in this moment of decision.

"Mr. Golightly speaks of roots. Well, let us go back to roots. We, as a people, have always identified with the children of Israel, their bondage in Egypt, their emancipation by Moses with God's help. Well, we are not walking on the hot sands of the Egyptian desert. We are hurtling through the heavens in vehicles from another world, having been set free from the bondage of our American Egypt by the intervention of outside forces. Even as the Egyptians, realizing their loss, tried to recapture the Israelites by force, so if whites in America do permit us to return, they will be doing so not for our sake but out of greed.

"Did not the Lord promise the Israelites a home, a land of their own? Is He not now, at long last, offering us a home beyond the corrupting influence of capitalism, colonialism, and racism? The slave singers, bowed down and heavy burdened, sang of a City called Heaven, one they had started to make their home. . . . Let us go on with the Space Traders to a home free of oppression, where each of us has the same opportunity as everyone else to fulfill himself or herself." . . .

As she finished speaking, a light flashed.

"It is time to vote," said the hidden voice. "We will monitor your votes as we monitor your thoughts. When the light flashes again, whisper the words 'Going on' or 'Going home' over and over like a mantra. Stop when the light flashes again."

Between the two flashes of light, I heard a sound, as faint but distinct as the rustling of leaves in a forest in a quiet breeze. Thus, the millions of people in my ship and in all the others cast their votes.

After the second flash of light, the voice announced the poll's result. "Of those who wish to continue with us, seventy percent. Of those who wish to return to America, thirty percent.

"This vote is not as decisive as it seems," the voice went on. "In monitoring your thoughts when you were listening to Mr. Golightly and Ms. Crenshaw, we found that a considerable proportion of you favored whomever was speaking at a particular moment. Thus, we must assume that if Mr. Golightly had spoken last, you would have voted to return home rather than continue with us.

"Such ambivalence disturbs us. . . . We are deeply disappointed.

"And now we have just learned that we do not have with us all African Americans. At the time of the roundup of blacks in the United States two months ago, some hundreds of thousands either escaped to other countries or were successfully hidden by friendly whites. Some of those who had fair complexions passed themselves off as whites. These black people have actually been permitted to return to their communities, and we understand that most of them long for the return of their relatives and friends we have carried away with us."

At that point, someone began singing the André Crouch gospel song "Soon and Very Soon." Other voices picked it up,

> Soon and very soon,
> We are going to see the King.
> Hallelujah! Hallelujah!
> We're going to see the King.

By the second verse, whole hosts of people had joined in exuberantly, even joyfully—but had changed the refrain to "We're going to see our home."

The next announcement expressed a familiar exasperation—my own when, in the past, I had tried with little obvious success to get an important point through the heads of obstinate students. "Seventy percent of you are now ready to return. With every second that passes, more of you are veering around to that view. Indeed, your heads are filled with thoughts of home. . . . But do you really suppose that America's leaders will invite or welcome you back?

"So far as we are concerned, whether America wants you back is irrelevant. It is a sign perhaps of our emotional unenlightenment, but we cannot risk disrupting our more advanced world with immigrants who could not accept it wholeheartedly, without regret."

A pause ensued, during which I thought I heard a faint sigh. Then a tremendous roar filled the space overhead and echoed through all our bodies. Somewhere huge mechanisms were shifting.

"We will circle your galaxy," the voice resumed, "until we decide what to do with you."

The ship settled into its new course. The only sound was Geneva singing the old hymn "Amazing Grace." Written in the eighteenth century by John Newton, a former slave-ship captain, it seems more than speculation that that melody may have emanated from the sounds of sorrow and strength rising from the holds of Newton's ship. As darkness fell, another voice joined Geneva, then another and another—all swelling into a great chorus as they reached the verse:

> Through many dangers, toils, and snares
> I have already come;
> 'Twas grace that brought me safe thus far,
> And grace will lead me home.

The Chronicle of
the Amber Cloud

The Amber Cloud descended upon the land without warning. Its heavy, chilling mist was clearly visible throughout the long night in which it rolled across the nation. By morning, it was gone, but in its wake it left a social transformation. The most fortunate young people in the land— white adolescents with wealthy parents—were stricken with a debilitating affliction, unknown to medical science, but whose symptoms were all too familiar to parents whose children are both poor and black.

The media called it "Ghetto Disease," a term that made up in accuracy what it lacked in elegance. Within days, the teenaged offspring of the nation's most prosperous families changed drastically in both appearance and behavior. Their skins turned a dull amber color. Those afflicted by the disease could not hide it. Because its cause and contagious potential were unknown, its victims, after an initial wave of sympathy, were shunned by everyone not afflicted.

Perhaps the victims' bizarre personality changes were a direct result of the Amber Cloud itself; perhaps they simply reflected the youths' reaction to being treated as lepers, both in public and in all but the most loving of homes. Whatever the cause, the personality changes were obvious and profound. Youngsters who had been alert, personable, and confident became lethargic, uninterested, suspicious, withdrawn, and hopelessly insecure. Their behavior resembled that of many children in the most disadvantaged and poverty-ridden ghettoes, barrios, and reservations.

The calamity dominated all discussion. The wealthy felt the effects directly and were distraught. Before the crisis ended, more than one parent

From Foreword: The Civil Rights Chronicles (Supreme Court 1984 Term), 99 Harv. L. Rev. 4 (1985). Copyright © 1985 by the President and Fellows of Harvard College. Reprinted by permission.

had publicly expressed envy for their ancient Egyptian counterparts whose first born were singled out and slain during the night of the Passover. Attendance and achievement in the finest schools plummeted. Antisocial behavior rose sharply as parents whose childrearing credo had been "privileged permissiveness" lost the status-based foundation of their control. Apathy was the principal symptom of the afflicted, but in many cases undisciplined behavior in the home escalated to gang warfare in suburban streets. Police had difficulty coping with serious crimes committed by those who earlier had committed only minor misdemeanors. Upper-income enclaves, which had long excluded blacks and the poor, now were devastated from within.

Working-class whites, although not directly affected by the cloud, sympathized deeply with the plight of the wealthy. Long accustomed to living the lives of the well-to-do vicariously through television and tabloids, they reacted with an outpouring of concern and support for their distressed upper class counterparts.

Private efforts raised large sums to further Ghetto Disease research. At the same time, governmental welfare programs extended their operations from the inner-city poor to the suburban rich. No one questioned the role of government in the emergency. Even those far to the political right urged state involvement. Public aid was not "welfare," they said, for the nation's future—now in danger—must be secured.

The young victims did not blame their plight on blacks. But many of their well-to-do and powerful parents charged that subversive black elements were responsible for the disaster. They supported the accusation by noting that no children of color were afflicted and by recalling that some civil rights leaders recently had expressed bitterness at the government's failure to improve the conditions in which ghetto children were raised and educated. Police officials soon responded to political pressures to "do something" about the crisis by rounding up civil rights leaders on a variety of charges. During the next few months, a growing number of whites urged even greater retaliatory measures against black leaders and their constituents.

Racial hostility did not extend to a group of black social scientists, all experts on the destructive behavior of black ghetto life, who worked with government experts to develop an effective treatment plan. During the search for a cure, hundreds of blacks volunteered for extensive psychiatric testing designed to determine the precise nature of Ghetto Disease.

After a year of strenuous effort, the President announced the develop-
ment of a psychological conditioning process and a special synthesis of
mind-altering chemicals that appeared capable of curing Amber Cloud
victims. Both the treatment and the new medicine were very expensive;
together they would cost up to one hundred thousand dollars per person.
But a nation that had prayed for a "cure at any cost" proved willing to
assume the burden.

Civil rights leaders hailed the discovery and urged that the treatment
be made available to nonwhite youths whose identical behavioral symp-
toms were caused by poverty, disadvantage, and racial prejudice. They
cited scientific appraisals predicting that the treatment would prove as ef-
fective in curing minority youths as Amber Cloud victims. They also ar-
gued that society owed minorities access to the cure, both because blacks
had been instrumental in developing it and because the nation was re-
sponsible for the ghetto pathology afflicting poor minorities.

The public responded indignantly to this initiative, criticizing the at-
tempt to "piggyback" the long-standing problems of minority youth onto
the Amber Cloud problem. More moderate critics felt that minority lead-
ers were moving too fast; the more vehement openly charged that the
problem with ghetto youths was not disease but inherent sloth, inferior
I.Q., and a life-long commitment to the "black lifestyle."

A presidential task force recommended legislative action authorizing
the billions needed to effectuate the cure. Congress budgeted the costs
largely by cutting appropriations for defense systems. "Defense," it
was argued, "must begin at home." The Amber Cloud Cure bill in-
cluded a "targeting" provision that specifically limited access to the
treatment to victims of the Amber Cloud. Over the furious objections
of minority group legislators, the Amber Cloud Cure bill quickly be-
came law.

Civil rights litigators prepared and filed lawsuits challenging the ex-
clusion of minority youths from coverage under the Amber Cloud Cure
Act. The lower courts, however, dismissed the suits on a variety of pro-
cedural grounds. The treatment program was marked by a high level of
efficiency and patriotic pride. The nation had faced and overcome the
strange, still-unexplained phenomenon. Following the cure of the last
Amber Cloud victim, the nation observed a national day of prayer and
thanksgiving. The treatment supply was exhausted; the nation and its
most privileged youth returned to normalcy.

· · ·

Geneva sat back in her chair. Recounting her Chronicles was physically tiring and emotionally taxing. This Chronicle had cast doubt upon my theory that progress for blacks might evolve out of a common crisis. I was reluctant, however, to accept the full implications of the Chronicle and discard my theory entirely. If an actual crisis threatened both blacks and whites alike more clearly than did the Amber Cloud, and if immediate and collective action were required, then perhaps the country might rise above its usual priorities and address common needs without racial bias.

I tried to break the silence without disturbing the calm. "Your Chronicle, were it not so tragic, would make an interesting question for my constitutional law course. I fear, though, that students might rebel against the facts or be so disturbed that they would be unable to address the legal issues calmly."

[Eds. The professor and Geneva discuss whether limiting the cure to upper class whites would be constitutional, concluding as follows:]

. . . .

"Look, Geneva," I said, "we may lose the case for all the reasons you have mentioned. Suspect classification doctrine has helped relatively powerless minorities, but only when the classification under review is so blatantly and arbitrarily discriminatory that the Court could strike it down under a much less exacting standard of review. Strict scrutiny under the equal protection clause has not served to protect minorities against the operation of laws and governmental policies that are racially neutral on their face, but very burdensome in effect.

"The Court rightly sought to maintain heightened equal protection review for minorities after its post-*Lochner* adoption of a lenient 'reasonableness' standard of review for most governmental actions. What it perhaps could not have foreseen was that overt exploitation and subordination are not the only forms of racial discrimination and that facially neutral social and economic legislation may wreak havoc on blacks because of their past deprivation. Thus, as it is with so many civil rights principles, the symbolic value of the suspect classification standard is reassuring, but in practice it provides no protection at all.

"I admit the prospects are not good, but, Geneva, perhaps we could convince the Court to undertake a full-scale review of equal protection jurisprudence and its usefulness in contemporary racial cases. Such a review, conducted in the dynamic and volatile context presented in the Amber Cloud Chronicle, could prove enlightening to everyone. Even in defeat, as we learned in *Korematsu*, the Court may yet gain new insight into the problems of modern racism and devise an improved method of addressing those problems in future cases."

Geneva smiled. "My friend," she said at last, "I remember when I shared your never-say-die enthusiasm. But I have been away too long and experienced too much. I am no longer certain that your earnest commitment is a help to our people. In fact, I fear that your efforts to effect change through the law and the courts place you not on the side of black people, but rather in their way."

Seeing that I was unwilling and really unable to respond to her skepticism, Geneva glanced out the window where the sun had already disappeared. "It has been a long day, and that last comment was not kind. Perhaps the final Chronicle will make clear why I have lost the optimism you still hold."

The Chronicle of the
Black Reparations Foundation

After months of excitement, the big day had arrived. The news conference was packed and hot. Television spots, like tiny orbitless suns, bathed the big stage where two dozen civil rights luminaries sat on folding chairs in a blinding glare of hot light. None of them seemed uncomfortable or even slightly put out that all eyes at this media event were on the large, balding white man who walked purposefully to the podium bristling with microphones, shuffled through a stack of notes, and then, in a deep, firm voice, began to give details of what had been rumored for months.

One of the world's richest men, Ben Goldrich was accustomed to attention. To paraphrase a popular television commercial, "when Ben Goldrich spoke, people *really* listened"—but not always. Goldrich was here now, he told the televised news conference, because so few had heeded his warnings that the growing black underclass represented both a disgrace to the nation and a potential danger far more serious than any foreign enemy.

The son of an immigrant Jewish tailor, Goldrich said that the familiar statistics regarding the ever-worsening plight of roughly ten million black people living at or below the official poverty level provided a poignant proof that "for those whose ruined lives are reflected in these statistics, the oft-heralded Supreme Court decisions and civil rights laws protecting against overt discrimination had come too late." He quoted a famous economist's conclusion that the "pattern of racial oppression in the past created the huge black underclass, as the accumulation of disadvantages were passed on from generation to generation, and the technological and economic revolution of advanced industrial society combined to insure it a permanent status."[1]

"I credit my success to hard work, faith in my ability, and the opportunity this country provided me when I was young. But," Goldrich asserted, "were I both poor and black, starting out in today's economy, I would fail: my hard work exploited by dead-end service jobs, my faith exploded by the society's still-virulent racism, my promised opportunity exposed as an unobtainable myth for all but a few people of color."

Whatever the benefits of affirmative action for blacks with educational skills and potential, Goldrich warned, these programs "are not designed to deal with the problem of the disproportionate concentration of blacks in the low-wage labor market. Their major impact has been in the higher-paying jobs of the expanding service-producing industries in both the corporate and government sectors." As a result, a "deepening economic schism . . . is developing in the black community, with the black poor falling further and further behind middle- and upper-income blacks."[2]

As Goldrich spoke, the black leaders on the platform nodded, more out of courtesy than surprise. For years Goldrich had been making similar statements, to which few beyond the civil rights community had listened very closely. No government or industry leader believed that anything more was needed than the existing social welfare programs. While expressing concern about the growing black underclass, their main commitment remained with their personal and corporate "bottom lines"— their *sine qua non* for success and achievement and worth. It was, his critics pointed out, easy enough for Ben Goldrich to play humanitarian, but he was speaking as a man whose wealth was reputed to exceed five billion dollars. "Let him put *his* money on the poverty firing line. Then, perhaps, we'll take him seriously."

Frustrated by this response, Goldrich had withdrawn from active engagement in his many business holdings to dedicate his life to righting what he believed was the nation's crucial sin. "I have been mightily disappointed in those liberals who, in the 1960s—when it was fashionable —joined blacks in their churches to sing 'We Shall Overcome,' but refuse to make way for them in the workplaces of the 1980s. All of Jewish history," he said, "counsels my commitment to defend any group designated as society's scapegoat, and condemns those long the victims of oppression who now feel so accepted in America that they can join in—even lead— the hypocrisy that urges blacks to forgo government help and pull themselves up on rungs of the economic ladder that no longer exist.

"Today," he continued, "with the active participation of those sitting behind me, I am responding to the righteous need of blacks and the sorry hypocrisy of whites by establishing the Black Reparations Foundation, whose simple purpose is to bring economic justice to those whose forebears were refused justice after the Civil War. It is with great humility and a strong sense of purpose that I stand here to carry on the work of the greatest abolitionist of them all, the nineteenth-century Radical Republican Thaddeus Stevens of Pennsylvania. You all remember"—Goldrich gave most of his listeners undue credit for a knowledge of American history—"how, in and out of Congress, Congressman Stevens, known as the 'Great Commoner,' urged the nation to break up all the Confederate-owned plantations and, under what was called the 'Forty Acres and a Mule' plan, distribute the land to the freedmen in forty-acre lots. The great Massachusetts senator Charles Sumner made a similar fight in the Senate. But neither of these men was able to persuade the Congress or the country to act. Land that the Freedman's Bureau, the federal agency set up to administer the emancipation process, had distributed to the former slaves was reclaimed and given back to the original Confederate owners.

. . . .

"Here," said Goldrich, with a dramatic flourish, "I pause to allow you to consider the enormous price this country has paid over the last century because it failed to heed the pleas for economic justice so eloquently voiced by Stevens, Sumner, and other ardent abolitionists. Though I, too, have tasted the bitter defeat on the issue of black reparations which these men knew so well, I am convinced that their goal was right, but their vehicle, government, was wrong."

Goldrich quickly went on to explain his reason for rejecting federal funding—the twentieth-century version of the rejected nineteenth-century reparations plan the reporters had anticipated. "First," he said, "for better or worse, we live in an era when the public support spending billions for military defense to protect against foreign threats, but oppose any spending for social programs to guard against domestic disruption.

. . . "Moreover," he said, "even if our sensitivities to justice for blacks and real security for us all were greater, my second reason for eschewing government in a reparations plan would retain its validity." Referring to the motivations and the performance of Germany in paying $820 million in reparations to Israel for the resettlement of five hundred thousand Jews, Goldrich referred to the warning of a scholar who had studied the Jewish experience: "Moral commitment to redress of historic wrongs against humanness can be badly compromised in the political and legislative process by which moral commitment is translated into programs and financial support. This means," Goldrich explained, "that politics and moral rhetoric tend to become confused in the legislative process. We talk about the 'good' reason, while that reason is contradicted by the 'real' reason for political action reflected in the legislation. As a result, 'we are caught off guard, and the legislative actions supposedly designed to correct social and political in-justice actually result in greater injustice.'"

Looking up from his text, Goldrich noted that the reporters were getting nervous, looking at their watches, feverishly dashing off to phone their editors and program directors. This, after all, was not simply news; it was racial drama—a subject, more likely than any, save perhaps sex, to hold the attention of readers and viewers.

Goldrich sensed that it was time for specifics. "For the reasons I have just described, I have decided that this program must be privately funded. I'm pleased to report that several wealthy individuals who wish to remain anonymous have contributed to this effort, and it's my fervent hope that many others will join in it. But whether or not such assistance is forthcoming, I am prepared to proceed and have transferred virtually all of my resources—the total assets will exceed twenty-five billion dollars—to the Black Reparations Foundation."

Although Goldrich announced his gift without any special emphasis, the enormous sum shocked even seasoned reporters, who spontaneously joined the blacks on the platform in applause. Without waiting for the applause to die down, Goldrich continued. "With the help of experts in several fields, the Foundation has prepared a complex formula that will move blacks at the poverty level and below up to the economic levels they likely would have held but for slavery and continuing racism.

"I am concerned about the corrupting effect of windfall wealth, such as raffles and lotteries. Experience shows that the sudden acquisition of large sums can be destructive to the recipients and endanger relationships with family and friends. For this reason, reparations grants will be based on free-enterprise models in which monthly payments are a percentage of currently earned income. Minimum-wage workers will receive grants supplementing their pay by an amount representing what they would have been paid had they been unionized and their wages set through collective bargaining. Unemployed blacks or those unable to work will receive grants sufficient to raise them above poverty level. Additional sums will enable grantees to obtain remedial schooling, job training, job placement, and child care."

Pointing to Black Reparations Foundation associates who were now distributing informational reports to the media members, Goldrich explained that the brochures contained program details as well as answers to their questions. "You will find that the complicated computer algorithms used in the grant formula will not turn the poor into fat cats, but will produce some satisfying results. For example, sharecroppers, exploited by their landowners over the generations, may come into sufficient sums to gain real independence in bargaining, and some may be able to buy the land on which they have labored so long for little return.

"As another example, little-known rhythm and blues singers and jazz musicians, whose work has been systematically copied and presented by whites over the years, may suddenly become wealthy. As they invest earnings to get exposure once denied them, they may also achieve the recognition their talents and skills justify. On the other hand, some well-known white singers and musicians, whose work is simply derivative, may be rejected and fall swiftly not only in fame but in income. The same phenomenon may occur," he predicted, "in other areas where the social vulnerability of black people has made them ready targets of exploitation by whites and, sometimes, by other blacks."

Some in the audience laughed nervously, but Goldrich did not smile. "I want to make clear that the purpose of the Black Reparations Foundation is to do justice to blacks and not cause mischief or sow misery among whites. We must expect readjustments in our social status and in our expectations. It isn't possible to do justice to a long-exploited minority without cost to the majority, all of whom have benefited directly or indirectly. With the understanding and cooperation of all, the dislocations will prove minimal and will soon be forgotten as all our citizens prosper. I thank you."

Blacks at all economic levels were overjoyed by the announcement that the Black Reparations Foundation was scheduled to begin functioning in one year. One observer noted that, in black communities across the country, "optimism is up and blood pressure levels are down." "Thanks to the Black Reparations Foundation," a black construction worker said, "I feel now I can make it in America." "The racism remains," a civil rights leader cautioned, while acknowledging that "the economic component of that racism has been neutralized for the black poor."

Predictably, the reaction of much of white America was far less positive. The government launched an official investigation of Ben Goldrich's holdings and scrutinized his reparations plan for legal flaws. None was found. Still, many expressed concern and resentment despite the foundation's expensive, low-key advertising campaign designed to broaden awareness of blacks' historic disadvantages.

The implications and threat to the socio-economic status quo were not lost on the nation's policy makers, who tried to dissuade Goldrich with arguments that his reparations program would disrupt the economy and increase racial hostility as white workers saw their black counterparts doing the same work but in effect earning more money through reparations grants.

Opponents were planning several legal attacks. One challenge would assert that the Black Reparations Foundation was practicing racial discrimination and thus was not entitled to its charitable status under the tax laws. These opponents also contended that, while the foundation was not a government entity bound by the Fifth and the Fourteenth Amendments, the scale of the Goldrich holdings was so large, its potential impact on people's lives so mammoth, that it was both appropriate and necessary to bring the foundation under governmental control. In addition, several state legislatures were studying anti-reparations bills which, while racially neutral on their face, would prohibit foundations from distributing assets according to the race of the recipient. Supporters characterized both approaches as upholding integration.

Concerned black groups met with Black Reparations Foundation officials about the opposition. Some representatives recommended canceling the program and agreed with its opponents that it would do more harm than good. Others urged broadening it to include all economically disadvantaged Americans, even though this change would substantially dilute the benefits slated for poor blacks. Most urged the foundation to go forward with its plans.

Widely condemned as both a traitor to his class and an enemy of his race, Ben Goldrich now determined even more vigorously to proceed with the implementation of his reparations plans. As he put it, "only an act of Congress sustained by a definitive U.S. Supreme Court decision will bring the program to a halt."

NOTES

1. William J. Wilson, The Declining Significance of Race 120 (1978).

2. *Id.* at 110, 152.

Beyond Despair

Dear Geneva,

I am reminded that our forebears — though betrayed into bondage — survived the slavery in which they were reduced to things, property, entitled neither to rights nor to respect as human beings. Somehow, as the legacy of our spirituals makes clear, our enslaved ancestors managed to retain their humanity as well as their faith that evil and suffering were not the extent of their destiny — or of the destiny of those who would follow them. Indeed, we owe our existence to their perseverance, their faith. In these perilous times, we must do no less than they did: fashion a philosophy that both matches the unique dangers we face, and enables us to recognize in those dangers opportunities for committed living and humane service.

The task is less daunting than it might appear. From the beginning, we have been living and working for racial justice in the face of unacknowledged threat. Thus, we are closer than we may realize to those in slavery who struggled to begin and maintain families even though at any moment they might be sold and separated, never to see one another again. Those blacks living in the pre–Civil War North, though deemed "free," had to live with the ever-present knowledge that the underground railroad ran both ways. While abolitionists provided an illegal network to aid blacks who escaped slavery, Southern "slave catchers" had an equally extensive system that enabled them to kidnap free blacks from their homes or the streets and spirit them off to the South and a life in bondage.

In those times, racism presented dangers from without that were stark and terrifying, but they were hardly more insidious than those blacks face today in our inner cities—all too often from other blacks. Victimized themselves by an uncaring society, some young blacks vent their rage on victims like themselves, thereby perpetuating the terror that whites once had to visit directly. We should not be surprised that a society that once legalized slavery and authorized pursuit of fugitive slaves with little concern about the kidnaping of free blacks now views black-on-black crime as basically a problem for its victims and their communities.

. . . The late Harvard historian Nathan Huggins points out in *Black Odyssey* . . . that Americans view history as linear and evolutionary and tend to see slavery and racism as aberrational: "Our national history has continued to amplify the myths of automatic progress, universal freedom, and the American dream without the ugly reality of racism seriously challenging the faith."[1] Those who accept these myths consider our view that racism is permanent to be despairing, defeatist, and wrong. In so doing, they overlook that the "American dogma of automatic progress fails those who have been marginalized. Blacks, the poor, and others whom the myth ignores are conspicuously in the center of the present, and they call for a national history that incorporates their experience."[2]

Such a new narrative, and the people who make it—including civil rights lawyers—must find inspiration not in the sacrosanct, but utterly defunct, glory of ideals that for centuries have proven both unattainable and poisonous. Rather, they must find it in the lives of our "oppressed people who defied social death as slaves and freedmen, insisting on their humanity despite a social consensus that they were 'a brutish sort of people.'"[3] From that reality, Huggins takes—as do you and I, Geneva—hope rather than despair. Knowing that no escape, no way out offered itself, the slaves, nonetheless continued to struggle. To carve out a humanity. To defy the murder of selfhood. Their lives were brutally shackled, certainly—but *not without meaning despite being imprisoned*.[4]

We are proud of our heroes, but we must not forget those whose lives were not marked by extraordinary acts of defiance. Though they lived and died as captives within a system of slave labor, "they produced worlds of music, poetry, and art. They reshaped a Christian cosmology to fit their spirits and their needs, transforming

Protestantism along the way. They produced a single people out of what had been many. . . . Their ordeal, and their dignity throughout it, speak to the world of the indomitable human spirit."[5]

Perhaps those of us who can admit we are imprisoned by the history of racial subordination in America can accept—as slaves had no choice but to accept—our fate. Not that we legitimate the racism of the oppressor. On the contrary, we can only *de*legitimate it if we can accurately pinpoint it. And racism lies at the center, not the periphery; in the permanent, not in the fleeting; in the real lives of black and white people, not in the sentimental caverns of the mind.

Armed with this knowledge, and with the enlightened, humility-based commitment that it engenders, we can accept the dilemmas of committed confrontation with evils we cannot end. We can go forth to serve, knowing that our failure to act will not change conditions and may very well worsen them. We can listen carefully to those who have been most subordinated. In listening, we must not do them the injustice of failing to recognize that somehow they survived as complete, defiant, though horribly scarred beings. We must learn from their example, learn from those whom we would teach.

If we are to extract solutions from the lessons of the slaves' survival, and our own, we must first face squarely the unbearable landscape and climate of that survival. We yearn that our civil rights work will be crowned with success, but what we really want —want even more than success—is meaning. "Meaningfulness," as the Stanford psychiatrist Dr. Irvin Yalom tells us, "is a by-product of engagement and commitment."[6] This engagement and commitment are what black people have had to do since slavery: making something out of nothing. Carving out a humanity for oneself with absolutely nothing to help—save imagination, will, and unbelievable strength and courage. Beating the odds while firmly believing in, *knowing* as only they could know, that all those odds are stacked against them.

. . . .

. . . Continued struggle can bring about unexpected benefits and gains that in themselves justify continued endeavor. We can recognize miracles we did not plan and value them for what they are, rather than always measure their worth by their likely contribution to our traditional goals. As a former student, Erin Edmonds, concludes, it is not a matter of choosing between the pragmatic recognition that racism is permanent no matter what we do, or an idealism based on the long-held dream of attaining a society free of racism. Rather, it is a question of *both, and*. *Both* the recognition of the futility of action—where action is more civil rights strategies destined to fail—*and* the unalterable conviction that something must be done, that action must be taken.

This is, I believe, a more realistic perspective from which to gauge the present and future worth of our race-related activities. Freed of the stifling rigidity of relying unthinkingly on the slogan "we shall overcome," we are impelled *both* to live each day more fully *and* to examine critically the actual effectiveness of traditional civil rights remedies. Indeed, the humility required by genuine service will not permit us to urge remedies that we may think appropriate and the law may even require, but that the victims of discrimination have rejected.

That, Geneva, is the real black history, all too easily lost in political debates over curricular needs. It is a story less of success than of survival through an unremitting struggle that leaves no room for giving up. We are all part of that history, and it is still unfolding. With you and the slave singers, "I want to be in that number."

Your friend as ever

NOTES

1. Nathan Huggins, Black Odyssey xvi (1990).
2. *Id.* at xiii.
3. *Id.* at lvi.
4. *Id.* at lxxiv.
5. *Id.*
6. Irvin Yalom, Love's Executioner & Other Tales of Psychotherapy 12 (1989).

The Afrolantica Awakening

The first oceanographers to report unusual rumblings in the middle of the Atlantic Ocean, some nine hundred miles due east of South Carolina, speculated that some sort of land mass was rising up from the ocean bottom. Naturally, these reports were dismissed as the work of crazies or, worse, of publicity-seeking scientists. Even more outrageous seemed these scientists' further hypothesis that this land mass was the fabled Atlantis —a body of land the ancients accepted as real, Plato describing it as the "lost continent of Atlantis." But gradually people began to take seriously the message of the insistent churning that made a hundred-mile area of the ocean impossible for even the most powerful ships to navigate. Night after night for several months, Americans sat glued to their television screens to watch the underwater camera pictures of a huge mass rising slowly out of the ocean depths. Then, one evening, a vast body of land roared into view like an erupting volcano.

For several weeks, the area was cloaked in boiling-hot steam and impenetrable mist. When the air finally cleared, observers in high-flying planes saw a new land, complete with tall mountains that sheltered fertile valleys and rich plains already lush with vegetation. The new Atlantis was surrounded by beautiful beaches punctuated by deep-water harbors. From all indications, the land—roughly the size of New England—was uninhabited by humans, though from afar you could see that fish filled its streams and animals in great abundance roamed its fields. Less picturesque but of more interest to potential developers, scientific tests performed from planes and space satellites suggested that the earth on this Atlantis contained substantial deposits of precious minerals, including gold and silver.

The United States and several other countries wasted no time in dispatching delegations to claim the land or portions of it. Several skirmishes by well-armed expeditions indicated that major nations would bitterly contest ownership of the new land. Nature, however, proved a more serious barrier to occupancy than did greed-motivated combat.

The first explorers, an American force escorted by a heavily armed battle crew, landed by helicopter. They barely escaped with their lives. The crew members had a hard time breathing and managed to take off just as they were beginning to lose consciousness. The experience was sufficiently painful and scary that none of those who came out of it wanted to try a second time. Subsequent efforts by the United States, other major nations, and independent adventurers to land either by air or by water also failed, even though the landing parties were equipped with space suits and breathing equipment that had sustained human life on the moon or hundreds of feet under the sea. On the new continent, the air pressure —estimated at twice the levels existing at the bottom of the sea—threatened human life. One survivor explained that it was like trying to breathe under the burdens of all the world—a description that was to take on special significance later.

What frustration! This beckoning new land mass seemed to be aching for exploration and, of course, development. Ceasing their competition, the major powers cooperated in one enormously expensive effort after another, all intended to gain access to Atlantis. All failed. Not even the world's most advanced technology allowed human beings to survive on those strange shores, so inviting seen from afar; and they proved totally inhospitable to a series of approaches.

Then a team of four U.S. Navy divers tried to reach the new land under water. A submarine entered a deep harbor and discharged the divers through a special chamber. They swam underwater through the harbor and into the mouth of a large river. All seemed to go well until, a few hundred yards up the river, the divers suddenly began to experience the same breathing difficulties that had thwarted earlier explorers. Turning immediately, they started back to the submarine; but they had gone too far and, long before reaching the harbor, began to lose consciousness.

The crew chief, Ensign Martin Shufford, managed to link the three groggy team members together with a slender cable and to tow them back to the submarine. When the divers revived, they hailed Shufford as a hero. He declined the honor, insisting that he had not had trouble breathing— that, in fact, he'd felt really invigorated by the new land's waters. And a medical check found him normal. The only difference between Shufford and the members of his crew (and, indeed, all those who had tried previously to land on Atlantis) was race. Martin Shufford was an American black man.

Initially, neither the military nor government officials viewed this fact as significant. After all, peoples of color from other countries, including Africa, had tried to land on the new land with the usual near-fatal results. Even so, there was no denying the evidence of the Martin Shufford rescue. African Americans did appear immune to the strange air pressures that rendered impossible other human life on the new Atlantis.

In an effort to determine whether other African Americans could survive on Atlantis—a possibility many believed, given the new land's importance, highly inappropriate—the next helicopter expedition carried on board three African American men and, as pilot, an African American woman. An amazed world watched the landing, filmed by a crew member and beamed back via satellite for televising. After a cautious first few steps, the crew discovered that they needed neither their space suits nor special breathing equipment. In fact, the party felt exhilarated and euphoric—feelings they explained upon their reluctant return (in defiance of orders, they spent several days exploring the new land) as unlike any alcohol- or drug-induced sensations of escape. Rather, it was an invigorating experience of heightened self-esteem, of liberation, of waking up. All four agreed that, while exploring what the media were now referring to as "Afrolantica," they felt *free.*

Cautiously, blacks began wondering whether Afrolantica might not be their promised land. Incredulity changed to excitement as more and more African Americans visited it and found it both habitable and inviting. Many people drew a parallel with the Hebrews' experiences in the Book of Exodus (13:21), as did one black minister in an oft-quoted sermon after a trip to Afrolantica:

"For the Israelites of old, the Lord made Himself into a pillar of cloud by day and a pillar of fire by night to lead them to the light. Are we less needy than were they? We, like they, have wandered in a hostile wilderness for not forty but closer to four hundred years. We, like they, have suffered the destruction of slavery—and, in addition, the second-class status of segregation. Now we endure the hateful hypocrisy of the equal-opportunity era that, like the "separate but equal" standard it replaced, denies the very opportunity its name proclaims. But at long last the Lord has sent us a home that is as hostile to others as America has been to us. Let

us go there and show what—given the chance—we might have done
here!"

Many, but far from all, African Americans shared this minister's enthusiasm. [One opponent warned that] "Emigrating to Afrolantica would
be to abandon a civilization we have helped create for a wilderness that
could prove an enticing trap. Life in America is hard for African Americans," she acknowledged, "but, my friends, be warned. For us, the Exodus story is both inaccurate as analogy and frightening as prediction.

"First, it is inaccurate as a measure of our present condition: we are
not slaves to any pharaoh. Second, the forty years the Israelites wandered
in the wilderness after leaving Egypt was a dire experience few of us
would view as an acceptable substitute for life in America. We must not
surrender the gains made through our civil rights efforts. We must not relinquish the labor of the generations who came before us and for whom
life was even harder than it is for us. America, whether whites like it or
not, is our land, too. We would like to visit Afrolantica, but our home is
here."

A pro-emigration group introduced a bill that would provide twenty
thousand dollars to each African American citizen wishing to emigrate to
Afrolantica. This federal "Reparations Subsidy" would finance the move
and was to be repaid if a recipient sought to return in less than ten years.
Emigration opponents attacked the legislation as both bad policy and unconstitutional because it created and offered benefits based on a recipient's race without citing a compelling state interest to justify a suspect
racial classification. This legislation—though never enacted—sparked a
debate on Afrolantica which pre-empted all other civil rights issues in
households across America.

Each side found support for its arguments in the nearly two hundred
years of efforts—led by whites as well as blacks—to establish a homeland
on the continent of Africa where slaves or ex-slaves might go or be sent.
Both sides were as divided over the issue as were their forebears, though
both acknowledged that whites had, from the beginning, fostered efforts
at black emigration in an "endless cycle" of pushing blacks around in accordance with the political and economic needs of the moment.

Supporters of Afrolantican emigration took as their models three key
advocates of emigration between the early nineteenth century and the
1920s: Paul Cuffe, Martin R. Delany, and Marcus Garvey. The first, Paul
Cuffe, was a black shipowner from Massachusetts who, himself a constant victim of persecution (he was jailed for his refusal to pay taxes,

which he withheld to protest being denied the vote and other privileges of citizenship), had determined to "emancipate" Africa. Between 1811 and 1816, Cuffe had, at his own expense, led voyages of blacks to Sierra Leone (the British having already established a colony there for the purpose of resettling several hundred destitute and friendless blacks who had gone to England after fighting on its side in the Revolutionary War in return for their freedom). That Cuffe's movement had been curtailed by his death in 1817 scarcely dampened the enthusiasm of the blacks who wanted to emigrate to Afrolantica. Indeed, it merely heightened their enthusiasm to revive the memory of this early black hero.

Later, in the mid-1850s, the black leader, physician, and journalist Martin R. Delany had—in line with the preference of contemporary black leaders for Central America or Haiti over Africa as a place for black resettlement—arranged for two thousand black people to sail to Haiti. But the most potent of these great advocates of black emigration was certainly Marcus Garvey. In the 1920s, this charismatic Jamaican immigrant had founded the Universal Negro Improvement Association, which managed to raise, in only a few years, ten million dollars and attracted at least half a million members. Although Garvey made definite plans for emigration to Africa, buying and equipping ships, they were frustrated when —in a highly controversial case—he was convicted of using the mails to defraud and sentenced to five years in prison, fined one thousand dollars, and required to pay court costs. Though pardoned by President Calvin Coolidge in 1927, he was deported as an undesirable alien; and his subsequent efforts to revive his movement failed.

The blacks who wanted to emigrate to Afrolantica pointed out that all these earlier advocates of emigration had themselves been driven to take their stand by their experience of slavery or segregation and by their perception that the discrimination, exclusion, and hostility from whites was never going to end. Garvey himself had told blacks that racial prejudice was so much a part of the white civilization that it was futile to appeal to any sense of justice or high-sounding democratic principles.

On the other side, American blacks opposing Afrolantican emigration pointed out that, while some blacks had indeed been interested in emigration over the last two centuries, relatively few had actually left. Moreover, the initial impetus had come from whites, who had by the 1830s managed to place some fourteen hundred blacks in Liberia. Then the movement lost steam, though it was endorsed in the 1850s by the Republican party and some abolitionists supported it. These anti-Afrolantica blacks maintained that African Americans must not give up their long equality struggle: after all, it had transformed the Constitution from being a document primarily protective of both property and its owners, to one aimed to protect individual rights—and as such was a shield that, however flawed, was the envy of the free world. The slavery and segregation eras were important history, but they were just that—history. They were not cast from some eternal, social mold determining all of America's racial policies.

. . . .

Then pro-emigration blacks moved forward their big gun: Abraham Lincoln. They noted the historian John Hope Franklin's comment that Negro colonization seemed almost as central to Lincoln as emancipation itself. . . . In an 1862 bill that sought to emancipate slaves in the District of Columbia, Lincoln included a provision of one hundred thousand dollars for the voluntary emigration, to Haiti and Liberia, of former slaves; the bill was eventually enacted. In the same year, he called a group of black leaders to the White House and urged them to support colonization, stating, "Your race suffer greatly, many of them, by living among us, while ours suffer from your presence. In a word we suffer on each side. If this is admitted, it affords a reason why we should be separated."

For their part, blacks opposed to Afrolantica emigration cited Frederick Douglass, the most influential of the black leaders of the time. He had always opposed emigration and, in November 1858, set out his position in his newspaper, *North Star,* with spine-tingling clarity. . . .

To counter this black patriotism, emigration advocates vehemently recalled the hopes so often dashed as, over the years, thousands of blacks had left their homes to seek elsewhere in America some better place, a place they could call their own, where they would not be harassed—or lynched; where they could live as the free citizens the government assured them they were. But these efforts had been almost always met by opposition and further harassment.

Strongly promoting emigration to Afrolantica were black nationalist groups, who have traditionally made emigration or separation a major goal. They were especially attracted by the idea of an island of their own because their efforts to establish black communities in this country had met harsh opposition, particularly from law enforcement officials. For example, when in November 1969, white residents of St. Clair County, Alabama, learned that black Muslims had purchased two large farms in the area, they organized a "Stop the Muslims" movement. Almost immediately Muslim members were subjected to criminal prosecution on various charges: trespass, "failure to register as a Muslim," acting as agent for an unlicensed foreign corporation, and "permitting livestock to run at large." Whites filed a civil suit for five hundred thousand dollars against them, charging aggravated trespass and infringement upon use of land. The Muslims challenged these actions in a federal suit and obtained partial relief from a three-judge federal court.

. . . .

Thus the debate raged on, as each side marshaled something out of history or experience to support its point of view. After some months, many outspoken blacks were quite ready to emigrate, but most were not. Whether ready to go or determined to stay, clearly all black people felt good about the opportunity. Blacks' enslaved forebears had, after learning of the Emancipation Proclamation, gained the courage to leave their masters' plantations. Now, the very idea of a continent emerged from the ocean and habitable only by black Americans awakened black pride—a term not much heard since the sixties. . . .

While black people pondered, white Americans grew increasingly troubled by the blacks' new confidence: some whites thought it arrogant; others, "uppity"; all found it unnerving. The linking of Afrolantica and freedom for African Americans, coming as new racial oppression swept the country, heightened racial tensions. Televised reports showing American blacks able to function normally on the rich new land sparked racial clashes and several attacks by white hoodlums on black communities. A man arrested at the scene of a race riot spoke for all hostile whites: "Damn! It ain't right! The niggers got sports and pop music all tied up. Now this! It's more than this God-fearing, America-loving white man can take!"

. . . .

Some conservatives feared Afrolantica could become another Cuba and a rallying point for other third-world peoples who might conclude that white influence, rather than colored incompetence, was responsible for their poverty and powerlessness. . . .

Before long, Afrolantica became a national obsession. Government officials hinted ominously about a dire plot to undermine world stability, economic security, and the American Way of Life. The government launched a quiet search for black leaders or academics who would support the conspiracy theory and condemn the emigration movement as subversive. Surprisingly, none could be found, though the undercover agents offered the usual rewards of money and prestige. In the past, such rewards had proven adequate to attract blacks all too ready to please whites regardless of the adverse consequences for their people.

In the meantime, a large group of blacks turned their energies to planning for emigration. . . . Pooling their resources to obtain transportation and equipment needed to sustain life and build new communities in the new land, the Afrolantica emigration programs, like the Jewish movements to support Israel, gained the support of even blacks who did not wish to move there. The uniformity of this support served to heighten the fears of many whites that the new continent posed both a political and an economic threat. Together, government and corporate institutions erected innumerable barriers in the paths of blacks seeking to leave the country. Visas were not available, of course; and immigration officials warned that since Afrolantica did not exist as a governmental entity, blacks moving there might sacrifice both their citizenship and the right to return to America—even to visit relatives and friends.

Soon these pro-emigration leaders found themselves facing an array of civil suits and criminal charges. Remembering how Marcus Garvey had been similarly hounded, blacks determined to avoid his fate. They fought the anti-emigration policies with protests and boycotts. Unlike the Israelites of ancient Egypt before the first Passover, black people during this period did not rely on one leader or seek deliverance through one organization. Rather, they worked together in communities.

"There is," one black woman observed, "something of Moses within each of us that we must offer as a service, as a living sacrifice to those like ourselves."

And out of this miracle of cooperative effort came the Afrolantica Armada: a thousand ships of every size and description loaded with the first wave of several hundred thousand black settlers. It set out for Afrolantica early on one sunny Fourth of July morning.

They never made it. Within hours of their departure, they received weather reports of severe disturbances in the ocean around Afrolantica. The island that had stood for a year in clear sunlight, a beacon of hope to long-besieged blacks, was—for the first time since its emergence—enveloped in a thick mist. The emigrants pressed on, hoping they would not have to land in bad weather. . . .

Then the mist rose. The sight that met the eyes of the blacks on the emigrant armada was amazing, terrifying. Afrolantica was sinking back into the ocean whence it had arisen. The blacks on the ships knew they were witnessing the greatest natural spectacle in world history. "My God, what's happening?" was the universal question. It was replaced almost immediately, in the minds of those watching from the safety of their television sets in America, by another: Was Afrolantica, after all, no more than a cruel hoax, Nature's seismic confirmation that African Americans are preordained to their victimized, outcast state?

But, to their surprise, the black men and women on board the armada felt neither grief nor despair as they watched the last tip of the great land mass slip beneath the waves, and the ocean spread sleek and clear as though Afrolantica had never been. They felt deep satisfaction—sober now, to be sure—in having gotten this far in their enterprise, in having accomplished it together. As the great ships swung around in the ocean to take them back to America, the miracle of Afrolantica was replaced by a greater miracle. Blacks discovered that they themselves actually possessed the qualities of liberation they had hoped to realize on their new homeland. Feeling this was, they all agreed, an Afrolantica Awakening, a liberation—not of place, but of mind.

One returning black settler spoke for all: "It was worth it just to *try* looking for something better, even if we didn't find it."

As the armada steamed back to America, people recalled the words of Frederick Douglass that opponents of emigration had cited to support their position: "We are Americans. We are not aliens. We are a component part of the nation. We have no disposition to renounce our nationality." Even though they had rejected that argument, it was nevertheless possible to affirm it, because they understood they need no longer act as the victims of centuries of oppression. . . .

Their faces glowed with self-confidence, as they walked, erect and proud, down the gangplanks the next day when the ships returned to their home ports. The black men and women waiting to greet them, expecting to commiserate with them, were instead inspired. The spirit of cooperation that had engaged a few hundred thousand blacks spread to others, as they recalled the tenacity for humane life which had enabled generations of blacks to survive all efforts to dehumanize or obliterate them. Infectious, their renewed tenacity reinforced their sense of possessing themselves. Blacks held fast, like a talisman, the quiet conviction that Afrolantica had not been mere mirage—that somewhere in the word *America*, somewhere irrevocable and profound, stands as well the word *Afrolantica.*

CHAPTER 15

Critiques

Over the years, Bell has drawn his share of criticism, both positive and negative. The following excerpts critique Bell as a closet theologian, and as an Afrocentrist who misses a few good avenues by not attending to the broader aspects of white-over-black-brown-and-yellow subordination. One commentator employs the device of a fictional selection of Derrick Bell to be a justice of the United States Supreme Court to review his life and accomplishments.

Racism as Original Sin

Derrick Bell and Reinhold Niebuhr's Theology

George Taylor

At the heart of Derrick Bell's work lies a conundrum. He argues that racism is permanent and yet at the same time insists that the struggle against racism remains worthwhile and valuable. A number of critics find Bell's thesis about racism's permanence to be so despairing that, on its own terms, it renders any meaningful possibility of action against racism pointless. My goal is to try to make sense of the paradox that lies so deep at the core of Bell's work and show how antiracist action can coexist with racism's perdurance. . . . I draw an analogy from Christian theology, in particular from the work of the twentieth century American Protestant theologian, Reinhold Niebuhr,[1] who addressed a similar paradox: sin is an inextricable structure of human life, and yet human action remains meaningful. As in Bell, the paradox is not overcome; the tension between sin and action is one that has challenged Christianity since its origins. As will be seen, the relation between sin and action may illuminate the dynamics of the relation between racism and action . . . and, in particular, Bell's conundrum—that racism is permanent and yet must be continually fought.

Bell's thesis is direct and searing: "[R]acism is an integral, permanent, and indestructible component of this society."[2] This thesis of "the permanence of racism" is asserted as the subtitle of his book, *Faces at the Bottom of the Well,* and reiterated in the title of several of his articles. In *Faces,* Bell's position is emphatic and unremitting:

9 Mich. J. Race & Law 269 (2004). Used by permission.

- "[R]acism in America is not a curable aberration. . . ." (x)
- "[T]he sources of racial problems . . . grow more intractable with time." (xii)
- "Black people will never gain full equality in this country." (12)
- "[R]acism is a permanent component of American life." (13)
- "[R]acism is a permanent part of the American landscape." (92)
- "[O]ppression on the basis of race returns time after time—in different guises, but it always returns." (97)
- "[R]acism is permanent, the ultimate betrayal. . . ." (108)
- "[R]acism lies at the center, not the periphery; in the permanent, not in the fleeting. . . ." (198)

. . . .

The severity of Bell's indictment is perhaps most keenly reflected in his best-known fictional chronicle, *The Space Traders*. There Bell offers the story of alien visitors to the United States who promise the country wealth, environmental decontaminants, and alternatives to fossil fuel. The gifts will assure the country's prosperity for the foreseeable future— except for one catch. In return for the gifts, the space traders want to take home all of this country's blacks. After significant debate, the nation votes conclusively for the trade. The country does not decide on the basis of what is moral or right but of white self-interest. . . . Bell reports that significant majorities of his lecture audiences agree that were such a vote actually to be taken, the result would agree with that in the fable. And a number of blacks have related to Bell that if they had the choice, they would gladly choose to go. . . .

The Evidence

Bell's thesis is undeniably forceful, but what evidence does he provide in support? . . . First, despite the entrance of certain blacks to the middle and professional classes, the actual economic plight of blacks as a class is no better than it was and may be worse. Second, the structure of racism persists. As to the first, the figures are dire: black unemployment has been twice that of whites; black income has been a little over half that of whites; joblessness has ravaged not only individuals, but also their families and their larger communities; one-third of young black men are either in prison or in the hands of the criminal justice system; more black men are in prison than in college. Schools are now more segregated than they were three decades ago. The courts are increasingly resistant to claims for racial redress. . . .

These facts demonstrate the failures of change. *Why* then is it that for African Americans "nothing has changed"? For Bell, the answer lies not in the legacy of slavery or some "intrinsic weakness" in blacks themselves, but in a social system where the subordination of blacks serves as a source of protection for the identity and social stability of whites. The permanence of racism thesis recognizes racism's deepest roots. Racism is not a lingering vestige of a historical past; it is a present, ongoing system of subordination. . . . Any reforms that arise as a result of civil rights litigation must cohere with white self-interest. Even though some individual blacks may have advanced due to the abandonment of formal barriers, these advances ironically serve to enhance rather than undermine social stability serving as proof that racism is no more, is dead. . . .

Part of Bell's great frustration and deep disappointment is that his interest-convergence thesis suggests that whites low on the economic ladder might have sought alliance with blacks in similar conditions. That, however, has not occurred. Rather than recognize and work together with similarly situated blacks to redress their common plight, whites at the economic bottom identify with whites at the economic top and blame blacks of a class similar to their own as the source of their problem. . . . Because of their racial bond, they place themselves "'in the dominant circle—an area in which most hold no real power, but only their privileged racial identity.' (8)" Whiteness as a property right is an essential element of American social stability.

. . . .

The Possibilities of Action

As Bell is only too aware, his indictment that racism is permanent can have a shattering impact on readers and listeners who had hoped for racism's end. . . . If racism is permanent, then isn't struggle hopeless? (xi). . . . Bell insists that racism is permanent, and at the same time "that something must be done, that action must be taken" (114). . . . The acid bath of Bell's thesis of racism's permanence lays reality bare; it strips away our illusions. To lay reality bare is a virtue unto itself. . . .

... "[W]e risk despair as the necessary price of much-needed enlightenment. Facing up to the real world is the essential prerequisite for a renewed vision, and for a renewed commitment to struggle based on that vision (xi)."

Action that has faced the discipline of necessity takes three forms in Bell's work and life. The first is action as protest. Action here recognizes reality but challenges it, protests it, defies it, even as this action understands that it will likely end in defeat. . . .

. . . Others may be inspired by the protest to take up the cause or similar causes; still others may be moved to support those who protested. . . .

The second form action takes in Bell's work and life is as "racial realism," which acknowledges the present reality of blacks' subordinate status and argues that only economic change will provide redress to poverty, joblessness, and other similar ills. . . . The prototypical example of Bell's realism is his long-standing resistance to *Brown,* its enforcement, and its continued advocacy by the civil rights community. From at least 1976, Bell has consistently—and, obviously, quite controversially—insisted that the educational focus for blacks should not be on school integration but on high quality education.

Bell's writings provide some provocative proposals for how economic change could occur. Bell argues, for example, for recognition of "entitlement to basic needs—jobs, housing, health care, education, security in old age—as an essential property right of all."[3] Elsewhere, Bell proposes . . . that business establishments that wish to discriminate should be permitted to do so, but must pay a tax, which would go to support black businesses and the black community (48–49). In another story, Bell proposes that companies that draw on African American music, dance, hairstyles, and language would be charged a royalty fee that would be funneled into urban redevelopment.

Despite a certain irony in Bell's advocacy of these actions as racial "realism," . . . Bell remains serious about the goals of economic change, both on the basis of black self-help and the possibility—even if remote—of support from working-class whites. . . .

Action as Writing

A third form of action in Bell's work and life is his writings themselves. . . . "We're a race of Jeremiahs, prophets calling for the nation to repent

(157)." Bell also acknowledges throughout his work that his message may fail. . . . Bell recalls his late wife Jewel's admonition that "trying to teach the [w]hite folks" was folly. Bell recognizes as well the quixotic character of fighting with words against structures of oppression and economic and political power.

Yet a deeper purpose informs Bell's writings, one that does not reject the limitations just raised but carves out its own space nevertheless. . . . First, as with other writings of a comparable perspective, Bell's stories can provide understanding and reassurance for those, such as many blacks, who have walked a similar path. Bell's truthtelling is the telling of *their* stories. These "counterstories" at the same time contest majoritarian stories and "strike a chord" with the ready listener.[4] The stories can provide a sense of "homeland" in readers' minds and hearts. By contrast, for those readers, mainly white, who have not trod Bell's path, Bell's writings —particularly the fictional narratives—serve a second function. . . .

. . . Racism is elemental to "what is," but we do not know what "may be." Bell does not want to discard or escape his thesis of racism's permanence, and yet he has hopes for the future. This is an indissoluble tension. . . . His work is disruptive both to challenge what is and to open the way for what may be . . . for new, real, but yet unknown possibilities.

. . . .

Niebuhr's Theology

Produced during the 1930s and early 1940s[5] against the backdrop of World War I, the Depression, social and political unrest, and the sweep of history toward World War II,

> Niebuhr's theology seemed to present the possibility of a social realism that maintained its moral nerve and did not become either cynical or despairing, even when self-interest appeared to rule everywhere. [I]t also promised an answer to work for the question: How is it possible to have hope and to maintain the struggle for justice in a world so filled with self-interest.[6]

We can easily sense a strong resonance between Niebuhr and Bell. Although each writes in a different historical moment, similar themes predominate: evil and self-interest, the struggle for justice, and the drive toward new possibilities. Niebuhr's "social realism" corresponds, as well, to Bell's "racial realism." . . .

A Political Theology

Christianity often preoccupies itself with the individual: his or her own individual sin, individual relation to God, and individual salvation in a life hereafter. Niebuhr's focus, however, is *social* existence and *historical* meaning. For Niebuhr, "[t]he obligations that faith entails are those that mainly involve the creation of justice and love in our own historical communities"; the primary result of sin is not distance from God "but injustice toward the neighbor in historical time."[7] At the heart of his thought is a "passion for social justice and for historical renewal"; his theology's aim is to provide "a foundation for creative action in the world."[8] Niebuhr's is therefore a political theology.

Like Bell's fight against the prevailing liberal civil rights doctrine of his era, Niebuhr had to fight against the prevailing liberal theological and social doctrine of his own. Niebuhr, like Bell, contested what Niebuhr called the "modern optimism [in] a philosophy of history expressed in the idea of progress."[9] Liberal doctrine did not regard evil as a serious or persisting problem. Niebuhr, like Bell, argued that this optimism found little support in the world around him. Liberalism's failure to attend the seriousness of evil also left it unable to function as a source of insight, understanding, or possible answer when the pervasiveness of evil could no longer be denied. . . .[10]

. . . .

Guilt

. . . Niebuhr's account seems to present a problem on its own terms. As Niebuhr acknowledges, sin's universality seems to imperil the possibility of social judgment and action. How does one judge between individuals or between groups if everyone is a sinner? Niebuhr answers by differentiating between sin and guilt. Guilt represents the actual consequences of sin in the historical, horizontal dimension. And, Niebuhr argues, although there may be equality of sin, there is inequality of guilt. "[T]hose who hold great economic and political power are more guilty of pride against God and of injustice against the weak than those who lack power and prestige."[11] The acts of those in power result in a greater number of unjust historical consequences. They are therefore more guilty.

> White men sin against Negroes in Africa and America more than Ne-groes sin against [w]hite men. Wherever the fortunes of nature, the acci-dents of history or even the virtues of the possessors of power endow an individual or a group with power, social prestige, intellectual eminence or moral approval above their fellows, there an ego is allowed to ex-pand. . . . Its horizontal expansion involves it in an unjust effort to gain security and prestige at the expense of its fellows.[12]

If we want to pursue justice, we can choose between historical actors and align ourselves with those having the least guilt.

Possibilities of Action

As we come to understand the functioning of power and self-righteous-ness in the world, we recognize the dimension of sin and the injustices it creates. Challenge of and resistance to these injustices signify one real measure of the possibilities of action in this world. . . . What is our ca-pacity to know and do good?

In his response to these questions, Niebuhr returns to his juxtaposition of freedom and sin and his claim that liberal doctrine had underestimated the capacity of both. He argues, "Both the majesty and the tragedy of human life exceed the dimension within which modern [i.e. liberal] cul-ture seeks to comprehend human existence."[13] It is the human spirit's "yearning for the infinite" that is "the source of both human creativity and human sin."[14] Humans are sinful but not solely so. Freedom is the basis of sin, but sin is not the whole of freedom. That sin is not the sum of human existence keeps alive the possibility of meaningful earthly ac-tion; earthly existence is not simply or solely evil. Second, this creativity is part of our earthly freedom: the human capacity for imagination, in-vention, and breakthrough, in issues ranging from the sciences to the arts to government to social relations.

Just as creativity and freedom coexist with sin, the *realism* of social ac-tion must confront the capacities for human sin—power, self-righteous-ness—in human action. Contrary to liberalism, social reform will not occur principally due to "the power of education and moral suasion"[15] but will require employment of politics and power. Niebuhr calls on the use of boycotts, for instance. He is cognizant that groups in power will not surrender their power voluntarily. Recall Niebuhr's comment on the prospect for racial reform: "[T]he [w]hite race in America will not admit the Negro to equal rights if it is not forced to do so. Upon that point one may speak with a dogmatism which all history justifies." . . .

. . . .

Niebuhr has no doubt that the interrelation he describes between the pervasiveness of sin and the possibilities of human action—between "fate and freedom"—remains paradoxical. And Niebuhr recognizes that our tendency would be to reject the paradox precisely because it seems non-rational and absurd. He asks us to consider, though, the limits of human rationality and to be open to the possibility "that a rationally irresolvable contradiction may point to a truth which logic cannot contain. . . ."[16]

. . . .

Bell, Theology, and Beyond

What are the possible resonances between Niebuhr and Bell's portrayals of human existence? . . .

. . . .

When Bell finds value in action as protest, the vocabulary is not simply existentialist, but religious. Even as he reiterates that protest will likely lead to defeat, he talks of it as "a kind of spiritual salvation," that "can bring an inner triumph of the spirit (xii)." In it lies "the salvation of spirit, of mind, of soul."[17] . . . Unlike Camus' existentialism, which expresses defiance in the face of what is viewed to be the ultimate meaningless of the world, Bell expresses a belief that even if his protest defies the realities of the social world, it comports with the truths of a more far-reaching world.[18] Bell remains existentialist, but his existentialism has a strongly religious component.

Bell's Religiosity

The centrality of religion in Bell's writings has become increasingly overt in books such as *Gospel Choirs* and *Ethical Ambition*. Bell has documented his religious upbringing in the Protestant black church and his continuing religious faith. He describes himself as Christian, but his faith is not cabined by traditional Christian doctrine. Bell finds Christian literalism to "trivialize the depths of [the Bible's] meaning and the universality of its message."[19] For Bell, "God is there, even if not in the form I had long imagined."[20] This faith that takes on the challenges of contemporary criticism is one that Bell also locates in Niebuhr.[21] Bell's drawing upon the music and message of the spirituals and gospel hymns, what he has often called a "theology in song," is particularly revealing. This music provides a "spiritual nourishment . . . a universality that is capable of touching all who hear and need its comfort, its consolation."[22]

. . . To what degree does Niebuhr's discussion of the paradox between sin and action help us to understand better Bell's paradox between action and racism's permanence?

. . . Bell's writings explicitly employ the term "sin" only rarely, although he fairly frequently uses the term "evil," particularly to characterize slavery and racism. Bell's invocation of racism as an "evil" may not seem surprising, but it reinforces his point that racism is not something superficial, occasional, or a matter of perception but rather something deep and enduring. . . .

At the few points where Bell's work directly discusses the universality of sin, it is typically critical. Commenting on another legal scholar's statement that imperfection and evil are a heritage shared by all of humanity, Bell remarks: "I have often heard similar explanations, and they have never eased either the pain or bitterness of racist policies condoned in a nation that boasts endlessly of its equality and justice."[23] Similarly, he finds woefully insufficient "confessions of guilt" by those who have engaged in racial oppression; these confessions do nothing to solve the real economic problems blacks are facing.[24] For Bell, sin's universality easily becomes a rationalization for acquiescence, accommodation, and inaction. Similarly, Niebuhr differentiates sin from guilt.

. . . .

Additional light on the universality of sin appears in his reflections on his own activism. As Bell emphasizes repeatedly, he has been constantly aware that his own actions may not only end in defeat or in unanticipated consequences, but in harmful results: "Each action intended to help some will unintentionally harm or disadvantage others who, as a result of our well-intended efforts, will feel—and may well be—less well off."[25] One of the most vivid and poignant examples of this dilemma arose as a result of Bell's protest against Harvard Law School's failure to hire to its permanent teaching ranks a woman of color. As Bell recounts, a black law professor . . . was then visiting at Harvard, and Bell's actions were interpreted in part as advocacy on her behalf. Bell had not consulted in advance with [her] about his protest, which a number of minority women law faculty resented, and Bell acknowledges that the publicity and backlash surrounding his protest may in fact have eliminated [her] ability to gain a permanent position at Harvard.[26] Bell also grants that despite his good intentions, "[i]t is not difficult to find my failure to consider the effect of my protest on [the visitor] both selfish and sexist."[27] He as well recognizes that in the eyes of some, his actions may have delayed the hiring of women of color for more years to come. Bell defends his actions but knows that they also caused pain and may have led to some unwanted consequences.

Elsewhere in his work, Bell frequently recurs to a statement he heard from Reverend Peter Gomes on Bell's move in 1980 from Harvard to become a dean at the University of Oregon School of Law. Gomes told Bell that as a dean he would be an evil; he would find himself rewarding those he should disappoint and disappointing those he should reward. The task was to become a "necessary evil."[28] As in his comments about his protests, the insight in these statements may in part be existentialist: action is necessary but if undertaken may lead to the evil of injuring others we had wanted to assist. In part the message may also be an insistence on humility. The insight may be as well that in order to act for social justice, tools such as power must necessarily be employed. It is unclear whether Bell would say that, as a social actor, he must necessarily employ means that are sinful, and it is additionally unclear whether he would also acknowledge that this employment demonstrates sinfulness in the vertical dimension as well. He did acknowledge that "Power in the hands of the reformer is no less potentially corrupting than in the hands of the oppressor."[29]

. . . .

Recall how Bell cites Niebuhr's insight that whites will not grant blacks equal rights as a matter of morality but only if forced to do so. . . . Niebuhr's formulation, of course, recalls Bell's characterization of whiteness as a property right. Niebuhr endorsed the civil rights activities of Martin Luther King, Jr., and urged that it was grossly mistaken for the country to prioritize military expense in the "futile war" in Vietnam particularly while at the same time the needs of the black community were not being met. . . .

Having discussed possible points of comparison between Bell and Niebuhr on the plane of social action, one last source of potential resemblance remains, and that lies on the vertical plane of faith. If Niebuhr finds in his faith a transcendent ground of meaning, so does Bell. Bell frequently quotes the following passage from Patricia Williams:

> [B]lacks always believed in rights in some larger, mythological sense—as a pantheon of possibility. It is in this sense that [b]lacks believed in rights so much and so hard that we gave them life where there was none before; held onto them, put the hope of them into our wombs, mothered them, not the notion of them; we nurtured rights and gave rights life. . . . This was the story of Phoenix; the parthenogenesis of unfertilized hope (25).[30]

At first glance, the statement of "an unfertilized hope" appears existential, not religious. . . . The context seems so because there is victory regardless whether of outward success or the world's indifference. Struggle can bring "an inner triumph of the spirit even as, outwardly, one suffers defeat after defeat (xii)." . . .

Bell gleans from the spirituals that enslaved ancestors retained a faith, a faith that was their only "property." The faith was that "evil and suffering were not the extent of their destiny—or of the destiny of those who would follow them (195)." This seems Bell's faith also. He relies, he says, on what Protestant theologian Paul Tillich has described as "a faith beyond the unbelievable."[31] Despite the permanence of racism and life's defeats, . . . Bell's faith provides a key to comprehending why this tension is a paradox and not a contradiction. His faith holds out a hope that both hews to Bell's realism and requires humility in acting upon it.

NOTES

1. *See* Reinhold Niebuhr, Moral Man and Immoral Society (1932) [hereinafter Niebuhr, Moral Man and Immoral Society]; 1–2 Reinhold Niebuhr, The Nature and Destiny of Man (Charles Scribner's Sons 1964) (1943) [hereinafter Niebuhr, Nature and Destiny of Man].

2. Bell, Faces at the Bottom of the Well xiii (1992).

3. Derrick Bell, *Remembrances of Racism Past: Getting Beyond the Civil*

Rights Decline, in Race in America 73, 81 (Herbert Hill & James E. Jones, Jr. eds., 1993).

4. Richard Delgado, *Derrick Bell's Racial Realism: A Commentary on White Optimism and Black Despair,* 24 Conn. L. Rev. 527, 530 (1992) ("It is no accident that Bell has a tremendous underground circulation and status in the minority community of color. We know that his message is true").

5. See Moral Man and Immoral Society, *supra* note 1, published in 1932, and the two volumes of The Nature and Destiny of Man, *supra* note 1, published, respectively, in 1941 and 1943.

6. See Langden Gilkey, On Niebuhr xxi (2001).

7. *Id.* at 228.

8. *Id.* at 22.

9. 1 Niebuhr, Nature and Destiny of Man, *supra* note 1, at 24.

10. *See* Gilkey, On Niebuhr, *supra,* at 78.

11. 1 Niebuhr, Nature and Destiny of Man, *supra* note 1, at 225.

12. *Id.* at 226.

13. *Id.* at 122.

14. *Id.*

15. Niebuhr, Moral Man and Immoral Society, *supra* note 1, at 253.

16. 1 Niebuhr, Nature and Destiny of Man, *supra* note 1, at 1250.

17. Derrick Bell, Ethical Ambition 177 (1993).

18. *See, e.g., id.* at 4.

19. Bell, Ethical Ambition, *supra* at 85.

20. *Id.* at 88.

21. *Id.* at 85.

22. Derrick Bell, Gospel Choirs 3 (1996).

23. Derrick Bell, *Preaching to the Choir: American As It Might Be,* 37 UCLA L. Rev. 1025, 1032 (1990) (reviewing Kenneth L. Karst, Belonging to America (1989)).

24. Bell, Gospel Choirs, *supra,* at 47.

25. Derrick Bell, Confronting Authority xii, 7, 185 (1994); *see also* Derrick Bell, Afrolantica Legacies 62 (1998) ("Our most unselfish work may turn out to do harm as great as the injustices we tried to end."); Bell, Faces, *supra,* at 198–99 ("our actions . . . may indeed, despite our best efforts, be of more help to the system we despise than to the victims of that system whom we are trying to help"); Bell, *Public Education for Black Children,* in Quality Education for All in the 21st Century 25, 47–48 (1994) ("What we have to do, [B]lack and [W]hite who are concerned, is to recognize our potential in this society for doing harm even as we seek to do good.") (question and answer session).

26. Confronting Authority, *supra,* at 114–19.

27. *Id.* at 116.

28. Bell, Ethical Ambition, *supra,* at 159–60.

29. *Id.* at 159.

30. Bell, Faces, *supra,* at 25 (quoting Patricia Williams, *Alchemical Notes: Reconstructing Ideals from Deconstructed Rights,* in A Less Than Perfect Union: Alternative Perspectives on the United States Constitution 64 (Jules Lobel ed., 1988)).

31. Bell, Ethical Ambition, *supra,* at 77 (referring to Paul Tillich, The Courage to Be 172 (1952)).

Derrick Bell's Toolkit—Fit to Dismantle That Famous House?

Richard Delgado

Bluebeard's Castle

In the world of literature and music, *Bluebeard's Castle* is both a French fairy tale and an opera by Bela Bartók. Both tell the story of a nobleman who marries a series of women and spirits them away to his castle, where they remain hidden for the rest of their lives. In Bartók's version, the principal character, Judith, Bluebeard's fourth wife, is attracted to the "strange and awe-inspiring" noble whose heart she hopes to touch with the humanizing power of her love. Despite her family's warnings and the evidence of her senses, she allows herself to become entranced with Bluebeard and takes increasing risks as their relationship develops. When Judith visits Bluebeard's castle, she finds a forbidding, windowless fortress, so damp and sunless that, in a signature aria, she sings that the very stones must be weeping.

Walking along a central hallway, Judith spies a series of seven locked doors. Hoping to find a ray of light to relieve the castle's gloom, Judith asks Bluebeard to throw them open. He refuses, asking her to accept him on faith. But she persists, certain that the rooms will contain what her hopes tell her must be there—some sign that life with Bluebeard will contain more than the all-pervading dreariness that envelops his castle. When she finally persuades Bluebeard to open the doors and peers inside, she discovers a series of vistas each more horrifying than the last—instruments of torture and hoards of wealth, all stained by blood. Undaunted, Judith insists on admission to the final room. Over Bluebeard's objections

75 NYU L. Rev. 283 (2000). Used by permission.

she enters, fearing the worst—that she will find the murdered corpses of Bluebeard's three previous wives. Instead, the door opens to reveal that Bluebeard has not murdered them. They are quite alive, pale and bedecked in jewels, crowns, and splendid dresses. As they advance, Bluebeard seizes the wide-eyed Judith, who pleads for mercy. But to no avail: Bluebeard drapes her with shining raiment, crown, and jewels, and she slowly, inevitably, takes her place with the others behind the closed doors.

For Derrick Bell, Judith's fate is an allegory for blacks' hopes and fears and a metaphor for American racial progress.[1] The six locked rooms of the castle correspond to major developments in civil rights history, such as *Brown v. Board of Education* and 1960s-era civil rights laws. Judith's hope as she opens each door mirrors the black community's celebrations following each milestone; her disappointment, that of African Americans as each advance inevitably is cut back by narrow judicial interpretation, foot dragging, and delay. Bell takes issue with Martin Luther King, Jr., who wrote that "the line of progress [may] never [be] straight," but that a traveler who perseveres will nevertheless "see the city again, closer by."[2] Instead, just as Bluebeard shuts Judith away when she opens the final door, so America will always shrink from the light so that "[d]isappointed, resigned to our fate, we will watch as the betrayal of our dreams is retired to some somber chamber while the stage grows dark and the curtain falls."[3]

Judith's Predicament as Metaphor for African American Hopes

Why did Bell choose a French fairy tale to illustrate a point about African American history and experience? Perhaps to illustrate a universal truth about empowered groups' cynical use of hope to keep the peasantry in line. Perhaps, too, Bell was drawn to the story of Bluebeard because he saw himself in Judith, whose transformation from besotted idealist to disillusioned bride mirrors, in some respects, Bell's own path. As the opera opens, Judith entertains a vision of an ideal life with Bluebeard and, despite warnings, takes risks to achieve it. When finally allowed access to the castle, she recognizes it for what it is—just as Bell, despite his early hopes, now recognizes the reality of a persistently racist country. The castle may also represent, on one level or another, Harvard Law School, whose hallways resisted, to the end, Bell's efforts to bring humanism and light. Despite her growing horrific realization, Judith clings to the faith that her marriage will succeed, just as civil rights activists once clung to the hope of a better world.

As Bell recounts it, the force of Bluebeard's story lies in its use of repetition, the seven doors standing in for milestones in black history, but also serving to highlight the maddening similarity of each step, with its repeat cycle of curiosity, hope, revelation, and disappointment. Similarly, the eerie image of the imprisoned brides, coma-like in their consciousness, is driven home through repetition. Three, now four, seemingly identical, pale, imprisoned women forcefully remind us of the fate of a people who fail to grasp their situation or who listen to dreamers who tell them that salvation lies just around the corner.

Bluebeard's Castle and the Architecture of Race

In Bell's allegory, Judith could have avoided her predicament by staying home and tending her garden, just as Bell, the sometime cultural nationalist, has encouraged his fellow African Americans to foreswear integration and settle instead for building strong black communities. As I will argue later, she need not abjure love entirely but instead seek it with a different, more steadfast suitor.

We might begin by taking a closer look at the architecture of that castle, its arrangement of rooms, and the relationships they set up among Bluebeard's four wives. Like an Eastern potentate with a harem, Bluebeard may be playing them off against each other, maintaining everything nicely under his control. Recall how at the very time *Brown v. Board of Education* announced a ringing breakthrough for black schoolchildren, U.S. Attorney General Herbert Brownell was ordering Operation Wetback, a massive roundup of Mexicans, many of them United States citizens, for deportation to Mexico, and how just a few years earlier, a presidential decree had ordered all Japanese Americans living on the West Coast to wartime detention centers, many losing farms and businesses in the process.

By the same token, during Reconstruction southern planters refused to hire the newly freed blacks, instead bringing in Mexicans and Asians to carry out the work the slaves previously performed. In similar fashion, Texas school authorities in the wake of *Brown* certified certain schools desegregated after cynically arranging pupil assignment so that the schools were fifty percent black, fifty percent Mexican American.

Ignoring how society racializes one group at the expense of another, then, is risky business. To understand when one is being manipulated or used to suppress someone else, each minority group must attend to the broader picture. Castle doors may be opening and shutting in a more complex sequence than we will realize if we focus only on the fortunes of one occupant.

When Bell carries out this larger exploration, the desperate urgency that he illustrated through the Bluebeard metaphor will gain even more force. He will be able to show that what minorities saw as social and legal advances actually moved us closer to the forfeiture of our dreams, and how the dominant society arranged it so. Like Judith, then, we will learn to be skeptical because "neither love nor life can be sustained on unearned trust."[4] This is even more so because the tyrannical Bluebeard, like some of today's conservatives, rationalizes that he did his bedecked, bejeweled, but still imprisoned wives a favor.

Knocking on the Castle Door: The Black/White Binary of Race

Judith's entrancement with Bluebeard may stand as a metaphor for the dichotomous quality that afflicts much racial thought today. As scholars . . . have pointed out, traditional civil rights thinking deems a single group paradigmatic, with the experiences and concerns of other groups receiving attention only insofar as they may be analogized to those of this group. Binary thinking often accompanies what is called "exceptionalism," the belief that one's group is, in fact, so unusual as to justify special treatment, as well as nationalism, the belief that the primary business of a minority group should be to look after its own interests.

Consider now the many ways that binary thinking—like Judith's initial refusal to consider the fates of Bluebeard's three previous wives—can end up harming even the group whose fortunes one is inclined to place at the center. . . .

The history of minority groups in America reveals that while one group is gaining ground, another is often losing it. From 1846 to 1848, the United States waged a bloodthirsty and imperialist war against Mexico in which it seized roughly one-third of Mexico's territory (and later colluded with crafty lawyers and land-hungry Anglos to cheat the Mexicans who chose to remain in the United States of their lands guaranteed under the Treaty of Guadalupe Hidalgo). Yet only a few years later, the

North fought an equally bloody, and gallant, war against the South, ostensibly to free the slaves. During Reconstruction (1865 to 1877), slavery was disbanded, the Equal Protection Clause was ratified, and black suffrage was written into law. Yet, this generosity did not extend to Native Americans: In 1871, Congress passed the Indian Appropriations Act, providing that no Indian nation would be recognized as independent and capable of entering into a treaty with the United States. A few years later, the Dawes Act broke up land held jointly by tribes, resulting in the loss of nearly two-thirds of Indian lands. In 1879, Article XIX of the California constitution made it a crime for any corporation to employ Chinese workers. And in 1882 Congress passed the Chinese Exclusion Laws that were soon upheld in *Chae Chan Ping v. United States*.[5] Good will toward one group, then, does not necessarily translate into the same for others.

In 1913, California's Alien Land Law made it illegal for aliens ineligible for naturalization to lease land for more than three years, a measure that proved devastating for the Japanese population, many of whom derived their livelihood from agriculture. A few years later, Congress *eased* immigration quotas for Mexicans because they were needed by large farm owners. Go figure.

During the first half of this century, Indian boarding schools sought to erase Indian history and culture, while California segregated black and Chinese schoolchildren to preserve the purity of young Anglo girls. Yet, in 1944, *Lopez v. Seccombe*[6] found segregation of Mexicans from public parks to violate the Equal Protection Clause, and a short time later a federal court declared California's practice of requiring Mexican American children to attend separate schools unconstitutional. And, in a horrific twist, in the 1940s, the United States softened its stance toward domestic minorities, who were needed in the war industries and as cannon fodder on the front, but turned its back on Jews fleeing the Holocaust. . . .

. . . Even today, the patchwork of progress for one group coming with retrenchment for another continues. For example, at a time when Indian litigators are winning striking breakthroughs for tribes, California has been passing a series of anti-Latino measures, including English-Only, Proposition 187, and restrictions on bilingual education.

Not only does binary thinking conceal the checkerboard of racial progress and retrenchment, it can hide the way dominant society casts minority groups against one another, to the detriment of both. For example, in colonial America, white servants had been treated poorly. In 1705, however, when the slave population was growing, Virginia gave white servants more rights than they had enjoyed before, to keep them from joining forces with slaves. In the same era, plantation owners treated house slaves (frequently lighter skinned than their outdoor counterparts) slightly better than those in the fields, recruited some of them to spy on their brothers and sisters in the field, and rewarded them for turning in dissidents.

In the years immediately following the Civil War, southern plantation owners urged replacing their former slaves, whom they were loath to hire for wages, with Chinese labor. They succeeded: In 1868, Congress approved the Burlingame Treaty with China, under which larger numbers of Chinese were permitted to travel to the United States. Immediately following the Civil War, the Army recruited newly freed slaves to serve as Buffalo Soldiers putting down Indian rebellions in the West.

In *People v. Hall*,[7] the California Supreme Court used legal restrictions on blacks and Native Americans to justify banning Chinese from testifying against whites in criminal trials. The court wrote:

> It can hardly be supposed that any Legislature would attempt . . . excluding domestic negroes and Indians, who not unfrequently have correct notions of their obligations to society, and turning loose upon the community the more degraded tribes of the same species, who have nothing in common with us, in language, country or laws.

Similarly, Justice Harlan's dissent in *Plessy v. Ferguson* staunchly rebuked segregation for blacks, but supported his point by disparaging the Chinese, who had the right to ride with whites.[8] And, in 1912, when the House of Representatives debated the question of American citizenship for Puerto Ricans, politicians used the supposed failure of other minority groups to justify withholding rights from the newly colonized.

During California's Proposition 187 campaign, proponents curried black votes by portraying Mexican immigrants as competitors for black jobs. Earlier, even the well regarded George Sánchez exhorted his fellow Mexican Americans to oppose further emigration from Mexico, on the ground that it would hurt Mexican Americans already here.

Sometimes the pitting of one minority group against another, inherent in binary approaches to race, takes the form of exaggerated identification with whites at the expense of other groups. For example, early in Mississippi's history, Asians sought to be declared white so that they could attend schools for whites. Early litigators followed a similar "other white" policy on behalf of Mexican Americans, arguing that segregation of Mexican Americans was illegal because only the variety directed against blacks or Asians was expressly countenanced by law.

Chinese on the West Coast responded indignantly to *People v. Hall,* the Chinese testimony case, on the grounds that it treated them the same as supposedly inferior Negroes and Indians. Later, Asian immigrants sought to acquire United States citizenship but learned that a naturalization statute that had stood on the books for 150 years, beginning in 1790, denied citizenship to anyone other than whites. In a series of cases, some of which reached the United States Supreme Court, Asians from China, Japan, and India sought to prove that they were white.

Anglocentric norms of beauty divide the Latino and black communities, enabling those who most closely conform to white standards to gain jobs and social acceptance, and sometimes to look down on their darker-skinned brothers and sisters. Box-checking also enables those of white or near-white appearance to benefit from affirmative action without suffering the worst forms of social stigma and exclusion.

. . . .

Binary thinking can easily allow one to believe that America made only one historical mistake—for example, slavery. If so, the prime order of business is to redress that mistake by making its victims whole; the concerns of other groups would come into play only insofar as they resemble, in kind and seriousness, that one great mistake. But simplifications of that form are always debatable, never necessary, and rarely wise. As a leading Native American scholar put it: "To the Indian people it has seemed quite unfair that churches and government agencies concentrated their efforts primarily on the blacks. By defining the problem as one of race and making race refer solely to black, Indians were systematically excluded from consideration."[9]

The truth is that all the groups are exceptional; each has been racialized in different ways; none is the paradigm or template for the others. Blacks were enslaved. Indians were massacred and then removed to the West. Japanese Americans were relocated in the other direction. African Americans are stereotyped as bestial or happy-go-lucky, depending on society's shifting needs; Asians, as crafty, derivative copycats or soulless drones; Mexicans as hot-tempered, romantic, or close to the earth. Blacks are racialized by reason of their color; Latinos, Indians, and Asians on that basis but also by reason of their accent, national origin, and, sometimes, religion as well. All these groups were sought as sources of labor;

Indians and Mexicans, as sources of land. Puerto Ricans, Indians, and Mexicans are racialized by reason of conquest. Latinos, Indians, and Asians are pressured to assimilate; blacks to do the opposite. The matrix of race and racialization thus is constantly shifting, sometimes overlapping, for the four main groups. This differential racialization renders binary thinking deeply problematic. . . .

Black/white or any other kind of binary thinking can also warp minorities' views of themselves and their relation to whites. As social scientists know, Caucasians occasionally select a particular minority group as a favorite, usually a small, non-threatening one, and make that group overseers of the others or tokens to rebut any inference that the dominant group is racist. Minorities may also identify with whites in hopes of gaining status or benefits under specific statutes, such as the naturalization statute, that limit benefits to whites. The siren song of specialness may also predispose a minority group to believe that it is uniquely victimized and entitled to special consideration from iniquitous whites. Latino exceptionalists, for example, sometimes point out (if only privately) that Latinos have the worst rates of poverty and school dropout; are now the largest group of color in the United States; fought bravely in many foreign wars and earned numerous medals and commendations; and are racialized in perhaps the greatest variety of ways of any group, including language, accent, immigration status, perceived foreignness, conquered status, and certain particularly virulent stereotypes. Needless to say, specialness lies entirely in the eye of the beholder. . . .

Binary thinking and exceptionalism also impair the ability to learn from history; they doom one to reinvent the wheel. For example, when Derrick Bell put forward the theory of interest convergence to account for the ebb and flow of black fortunes, the theory came as a genuine breakthrough, enabling readers to understand a vital facet of blacks' experience. Yet, the long train of Indian treaty violations, as well as Mexicans' treatment in the wake of the Treaty of Guadalupe Hidalgo, might have led commentators to arrive at that insight earlier and to mold it into a broader, more powerful form. By the same token, the treatment of Asians, with one group first favored, then disfavored when conditions change, might have inspired a similar, more nuanced theory. And in Mexican American jurisprudence, *Westminster School District v. Mendez*,[10] decided seven years before *Brown v. Board of Education,* marked the first time a major court expressly departed from the rule of *Plessy v. Ferguson* in a challenge to de jure segregation. Had it not been for a single alert litigator on the staff of the NAACP Legal Defense Fund who recognized the case's importance and insisted that the organization participate in *Mendez* as amicus, *Mendez* would have been lost to African Americans and the road to *Brown* would have been harder and longer. Finally, when Mexican Americans were demanding their rights, George Sánchez, anticipating one of the arguments that the NAACP used to great effect in *Brown*—namely, that continued discrimination against blacks endangered the United States's moral leadership in the uncommitted world—argued that mistreatment of Latinos in the United States could end up injuring the country's relations with Latin America. Earlier, the Japanese in California had effectively deployed a similar argument when San Francisco enacted a host of demeaning rules.

Writings by Derrick Bell and Gerald Rosenberg pointing out the limitations of legal reform for minorities are foreshadowed in the experience of American Indians when the state of Georgia refused to abide by the Supreme Court's ruling in *Worcester v. Georgia*[11] and President Andrew Jackson did nothing to enforce it. After Bell wrote his signature Chronicle of the Space Traders, Michael Olivas observed that Latino and Cherokee populations had experienced literal removal several times in history.

Finally, dichotomous thought impairs groups' ability to forge useful coalitions. For example, neither the NAACP nor any other predominantly African American organization filed an amicus brief challenging Japanese internment in *Korematsu v. United States*,[12] or in any of the other cases contesting that practice. Earlier, the League of United Latin American Citizens (LULAC), a politically moderate litigation organization for Latinos, distanced itself from other minority groups and even from darker-skinned Latinos by pursuing the "other white" strategy. And in Northern California, Asians, Mexican Americans, and blacks recently have been at loggerheads over admission to Lowell High School and UC-Berkeley.

Sometimes, minority groups do put aside differences and work together successfully. For example, Chinese- and Spanish-speaking parents successfully challenged monolingual instruction in San Francisco in *Lau v. Nichols*.[13] Jews and blacks marched hand in hand in the sixties. A coalition of California Latinos and Asians collaborated in litigation striking down Proposition 187, which denied social services and public education to undocumented immigrants. And another coalition of minority groups has been working to change the nearly all-white lineup on current television programs.

The school desegregation case *Mendez v. Westminster School District,* which was a rare exception to the inability of minority groups to generalize from other groups' experiences, is worth recounting in some detail. . . . By the 1920s, Mexican immigration had made Mexican Americans the largest minority group in California. Although state law did not require school districts to segregate Mexican American schoolchildren, pressure from parents led most school boards to do so on the pretext that the Mexican children's language difficulties made this in their best educational interest. On March 2, 1945, a small group of Mexican American parents filed suit in federal district court to enjoin that practice. The court ruled, nearly a year later, that because California lacked a segregation statute, the doctrine of "separate but equal" did not apply. Moreover, it found that sound educational reasons did not support separation of the Mexican children, that separation stigmatized them, and ruled the practice unconstitutional.

The school districts appealed to the Ninth Circuit Court of Appeals, at which point the case came to the attention of the American Jewish Congress and the NAACP Legal Defense Fund. The NAACP's amicus brief, prepared by Robert Carter, advanced many of the same arguments the attorneys for the Mexican plaintiffs had put forward in the trial court, but added a new one based not on legal doctrine or precedent, but on social science. Relying heavily on data collected by Ambrose Caliver, an African American researcher employed by the U.S. Department of Education, Carter argued that racial segregation would inevitably lead to inferior schools for minorities because few school districts could afford the cost of a dual system and would inevitably cut corners with the schools for Mexicans and blacks. Citing the work of Gunnar Myrdal and others, Carter also argued that racial segregation demoralized and produced poor citizenship among minority individuals and thus contravened public policy.

The NAACP's brief was cautious and incremental in arguing that segregation invariably led to spending differentials. At the same time, its social science was rudimentary, relying as it did on studies of the adverse effects of segregation in general, rather than on studies showing that segregated education harmed minority schoolchildren. A second brief authored by a group of social scientists and submitted by lawyer and historian Carey McWilliams supplied many of the links missing from the NAACP's brief. The social scientists marshalled studies showing that young children were especially vulnerable to the crippling effects of forced racial separation and were quick to absorb the lesson of their own inferiority. Segregation became a psychologically damaging "badge of inferiority" that could not be squared with the Fourteenth Amendment. This more narrowly targeted argument was the very one the NAACP would adopt, years later, in *Brown v. Board of Education*.

Although the Ninth Circuit affirmed the trial court opinion, it did so on the narrow ground that California law lacked any provision for the segregation of the Mexican schoolchildren. Two months later, Governor Earl Warren eliminated that loophole by signing a bill repealing all of California's statutes requiring racial segregation. Thus, official segregation in California came to an end.

While the appeal was pending, the NAACP sent their brief to William Hastie, one of the principal figures in the campaign against segregated schooling. Appreciating its significance, Hastie wrote to Thurgood Marshall, encouraging him to develop the argument contained in the social scientists' brief, "with as little delay as possible." Marshall agreed, and assigned Annette H. Peyser, a young staff member with a background in social science, to do so. She did, and other social scientists, learning of the NAACP's interest, pursued their own studies of the intrinsic harm of forced racial separation, many of which found their way into the graduate school litigation cases, and ultimately into *Brown* itself.

The *Mendez* case demonstrates that narrow nationalism not only deprives one of the opportunity to join with other groups, it also closes one off from the experiences and lessons of others. It can conceal how the American caste system, in a complex dance, disadvantages one group at one time and advantages it at another. It can disguise the way American society often affirmatively pits groups against one another, using them as agents of each other's subordination, or uses mistreatment of one group as a template for discrimination against another. Because almost all racial binaries consist of a nonwhite group paired with whites, they predispose outgroups to focus excessively on whites, patterning themselves after and trying to gain concessions from them, or aiming to assimilate into white society.

Minority groups in the United States should consider abandoning all binaries, narrow nationalisms, and strategies that focus on cutting the most favorable possible deal with whites, and instead set up a secondary market in which they negotiate selectively with each other. For example, instead of approaching the establishment supplicatingly, in hopes of a more favorable admission formula at an elite school or university system,

Asians might approach African Americans with the offer of a bargain. That bargain might be an agreement on the part of the latter group to support Asians with respect to an issue important to them—for example, easing immigration restrictions or supporting bilingual education in public schools—in return for their own promise not to pursue quite so intently rollbacks in affirmative action or set-asides for black contractors. The idea would be for minority groups to assess their own preferences and make tradeoffs that will, optimistically, bring gains for all concerned. Some controversies may turn out to be polycentric, presenting win-win possibilities so that negotiation can advance goals important to both sides without compromising anything either group deems vital. Like a small community that sets up an informal system of barter, exchanging jobs and services moneylessly, thus reducing sales and income taxes, this approach would reduce the number of times minorities approach whites hat in hand. Some gains may be achievable by means of collective action alone. When it *is* necessary to approach whites for something, a nonbinary framework allows that approach to be made in full force. It also deprives vested interests of the opportunity to profit from flattery, false compliments, and mock sympathy ("Oh, your terrible history. Your group is so special. Why don't we. . . .").

Ignoring the siren song of binaries opens up new possibilities for coalitions based on level-headed assessment of the chances for mutual gain. It liberates one from dependence on a system that has advanced minority interests at best sporadically and unpredictably. It takes interest convergence to a new dimension.

Bluebeard's Castle could just as easily have served as an allegory about gender imbalance and the social construction of marriage between unequals. Although Bell does not draw this lesson from it, it is certainly as implicit in the French fairy tale as the lesson Bell extracts about black progress. Seen through this other lens, a straightforward solution, one that Judith apparently never contemplated, would have been to engage in collaborative action with Bluebeard's three previous wives against their common oppressor, the gloomy noble bent on subjugating them all —in short, an injection of feminist solidarity. Persisting in an unsuccessful strategy, waging it with more and more energy, can prove a counsel of despair. Sometimes, as with the black/white binary, one needs to turn a thought structure on its side, look at it from a different angle, and gain some needed distance from it, before the path to liberation becomes clear.

NOTES

1. Afrolantica Legacies 155 (1998). [See chapter 4, "An American Fairy Tale: The Income-Related Neutralization of Race Law Precedent," this book].

2. *Id.* at 166.

3. *Id.* at 168.

4. *Id.* at 156.

5. 130 U.S. 581 (1889).

6. 71 F. Supp. 769 (S.D. Cal. 1944).

7. 4 Cal. 399 (1854).

8. 163 U.S. 537, 561 (1896) (Harlan, J., dissenting).

9. Vine Deloria, Jr., Custer Died for Your Sins 168 (1969).

10. 161 F.2d 774, 781 (9th Cir. 1947) (ordering end of school segregation of Mexican American children because California law did not explicitly provide for "separate but equal" treatment).

11. 31 U.S. (6 Pet.) 515, 561 (1932).

12. 323 U.S. 214, 215 (1944).

13. 414 U.S. 563 (1974).

Nomination of Derrick A. Bell, Jr., to Be an Associate Justice of the Supreme Court of the United States

Ilhyung Lee

Professor Derrick Bell is widely known for his outspoken and sometimes controversial views regarding race and law. In his many publications, Bell has attracted attention not only for his substantive message but also the manner in which he delivers it. Bell often departs from conventional law review style, favoring instead a storytelling method of discourse, one that brings to light issues in fictional or hypothetical form.

Consider the following, where Professor Bell himself is the subject of a fictional narrative. Employing a style similar to that of Bell's works, the story has Derrick Bell nominated to the United States Supreme Court. The confirmation process begins. The tale encourages consideration of Bell's views on the proper development of civil rights law, the role of race in American politics and jurisprudence, and the confirmation of Supreme Court nominees.

The Announcement

The President's trip to New York City came as no surprise. . . . It had been planned months before, as the *New York Times* reported that morning.

22 Ohio N.U. L. Rev. 363 (1995). Used by permission.

But this visit drew special attention, as it came the day after the surprise announcement by a Supreme Court justice that he would retire. The President's press secretary had promptly issued a statement commending the justice for his years of service on the Court, devotion to country, and contribution to American jurisprudence. . . .

Then came the announcement that the President would make an unscheduled visit to New York University School of Law, where he would offer his comments on the retirement and perhaps the selection of a replacement. Given just enough notice to provide coverage of the event, the media descended on Washington Square. Word spread quickly throughout the law school and the university campus: the President would be coming. A lecture hall in Vanderbilt Hall quickly filled with an odd array of undergraduate youth, law students, reporters, the academic old guard, city officials, and security personnel.

The President emerged to a warm greeting and approached the lectern. He repeated the remarks that his press secretary had made the previous day . . . noting that when the Justice, then a court of appeals judge, was first considered for the Supreme Court post in the 1970s, he was considered a judge's judge, and before that, a lawyer's lawyer. . . . The President then paused to acknowledge a smattering of applause. Continuing, he said, "I have given my assurance to the justice that I will make every effort to select as his successor an individual with his commitment to justice, his compassion, and his intellect. The American people ask for, and are entitled to, no less." Then came the announcement that set off an audible stir in the large hall: "Each age brings new challenges; America faces new tasks every day. The country and the times demand an individual who can lead us into the next century. With that in mind, I shall submit to the Senate my nomination of Professor Derrick A. Bell, Jr., visiting professor of law at the New York University School of Law, to be an Associate Justice of the United States Supreme Court."

. . . It would come out later that the President had consulted only his Attorney General during the selection process; other advisors did not receive word of the selection until shortly before the announcement. Some in attendance broke out in applause; others sat in silence, wondering if they had correctly heard what the President said. A few gasped. . . . The President continued:

> In Derrick Bell, we have an individual eminently qualified for the position of Associate Justice of the Supreme Court of the United States. He

has enjoyed a distinguished career as a lawyer, advocate, and scholar. Upon graduation from law school, he served honorably as a government lawyer at the Justice Department, and later, at the Department of Heath, Education and Welfare in the Johnson Administration. Most notably, Professor Bell served as a civil rights attorney in the South, as one of the original crusaders of the NAACP. Derrick Bell then became Professor Bell, beginning a teaching career for the next twenty-five years that continues today. Professor Bell was the first tenured African American at Harvard Law School. He left Harvard for his next calling, to serve as dean at Oregon Law School. Harvard asked him to return, and he did so, teaching for several more years there. He is now a distinguished visiting professor at NYU. Throughout his career, Derrick Bell has earned his stripes, much of it the hard way. He is living proof that an individual committed to excellence, with vision, can reach unlimited heights. This is a man of conviction, of conscience, and of courage, the type of figure America needs to have as a leader.

. . . Like Felix Frankfurter, this is a learned man who can offer his keen knowledge of the law from the first day. Like Thurgood Marshall, he brings to the Court the human experience of seeing those less fortunate in society, and an understanding that the Constitution guarantees certain protections for the individual. I could go on, but let me now introduce to you Professor Derrick Bell.

There was no mistake in what the audience heard. It was real. The next round of applause was more sustained. Professor Bell then approached the lectern. For a person whose words had provoked so much discussion and controversy and had inflamed so many, Bell was, on this occasion, a man of relatively few words. He had been given only short notice that he was under consideration, he said. He did not have time to appreciate fully the situation at hand. He thanked the President for the opportunity to serve on the Court and promised to do his very best if confirmed. He thanked his family members for their support, then remarked that this occasion was only the beginning, and that he looked forward to the many challenges that lay ahead. Astute observers wondered whether Bell was referring to the bruising confirmation process that would follow or a long career that he hoped to have on the bench. A reporter who had been present at the press conference announcing the last black nominee to the Supreme Court noted that unlike that nominee, this one shed no tears.

With his concluding remarks, Professor Bell took a step back, and taking a cue from one of the President's staffers, retreated to the President's side. Almost instantly, reporters leapt to their feet with a fusillade of questions: "Was the nominee's race a consideration in the selection process?" "Is Derrick Bell best qualified for the job?" "Mr. President, are you aware of Professor Bell's writings and legal theories?"

. . . The President raised a hand to request order. "Professor Bell, with his years of experience as a civil rights lawyer, as a scholar, and as a tireless advocate, is uniquely qualified to serve on the United States Supreme Court. Some have called him the nation's most renowned black scholar. The fact of the matter is that Professor Bell is a renowned legal scholar of any race. His energy, intellectual wisdom, and seasoned approach to the law are what this country needs."

"Mr. President, is Professor Bell the *best qualified* person for the job?" A reporter asked again.

The President responded evenly, "I'll leave it to you experts to decide what it means to be 'best qualified,' and how we should go about ranking individual candidates over others. In selecting Professor Bell, I looked for someone who can best undertake the enormous tasks and the awesome responsibilities facing a Supreme Court Justice. It is a unique honor that we have a man of his capability, compassion, and humility to serve on the Supreme Court."

Another reporter leaped to his feet. "Are you aware of Professor Bell's writings, Mr. President?"

The President answered with a question:

Do you know how many articles the Professor has written? Professor Bell is one of the most prolific legal writers in the country. It would be a herculean task to read everything he has written. I am confident that a reading of those articles in full will prove to the American public that he is an eminent scholar, a man of powerful intellect who has the temerity to take on controversial issues. There is not a tough question in the field on which he has not taken a position.

The President lifted his right hand in an effort to prevent the session from turning into a full press conference, but a reporter pressed on: "Do you think the writings will come back to haunt Professor Bell, as Judge Bork's articles did for him?"

Realizing that this was an issue that he could not dodge, at least not so early in the process, the President addressed the matter:

> As I said, this is a man of immense intellect and keen legal insight. Derrick Bell will not be the first law professor to join the Court. We have had distinguished scholars, law professors who had written extensively and who went on to lead outstanding careers on the bench. Justice Felix Frankfurter comes to mind. Today, three members of the Court were previously full-time professors at law schools. I do not see Professor Bell's work as a hindrance, but rather, as a positive indication of his legal thinking and articulation.

. . . .

The President soon closed the session, assuring his audience that there would be ample opportunity to probe the nominee on all matters relevant to his nomination. . . . But as Derrick Bell himself had mentioned just moments before, this was only the beginning.

The Reaction

The reaction to the President's announcement came loudly and from the expected sources. . . . Within hours of the President's announcement at NYU, a Congressman visiting his home district in the West Coast hastily called a press conference, and in an emotion-filled discourse expressed his views on the Bell nomination:

> The President has just announced Derrick Bell as a nominee to the Supreme Court. The American people may not know now, but they will know in short order, that Derrick Bell is simply unfit to be a Justice on the Supreme Court of the United States. A dangerous radical? An extremist? Those words don't begin to describe Mr. Bell. This is a man with fanatical views about law, about race, about society. Beyond the pale? Out of the mainstream? He is on a dry dock all by himself. To call him a "quota king" doesn't begin to describe the man. This is a person who sees everything in black and white. White is evil. White is mean. White is bad. And he is the President's man for the Supreme Court. The President calls him a great scholar, a great

thinker. Well let him stay in school. We don't need an extremist on the Supreme Court.

The President has described him as "uniquely qualified." Uniquely qualified for what? To be a racist? To be a dangerous radical? Are the American people to believe that this is the most qualified candidate in the country? This is an insult. The President couldn't find a more competent black liberal than Derrick Bell? There are thousands of liberals more qualified than Derrick Bell, thousands of black liberals more in the mainstream than Derrick Bell. The nominee would be in trouble if he ever visited my district, I assure you. Mr. President, I ask you to withdraw the nomination of Derrick Bell before it is too late.

The negative response to the President's announcement came also from Washington. A senator from the South, that part of the country that had been a source of both anguish and triumph for Derrick Bell, offered his views. In a voice more stately than that of his House colleague, but no less emphatic, the senator declared:

> Derrick Bell's America is a land in which nothing is more important than one's race, and nothing less so than the United States Constitution. In Derrick Bell's America, workers would be denied jobs or fired from jobs they already have, students would lose their place in colleges and universities, property would be seized and redistributed, and all of this without good cause, and without any consideration of due process or equal protection under the laws, all in the name of Derrick Bell's idea of "equality."[1]

It was just the beginning. Not yet a day had passed since the announcement of the nomination, and fierce opposition was already mounting. Other legislators, joined by groups representing conservative causes, came out in opposition, characterizing Bell as "extremist," "a dangerous radical," and "far out of the mainstream"—terms that would be heard again and again throughout the confirmation deliberations process. Some grimly vowed a fight to the end, while others called for the President to withdraw the nomination to spare the country from a crisis that would scar the nation's psyche.

Others, not prone to name-calling or hysteria, voiced different concerns about the nominee. They preferred a nominee with some judicial experience. "Supreme Court Judgeship Is Not Entry Level Position," read one newspaper editorial. Indeed, Bell would be the first to be sworn in as a Justice of the Supreme Court with no prior judicial experience at either the state or federal level, since then-Assistant Attorney General William H. Rehnquist became Associate Justice in 1971. Still others questioned whether Derrick Bell's age should have made the President look for someone younger. . . . "Supreme Court No Place for Professor's Retirement," read one op-ed piece.

Liberal and minority groups, on the other hand, were ecstatic. . . . But even they wondered if the President would have been wiser to make a more "safe" choice, one who did not have such pronounced views on race, one who was more identifiable as a moderate, one who could, in short, win easier confirmation. Bell, after all, was an academic with a long paper trail, whose positions and political leanings were well-known, who had complained loudly about the state of race relations in the country, and who had blamed for it the Founding Fathers, the Supreme Court, presidential politics, and society at large. Bell was hardly a "stealth candidate," whose positions could not be easily ascertained.

. . . .

Washington swirled with speculation. . . . One theory saw the nomination as a risky attempt by the President to confront squarely the thorny and troublesome debate over affirmative action programs, and to diffuse it before it became an explosive issue in the next election. Derrick Bell was widely known as an outspoken advocate of race-based preferential programs at all levels. . . .

Others theorized that Bell's was a "buffer nomination" that would exhaust the Senate and the country's resources, so that a second liberal nominee (though less controversial than Derrick Bell) could sail through. Indeed, history has shown that bruising confirmation battles were followed by nominees who won easy Senate approval. Justice Kennedy won quick confirmation after the failed Bork and Ginsburg nominations; Justice Blackmun likewise had an easy time after Haynsworth and Carswell went down in defeat in 1969 and 1970, respectively.

Yet another theory focused exclusively on the nominee's race. Those behind it speculated that the President, who had declared at the outset of his Administration that he would fill Cabinet posts with qualified women and minorities, had, over time, strayed from his stated goal. Perhaps the President felt he could not end his Presidency without nominating a black person to the Supreme Court. Left uncorrected, history would remember Presidents Johnson and Bush, the latter hardly perceived as a champion of minority representation in government, as the only Chief Executives to send African Americans to the High Court.

. . . .

But why Derrick Bell? In the final analysis, all agreed that the appointment of a Supreme Court Justice, from Presidential selection to Senate confirmation, is a deeply political process. Accordingly, only the President could know the reasons for the nomination of Derrick Bell, or, indeed, any individual.

. . . On the fourth day after the announcement, the White House issued a statement:

> The President stands by the nomination of Derrick Bell, and expects the professor to be confirmed, and to take his seat as the next Associate Justice of the United States Supreme Court. The President has met privately with the Chairman of the Senate Judiciary Committee. The Chairman has assured that a full and fair examination of the record of the nominee will take place, pursuant to the Senate duty to advise and consent. There will be open and frank discussion of the nominee's record and fitness for a position on the Supreme Court. Professor Bell will have his say as will all interested parties.

Thus, the first round ended. The nomination of Derrick Bell to be an Associate Justice of the Supreme Court of the United States would go forward. Liberals were overjoyed. For them the day was long overdue for a true liberal on the Court. Justices Brennan, Marshall and Blackmun had left the Court, and no one of equal or similar commitment to civil rights and individual liberties had replaced them. If the right could have Rehnquist and Scalia, as well as a black Justice in Thomas, surely the Court had room for a Justice with the philosophy of Derrick Bell, they reasoned. They assumed that Bell would deliver, although his positions on privacy and First Amendment protections were not readily known. Bell had not written extensively on those issues, at least where race was not concerned. Black leaders also praised the nomination. Black Americans feared that they would not see another black Justice on the Supreme Court during their lifetimes, leaving them only memories of Thurgood Marshall and attempts to reconcile with Clarence Thomas. They would pay any price to see Derrick Bell, a true civil rights advocate, take a seat on the Court. At some point, they reasoned, the charges and the distortion would halt, the sound-bites would have their last airing, the hearings would conclude, the debate would cease, and the Senate will cast its vote. The vote would be close, even the most optimistic had conceded, but only a simple majority would be needed. Moreover, the prospect of Justice Bell debating the finer points of civil rights law with Justice Thomas was, to many, simply too delectable.

Conservatives, too, were secretly delighted with the Bell nomination, albeit for very different reasons. . . . This nomination would mark the first time since the Bork debacle that an unashamed, unabashed liberal had been nominated to the Supreme Court. The opportunity to avenge the defeat of Robert Bork was in their grasp. . . .

Who Is This Man?

Shortly after the President's announcement, news organizations quickly dispatched correspondents to the many places where Derrick Bell had once lived: Pittsburgh, where Derrick Bell was born and raised; to various locations in the South, sites of Bell's early career as a civil rights lawyer; to Harvard, where he had taught for fifteen years, some of them tumultuous, and departed under protest; to Eugene, Oregon, where he served as dean of Oregon Law School; to New York University and other law schools where he had taught as a visiting professor; and to various other localities to interview relatives, colleagues, former students, and adversaries. . . . They looked hard at the first twenty-five years of his life to ascertain the early forces that shaped a man who would later be excoriated by some, worshipped by others.

. . . .

Writings

They also examined his writings. . . . Beginning from the early 1970s, the professor had compiled a remarkable record, publishing several books and over 100 law review articles, almost all of them on race issues. But as the nomination of Robert Bork taught, a nominee's paper trail will attract intense scrutiny during the confirmation process. . . .

In the case of Professor Bell, both the substance and the style of his writings prompted discussion, debate, and concern. Bell, who has made the interrelationship among race, racism, and law a life study, is universally credited as the originator and force behind the movement known as Critical Race Theory (CRT); his works are widely cited as illustrative, if not prototypical works of CRT scholarship. Richard Delgado, a principal figure in current Critical Race thought, explains Bell's role in the development of the movement:

> Critical Race Theory sprang up with the realization that the civil rights movement of the 1960s had stalled and needed new approaches to deal with the complex relationship among race, racism, and American law. Derrick Bell and others began writing about liberalism's defects and the way our system of civil rights statutes and case law reinforces white-over-black domination.[2]

As developed by Bell, Critical Race Theory argues that law, under the guise of abstract, neutral principles, actually leads to "legal results that harm blacks and perpetuate their inferior status."[3] CRT challenges the notion that law is applied with detached impartiality; rather, law is seen as "conceal[ing] the partisan exercise of power," and acting as "an instrument of subordination and an agent for silencing minority voices." CRT thus offers oppositional scholarship that is more "contextualized and based on narrative and experience."[4] Critical Race Theory therefore is distinct and removed from traditional or "liberal" civil rights law (once known as antidiscrimination law), which depends on "the premise of formal equality" to protect minorities, women and the poor from continued subjugation. Once a fledgling, revolutionary school of thought, CRT now boasts a substantial library of illustrative works, followers who hold membership in the faculties of the nation's leading law schools, and annual workshops bringing disciples together to advance the movement.

Articles exhibiting Critical Race Theory thought read quite differently than traditional legal scholarship. Rather than the turgid, jargon-filled mode of writing seen in many law review publications, CRT thought often takes the form of storytelling. Thus, many of Bell's writings are presented as fictional accounts, or allegories, which provide a comfortable setting for dialogue between characters. Readers are asked temporarily to suspend judgment and the rules of technical feasibility, and listen in. The dialogue often represents the views and voices of Bell himself and his colleagues in the Critical Race Theory movement. Analysis, argumentation and criticism merge with hypotheticals that pose difficult legal questions.

Supporting authority, where not provided in the fictional dialogue, appears in the footnotes. . . .

Storytelling

Perhaps the best known of Bell's unique writings is an article that appeared as a foreword in the *Harvard Law Review*. In the article, the narrator, who, many presume, is Bell himself, offers a series of fictional scenarios, or "Chronicles," that raise compelling issues concerning race and law. Each Chronicle features a discussion between the narrator and Geneva Crenshaw, a former colleague from the NAACP Legal Defense Fund in the 1960s. For example, in the "Chronicle of the DeVine Gift,"[5] Crenshaw relates her experiences as the token black on the faculty of a prestigious law school. She is approached by a wealthy, successful black entrepreneur (Taylor DeVine), who offers his vast resources in capital and networking to assist Crenshaw in seeking and attracting other minorities to the school's faculty. As a result of their efforts, three more blacks (two men and one woman), a Hispanic man and an Asian woman join the faculty, bringing the total number of minority faculty members to six. DeVine and Crenshaw then discover a "Seventh Candidate." . . .

. . . .

White Self-Interest

Bell has described as a maxim of American law that "white self-interest will prevail over black rights." Beginning with the founding of the Republic, it was in white interest to continue the enslavement of blacks for many years, and to have the might of political and legal institutions behind it to ensure its protection and continued implementation. It was simply a question of economics. Segregation followed slavery, for whites were not quite ready for an integrated society. But slavery ended many years ago; what of those "civil rights victories," measures designed to advance "racial progress"? According to Bell, they were motivated not by concern for injustices to blacks, but by white self-interest: "[T]he most significant political advances for blacks resulted from policies which were intended and had the effect of serving the interests and convenience of whites rather than remedying racial injustices against blacks." To Bell, the abolition of slavery in the North, the Reconstruction Amendments, as well as *Brown v. Board of Education* and related school desegregation cases are examples of this pattern.

. . . .

Property Right in Whiteness

It is a staple of Critical Race thought that American law has subordinated and oppressed blacks. In addition, Bell has specifically stated that government was created and sustained primarily to protect property rights of whites. . . . First incorporated in *Plessy v. Ferguson*, "[t]he law has [since] mostly encouraged and upheld . . . a property right in whiteness." According to Bell, the Supreme Court has continued to reinforce and protect that property right nearly a century after *Plessy* in cases affecting racial classifications in affirmative action, capital punishment, and employment discrimination. Over the years, the Court, and society too, has become more sophisticated in protecting such a right, Bell contends. Today, the passwords for gaining judicial recognition of the still viable property right to the advantages of being white include higher entrance scores, merit, seniority, and neighborhood schools.

Permanence of Racism

For a time, Derrick Bell once held out the hope that racial reform and racial justice were possible ends. Consider the subtitle of his text, *And We Are Not Saved: The Elusive Quest for Racial Justice*, for example. The quest was "elusive," but the much savored end of justice for all races made continuing the quest worthwhile. Bell has since given up. After years of leading the quest, Bell has concluded that racism in America is permanent; racism is an "integral" and "indestructible component of this society"; and racial equality is, in fact, not a realistic goal.[6]

. . . .

Bell's Tone

Bell's expositions on issues of race and racism in America over the years exhibit a persistent undertone of pessimism, sometimes verging on a hyperbolic cynicism. In addition to those who charge Bell with undue pessimism, others have complained that he is simply blind to the actual consequences of law and legal precedent. Occasionally, reviewers wonder if Bell can possibly mean what he says, and whether he has gone too far. All of these would be grist for the confirmation hearings mill.

. . . .

Preliminary Questioning

[Eds. The days leading up to Bell's confirmation hearing, and the early rounds of that hearing, featured grueling reviews of the nominee's views. Was he a racial extremist? An irresponsible critic who rejected everything white America offered? Did he live to harass white folks? Really believe white America would send blacks on a spaceship if the opportunity presented itself? The author draws on the confirmation proceeding that rejected Robert Bork and accepted Clarence Thomas to paint the scathing questioning Bell would face. He then continues as follows:]

Hearings before the Senate Judiciary Committee

The date of the hearings before the Senate Judiciary Committee had arrived at last. From the time the President first made the surprise announcement, much had been said about Bell, both in support and in opposition. . . . Many had drawn comparisons to the failed Bork nomination; others still could not believe the President's selection. The Chairman of the Judiciary Committee opened the hearings. He recognized and thanked the dignitaries in attendance for this occasion. The formalities and protocol were followed. Following custom, a senator introduced the nominee to the Committee. Then the members of the Committee, in order of seniority beginning with the Chairman, made their opening statements. There were the usual remarks about the Constitutional mandate for Senatorial advice and consent, the grave responsibility of the Senate to examine closely the nominee's qualifications, character, judicial philosophy, and fitness for a position with lifetime tenure. A few senators offered flowery praise for the nominee's accomplished career as a civil rights advocate, public servant, scholar, and teacher. One stated, "Professor Bell, you have committed your life to equality and justice for all Americans; you have taken it on as a crusade, at great personal sacrifice, and for that, the Nation owes you a note of gratitude." Another senator, as expected, stated his opposition to the nominee and urged the Committee and the Senate to reject the nomination:

> From the beginning, America has set the highest standards for our highest Court. We insist that a nominee should have outstanding ability and integrity. But we also insist on even more: that those who sit on the Supreme Court must deserve the special title we reserve for only nine federal judges in the entire country, the title that sums up in one word the awesome responsibility on their shoulders—the title of "Justice."
>
> Historically, America has set this high standard because the Justices of the Supreme Court have a unique obligation: to serve as the ultimate guardians of the Constitution, the rule of law, and the liberty and the equality of every citizen.
>
> Derrick Bell . . . falls far short of what Americans demand of a man or woman as a Justice on the Supreme Court. The strongest case against this nomination is made by the words of Mr. Bell himself.
>
> In article after article, speech after speech, Professor Bell has criticized the constitutional decisions of the Supreme Court—not once, not a few times, not a dozen, but in scores of decisions. He has called these decisions "mind boggl[ing]," "not only wrong[, but] . . . also capricious," legally inconsistent and intellectually dishonest. With respect to other decisions, he has accused the Supreme Court of "constitutionally sanction[ing] . . . [the] exclu[sion of] the poor and . . . minorities," and "refus[ing] to . . . strike down laws, which . . . promote racial discrimination."
>
> In yet other articles, Derrick Bell has written that the Constitution does not, and indeed, cannot work for people. He believes that laws cannot be fairly applied. Only three years ago, he stated that it is unrealistic for minorities to achieve equality under the law.
>
> These views are fundamentally at odds with the express understanding of the Framers and with the history of the Supreme Court in building our tradition of constitutionalism. Our nation demands that the Supreme Court exercise wisdom and statesmanship in mediating conflicts spurred by growth and change in a dynamic society. His writings raise grave concerns that he would do so.
>
> In Derrick Bell's America, there is no room at the inn for both blacks and whites, no room anywhere where blacks and whites can work side by side, or live as neighbors, and no place in the Constitution for a

color-blind approach to the law; and in our America, there should be no seat on the Supreme Court for Derrick Bell.

The fact of the matter is that Professor Bell is out of step with the Congress, out of step with the country, out of step with the Constitution and many of the most fundamental issues facing America. Professor Bell is a walking constitutional amendment and he should not be confirmed by the Senate.

. . . Professor Bell, I am sure you know the one question to be raised in these hearings is whether or not you are going to read new rights into the Constitution, without regard to the text of the Constitution, judicial precedent, or the amendment process.

In addition, you have said whites who know your record . . . need not fear you. But the fact is, Professor Bell, they do fear you. They are concerned. They are frightened. . . . The whites of America, in my opinion, have much to be worried about in connection with your appointment. . . . And it is only fair to say that you have made it quite clear . . . that you are not a frightening man, but you are a man with frightening views.

I strongly encourage you, Professor Bell, to be straightforward and clear with this committee. The record is voluminous. It would be a disservice to you and the country to distort it. . . . The Senate's inquiry follows more than just a consideration of Professor Bell's professional credentials. In the end each Senator [m]ust search his or her conscience and ask, is the confirmation of Derrick Bell in the best interest of this country?

With that, the stage was set. The Chairman turned to Derrick Bell and asked if the nominee wished to make an opening statement. It was not that Derrick Bell had been waiting all his life for this moment. He certainly had not. Issues of race and racism had deeply troubled him, and he had said so. He had done what he could to effect change. The judicial system provided an early forum. A civil rights lawyer in the South in the 1960s, he saw firsthand the resistance of some Americans to racial equality. Later, he sought new audiences in academia, spreading his message to students, to friend and foe in the community, with his writings and ideas. He would do it through dialogue, argument, persuasion, and if necessary, protest. Some deified him; others barely acknowledged him. If reform would entail risk, it was a small price to pay. But after those efforts came reflection and some resignation. Better blacks accept the permanence of racism and deal with it accordingly than flail aimlessly with unattainable expectations. Yet in the same breath he encouraged the fight to go on. Bell saw no inconsistency in that. Bell's cause, was, in a sense, like that of Moses, "perhaps destined never to see the promised land, but committed to working toward that goal." Then had come the call from the President.

It was Derrick Bell's turn. [He smoothed a single sheet of bullet points on the lectern in front of him, looked up at his audience, and began.]

NOTES

1. Compare these comments to those by Senator Edward Kennedy in response to President Reagan's nomination of Judge Bork some years before:

Robert Bork's America is a land in which women would be forced into back alley abortions, blacks would sit at segregated lunch counters, rogue police could break down citizens' doors in midnight raids, school children could not be taught about evolution, writers and artists could be censored at the whim of government, and the doors of the federal courts would be shut on the fingers of millions of citizens for whom the judiciary is—and is often the only—protector of the individual rights that are the heart of our democracy.

113 Cong. Rec. 18,519 (1987).

2. Richard Delgado, *The Inward Turn in Outsider Jurisprudence*, 34 Wm. & Mary L. Rev. 741, 745 (1993).

3. Bell, *Racial Realism, supra* this volume.

4. Delgado, *Outsider Jurisprudence, supra*, at 745. "[CRT] challenges the universality of white experience/judgment as the authoritative standard that binds people of color, and normatively measures, directs, controls, and regulates the terms of proper thought, expression, presentment, and behavior."

5. See chapter 6, this volume.

6. Bell, Faces at the Bottom of the Well, *supra*, at 12.

Bibliography

ARCHIVES

New York University. Elmer Holmes Bobst Library. Archives. Guide to the Derrick A. Bell, Jr. Papers, 1959–1999 (contains correspondence, speeches and writings, subject files, course materials, book materials, 116 linear feet (116 boxes)).

BOOKS

Race, Racism, and American Law, 5th Edition, New York: Aspen Law and Business, 2004.

Silent Covenants: *Brown v. Board of Education* and the Unfulfilled Hopes for Racial Reform, New York: Oxford University Press, 2004.

Ethical Ambition: Living a Life of Meaning and Worth, New York & London: Bloomsbury, 2002.

Afrolantica Legacies, Chicago: Third World Press, 1998.

Constitutional Conflicts: Part 1, Cincinnati: Anderson Publishing Co., 1997.

Gospel Choirs: Psalms of Survival for an Alien Land Called Home, New York: Basic Books, 1996.

Confronting Authority: Reflections of an Ardent Protester, Boston: Beacon Press, 1994.

Faces at the Bottom of the Well: The Permanence of Racism, New York: Basic Books, 1992.

And We Are Not Saved: The Elusive Quest for Racial Justice, New York: Basic Books, 1987.

Civil Rights: Leading Cases (Editor), Boston: Little, Brown, 1980.

Shades of Brown: New Perspectives on School Desegregation (Editor), New York: Teachers College Press, Columbia University, 1980.

ARTICLES

Diversity's Distractions, 103 Colum. L. Rev. 1622 (2003).

Learning from Living: The University of Michigan Affirmative Action Cases, Jurist, Sept. 5, 2003, at http://jurist.law.pitt.edu/forum/symposium-aa.

Racism: A Major Source of Property and Wealth Inequality in America ([Symposium]: Property, Wealth, and Inequality), 34 Ind. L. Rev. 1261 (2001).

Brown v. Board of Education: Forty-Five Years after the Fact (2000 Kormendy Lecture), 26 Ohio N.U. L. Rev. 171 (2000).

Wanted: A White Leader Able to Free Whites of Racism (Edward L. Barrett, Jr. Lecture on Constitutional Law), 33 U.C. Davis L. Rev. 527 (2000).

A Colony at Risk, 15 Touro L. Rev. 347 (1999).

Getting Beyond a Property in Race ([Special Issue]: Access to Justice: The Social Responsibility of Lawyers), 1 Wash. U. J.L. & Pol'y 27 (1999).

"Here Come de Judge": The Role of Faith in Progressive Decision-Making (Justice Matthew O. Tobriner Memorial Lecture), 51 Hastings L.J. 1 (1999).

The Power of Narrative (Symposium: Law, Literature, and Science Fiction), 23 Legal Stud. F. 315 (1999).

Constitutional Conflicts: The Perils and Rewards of Pioneering in the Law School Classroom, 21 Seattle U. L. Rev. 1039 (1998).

California's Proposition 209: A Temporary Diversion on the Road to Racial Disaster, 30 Loy. L.A. L. Rev. 1447 (1997).

A Gift of Unrequited Justice (Symposium: Speaking Truth to Power: The Jurisprudence of Julia Cooper Mack), 40 How. L.J. 305 (1997).

A Pre-Memorial Message on Law School Teaching, 23 N.Y.U. Rev. L. & Soc. Change 205 (1997).

Racial Libel as American Ritual (The Foulston & Siefkin Lecture), 36 Washburn L.J. 1 (1996).

Black History and America's Future (The Edward A. Seegers Lecture), 29 Val. U. L. Rev. 1179 (1995).

1995 Commencement Address: Howard University School of Law, 38 How. L.J. 463 (1995).

The Triumph in Challenge, 54 Md. L. Rev. 1691 (1995).

Who's Afraid of Critical Race Theory? (David C. Balm Memorial Lecture), 1995 U. Ill. L. Rev. 893. Reprinted in Critical White Studies: Looking behind the Mirror (Richard Delgado & Jean Stefancic eds., 1997) as Thank You, Doctors Murray and Herrnstein.

Diversity and Academic Freedom ([Special Issue]: Academic Freedom and Legal Education), 43 J. Legal Educ. 371 (1993).

Learning the Three "I's" of America's Slave Heritage (Symposium on the Law of Slavery), 68 Chi.-Kent L. Rev. 1037 (1993). Reprinted in Slavery and the Law 29 (Paul Finkelman ed., 1997).

Making a Record, 26 Conn. L. Rev. 265 (1993) (with Linda Singer).

The Permanence of Racism, 22 Sw. U.L. Rev. 1103 (1993).

Political Reality Testing: 1993, 61 Fordham L. Rev. 1033 (1993).

The Racism Is Permanent Thesis: Courageous Revelation or Unconscious Denial of Racial Genocide, 22 Cap. U.L. Rev. 571 (1993).

Students as Teachers, Teachers as Learners (Symposium: Legal Education), 91 Mich. L. Rev. 2025 (1993) (with Erin Edmonds).

The Racial Preference Licensing Act: A Fable about the Politics of Hate, 78 A.B.A.J., Sept. 1992, at 50.

Racial Realism, 24 Conn. L. Rev. 363 (1992). Reprinted in Critical Race Theory: The Key Writings That Formed the Movement 302 (Kimberlé Crenshaw et al. eds., 1995); also in Philosophical Problems in the Law, 3d ed. 136 (David M. Adams ed., 2000).

Reconstruction's Racial Realities (Symposium: The Reconstruction Amendments: Then and Now), 23 Rutgers L. J. 261 (1992). Published as The Fourteenth Amendment in a bicentennial issue of the N.Y. Times Sunday Magazine, Sept. 13, 1987.

The Last Black Hero: A Chronicle of Interracial Love and Sacrifice ([Special Issue]: Personal Reflections on the Struggle for Equality), 8 Harv. BlackLetter J. 275 (1991).

The Law of Racial Standing, 2 Yale J. L. & Liberation 117 (1991).

Racism Is Here to Stay: Now What? (Thurgood Marshall Commemorative Issue), 35 How. L.J. 79 (1991).

After We're Gone: Prudent Speculations on America in a Post-Racial Epoch (1989 Sanford E. Sarasohn Memorial Lecture) (A Forum on Derrick Bell's Civil Rights Chronicles), 34 St. Louis U. L.J. 393 (1990). Reprinted in part in Critical Race Theory: The Cutting Edge, 2d ed. 2 (Richard Delgado & Jean Stefancic eds., 2000); also in Dark Matter: A Century of Speculative Fiction from the African Diaspora (Sheree R. Thomas ed., 2000); also in Reflections: An Anthology of African American Philosophy 325 (James A. Montmarquet & William H. Hardy eds., 2000).

Dividends of Diversity, 23 Bill of Rights J. 16 (Dec. 1990).

Racial Reflections: Dialogues in the Direction of Liberation, 37 UCLA L. Rev. 1037 (1990) (with Tracy Higgins and Sung-Hee Suh). Reprinted in Critical White Studies 106 (Richard Delgado & Jean Stefancic eds., 1997).

An Epistolary Exposition for a Thurgood Marshall Biography, 6 Harv. BlackLetter J. 51 (1989). Reprinted in Southern University Law Review, see 20 So. U. L. Rev. 83 (1993).

The Final Report: Harvard's Affirmative Action Allegory ([Symposium]: Legal Storytelling), 87 Mich. L. Rev. 2382 (1989).

Racism: A Prophecy for the Year 2000 (C. Willard Heckel Lecture), 42 Rutgers L. Rev. 93 (1989).

The Constitution at 200: Reflections on the Past—Implications for the Future, 5 N.Y.L. Sch. J. Hum. Rts. 331 (1988).

The Republican Revival and Racial Politics (Symposium: The Republican Civic Tradition), 97 Yale L.J. 1609 (1988) (with Preeta Bansal).

White Superiority in America: Its Legal Legacy, Its Economic Costs, 33 Vill. L.

Rev. 767 (1988). Reprinted in African Americans and the Living Constitution 183 (John Hope Franklin & Genna Rae McNeil eds., 1995) as The Real Costs of Racial Discrimination; also in Critical White Studies: Looking behind the Mirror 596 (Richard Delgado & Jean Stefancic eds., 1997); also in Black on White: Black Writers on What It Means to Be White 138 (David R. Roediger ed., 1998); also in Critical Race Theory: The Cutting Edge, 2d ed. 71 (Richard Delgado & Jean Stefancic eds. 2000) as Property Rights in Whiteness: Their Legal Legacy, Their Economic Costs.

Application of the "Tipping Point" Principle to Law Faculty Hiring Policies (Transforming Legal Education: A Symposium of Provocative Thought), 10 Nova L.J. 319 (1986).

The Dilemma of the Responsible Law Reform Lawyer in the Post–Free Enterprise Era (The Inaugural Presentation of the Charles H. Revson Urban Law and Policy Lectures, Nov. 21, 1985), 4 Law & Ineq. 231 (1986).

Strangers in Academic Paradise: Law Teachers of Color in Still White Schools (The 1985 Minority Law Teachers' Conference), 20 U.S.F. L. Rev. 385 (1986).

An American Fairy Tale: The Income-Related Neutralization of Race Law Precedent, 18 Suffolk U. L. Rev. 331 (1984). Reprinted in Beyond Racism: Race and Inequality in Brazil, South Africa, and the United States 553 (Charles V. Hamilton et al. eds., 2001).

A Holiday for Dr. King: The Significance of Symbols in the Black Freedom Struggle, 17 U.C. Davis L. Rev. 433 (1984).

A Hurdle Too High: Class-Based Roadblocks to Racial Remediation (1983 James McCormick Mitchell Lecture), 33 Buff. L. Review 1 (1984) (includes responses by Alan Freeman, Monroe Fordham, and Sidney Willhelm).

The Law Student as Slave: One Dean's Perspective, 11 Student Lawyer (Oct. 1982), at 18.

The Dialectics of School Desegregation (Symposium: Judicially Managed Institutional Reform), 32 Ala. L. Rev. 281 (1981).

Law School Exams and Minority-Group Students, 7 Black L.J. 304 (1981).

Private Clubs and Public Judges: A Nonsubstantive Debate about Symbols, 59 Tex. L. Rev. 733 (1981).

Race, Class, and the Contradictions of Affirmative Action (Panel Discussion, Third Annual Conference on Critical Legal Studies, Nov. 10, 1979), 7 Black L.J. 270 (1981) (with Alan Freeman and Henry McGee).

Brown v Board of Education and the Interest-Convergence Dilemma, 93 Harv. L Rev. 518 (1980). Reprinted in Critical Race Theory: The Key Writings That Formed the Movement 20 (Kimberlé Crenshaw et al. eds., 1995); also in A Reader on Race, Civil Rights, and American Law: A Multiracial Approach 742 (Timothy Davis et al. eds., 2001).

Bakke, Minority Admissions, and the Usual Price of Racial Remedies, 67 Cal. L. Rev. 3 (1979).

Black Colleges and the Desegregation Dilemma (In Commemoration: The Twenty-Fifth Anniversary of *Brown*), 28 Emory L.J. 949 (1979).

The Legacy of W. E. B. Du Bois: A Rational Model for Achieving Public School Equity for America's Black Children, 11 Creighton L. Rev. 409 (1978).

The Referendum: Democracy's Barrier to Racial Equality, 54 Wash. L. Rev. 1 (1978).

Racial Remediation: An Historical Perspective on Current Conditions ([Special Issue]: Civil and Human Rights—Reflections 1976), 52 Notre Dame L. Rev. 5 (1976).

Serving Two Masters: Integration Ideals and Client Interests in School Desegregation Litigation, 85 Yale L.J. 470 (1976). Reprinted in Limits of Justice: The Court's Role in School Desegregation 569 (H. Kalodner and J. Fishman, eds., 1978); also in Critical Race Theory: The Key Writings That Formed the Movement 5 (Kimberlé Crenshaw et al. eds., 1995); also in Critical Race Theory: The Cutting Edge, 2d ed. 236 (Richard Delgado & Jean Stefancic eds., 2000).

The Burden of *Brown* on Blacks: History-Based Observations on a Landmark Decision, 7 N.C. Cent. L.J. 25 (1975).

Proceedings of Minority Group Law Teachers Planning Conference, Harvard Law School (September 1974), D. Bell, Editor. 4 BlackLetter L.J. 575 (1975).

Running and Busing in Twentieth-Century America, 4 J. L. & Educ. 214 (1975).

Waiting on the Promise of *Brown,* 39 Law & Contemp. Prob. 341 (1975).

The Real Cost of Racial Equality, 1 Civ. Lib. Rev. 79 (1974).

Racism in American Courts: Cause for Black Disruption or Despair, 61 Cal. L. Rev. 165 (1973).

Black Faith in a Racist Land: A Summary Review of Racism in American Law, 20 J. Public L. 409 (1971). Reprinted in Howard Law Journal, see 17 Howard L.J. 300 (1972).

Black Students in White Law Schools: The Ordeal and the Opportunity, 1970 U. Toledo L Rev. 539.

In Defense of Minority Admissions Programs: A Response to Professor Graglia, 119 U. Pa. L. Rev. 364 (1970). Reprinted in Black Law Journal, see 3 Black L.J. 241 (1974).

School Litigation Strategies for the 1970's: New Phases in the Continuing Quest for Quality Schools, 1970 Wis. L. Rev. 257.

BOOK REVIEWS

Meanness as Racial Ideology (1990 Survey of Books Relating to the Law), 88 Mich. L. Rev. 1689 (1990) (reviewing Robert L. Allen, The Port Chicago Mutiny: The Story of the Largest Mutiny Trial in U.S. Naval History (1989)).

Preaching to the Choir: America As It Might Be, 37 UCLA L. Rev. 1025 (1990) (reviewing Kenneth L. Karst, Belonging to America: Equal Citizenship and the Constitution (1989)).

Law, Litigation, and the Search for the Promised Land, 76 Geo. L.J. 229 (1987) (reviewing Mark V. Tushnet, The NAACP: Legal Strategy against Segregated Education, 1925–1950 (1987)).

A School Desegregation Post-Mortem, 62 Tex. L. Rev. 175 (1983) (reviewing David L. Kirp, Just Schools: The Idea of Racial Equality in American Education (1982)).

Civil Rights Lawyers on the Bench, 91 Yale L.J. 814 (1982) (reviewing Jack Bass, Unlikely Heroes (1981)).

Preferential Affirmative Action, 16 Harv. C.R.-C.L. L. Rev. 855 (1982) (reviewing Daniel C. Maguire, A New American Justice (1980)).

Britain, Blacks, and Busing, 79 Mich. L. Rev. 835 (1981) (reviewing David L. Kirp, Doing Good by Doing Little: Race and Schooling in Britain (1979)).

Book Review, 92 Harv. L. Rev. 1826 (1979) (reviewing Ray C. Rist, The Invisible Children: School Integration in American Society (1978); Gary Orfield, Must We Bus? Segregated Schools and National Policy (1978); David J. Armor, White Flight, Democratic Transition, and the Future of School Desegregation (1978); Sara Lawrence Lightfoot, Worlds Apart: Relationships between Families and Schools (1978)).

Book Review, 4 So. U. L. Rev. 114 (1977) (reviewing Lino Graglia, Disaster by Decree (1976)).

Book Review, 76 Colum. L. Rev. 350 (1976) (reviewing Robert M. Cover, Justice Accused: Antislavery and the Judicial Process (1975)).

Book Review, 25 Emory L.J. 879 (1976) (reviewing Nathan Glazer, Affirmative Discrimination: Ethnic Inequality and Public Policy (1975)).

Dissection of a Dream, 9 Harv. C.R.-C.L. L. Rev. 156 (1974) (reviewing Boris I. Bittker, The Case for Black Reparations (1973)).

Book Review, 9 Crim. L. Bull. 80 (1973) (reviewing Race, Crime, and Justice, Charles E. Reasons & Jack L. Kuykendall eds. (1972)).

Book Review, 18 U.C.L.A. L. Rev. 616 (1971) (reviewing Harold W. Horowitz & Kenneth L. Karst, Law, Lawyers, and Social Change: Cases and Materials on the Abolition of Slavery, Racial Segregation, and Inequality of Educational Opportunity (1969)).

AFTERWORDS, EPILOGUES, FOREWORDS, INTRODUCTIONS, AND TRIBUTES

Afterword: The Handmaid's Truth, in Crossroads, Directions, and a New Critical Race Theory 411 (Francisco Valdes et al. eds., 2002).

Epilogue, in When Race Becomes Real: Black and White Writers Confront Their Personal Histories 327 (Bernestine Singley ed., 2002).

Judge A. Leon Higginbotham, Jr.'s Legacy (Judge A. Leon Higginbotham, Jr.: A Tribute), 53 Rutgers L. Rev. 627 (2001).

Foreword, in Within the Veil: Black Journalists, White Media ix (Pamela Newkirk ed., 2000).

Foreword, in Documents of American Prejudice: An Anthology of Writings on Race from Thomas Jefferson to David Duke xiii (S.T. Joshi ed., 1999).

Introduction, in Black Mutiny: The Revolt on the Schooner Amistad, by William A. Owens vii (1997) (with Michael E. Dyson).

Foreword, in Critical Race Feminism: A Reader xiii (Adrien K. Wing ed., 1997).

Foreword, in Beyond a Dream Deferred: Multicultural Education and the Politics of Excellence ix (Becky W. Thompson & Sangeeta Tyagi eds., 1993).

Introduction: (Multiple Cultures and the Law: Do We Have a Legal Canon?), 43 J. Legal Educ. 1 (1993).

[Tribute]: Thurgood Marshall, 68 N.Y.U. L. Rev. 212 (1993).

Foreword: The Final Civil Rights Act (Symposium: Civil Rights Legislation in the 1990s), 79 Cal. L. Rev. 597 (1991).

Introduction: Minority Law Professors' Lives: The Bell-Delgado Survey, 24 Harv. C.R.-C.L. L. Rev. 349 (1989) (with Richard Delgado).

Xerces and the Affirmative Action Mystique (A Tribute to Prof. Arthur S. Miller), 57 Geo. Wash. L. Rev. 1595 (1989).

Foreword: Introduction to Gil Kujovich's *Equal Opportunity in Higher Education and the Black Public College: The Era of Separate But Equal,* 72 Minn. L. Rev. 23 (1987).

Foreword: The Civil Rights Chronicles (The Supreme Court, 1984 Term), 99 Harv. L. Rev. 4 (1985). Reprinted in part in Color, Class, Identity: The New Politics of Race 98 (John Arthur & Amy Shapiro eds., 1996); and in Critical Race Theory: The Cutting Edge, 2d ed. 468 (Richard Delgado & Jean Stefancic eds., 2000).

Introduction: Issue on Legal History, 63 Or. L. Rev. 557 (1984).

A Tragedy of Timing (A Tribute to the Memory of Clarence Clyde Ferguson, Jr. (1924–1983)), 19 Harv. C.R.-C.L. L. Rev. 277 (1984).

Foreword: (An Issue on Race Relations), 61 Or. L. Rev. 151 (1982).

Humanity in Legal Education, 59 Or. L. Rev. 243 (1980).

Introduction: Awakening after *Bakke,* 14 Harv. C.R.-C.L. L. Rev. 1 (1979).

Foreword: Equal Employment Law and the Continuing Need for Self-Help (Fair Employment Practices Symposium), 8 Loy. U. Chi. L.J. 681 (1977).

Foreword: Special Issue: *Brown* to *Defunis* Twenty Years Later, 3 Black L.J. 105 (1974).

SELECTED NON-LEGAL PUBLICATIONS

Professor Derrick Bell Discusses How to Live an Ethical Life (interview with Tavis Smiley), NPR, Los Angeles, Nov. 28, 2002.

Is the Legal Profession on the Trash Heap?, 1995 Bus. & Soc'y Rev. 14 (with others).

Injustice for All, 26 Essence (No. 5, Sept. 1995) (with Janet Dewart).

The Freedom of Employment Act, The Nation, May 23, 1994, at 708.

Is Diversity Training Worth Maintaining? 1994 Bus. & Soc'y Rev. 47 (with others).

Fear of Black Crime Is Political Tool, LA Daily J., Jan. 19, 1990, at 6.

The Effects of Affirmative Action on Male-Female Relationships among African Americans, 21 Sex Roles 13 (Nos. 1/2, 1989).

Does Discrimination Make Economic Sense? For Some, It Did—and Still Does (Special Report: What Color Is the Constitution?), 15 Hum. Rts. 38 (1988).

The Legacy of Racial Discrimination: Who Pays the Cost? (Symposium: Afro-Americans and the Evolution of a Living Constitution), 12 Update on L.-Related Educ., Fall, 1988, at 22 (with Claire Conway).

The Fourteenth Amendment: To Make a Nation Whole, NY Times Sunday Mag., Sep. 13, 1987, at 43. Published as Reconstruction's Racial Realities in Rutgers Law Journal, see 23 Rutgers L.J. 261 (1992).

Is the Constitution Out of Date? 73 A.B.A.J., Sept. 1, 1987, at 52 (discussion with Lino Graglia and Arthur Miller).

Whites Make Big Gains under Broadened Selection Criteria, LA Daily J., Sept. 1, 1987, at 4.

Desegregation, in 2 Encyclopedia of the American Constitution 557 (1986).

Brown v. Board of Education and the Black History Month Syndrome, Educ. Week, February 22, 1984, at 24. Reprinted in Harvard BlackLetter Journal, see 1 Harv. BlackLetter J. 13 (1984).

Remembering the Promise of *Brown v. Board of Education,* Educ. Week, June 6, 1984, at 28.

Facing Educational Facts: A Respectful Response to Kenneth Clark, 41 Educ. Leadership 86 (Dec.1983/Jan.1984).

Learning from Our Losses: Is School Desegregation Still Feasible in the 1980s? 64 Phi Delta Kappan 572 (Apr. 1983).

Time for the Teachers: Putting Educators Back into the *Brown* Remedy, 52 J. Negro Educ. 290 (1983).

A Reassessment of Racial Balance Remedies, 62 Phi Delta Kappan 177 (Nov. 1980).

Learning from the *Brown* Experience, 11 Black Scholar 9 (Sept./Oct. 1979).

The Chinese Challenge, 29 Harv. L. Sch. Bull. 14 (1978).

The Community Role in the Education of Poor, Black Children, 17 Theory into Practice 115 (No. 2, Apr. 1978).

The Curse of *Brown* on Black, 2 First World 14 (Spring 1978).

The High Price of Non-Representation, 58 Phi Kappa Phi J. 19 (1978).

Inside China: Conformity and Social Change, 8 Juris Doctor 23 (Apr. 1978).

School Desegregation: Seeking New Victories among the Ashes, 17 Freedomways 35 (No. 1, 1977). Reprinted in Freedomways Reader: Prophets in Their Own Country 229 (Esther Cooper Jackson & Constance Pohl eds., 2000).

Is *Brown* Obsolete? Yes! 14 Integrateducation No. 81, 28 (May–June,1976).

NAACP: Faith and an Opportunity, 13 Freedomways 330 (No. 4, 1973).

Integration: A No Win Policy for Blacks? 11 Inequality in Education 35 (1972). Reprinted in Harvard Law School Bulletin, see 23 Harv. L. Sch. Bull. 7 (1972).

CHAPTERS IN BOOKS

Simple Dialogue: The Potential Value of Losing *Brown v. Board,* in The Unfinished Agenda of *Brown v. Board of Education* 150 (Editors of Black Issues in Higher Education with James A. & Dara N. Byrne eds., 2004).

Defying the Norms: Teaching Large Law School Classes in Accordance with Good Pedagogy, in Engaging Large Classes 235 (Christine A. Stanley & M. Erin Porter eds., 2002).

Difficulty of Doing Good: Civil Rights Activism as Metaphor, in The New Politics of Race: From Du Bois to the 21st Century 175 (Marlese Durr ed., 2002).

Divining Our Racial Themes, in Understanding Inequality: The Intersection of Race/Ethnicity, Class, and Gender 25 (Barbara A. Arrighi ed., 2001). Reprinted from Faces at the Bottom of the Well.

Love's Labor Lost? Why Racial Fairness Is a Threat to Many White Americans, in Who's Qualified 42 (Lani Guinier and Susan Sturm eds., 2001).

Police Brutality: Portent of Disaster and Discomforting Divergence, in Police Brutality: An Anthology 88 (Jill Nelson ed., 2000).

Great Expectations: Defining the Divide between Blacks and Jews, in Strangers & Neighbors: Relations between Blacks & Jews in the United States 802 (Maurianne Adams and John Bracy eds., 1999).

Silent Acquiescence: The Too-High Price of Prestige, in Black Men on Race, Gender, and Sexuality: A Critical Reader 408 (Devon W. Carbado ed., 1999).

The Burger Court's Place on the Bell Curve of Racial Jurisprudence, in The Burger Court: Counter-Revolution or Confirmation? 57 (Bernard Schwartz ed., 1998).

Doing the State Some Service: Paul Robeson and the Endless Quest for Racial Justice, in Paul Robeson: Artist and Critic 49 (Jeffrey C. Stewart ed., 1998). Reprinted from Afrolantica Legacies.

Farrakhan Fever: Defining the Divide between Blacks and Jews, in The Farrakhan Factor: African-American Writers on Leadership, Nationhood, and

Minister Louis Farrakhan 211 (Amy Alexander ed., 1998). Reprinted from Afrolantica Legacies.

The Real Status of Blacks Today, in Race, Class, Gender, and Sexuality: The Big Questions 1 (Naomi Zack et al. eds., 1998).

Racial Realism in Retrospect, in Reason and Passion: Justice Brennan's Enduring Influence 199 (E. Joshua Rosenkranz & Bernard Schwartz eds., 1997).

Learning from the Past, in The Wisdom of the Elders 262 (Robert Fleming ed., 1996).

The Chronicle of the Sacrificed Black Children, in Jump Up and Say! A Collection of Black Storytelling 222 (Linda Goss & Clay Goss eds., 1995). Reprinted from And We Are Not Saved.

Faces at the Bottom of the Well, in Brotherman: Stories and Essays by and about Black Men 373 (Herb Boyd & Robert Allen eds., 1995).

Permanently Alienated, in One by One from the Inside Out: Essays and Reviews on Race and Responsibility in America 289 (Glenn C. Loury ed., 1995).

The Race-Charged Relationship of Black Men and Black Women, in Constructing Masculinity 193 (Maurice Berger et al. eds., 1995). Reprinted from And We Are Not Saved.

The Sexual Diversion: The Black Man/Black Woman Debate in Context, in Speak My Name: Black Men on Masculinity and the American Dream 144 (Don Belton ed., 1995); also in Black Men on Race, Gender, and Sexuality: A Critical Reader 237 (Devon W. Carbado ed., 1999); also in Traps: African American Men on Gender and Sexuality 168 (Rudolph P. Byrd & Beverly Guy-Sheftall eds., 2001).

A Semblance of Safety, in Blacks and Jews: Alliance and Arguments 258 (Paul Berman ed., 1994).

Question of Credentials, in Blacks at Harvard: A Documentary History of African-American Experience at Harvard and Radcliffe 467 (Werner Sollors et al. eds., 1993).

Remembrances of Racism Past: Getting beyond the Civil Rights Decline, in Race in America: The Struggle for Equality 73 (Herbert Hill & James E. Jones, Jr. eds., 1993).

An Allegorical Critique of the United States Civil Rights Model, in Discrimination: The Limits of the Law 3 (Bob Hepple & Erika M. Szyszczak eds., 1992). Reprinted from Faces at the Bottom of the Well.

Victims as Heroes: A Minority Perspective on Constitutional Law, in The United States Constitution: Roots, Rights, and Responsibilities, 163 (A. E. Dick Howard ed., 1992).

Ceremonies in Civil Rights: A Thirty-Year Retrospective on the Law and Race, in The State of Black America 1984, 119 National Urban League (1984).

The Racial Imperative in American Law, in The Age of Segregation: Race Relations in the South 1890–1945 3 (Robert Haws ed., 1978).

Index

About the Editors

Richard Delgado is University Distinguished Professor of Law and Derrick A. Bell Fellow at the University of Pittsburgh. Jean Stefancic is the Derrick A. Bell Scholar and Research Professor of Law at the University of Pittsburgh. They are the authors of many books, including *Critical Race Theory: An Introduction*, *The Latino/a Condition: A Critical Reader*, and *The Rodrigo Chronicles: Conversations about America and Race*.